Stories and Tales

'From the very first publication of Hans Christian Andersen's fairy tales in 1835 to the present day, his stories have intrigued old and young. All the more reason to greet the re-publication of the nineteenth-century Routledge Classics edition of Andersen's *Stories and Tales*, which includes most of his major narratives as well as the fine ink drawings by A. W. Bayes. Translated into quaint Victorian English, Andersen's tales are nevertheless very modern in tone and style. He was among the very first to introduce modern inventions that assumed lives of their own, and he did not shy from dealing with grave social problems and delicate personal concerns in his narratives. What makes his fairy tales distinct is the undercurrent of tragedy and melancholy. Though the ugly duckling may turn into a swan and the princess may survive the pea beneath the mattresses, other Andersen protagonists like the little mermaid or the girl in red shoes are mutilated, and many of them must use violent means to assert themselves. The Routledge edition includes a wide array of Andersen's most gratifying and disturbing tales, and in this regard, it is a classic collection worth reading over and over again.'

Jack Zipes

Hans Christian
Andersen

Stories and Tales

Translated by H. W. Dulcken

Illustrated by A. W. Bayes and engraved by the
Brothers Dalziel

London and New York

First published in 1865
by Routledge, Warne and Routledge

First published in Routledge Classics 2002
by Routledge
11 New Fetter Lane, London EC4P 4EE
29 West 35th Street, New York, NY 10001

Routledge is an imprint of the Taylor & Francis Group

Hans Christian Andersen, Hermann Hesse, Andersens Märchen, in:
Hermann Hesse, *Eine Literaturgeschichte in Rezensionen und Aufsätzen*
© 1970 Suhrkamp Verlag Frankfurt am Main

Typeset in Joanna by RefineCatch Limited, Bungay, Suffolk
Printed and bound in Great Britain by
TJ International, Padstow, Cornwall

British Library Cataloguing in Publication Data
A catalogue record for this book is available from the British Library

Library of Congress Cataloguing in Publication Data
A catalog record for this book has been requested

ISBN 0–415–28597–6 (hbk)
ISBN 0–415–28598–4 (pbk)

CONTENTS

HANS CHRISTIAN ANDERSEN

When we were little children, who had only just learnt to read, we owned, like all children, a beautiful, favourite book. It was called *Andersen's Fairytales*, and every time, once we had read it, we would pick it up again; it was our faithful companion till the end of our boyhood years, our dear childhood, with its treasures and fairies, kings and rich merchants, poor beggar-children and bold fortune-seekers. There, next to the incomparable "Ole Luk-Oie", was a favourite – the story of the little mermaid, even though it always made me sad. Its beginning was so mysterious and vivid, with the palace and the gardens on the sea-floor. "During a calm the sun could be seen; it appeared like a purple flower, from which all light streamed out." And how good and pithy and believable was the beginning of the wonderful story of the flying trunk. "There was once a merchant, who was so rich, that he could pave the whole street with gold, and almost have enough left for a little lane. But he did not do that; he knew how to employ his money differently. When he spent a shilling he got back a crown, such a clever merchant was he; and this continued till he died."

It is not the sentences, however, that have remained in my memory; I have only just looked them up. In my memory there were no sentences and words, only the things themselves, the whole, multi-coloured, magnificent world of old Andersen, and it was so well preserved in my remembrance and was so beautiful, that I took great care in later years not to open this book again (which seemed in any case to have been lost). For I had unfortunately already, at an early age, made that painful discovery: the books which in earliest childhood and youth were the source of all our bliss, should never be read again; otherwise their old shine and sparkle will be no more and they will appear changed, sad and foolish.

But the story which I read was good; it was not at all as fabulous and effusive and artificial as I had secretly been almost dreading; on the contrary, it looked with fully alert eyes at the real world and sent forth its fairy enchantment not out of vanity and foolish high spirits, but from experience and compassionate resignation. The enchantment was genuine, and as I read again and attended once more to many of the old stories, there reappeared the same beautiful magic sparkle as before; from the furrowed disappointment arose a joy and exuberance, and wherever it lacked something and failed to resound with its old completeness, the fault lay with me and not with old Andersen.

Now I read the volumes often, with joy; they stand in a good position, where they can never get dusty. And if somehow I were ever to meet old Andersen, I wouldn't just raise my hat, but with grateful admiration I would try to get to know him better; for he was a man of mystery, simplicity and purity, so it seems to me. What little one can discover seems wonderfully true of this man of stories. Brought up in poverty, early on he was supported by a patron on whom he became dependent. Full of wanderlust and ambition, but always in the style of the son in the fairytale, setting out in search of adventure, eventually he acquired fame and fortune, but never found warmth and completeness: his heart was always seeking, every love unhappy – such was the life of this uncommon man. And he was so much a child that in his disappointment and loneliness he sat down with the little ones and invented fairytales for them, and in the end, though his fame was largely the result of other works, all that remains of him are these fairytales, for they have the nature of immortal things.

HERMANN HESSE   1910
(translated by Roger Thorp)

PREFACE

The continually increasing popularity of that most genial of "children's friends," Hans Christian Andersen, whose circle of readers increases like a rolling snow-ball as his works become more generally known, has induced the publishers of the present edition of the Danish poet's *Stories and Tales* to offer this volume to the public, in the hope that it may prove an acceptable gift-book, alike to the children for whom Andersen originally wrote his charming fictions, and likewise to those "children of a larger growth," who can appreciate genius in a homely and simple garb.

The Selection comprises some Tales, which, it is supposed, have not yet appeared in any former edition. The Illustrations, eighty in number, have been most carefully engraved by the Brothers Dalziel, from drawings by A. W. Bayes; and in the general preparation of the book, the proprietors have done their best to enlist the good will of the readers of all ages.

H. W. D.

The witch induces the soldier to climb the tree

THE TINDER-BOX

There came a soldier marching along the high road—"*one, two! one, two!*"
He had his knapsack on his back, and a sabre by his side for he had
been in the wars, and now he wanted to go home. And on the way he
met with an old witch; she was very hideous, and her under-lip hung
down upon her breast. She said "Good evening, soldier! What a fine
sword you have, and what a big knapsack! You're a proper soldier!
Now, you shall have as much money as you like to have."

   "I thank you, you old witch!" said the soldier.

"Do you see that great tree?" quoth the witch; and she pointed to a tree which stood beside them. "It's quite hollow inside. You must climb to the top and then you'll see a hole, through which you can let yourself down and get deep into the tree. I'll tie a rope round your body, so that I can pull you up again when you call me."

"What am I to do down in the tree?" asked the soldier.

"Get money," replied the witch. "Listen to me; when you come down to the earth under the tree, you will find yourself in a great hall; it is quite light, for above three hundred lamps are burning there. Then you will see three doors; these you can open, for the keys are sticking there. If you go into the first chamber, you'll see a great chest in the middle of the floor; on this chest sits a dog; and he's got a pair of eyes as big as two tea-cups. But you need not care for that. I'll give you my blue-checked apron, you can spread it out upon the floor; then go up quickly and take the dog, and set him on my apron; then open the chest and take as many shillings as you like. They are of copper; if you prefer silver, you must go into the second chamber. But there sits a dog with a pair of eyes as big as mill-wheels. But do not you care for that. Set him upon my apron, and take some of the money. And if you want gold, you can have that too; in fact, as much as you can carry—if you go into the third chamber. But the dog that sits on the money-chest there has two eyes as big as round towers. He's a fierce dog, you may be sure. But you needn't be afraid for all that. Only set him on my apron, and he won't hurt you; and take out of the chest as much gold as you like."

"That's not so bad," said the soldier. "But what am I to give you, you old witch? For you will not do it for nothing, I fancy."

"No," replied the witch. "Not a single shilling will I have. You shall only bring me an old tinder-box, which my grandmother forgot when she was down there last."

"Then tie the rope round my body!" cried the soldier.

"Here it is," said the witch, "and here's my blue-checked apron."

Then the soldier climbed up into the tree, let himself slip down into the hole, and stood, as the witch had said, in the great hall where the many hundred lamps were burning.

Now he opened the first door. Ugh! There sat the dog with eyes as big as tea-cups, staring at him. "You're a nice fellow!" cried the soldier, and he set him on the witch's apron, and took as many copper shillings as his pockets would hold, and then locked the chest, set the dog on it again, and went into the second chamber. Aha! There sat the dog with eyes as big as mill-wheels.

"You should not stare so hard at me," said the soldier; "you might strain your eyes." And he set the dog upon the witch's apron. And when he saw all the silver money in the chest, he threw away all the copper money he had, and filled his pockets and his knapsack with silver only. Then he went into the third chamber. Ho! But that was horrid! The dog there had really eyes as big as towers, and they turned round and round in his head like wheels.

"Good evening!" said the soldier; and he touched his cap, for he had never seen such a dog as that before. When he had looked at him a little more closely, he thought, that will do,—and lifted him down upon the floor, and opened the chest. Mercy! What a quantity of gold was there. He could buy with it the whole town, and the sugar sucking-pigs of the cake-women, and all the tin soldiers, whips and rocking-horses in the whole world. Yes, that was a quantity of money! Now the soldier threw away all the silver coin with which he had filled his pockets and his knapsack, and took gold instead; yes, all his pockets, the knapsack, his boots and his cap were filled, so that he could scarcely walk. Now he had money. He put the dog on the chest, shut the door, and then called up through the tree, "Now pull me up, you old witch."

"Have you the tinder-box?" asked the witch. "Plague on it!" exclaimed the soldier. "I had clean forgotten that"—and he went and brought it.

The witch drew him up; and he stood on the high road again, with pockets, boots, knapsack and cap full of gold.

"What are you going to do with that tinder-box?" asked the soldier. "That's nothing to you," retorted the witch. "You've had your money, just give me the tinder-box."

"Nonsense!" said the soldier. "Tell me directly what you're going to do with it, or I'll draw my sword and cut off your head." "No!" cried the witch.

So the soldier cut off her head. There she lay! But he tied up all his money in her apron, took it on his back like a bundle, put the tinder-box in his pocket, and went straight off towards the town.

That was a splendid town! And he put up at the very best inn, and asked for the finest rooms, and ordered his favourite dishes, for now he was rich, as he had so much money. The servant who was to clean his boots certainly thought them a remarkably old pair for such a rich gentleman. But he had not bought any new ones yet. The next day he procured proper boots and handsome clothes. Now our soldier had become a fine gentleman; and the people told him of all the splendid things which were in their city, and about the king, and what a pretty princess the king's daughter was.

"Where can one get to see her?" asked the soldier. "She is not to be seen at all," said they all together; "she lives in a great copper castle, with a great many walls and towers round about it; no one but the king may go in and out there; for it has been prophesied that she shall marry a common soldier, and the king can't bear that."

"I should like to see her," thought the soldier; but he could not get leave to do so. Now he lived merrily, went to the theatre, drove in the king's garden, and gave much money to the poor; and this was very kind of him, for he knew from old times how hard it is when one has not a shilling. Now he was rich, had fine clothes, and gained many friends, who all said he was a rare one, a true cavalier. And that pleased the soldier well. But as he spent money every day and never earned any, he had at last only two shillings left; and he was obliged to turn out of his fine rooms in which he had dwelt, and had to live in a little garret under the roof, and clean his boots for himself, and mend them with a darning-needle. None of his friends came to see him; for there were too many stairs to climb.

It was quite dark, one evening, and he could not even buy himself a candle, when it occurred to him that there was a candle-end in the tinder-box which he had taken out of the hollow tree into which the witch had helped him. He brought out the tinder-box and the candle-end; but so soon as he struck fire and the sparks rose up from the flint, the door flew open; and the dog who had eyes as big as a couple of tea-cups, and whom he had seen in the tree, stood before him, and said: "What are my lord's commands?"

"What is this?" said the soldier. "That's a famous tinder-box, if I can get everything with it that I want! Bring me some money," said he to the dog: and whisk, the dog was gone, and whisk, he was back again, and had a great bag full of shillings in his mouth.

Now, the soldier knew what a capital tinder-box this was. If he struck it once, came the dog who sat on the chest of copper money; if he struck it twice, the dog came who had the silver; and if he struck it three times, then appeared the dog who had the gold. Now the soldier moved back into the fine rooms, and appeared again in handsome clothes; and all his friends knew him again, and cared very much for him indeed.

Once he thought to himself, "It is a very strange thing that one cannot get to see the princess. They all say she is very beautiful; but what is the use of that, if she has always to sit in the great copper castle with the many towers? Can I not get to see her at all? Where is my tinder-box?" And so he struck a light, and, whisk, came the dog with eyes as big as tea-cups.

"It is certainly midnight," said the soldier, "but I should very much like to see the princess, only for one little moment;" and the dog was outside the door directly, and before the soldier thought it, he came back with the princess. She sat upon the dog's back, and slept; and every one could see she was a real princess, for she was so lovely. The soldier could not refrain from kissing her; for he was a thorough soldier. Then the dog ran back again with the princess. But when morning came, and the king and queen were drinking tea, the princess said, she had had a strange dream, the night before, about a dog and a soldier; that she had ridden upon the dog, and the soldier had kissed her.

"That would be a fine history!" said the queen.

Now one of the old court ladies was to watch the next night by the princess's bed, to see if this was really a dream, or what it might be.

The soldier had a great longing to see the lovely princess again; so the dog came in the night, took her away, and ran as fast as he could. But the old lady put on water-boots, and ran just as fast after him. When she saw that they both entered a great house, she thought, "now I know where it is," and with a bit of chalk she drew a great cross on the door. Then she went home and lay down, and the dog came up with the princess; but when he saw that there was a cross drawn on the door where the soldier lived, he took a piece of chalk too, and drew crosses on all the doors in the town. And that was cleverly done; for

The princess arrives on the dog's back

now the lady could not find the right door, because all the doors had crosses upon them.

In the morning early came the king and the queen, the old court lady and all the officers, to see where it was the princess had been. "Here it is," said the king, when he saw the first door with a cross upon it. "No, my dear husband, it is there," said the queen, who descried another door which also showed a cross. "But there is one, and there is one!" said all, for wherever they looked there were crosses on the doors. So they saw that it would avail them nothing if they searched on.

But the queen was an exceedingly clever woman, who could do

more than ride in a coach. She took her great gold scissors, cut a piece of silk into pieces, and made a neat little bag; this bag she filled with fine wheat flour, and tied it on the princess's back, and when that was done, she cut a little hole in the bag, so that the flour would be scattered along all the way which the princess should take.

In the night the dog came again, took the princess on his back, and ran with her to the soldier, who loved her very much, and would gladly have been a prince so that he might have her for his wife. The dog did not notice at all how the flour ran out in a stream from the castle to the windows of the soldier, where he ran up the wall with the princess. In the morning the king and the queen saw well enough where their daughter had been; and they took the soldier and put him in prison.

There he sat. Oh, but it was dark and disagreeable there!—and they said to him, "To-morrow you shall be hanged!" That was not amusing to hear, and he had left his tinder-box in the inn. In the morning he could see through the iron grating of the little window, how the people were hurrying out of the town to see him hanged. He heard the drums beat, and saw the soldiers marching. All the people were running out; and among them was a shoemaker's boy with leather apron and slippers; and he galloped by so fast that one of his slippers flew off, and came right against the wall where the soldier sat looking through the iron grating.

"Halloo, you shoemaker's boy, you need not be in such a hurry," cried the soldier to him. "It will not begin till I come. But if you will run to where I lived, and bring me my tinder-box, you shall have four shillings, but you must put your best leg foremost." The shoemaker's boy wanted to get the four shillings; so he went and brought the tinder-box, and—well, we shall hear now what happened.

Outside the town a great gallows had been built; and round it stood the soldiers, and many hundred thousand people. The king and queen sat on a splendid throne, opposite to the judges and the whole council. The soldier already stood upon the ladder; but as they were about to put the rope round his neck, he said, that before a poor criminal suffered his punishment an innocent request was always granted to him. He wanted very much to smoke a pipe of tobacco; and it would be the last pipe he should smoke in the world. The king would not say "No," to this; so the soldier took his tinder-box, and struck fire.

One—two—three!—and there stood suddenly all the dogs; the one with eyes as big as tea-cups, the one with eyes as large as mill-wheels, and the one whose eyes were as big as round towers.

"Help me now, so that I may not be hanged!" said the soldier. And the dogs fell upon the judge and all the council, seized one by the leg and another by the nose, and tossed them all many feet into the air, so that they fell down and were all broken to pieces.

"I won't!" cried the king; but the biggest dog took him and the queen, and threw them after the others; then the soldiers were afraid, and all the people cried, "Little soldier, you shall be our king, and marry the beautiful princess!"

So they put the soldier into the king's coach, and all the three dogs darted on in front, and cried "Hurrah!" and the boys whistled through their fingers, and the soldiers presented arms. The princess came out of the copper castle, and became queen, and she liked that well enough. The wedding lasted a week, and the three dogs sat at the table too, and opened their eyes wide at all they saw.

LITTLE CLAUS AND GREAT CLAUS

There lived two men in one village, and they had the same name,—each was called Claus; but one had four horses and the other only a single horse. To distinguish them from each other, folks called him who had four horses Great Claus, and the one who had only a single horse Little Claus. Now we shall hear what happened to each of them; for this is a true story.

The whole week through Little Claus was obliged to plough for Great Claus, and to lend him his one horse; then Great Claus helped him out with all his four, but only once a week, and that on a holiday. Hurrah! How Little Claus smacked his whip over all five horses; for they were as good as his own on that one day. The sun shone gaily, and all the bells in the steeples were ringing, the people were all dressed in their best, and were going to Church with their hymn-books under their arms, to hear the clergyman preach;—and they saw Little Claus ploughing with five horses; but he was so merry

Little Claus deploring the death of his horse

that he smacked his whip again and again, and cried "Gee up, all my five!"

"You must not talk so," said Great Claus, "for only the one horse is yours!"

But when no one was passing, Little Claus forgot that he was not to say this, and he cried, "Gee up, all my horses!"

"Now, I must beg you to let that alone," cried Great Claus, "for if you say it again, I shall hit your horse on the head so that it will fall down dead, and then it will be all over with him." "I will certainly not say it any more," said Little Claus. But when people came by soon afterwards, and nodded "good day" to him, he became very glad, and thought it looked very well after all that he had five horses to plough his field; and so he smacked his whip again, and cried, "Gee up, all my horses!"

"I'll 'gee up' your horses!" said Great Claus; and he took the hatchet and hit the only horse of Little Claus on the head, so that it fell down, and was dead immediately. "Oh, now I haven't any horse at all!" said Little Claus, and began to cry. Then he flayed the horse, and let the hide dry in the wind, and put it in a sack and hung it over his shoulder, and went to the town to sell his horse's skin.

He had a very long way to go, and was obliged to pass through a great dark wood, and the weather became dreadfully bad. He went quite astray, and before he got into the right way again it was evening, and it was too far to get to the town or even home again before nightfall.

Close by the road stood a large farm-house. The shutters were closed outside the windows, but the light could still be seen shining out over them. "I may be able to get leave to stop here through the night," thought Little Claus, and he went and knocked. The farmer's wife opened the door; but when she heard what he wanted she told him to go away, declaring that her husband was not at home, and she would not receive strangers. "Then I shall have to lie outside," said Little Claus; and the farmer's wife shut the door in his face.

Close by stood a great hay-stack; and between this and the farm-house was a little out-house thatched with straw. "Up there I can lie," said Little Claus, when he looked up at the roof. "That is a capital bed; I suppose the stork won't fly down and bite me in the legs." For a living stork was standing on the roof, where he had his nest.

Now Little Claus climbed up to the roof of the shed where he lay, and turned round to settle himself comfortably. The wooden shutters did not cover the windows at the top, and he could look straight into the room. There was a great table, with the cloth laid, and wine and roast meat and a glorious fish upon it. The farmer's wife and the clerk were seated at table, and nobody besides. She was filling his glass, and he was digging his fork into the fish, for that was his favourite dish.

"If one could only get some, too," thought Little Claus, and stretched out his head towards the window. Heavens! what a glorious cake he saw standing there. Yes, certainly, that was a feast.

Now he heard some one riding along the high road; it was the woman's husband, who was coming home. He was a good man enough, but he had the strange peculiarity that he could never bear to see a clerk. If a clerk appeared before his eyes he became quite wild. And that was the reason why the clerk had gone to the wife to wish her good day, because he knew that her husband was not at home; and the good woman therefore put the best fare she had before him. But when they heard the man coming they were frightened, and the woman begged the clerk to creep into a great empty chest which stood there; and he did so, for he knew the husband could not bear the sight of a clerk. The woman quickly hid all the excellent meat and wine in her baking-oven; for if the man had seen that, he would have been certain to ask what it meant. "Ah, yes," sighed Little Claus, up in his shed, when he saw all the good fare put away.

"Is there anyone up there?" asked the farmer; and he looked up at Little Claus. "Who are you lying there? Better come with me into the room." And Little Claus told him how he had lost his way, and asked leave to stay there for the night. "Yes, certainly," said the peasant; "but first we must have something to live on."

The woman received them both in a very friendly way, spread the cloth on a long table, and gave them a great dish of porridge. The farmer was hungry, and ate with a good appetite; but Little Claus could not help thinking of the capital roast meat, fish and cake, which he knew were in the oven. Under the table, at his feet, he had laid the sack with the horse's hide in it; for we know that he had come out to sell it in the town. He could not relish the porridge, so he trod upon the sack, and the dry skin inside crackled quite loudly.

"Why, what have you in your sack?" asked the farmer. "Oh, that's a magician!" answered Little Claus. "He says we are not to eat porridge, for he has conjured the oven all full of roast meat, fish, and cake."

"Wonderful!" cried the farmer; and he opened the oven in a hurry, and found all the dainty provisions which his wife had hidden there, but which, as he thought, the wizard had conjured forth. The woman dared not say anything, but put the things at once on the table; and so they both ate of the meat, the fish, and the cake. Now Little Claus trod again on his sack, and made the hide creak.

"What does he say now?" said the farmer. "He says," replied Claus, "that he has conjured three bottles of wine for us, too; and that they are standing there in the corner behind the oven!" Now the woman was obliged to bring out the wine which she had hidden, and the farmer drank it, and became very merry. He would have been very glad to see such a conjuror as Little Claus had there in the sack.

"Can he conjure the demon forth?" asked the farmer. "I should like to see him, for now I am merry."

"Oh, yes," said Little Claus, "my conjuror can do anything that I ask of him. Can you not?" he added, and trod on the hide, so that it crackled. "He says 'Yes;' but the demon is very ugly to look at, we had better not see him."

"Oh, I'm not at all afraid. Pray what will he look like?"

"Why, he'll look the very image of a clerk."

"Ha!" said the farmer, "that's ugly! You must know I can't bear the sight of a clerk. But it doesn't matter, for I know that he's a demon, so I shall easily stand it. Now I have courage, but he must not come too near me."

"Now, I will ask my conjuror," said Little Claus; and he trod on his sack and held his ear down.

"What does he say?"

"He says you may go and open the chest that stands in the corner, and you will see the demon crouching in it; but you must hold the lid so that he doesn't slip out."

"Will you help me to hold him?" asked the farmer. And he went to the chest where the wife had hidden the real clerk, who sat in there and was very much afraid. The farmer opened the lid a little way, and peeped in underneath it. "Hu!" he cried, and sprung backward. "Yes, now I've seen him, and he looked exactly like our clerk. Ho, that was dreadful!"

Upon this they must drink. So they sat and drank until late into the night.

"You must sell me that conjuror," said the farmer. "Ask as much as you like for him. I'll give you a whole bushel of money directly."

"No, that I can't do," said Little Claus. "Only think how much use I can make of this conjuror."

"Oh, I should so much like to have him," cried the peasant; and he went on begging.

"Well," said Little Claus, at last, "as you have been so kind as to give me shelter for to-night, I will let it be so. You shall have the conjuror for a bushel of money;—but I must have the bushel heaped up."

"That you shall have," replied the farmer. "But you must take the chest yonder away with you. I will not keep it in my house an hour. One cannot know,—perhaps he may be there still."

Little Claus gave the farmer his sack with the dry hide in it, and got in exchange a whole bushel of money, and that heaped up. The farmer also gave him a big truck, on which to carry off his money and the chest.

"Farewell!" said Little Claus; and he went off with his money and the big chest, in which the clerk was still sitting.

On the other side of the wood was a great deep river. The water rushed along so rapidly that one could scarcely swim against the stream. A fine new bridge had been built over it; Little Claus stopped on the centre of the bridge, and said quite loud, so that the clerk could hear it:—

"Ho, what shall I do with this stupid chest? It's as heavy as if stones were in it. I shall only get tired if I drag it further, so I'll throw it into the river; if it swims home to me, well and good, and if it does not, it will be no great matter." And he took the chest with one hand, and lifted it up a little, as if he had intended to throw it into the river.

"No,—let be!" cried the clerk, from within the chest, "let me out first."

"Hu!" exclaimed Little Claus, and pretended to be frightened. "He's in there still. I must make haste and throw him into the river that he may be drowned."

"Oh, no! Oh, no!" screamed the clerk. "I'll give you a whole bushel full of money if you'll let me go."

"Why, that's another thing!" said Little Claus; and he opened the chest.

The clerk crept quickly out, pushed the empty chest into the water, and went to his house, where Little Claus received a whole bushel full of money. He had already received one from the farmer, and so now he had his truck loaded with money.

"See, I've been well paid for the horse," he said to himself, when he had got home to his own room, and was emptying all the money into a heap in the middle of the floor. "That will vex Great Claus when he hears how rich I have grown through my own horse; but I won't tell him about it outright." So he sent a boy to Great Claus to ask for a bushel-measure.

"What can he want with it?" thought Great Claus; and he smeared some tar underneath the measure, so that something of whatever was measured, should stick to it. And thus it happened; for when he received the measure back, there were three new eight-shilling pieces adhering thereto.

"What's this?" cried Big Claus; and he ran off at once to Little Claus.

"Where did you get all that money from?"

Great Claus beaten by the shoemakers and tanners

"Oh, that's for my horse's skin. I sold it yesterday evening."

"That's really well paid," said Great Claus; and he ran home in a hurry, took an axe, and killed all his four horses; then he flayed them, and carried off their skins to the town.

"Hides! hides!—who'll buy hides?" he cried through the streets.

All the shoemakers and tanners came running, and asked how much he wanted for them.

"A bushel of money for each!" said Great Claus.

"Are you mad?" said they. "Do you think we have money by the bushel?"

"Hides! hides!" he cried again; and to all who asked him what the hides cost, he replied, "A bushel of money."

"He wants to make fools of us," they all exclaimed; and the shoemakers took their straps, and the tanners their aprons, and they began to beat Great Claus.

"Hides! hides!" they called after him, jeeringly. "Yes, we'll tan your hide for you till the red broth runs down. Out of the town with him!" And Great Claus made the best haste he could, for he had never yet been thrashed as he was thrashed now.

"Well," said he, when he got home, "Little Claus shall pay for this. I'll kill him for it."

Now, at Little Claus's the old grandmother had died. She had been very hard and unkind to him; but yet he was very sorry, and took the dead woman and laid her in his warm bed to see if she would not come to life again. There he intended she should remain all through the night, and he himself would sit in the corner and sleep on a chair, as he had often done before. As he sat there in the night the door opened, and Great Claus came in with his axe. He knew where Little Claus's bed stood, and going straight up to it, hit the old grandmother on the head, thinking she was Little Claus. "D'ye see," said he, "you shall not make a fool of me again." And then he went home.

"That's a bad fellow, that man," said Little Claus. "He wanted to kill me. It was a good thing for my old grandmother that she was dead already. He would have taken her life." And he dressed his grandmother in her Sunday clothes, borrowed a horse of his neighbour, harnessed it to a car, and put the old lady on the back seat, so that she could not fall out when he drove; and so they trundled away through the wood. When the sun rose, they were in front of a great inn; there Little Claus pulled up, and went in to have some refreshment.

The host had very, very much money; he was also a very good man, but exceedingly hot, as if he had pepper and tobacco in him.

"Good morning!" said he, to Little Claus. "You've put on your Sunday clothes early to-day."

"Yes," answered Little Claus, "I'm going to town with my old grandmother; she's sitting there on the car without. I can't bring her into the room. Will you give her a glass of mead? But you must speak very loud, for she can't hear well."

"Yes, that I'll do," said the host; and he poured out a great glass of mead, and went out with it to the dead grandmother, who had been placed upright in the carriage.

"Here's a glass of mead from your son!" quoth mine host. But the dead woman replied not a word, but sat quite still. "Don't you hear?" cried the host, as loud as he could, "here is a glass of mead from your son."

Once more he called out the same thing,—but as she persisted in not hearing him he became angry at last, and threw the glass in her face, so that the mead ran down over her nose, and she tumbled backwards into the carriage, for she had only been put upright, and not bound fast.

"Halloo!" cried Little Claus, running out at the door, and seizing the host by the breast, "you've killed my grandmother now! See, there's a big hole in her forehead."

"Oh, here's a misfortune!" cried the host, wringing his hands. "That all comes of my hot temper. Dear Little Claus, I'll give you a bushel of money, and have your grandmother buried as if she were my own; only keep quiet, or I shall have my head cut off, and that would be so disagreeable!"

So Little Claus again received a whole bushel of money; and the host buried the old grandmother as if she had been his own. And when Little Claus came home with all this money he at once sent his boy to Great Claus to ask to borrow a bushel-measure.

"What's that?" said Great Claus. "Have I not killed him? I must go myself and see to this;" and so he went over himself with the bushel to Little Claus.

"Now, where did you get all that money from?" he asked, and opened his eyes wide when he saw all that had been brought together.

"You killed my grandmother, and not me," replied Little Claus; "I've been and sold her, and have got a whole bushel of money for her."

"That's really well paid!" said Great Claus; and he hastened home, took an axe, and killed his own grandmother directly. Then he put her on a carriage, and drove off to the town with her, to where the apothecary lived, and asked him if he would buy a dead person.

"Who is it, and where did you get him from?" asked the apothecary.

"It's my grandmother," answered Great Claus. "I've killed her to get a bushel of money for her."

"Heaven save us!" cried the apothecary. "You're raving. Don't say such things, or you may lose your head!" And he told him earnestly what a bad deed this was that he had done, and what a bad man he was and that he must be punished. And Great Claus was so frightened that he jumped out of the surgery straight into his carriage, and whipped the horses and drove home. But the apothecary and all the people thought him mad; and so they let him drive whither he would.

"You shall pay for this!" said Great Claus, when he was out upon the high road. "Yes, you shall pay me for this, Little Claus;" and directly he got home he took the biggest sack he could find, and went over to Little Claus, and said, "Now you've tricked me again! First I killed my horses, and then my old grandmother! That's all your fault; but you shall never trick me any more!" And he seized Little Claus round the body, and thrust him into his sack, and took him thus upon his back, and called out to him, "Now I shall go off with you and drown you."

It was a long way that he had to travel before he came to the river, and Little Claus was not too light to carry. The road led him close to the church; the organ was playing, and the people were singing so beautifully! Then Great Claus put down his sack with Little Claus in it, close to the church door, and thought it would be a very good thing to go in and hear a psalm before he went further; for Little Claus could not get out, and all the people were in church; and so he went in.

"Ah, yes! ah, yes!" sighed Little Claus in the sack, and turned and twisted; but he found it impossible to loosen the cord. Then there came by an old drover with snow-white hair, and a great staff in his hand; he was driving a whole herd of cows and oxen before him; they stumbled against the sack in which Little Claus was confined, so that it was overthrown.

"Oh, dear!" sighed Little Claus, "I'm so young yet, and am to go to Heaven directly."

"And I, poor fellow," said the drover, "I'm so old already, and can't get there yet."

"Open the sack!" cried Little Claus; "creep into it instead of me, and you will get to Heaven directly!"

"With all my heart," replied the drover; and he untied the sack, out of which Little Claus crept forth immediately.

"But will you look after the cattle?" said the old man; and he crept into the sack at once, whereupon Little Claus tied it up, and went his way with all the cows and oxen.

Soon afterwards, Great Claus came out of the church. He took the sack on his shoulders again,—although it seemed to him as if the sack had become lighter; for the old drover was only half as heavy as Little Claus.

"How light he is to carry now. Yes, that's because I have heard a psalm."

So he went to the river, which was deep and broad, threw the sack with the old drover in it into the water, and called after him, thinking that it was Little Claus, "You lie there! Now, you shan't trick me any more!"

Then he went home; but when he came to a place where there was a cross-road, he met Little Claus driving all his beasts.

"What's this!" cried Great Claus. "Have I not drowned you?"

"Yes," replied Little Claus, "you threw me into the river less than half an hour ago."

"But wherever did you get all those fine beasts from?" asked Great Claus.

"These beasts are sea-cattle," replied Little Claus. "I'll tell you the whole story,—and thank you for drowning me, for now I'm at the top of the tree. I am really rich! How frightened I was when I lay huddled in the sack, and the wind whistled about my ears when you threw me down from the bridge into the cold water. I sank to the bottom immediately; but I did not knock myself, for the most splendid soft grass grows down there. Upon that I fell,—and immediately; the sack was opened, and the loveliest maiden, with snow-white garments and a green wreath on her wet hair, took me by the hand, and said, 'Are you come, Little Claus? Here you have some cattle to begin with. A mile further along the road there is a whole herd more which I will give to you.' And now I saw that the river formed a great highway for the people of the sea. Down in its bed they walked and drove directly from the sea and straight into the land, to where the river ends. There it was so beautifully full of flowers and of the freshest grass; the fishes, which swam in the water, shot past my ears, just as here the birds in the air. What pretty people there were there, and what fine cattle pasturing on mounds and in ditches!"

"But why did you come up again to us directly?" asked Great Claus; "I should not have done that, if it is so beautiful down there."

"Why," replied Little Claus, "in that I just acted with good policy. You heard me tell you that the sea-maiden said, 'A mile further along the road,' and by the road she meant the river—for she can't go anywhere else—'there is a whole herd of cattle for you.' But I know what bends the stream makes—sometimes this way, sometimes that; there's a long way to go round; no, the thing can be managed in a shorter way by coming here to the land, and driving across the fields towards the river again. In this manner I save myself almost half a mile, and get all the quicker to my sea cattle!"

"Oh, you are a fortunate man!" said Great Claus. "Do you think I should get some sea-cattle too if I went down to the bottom of the river?"

"Yes, I think so," replied Little Claus. "But I cannot carry you in the sack as far as the river; you are too heavy for me! But if you will go there, and creep into the sack yourself, I will throw you in with a great deal of pleasure."

"Thanks!" said Great Claus; "but if I don't get any sea-cattle when I am down there, I shall beat you, you may be sure!"

"Oh, no; don't be so fierce!" And so they went together to the river. When the beasts, which were thirsty, saw the stream, they ran as fast as they could to get at the water.

"See how they hurry!" cried Little Claus. "They are longing to get back to the bottom."

"Yes, but help me first!" said Great Claus, "or else you shall be beaten."

And so he crept into the great sack, which had been laid across the back of one of the oxen.

"Put a stone in, for I'm afraid I shan't sink else!" said Great Claus.

"That can be done," replied Little Claus; and he put a big stone into the sack, tied the rope tightly, and pushed against it. *Plump!* There lay Great Claus in the river, and sank at once to the bottom.

"I'm afraid he won't find the cattle!" said Little Claus,—and then he drove homeward with what he had.

THE PRINCESS ON THE PEA

There was once a prince who wanted to marry a princess; but she was to be a *real* princess. So he travelled about, all through the world, to find a real one, but everywhere there was something in the way. There were princesses enough, but whether they were *real* princesses he could not quite make out. There was always something that did not seem quite right. So he came home again, and was quite sad; for he wished so much to have a real princess.

One evening a terrible storm came on. It lightened and thundered, the rain streamed down; it was quite fearful! Then there was a knocking at the town gate, and the old king went out to open it.

It was a princess who stood outside the gate. But, mercy! How she looked, from the rain and the rough weather! The water ran down from her hair and her clothes! It ran in at the points of her shoes, and out at the heels; and yet she declared that she was a real princess.

"Yes, we will soon find that out," thought the old queen. But she said nothing, only went into the bed-chamber, took all the bedding off, and put a pea on the flooring of the bedstead; then she took twenty mattresses and laid them upon the pea, and then twenty eider-down beds upon the mattresses. On this the princess had to lie all night. In the morning she was asked how she had slept.

"Oh, miserably!" said the princess. "I scarcely closed my eyes all night long. Goodness knows what was in my bed. I lay upon something hard, so that I am black and blue all over! It is quite dreadful!"

The princess complaining of the pea in her bed

Now they saw that she was a real princess; for through the twenty mattresses and the twenty eider-down beds she had felt the pea. No one but a real princess could be so delicate.

So the prince took her for his wife; for now he knew that he had a true princess; and the pea was put in the Museum, and it is there now unless somebody has carried it off.

Look you, this is a true story.

LITTLE IDA'S FLOWERS

"My poor flowers are quite dead!" said little Ida. "They were so pretty yesterday; and now all the leaves hang withered. Why do they do that?" she asked the student, who sat on the sofa; for she liked him very much. He knew the prettiest stories, and could cut out the most amusing pictures; hearts, with little ladies in them who danced, flowers, and great castles, in which one could open the doors; he was a merry student. "Why do the flowers look so faded to-day?" she asked again, and showed him a nosegay, which was quite withered.

"Do you know what's the matter with them?" said the student. "The flowers have been at a ball last night, and that's why they hang their heads."

"But flowers cannot dance!" cried little Ida.

"Oh yes," said the student, "when it grows dark, and we are asleep, they jump about merrily. Almost every night they have a ball."

"Can children go to this ball?"

"Yes," said the student, "quite little daisies, and lilies of the valley."

"Where do the beautiful flowers dance?" asked little Ida.

"Have you not often been outside the town-gate, by the great castle, where the king lives in summer, and where the beautiful garden is, with all the flowers? You have seen the swans, which swim up to you when you want to give them bread crumbs. There are capital balls there, believe me!"

"I was out there in the garden yesterday, with my mother," said Ida; "but all the leaves were off the trees, and there was not one flower left. Where are they? In the summer I saw so many."

"They are within, in the castle," replied the student. "You must know, as soon as the king and all the court go to town, the flowers run out of the garden into the castle, and are merry. You should see that. The two most beautiful roses seat themselves on the throne, and then they are king and queen; all the red coxcombs range themselves on either side, and stand and bow; they are the chamberlains. Then all the pretty flowers come, and there is a great ball. The blue violets represent little naval cadets; they dance with hyacinths and crocuses, which they

The student telling little Ida the story of the flowers

call young ladies; the tulips and the great tiger-lilies are old ladies who keep watch that the dancing is well done, and that everything goes on with propriety."

"But," asked little Ida, "is nobody there who hurts the flowers, for dancing in the king's castle?"

"There is nobody who really knows about it," answered the student. "Sometimes, certainly, the old steward of the castle comes at night, and he is to watch there. He has a great bunch of keys with him; but as soon as the flowers hear the keys rattle, they are quite quiet, hide behind the long curtains, and only poke their heads out. Then the old steward says, "I smell that there are flowers here," but he cannot see them.

"That is famous!" cried little Ida, clapping her hands. "But should not I be able to see the flowers?"

"Yes," said the student, "only remember when you go out again, to peep through the window; then you will see them. That is what I did to-day. There was a long yellow lily lying on the sofa and stretching herself. She was a court lady."

"Can the flowers out of the Botanical garden get there? Can they go the long distance?"

"Yes, certainly," replied the student, "if they like they can fly. Have you not seen the beautiful butterflies, red, yellow, and white? They almost look like flowers; and that is what they have been. They have flown off their stalks high into the air, and have beaten it with their leaves, as if these leaves were little wings, and thus they flew. And because they behaved themselves well, they got leave to fly about in the daytime too, and were not obliged to sit still upon their stalks at home; and thus at last the leaves became real wings. That you have seen yourself. It may be, however, that the flowers in the Botanical garden have never been in the King's castle, or that they don't know of the merry proceedings there at night. Therefore, I will tell you something; he will be very much surprised, the botanical professor who lives close by here. You know him, do you not? When you come into his garden, you must tell one of the flowers, that there is a great ball yonder in the castle. Then that flower will tell it to all the rest, and then they will fly away; when the professor comes out into the garden, there will not be a single flower left, and he won't be able to make out where they are gone."

"But how can one flower tell it to another? For you know flowers cannot speak."

"That they cannot, certainly," replied the student; "but then they make signs. Have you not noticed that when the wind blows a little, the flowers nod at one another, and move all their green leaves? They can understand that just as well as we when we speak together."

"Can the professor understand these signs?" asked Ida.

"Yes, certainly. He came one morning into his garden and saw a great stinging-nettle standing there, and making signs to a beautiful red carnation, with its leaves. It was saying, 'You are so pretty, and I love you with all my heart.' But the professor does not like that kind of thing, and he directly slapped the stinging-nettle upon its leaves, for those are its fingers, but he stung himself; and since that time he has not dared to touch a stinging-nettle."

"That is funny," cried little Ida; and she laughed.

"How can any one put such notions into a child's head!" said the tiresome privy councillor, who had come to pay a visit, and was sitting on the sofa. He did not like the student, and always grumbled when he saw him cutting out the merry funny pictures: sometimes a man hanging on a gibbet and holding a heart in his hand, to show that he stole hearts; sometimes an old witch riding on a broom, and carrying her husband on her nose. The councillor could not bear this, and then he said, just as he did now, "How can any one put such notions into a child's head? Those are stupid fancies!"

But to little Ida, what the student told about her flowers seemed very droll; and she thought much about it. The flowers hung their heads, for they were tired because they had danced all night; they were certainly ill. Then she went with them to her other toys which stood on a pretty little table, and the whole drawer was full of beautiful things. In the doll's bed lay her doll Sophia, asleep; but little Ida said to her, "You must really get up, Sophy, and manage to lie in the drawer for to-night. The poor flowers are ill, and they must lie in your bed; perhaps they will then get well again." And she at once took the doll out; but the doll looked cross, and did not say a single word; for she was cross because she could not keep her own bed.

Then Ida laid the flowers in the doll's bed, pulled the little coverlet quite up over them, and said they were to lie still and be good, and she would make them some tea, so that they might get well again, and be able to get up to-morrow. And she drew the curtains closely round the little bed, so that the sun should not shine in their eyes. The whole evening through, she could not help thinking of what the student had told her. And when she was to go to bed herself, she was obliged first to look behind the curtain which hung before the windows where her mother's beautiful flowers stood,—hyacinths as well as tulips;—then she whispered, "I know you're going to the ball to-night!" But the flowers made as if they did not understand a word, and did not stir a leaf; but still little Ida knew what she knew.

When she was in bed she lay for a long time thinking how pretty it must be to see the beautiful flowers dancing out in the king's castle. "I wonder if my flowers have really been there?" And then she fell asleep. In the night she awoke again; she had dreamt of the flowers and of the student, with whom the councillor found fault. It was quite quiet in the bed-room, where Ida lay; the night-lamp burned on the table, and father and mother were asleep.

"I wonder if my flowers are still lying in Sophy's bed?" she thought to herself. "How I should like to know it!" She raised herself a little, and looked at the door, which stood ajar; within lay the flowers and all her playthings. She listened, and then it seemed to her as if she heard some one playing on the piano in the next room, but quite softly and prettily, as she had never heard it before.

"Now all the flowers are certainly dancing in there!" thought she. "Oh, how glad I should be to see it!" But she dared not get up, for she would have disturbed her father and mother.

"If they would only come in!" thought she. But the flowers did not come, and the music continued to play beautifully; then she could not bear it any longer, for it was too pretty; she crept out of her little bed and went quietly to the door, and looked into the room. Oh, how splendid it was, what she saw!

There was no night-lamp burning, but still it was quite light; the moon shone through the window into the middle of the floor; it was almost like day. All the hyacinths and tulips stood in two long rows in the room; there were none at all left at the window. There stood the empty flower-pots. On the floor all the flowers were dancing very gracefully round each other, making perfect turns, and holding each other by the long green leaves as they swang round. But at the piano sat a great yellow lily, which little Ida had certainly seen in summer, for she remembered how the student had said, "How like that one is to Miss Lina." Then he had been laughed at by all; but now it seemed really to little Ida as if the long yellow flower looked like the young lady; and it had just her manners in playing; sometimes bending its long yellow face to one side, sometimes to the other, and nodding in tune to the charming music! No one noticed little Ida. Then she saw a great blue crocus hop into the middle of the table, where the toys stood, and go to the doll's bed and pull the curtains aside; there lay the sick flowers, but they got up directly, and nodded to the others, to say that they wanted to dance too. The old chimney-sweep doll, whose underlip was broken off, stood up and bowed to the pretty flowers; these did not look at all ill now; they jumped down to the others, and were very merry.

Then it seemed as if something fell down from the table. Ida looked that way. It was the birchrod which was jumping down! It seemed almost as if it belonged to the flowers. At any rate it was very neat; and a little wax doll, with just such a broad hat on its head as the Councillor wore, sat upon it. The birchrod hopped about among the flowers, on its three stilted legs, and stamped quite loud; for it was dancing the mazourka; and the other flowers could not manage that dance, because they were too light and unable to stamp like that.

The wax doll on the birchrod all at once became quite great and long, turned itself over the paper flowers and said: "How can one put such things in a child's head! Those are stupid fancies!" and then the wax doll was exactly like the councillor with the broad hat, and looked just as yellow and cross as he. But the paper flowers hit him on his thin legs, and then he shrank up again, and became quite a little wax doll. That was very amusing to see; and little Ida could not restrain her laughter. The birchrod went on dancing, and the councillor was obliged to dance too; it was no use, he might make himself great and long, or remain the little yellow wax doll with the big black hat. Then the other flowers put in a good word for him, especially those who had lain in the doll's bed, and then the birchrod gave over. At the same moment there was a loud knocking at the drawer, inside where Ida's doll, Sophy, lay with many other toys; the chimney-sweep ran to the edge of the table, lay flat down on his stomach, and began to pull the drawer out a little. Then Sophy raised herself and looked round quite astonished. "There must be a ball here—" said she, "Why did nobody tell me?"

"Will you dance with me?" asked the chimney-sweep. "You are a nice sort of fellow to dance!" she replied, and turned her back upon him. Then she seated herself upon the drawer, and thought that one of the flowers would come and ask her; but not one of them came. Then she coughed, "Hem, Hem, Hem!" but for all that not one came. The chimney-sweep now danced all alone, and that was not at all so bad.

As none of the flowers seemed to notice Sophy, she let herself fall down from the drawer straight upon the floor, so that there was a great noise. The flowers now came all running up, to ask if she had not hurt herself; and they were all very polite to her, especially the flowers that had lain in her bed. But she had not hurt herself at all; and Ida's flowers all thanked her for the nice bed, and were kind to her, took her into the middle of the room, where the moon shone in, and danced with her; and all the other flowers formed a circle round her. Now Sophy was glad, and said they might keep her bed; she did not at all mind lying in the drawer.

But the flowers said, "We thank you heartily, but in any way we cannot live long. To-morrow we shall be quite dead. But tell little Ida she is to bury us out in the garden, where the canary lies; then we shall wake up again in summer, and be far more beautiful."

"No, you must not die," said Sophy; and she kissed the flowers. Then the door opened, and a great number of splendid flowers came dancing in. Ida could not imagine whence they had come; these must certainly all be flowers from the King's castle yonder. First of all came two glorious roses, and they had little gold crowns on; they were a King and a Queen. Then came the prettiest stocks and carnations; and they bowed in all directions. They had music with them. Great poppies and peonies blew upon pea pods till they were quite red in the face. The blue hyacinths and the little white snow-drops rang just as if they had bells. That was wonderful music! Then came many other flowers, and danced all together; the blue violets and the pink primroses, daisies and the lilies of the valley. And all the flowers kissed one another. It was beautiful to look at!

At last the flowers wished one another good-night; then little Ida, too, crept to bed, where she dreamt of all she had seen.

When she rose next morning, she went quickly to the little table, to see if the little flowers were still there. She drew aside the curtains of the little bed; there were they all, but they were quite faded, far more than yesterday. Sophy was lying in the drawer where Ida had laid her; she looked very sleepy.

"Do you remember what you were to say to me?" asked little Ida. But Sophy looked quite stupid, and did not say a single word.

"You are not good at all!" said Ida. "And yet they all danced with you."

Then she took a little paper box, on which were painted beautiful birds, and opened it, and laid the dead flowers in it. "That shall be your pretty coffin," said she, "and when my cousins come to visit me by-and-by, they shall help me to bury you outside in the garden, so that you may grow again in summer, and become more beautiful than ever."

These cousins were two merry boys. Their names were Gustave and Adolphe; their father had given them two new cross-bows, and they had brought these with them to show to Ida. She told them about the poor flowers which had died, and then they got leave to bury them. The two boys went first, with their cross-bows on their shoulders, and little Ida followed with the dead flowers in the pretty box. Out in the garden a little grave was dug. Ida first kissed the flowers, and then laid them in the earth in the box, and Adolphe and Gustave shot with their cross-bows over the grave;—for they had not guns or cannons.

THUMBELINA

There was once a woman who wished for a very little child; but she did not know where she should procure one. So she went to an old witch, and said: "I do so very much wish for a little child; can you not tell me where I can get one?"

"Oh! That can easily be managed," said the witch. "There you have a barley-corn,—that is not of the kind which grows in the countryman's field, and which the chickens get to eat,—put that into a flowerpot, and you shall see what you shall see."

"Thank you," said the woman; and she gave the witch twelve shillings, for that is what it cost. Then she went home and planted the barley-corn, and immediately there grew up a great handsome flower, which looked like a tulip; but the leaves were tightly closed, as though it were still a bud.

"That is a beautiful flower," said the woman; and she kissed its yellow and red leaves. But just as she kissed it, the flower opened with a pop. It was a real tulip, as one could now see; but in the middle of the flower there sat upon the green velvet stamens a little maiden, delicate and graceful to behold. She was scarcely half a thumb's length in height, and therefore she was called Thumbelina.

A neat polished walnut-shell served Thumbelina for a cradle, blue violet leaves were her mattresses, with a rose-leaf for a coverlet. There she slept at night; but in the daytime she played upon the table, where the woman had put a plate with a wreath of flowers around it, whose stalks stood in water; on the water swam a great tulip-leaf, and on this the little maiden could sit, and row from one side of the plate to the other, with two white horse-hairs for oars. That looked pretty, indeed! She could also sing, and, indeed, so delicately and sweetly, that the like had never been heard.

Once as she lay at night in her pretty bed, there came an old toad creeping through the window, in which one pane was broken. The toad was very ugly, big, and damp; it hopped straight down upon the table, where Thumbelina lay sleeping under the rose-leaf.

"That would be a handsome wife for my son," said the toad; and she took the walnut-shell in which Thumbelina lay asleep, and hopped with it through the window down into the garden.

There ran a great broad brook; but the margin was swampy and soft, and here the toad dwelt with her son. Ugh! He was ugly, and looked just like his mother. "Croak, croak, brek-kek-kex!" that was all he could say when he saw the graceful little maiden in the walnut-shell.

"Don't speak so loud, or she will awake!" said the old toad. "She might run away from us, for she is as light as a bit of swan's-down. We will put her out in the brook upon one of the broad water-lily leaves. That will be just like an island for her, she is so small and light. Then she can't get away, while we put the state room under the marsh in order, where you are to live and keep house together."

Out in the brook there grew many water-lilies with broad green leaves, which looked as if they were floating on the water; the leaf which lay farthest out was also the greatest of all, and to that the old toad swam out and laid the walnut-shell upon it with Thumbelina. The little tiny Thumbelina woke early in the morning, and when she saw where she was, she began to cry very bitterly; for there was water on every side of the great green leaf, and she could not get to land at all. The old toad sat down in the marsh decking out her room with rushes and yellow weed; it was to be made very pretty for the new daughter-in-law; then she swam out, with her ugly son, to the leaf on which Thumbelina was. They wanted to take her pretty bed, which was to be put in the bridal chamber before she went in there herself. The old toad bowed low before her in the water, and said: "Here is my son; he will be your husband, and you will live splendidly together in the marsh."

"Croak, croak, brek-kek-kex!" was all the son could say.

Then they took the delicate little bed and swam away with it; but Thumbelina sat all alone upon the green leaf and wept, for she did not like to live at the nasty toad's, and have her ugly son for a husband. The little fishes swimming in the water below, had both seen the toad, and had also heard what she said; therefore they stretched forth their heads, for they wanted to see the little girl. So soon as they saw her they considered her so pretty; that they felt very sorry she should have to go down to the ugly toad. No! That must never be! They assembled together in the water around the green stalk which held the leaf, on which the little maiden stood, and with their teeth they gnawed away the stalk, and so the leaf swam down the stream; and away went Thumbelina far away, where the toad could not get at her.

Thumbelina sailed by many cities, and the little birds which sat in the bushes saw her, and said: "What a lovely little girl!" The leaf swam away with them, farther and farther—so Thumbelina travelled out of the country.

A graceful little white butterfly always fluttered round her, and at last alighted on the leaf. Thumbelina pleased him, and she was very glad of this, for now the toad could not reach them; and it was so beautiful where she was floating along—the sun shone upon the water, and the water glistened like the most splendid gold. She took her girdle and bound one end of it round the butterfly, fastening the other end of the ribbon to the leaf. The leaf now glided onward much faster; and Thumbelina too, for she stood upon the leaf.

There came a big cockchafer flying up;—and he saw her, and immediately clasped his claws round her slender waist, and flew with her up into a tree. The green leaf went swimming down the brook, and the butterfly with it; for he was fastened to the leaf and could not get away from it.

Mercy! How frightened poor little Thumbelina was when the

cockchafer flew with her up into the tree. But especially she was sorry for the fine white butterfly whom she had bound fast to the leaf, for if he could not free himself from it, he would be obliged to starve. The cockchafer, however, did not trouble himself at all about this. He seated himself with her upon the biggest green leaf on the tree, gave her the sweet part of the flowers to eat, and declared that she was very pretty, though she did not in the least resemble a cockchafer. Afterwards came all the other cockchafers who lived in the tree to pay a visit; they looked at Thumbelina, and said: "Why, she has not even more than two legs—that has a wretched appearance." "She has not any feelers," cried another. "Her waist is quite slender—fie! she looks like a human creature—how ugly she is," said all the lady cockchafers. And yet Thumbelina was very pretty. Even the cockchafer who had carried her off saw that; but when all the others declared she was ugly, he believed it at last, and would not have her at all—she might go whither she liked. Then they flew down with her from the tree, and set her upon a daisy, and she wept, because she was so ugly that the cockchafers would have nothing to say to her; and yet she was the loveliest little being one could imagine, and as tender and delicate as a rose-leaf.

The whole summer through poor Thumbelina lived quite alone in the great wood. She wove herself a bed out of blades of grass, and hung it up under a shamrock, so that she was protected from the rain; she plucked the honey out of the flowers for food, and drank of the dew which stood every morning upon the leaves. Thus summer and autumn passed away; but now came winter, the cold long winter. All the birds who had sung so sweetly before her flew away; trees and flowers shed their leaves; the great shamrock under which she had lived, shrivelled up, and there remained nothing of it but a yellow withered stalk; and she was dreadfully cold, for her clothes were torn, and she herself was so frail and delicate—poor little Thumbelina! she was nearly frozen. It began to snow, and every snow-flake that fell upon her was like a whole shovelful thrown upon one of us, for we are tall, and she was only an inch long. Then she wrapped herself in a dry leaf, and that tore in the middle, and would not warm her—she shivered with cold.

Close to the wood into which she had now come, lay a great corn-field, but the corn was gone long ago; only the naked dry stubble stood up out of the frozen ground. These were just like a great forest for her to wander through; and, oh! How she trembled with cold. Then she arrived at the door of the field-mouse. This mouse had a little hole under the stubble. There the field-mouse lived, warm and comfortable, and had a whole roomful of corn, a glorious kitchen and larder. Poor Thumbelina stood at the door just like a poor beggar girl, and begged for a little bit of a barley-corn, for she had not had the smallest morsel to eat for the last two days.

"You poor little creature," said the field-mouse,—for after all she was a good old field-mouse,—"come into my warm room and dine with me."

As she was pleased with Thumbelina, she said: "If you like, you may stay with me through the winter, but you must keep my room clean and neat, and tell me little stories, for I am very fond of those." And Thumbelina did as the kind old field-mouse bade her, and had a very good time of it.

"Now we shall soon have a visitor,—" said the field-mouse, "My neighbour is in the habit of visiting me once a week. He is even better off than I am, has great rooms, and a beautiful black velvety fur. If you could only get him for your husband you would be well provided for—you must tell him the prettiest stories you know."

But Thumbelina did not care about this; she thought nothing of the neighbour, for he was a mole. He came and paid his visit in his black velvet coat. The field-mouse told how rich and how learned he was, and how his house was more than twenty times larger than hers; that he had learning, but that he did not like the sun and beautiful flowers, for he had never seen them.

Thumbelina had to sing, and she sang: "Cockchafer, fly away:" and "When the parson goes afield." Then the mole fell in love with her, because of her delicious voice; but he said nothing, for he was a sedate man.

A short time before, he had dug a long passage through the earth, from his own house to theirs; and Thumbelina and the field-mouse obtained leave to walk in this passage as much as they wished. But he begged them not to be afraid of the dead bird which was lying in the passage. It was an entire bird, with wings and a beak. certainly must have died only a short time before, and was now buried just where the mole had made his passage.

The mole took a bit of decayed wood in his mouth, and it glimmered like fire in the dark; and then he went first and lighted them through the long dark passage. When they came where the dead bird lay the mole thrust up his broad nose against the ceiling, so that a great hole was made, through which the daylight could shine down. In the middle of the floor lay a dead swallow, his beautiful wings pressed close against his sides, and his head and feet drawn back under his feathers; the poor bird had certainly died of cold. Thumbelina was very sorry for this; she was very fond of all the little birds, who had sung and twittered so prettily before her through the summer; but the mole gave him a push with his crooked legs, and said: "Now he doesn't pipe any more! It must be miserable to be born a little bird. I'm thankful that none of my children can be that; such a bird has nothing but his 'tweet-tweet,' and has to starve in the winter!"

"Yes, you may well say that, as a clever man," observed the field-mouse. "Of what use is all his tweet-tweet to a bird when the winter comes? He must starve and freeze. But they say that's very aristocratic."

Thumbelina said nothing; but when the two others turned their backs on the bird, she bent down, put the feathers aside which covered his head, and kissed him upon his closed eyes.

"Perhaps it was he who sang so prettily before me in the summer," she thought. "How much pleasure he gave me, the dear beautiful bird!"

The mole now closed up the hole through which the daylight shone in, and accompanied the ladies home. But at night Thumbelina could not sleep at all; so she got up out of her bed and wove a large beautiful carpet of hay, and carried it and spread it over the dead bird, and laid the thin stamens of flowers, soft as cotton, and which she had found in the field-mouse's room, at the bird's sides, so that he might lie soft in the ground.

"Farewell, you pretty little bird!" said she. "Farewell! and thanks to you for your beautiful song in summer, when all the trees were green, and the sun shone down warmly upon us," and then she laid the bird's head on her heart. But the bird was not dead; he was only lying there torpid with cold; and now he had been warmed, and came to life again.

In autumn all the swallows fly away to warm countries; but if one happens to be belated, it becomes so cold, that it falls down as if dead, and lies where it fell, and then the cold snow covers it.

Thumbelina fairly trembled, she was so startled; for the bird was large, very large, compared with her, who was only an inch in height. But she took courage, laid the cotton closer round the poor bird, and brought a leaf that she had used as her own coverlet, and laid it over the bird's head.

The next night she crept out to him again—and now he was alive, but quite weak; he could only open his eyes for a moment, and look at Thumbelina, who stood before him with a bit of decayed wood in her hand, for she had not a lantern.

"I thank you, you pretty little child," said the sick swallow; "I have been famously warmed. Soon I shall get my strength back again, and I shall be able to fly about in the warm sunshine."

"Oh!" she said, "it is so cold without. It snows and freezes. Stay in your warm bed, I will nurse you."

Then she brought the swallow water in the petal of a flower; and the swallow drank, and told her how he had torn one of his wings in a thorn-bush, and thus had not been able to fly so fast as the other swallows, which had sped away, far away, to the warm countries. So at last he had fallen to the ground, but he could remember nothing more, and did not know at all how he had come where she found him.

The whole winter the swallow remained there, and Thumbelina nursed and tended him heartily. Neither the field-mouse nor the mole heard anything about it, for they did not like the poor swallow. So soon as the spring came, and the sun warmed the earth, the swallow bade Thumbelina farewell, and she opened the hole which the mole had made in the ceiling. The sun shone in upon them gloriously, and the swallow asked if Thumbelina would go with him; she could sit upon his back, and they would fly away far into the green-wood. But Thumbelina knew that the old field-mouse would be grieved if she left her. "No, I cannot!" said Thumbelina.

"Farewell, farewell, you good, pretty girl!" said the swallow; and he flew out into the sunshine. Thumbelina looked after him, and the tears came into her eyes, for she was heartily fond of the poor swallow.

"Tweet-weet, tweet-weet," sang the bird, and flew into the green forest. Thumbelina felt very sad. She did not get permission to go out into the warm sunshine. The corn which was sown in the field over the house of the field-mouse, grew up high into the air; it was quite a thick wood for the poor girl, who was only an inch in height.

"You are betrothed now, Thumbelina!" said the field-mouse. "My neighbour has proposed for you. What great fortune for a poor child like you—now you must work at your outfit, woollen and linen clothes both; for you must lack nothing when you become the mole's wife."

Thumbelina had to turn the spindle, and the mole hired four spiders to weave for her day and night. Every evening the mole paid her a visit; and he was always saying, that when the summer should draw to a close, the sun would not shine nearly so hot, for that now it burned the earth almost as hard as a stone. Yes, when the summer should have gone, then he would keep his wedding day with Thumbelina. But she was not glad at all, for she did not like the tiresome mole. Every morning when the sun rose, and every evening when it went down, she crept out at the door, and when the wind blew the corn ears apart, so that she could see the blue sky, she thought how bright and beautiful it was out here, and wished heartily to see her dear swallow again. But the swallow did not come back; he had doubtless flown far away, in the fair green forest. When autumn came on, Thumbelina had all her outfit ready.

"In four weeks you shall celebrate your wedding," said the field-mouse to her.

But Thumbelina wept, and declared she would not have the tiresome mole.

"Nonsense," said the field-mouse. "Don't be obstinate, or I will bite you with my white teeth. He is a very fine man, whom you will marry. The Queen herself has not such a black velvet fur; and his kitchen and cellar are full. Be thankful for your good fortune."

Now the wedding was to be held. The mole had already come to fetch Thumbelina; she was to live with him, deep under the earth, and never to come out into the warm sunshine, for that he did not like. The poor little thing was very sorrowful; she was now to say farewell to the glorious sun, which after all she had been allowed by the field-mouse to see from the threshold of the door.

"Farewell, thou bright sun!" she said, and stretched out her arms towards it; and walked a little way forth from the house of the field-mouse, for now the corn had been reaped, and only the dry stubble stood in the fields. "Farewell!" she repeated, twining her arms round a little red flower, which still bloomed there. "Greet the little swallow from me, if you see him again."

"Tweet-weet! tweet-weet!" a voice suddenly sounded over her head. She looked up; it was the little swallow, who was just flying by. When he saw Thumbelina he was very glad; and Thumbelina told him, how loth she was to have the ugly mole for her husband, and that she was to live deep under the earth, where the sun never shone. And she could not refrain from weeping.

"The cold winter is coming now," said the swallow. "I am going to fly far away into the warm countries. Will you come with me? You can sit upon my back, then we shall fly from the ugly mole and his dark room,—away, far away, over the mountains, to the warm countries, where the sun shines warmer than here, where it is always summer, and there are lovely flowers. Only fly with me, you dear little Thumbelina, you who have saved my life when I lay frozen in the dark earthy passage."

"Yes, I will go with you!" said Thumbelina; and she seated herself on the bird's back, with her feet on his outspread wing, and bound her girdle fast to one of his strongest feathers; then the swallow flew up into the air over forest and over sea, high up over the great mountains, where the snow always lies; and Thumbelina felt cold in the bleak air, but then she hid under the bird's warm feathers, and only put out her little head, to admire all the beauties beneath her.

At last they came to the warm countries. There the sun shone far brighter than here; the sky seemed twice as high, and in ditches and on the hedges grew the most beautiful blue and green grapes; lemons and oranges hung in the woods; the air was fragrant with myrtles and balsams, and on the roads the loveliest children ran about, playing with great, gay butterflies. But the swallow flew still further, and it became more and more beautiful. Under the most glorious green trees, by the blue lake, stood a palace of dazzling white marble, from the olden time. Vines clustered around the lofty pillars; at the top were many swallows' nests, and in one of these the swallow lived who carried Thumbelina.

"That is my house," said the swallow. "But it is not right that you should live there. It is not yet properly arranged, by a great deal, that

you can be content with it. Select for yourself one of the splendid flowers which grow down yonder; then I will put you into it, and you shall have everything as nice as you can wish."

"That is capital," cried she, and clapped her little hands.

A great marble pillar lay there, which had fallen to the ground and had been broken into three pieces; but between these pieces grew the most beautiful great white flowers. The swallow flew down with Thumbelina, and set her upon one of the broad leaves. But what was the little maid's surprise? There sat a little man in the midst of the flower, as white and transparent as if he had been made of glass; he wore the neatest of gold crowns on his head, and the brightest wings on his shoulders; he himself was not bigger than Thumbelina. He was the angel of the flower. In each of the flowers dwelt such a little man or woman, but this one was King over them all.

"Heavens! How beautiful he is!" whispered Thumbelina to the swallow.

The little Prince was very much frightened at the swallow; for it was quite a gigantic bird to him, who was so small. But when he saw Thumbelina he became very glad; she was the prettiest maiden he had ever seen. Therefore he took off his golden crown, and put it upon her, asked her name, and if she would be his wife, and then she should be

Queen of all the flowers. Now this was truly a different kind of man to the son of the toad, and the mole with the black velvet fur. She therefore said "Yes!" to the charming Prince. And out of every flower came a lady or a lord, so pretty to behold that it was a delight; each one brought Thumbelina a present; but the best gift was a pair of beautiful wings, which had belonged to a great white fly; these were fastened to Thumbelina's back, and now she could fly from flower to flower. Then there was much rejoicing; and the little swallow sat above them in his nest, and was to sing the marriage song, which he accordingly did, as well as he could; but yet in his heart he was sad, for he was so fond, oh! so fond of Thumbelina, and would have liked never to part from her.

"You shall not be called Thumbelina," said the flower angel to her. "That is an ugly name, and you are too fair for it—we will call you Maia."

"Farewell, farewell!" said the little swallow, with a heavy heart; and he flew away again from the warm countries, far away back to Denmark. There he had a little nest over the window of the man who can tell fairy tales. Before him he sang "Tweet-weet, tweet-weet,"—and from him we have the whole story.

THE NAUGHTY BOY

There was once an old poet—a very good old poet. One evening, as he sat at home there was dreadfully bad weather without. The rain streamed down: but the old poet sat comfortably by his stove, where the fire was burning and the roasting apples were hissing.

"There won't be a dry thread left on the poor people who are out in this weather!" said he—for he was a good old poet.

"Oh, open to me! I am cold, and quite wet," said a little child outside; and it cried, and knocked at the door, while the rain streamed down and the wind made all the casements rattle.

"You poor little creature!" said the poet; and he went to open the door. There stood a little boy; he was quite naked, and the water ran in streams from his long fair curls. He was shivering with cold; had he

The old poet shot through the heart by Cupid

not been let in, he would certainly have perished in the bad weather.

"You little creature!" said the poet, and took him by the hand. "Come to me, and I will warm you. You shall have wine and an apple, for you are a capital boy."

And so he was. His eyes sparkled like two bright stars, and though the water ran down from his fair curls, they fell in beautiful ringlets. He looked like a little angel child, but was white with cold and trembled all over. In his hand he carried a famous bow, but it looked quite spoiled by the wet; all the colours in the beautiful arrows had been blurred together by the rain.

The old poet sat down by the stove, took the little boy on his knees, pressed the water out of the child's curls, warmed its hands in his own, and made it some sweet wine-whey; then the boy recovered himself and his cheeks grew red, and he jumped to the floor and danced round the old poet.

"You are a merry boy!" said the old poet. "What is your name?" "My name is Cupid," he replied. "Don't you know me? There lies my bow—I shoot with that, you may believe me! See, now the weather is clearing up outside, and the moon shines."

"But your bow is spoilt," said the old poet. "That would be a pity," replied the little boy, and he took the bow and looked at it. "Oh, it is quite dry, and has suffered no damage; the string is quite stiff: I will try it!" Then he bent it, and laid an arrow across, aimed and shot the good old poet straight through the heart. "Do you see now, that my bow was not spoiled?" said he, and laughed out loud and ran away. What a naughty boy, to shoot the old poet in that way, who had admitted him into the warm room, and been so kind to him, and given him the best wine and the best apple!

The good poet lay upon the floor and wept; he was really shot straight into the heart. "Fie!" he cried, "what a naughty boy this Cupid is! I shall tell that to all good children, so that they may take care, and never play with him, for he will do them a hurt!"

All good children, girls and boys, to whom he told this, took good heed of this naughty Cupid; but still he tricked them, for he is very cunning! When the students come out from the lectures, he runs at their side with a book under his arm, and has a black coat on. They cannot recognize him at all. And then they take his arm and fancy he is a student too; but he thrusts the arrow into their breasts; yes, he is always following people! He sits in the great chandelier in the theatre and burns brightly, so that the people think he is a lamp; but afterwards they see their error. He runs about in the palace garden and on the promenades! Yes, he once shot your father and your mother straight through the heart! Only ask them, and you will hear what they say. Oh, he is a bad boy, this Cupid; you must never have anything to do with him. He is after every one. Only think, once he shot an arrow at old grandmamma; but that was a long time ago. The wound has indeed healed long since, but she will never forget it. Fie on that wicked Cupid! But now you know him, and know what a naughty boy he is.

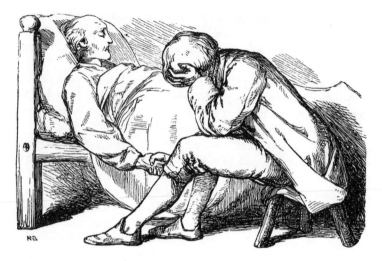

John at the death-bed of his father

THE TRAVELLING COMPANION

Poor John was in great tribulation, for his father was very ill, and could not get well again. Except these two, there was no one at all in the little room: the lamp on the table was nearly extinguished, and it was quite late in the evening.

"You have been a good son, John!" said the sick father. "Providence will help you through the world." And he looked at him with mild earnest eyes, drew a deep breath, and died; it was just as if he slept. But John wept; for now he had no one in the world, neither father nor mother, neither sister nor brother. Poor John! He lay on his knees before the bed, kissed his dead father's hand and shed very many bitter tears; but at last his eyes closed, and he went to sleep, lying with his head against the hard bedpost.

Then he dreamed a strange dream: he saw the sun and moon shine upon him, and he beheld his father again, fresh and well, and he heard his father laugh as he had always laughed when he was very glad. A beautiful girl, with a golden crown upon her long shining hair, gave him her hand; and his father said, "Do you see what a bride you have gained? She is the most beautiful in the whole world!" Then he awoke, and all the splendour was gone. His father was lying dead and cold in the bed; and there was no one at all with them. Poor John!

In the next week the dead man was buried. The son walked close behind the coffin, and could now no longer see the good father who had loved him so much. He heard how they threw the earth down upon the coffin, and stopped to see the last corner of it; but the next shovelful of earth hid even that; then he felt just as if his heart would burst into pieces, so sorrowful was he. Around him they were singing a psalm; those were sweet holy tones that arose, and the tears came into John's eyes; he wept, and that did him good in his sorrow. The sun shone magnificently on the green trees, just as if it would have said, "You may no longer be sorrowful, John! Do you see how beautiful the sky is? Your father is up there and prays to the Father of all, that it may always be well with you."

"I will always do right, too," said John, "then I shall go to Heaven to my father; and what joy that will be, when we see each other again! How much I shall then have to tell him! and he will show me so many things, and explain to me the glories of Heaven, just as he taught me here on earth. Oh, how joyful that will be!"

He pictured that to himself so plainly, that he smiled, while the tears were still rolling down his cheeks. The little birds sat up in the chestnut trees, and twittered, "Tweet-weet, tweet-weet!" They were joyful and merry, though they had been at the burying; but they seemed to know that the dead man was now in Heaven; that he had wings, far larger and more beautiful than theirs; that he was now happy, because he had been good upon earth, and that they were glad at it. John saw how they flew from the green tree out into the world, and he felt inclined to fly too. But first he cut out a great cross of wood to put on his father's grave; and when he brought it there in the evening the grave was decked with sand and flowers; strangers had done this; for they were all very fond of the good father who was now dead.

Early next morning John packed his little bundle, and put in his belt his whole inheritance, which consisted of fifty dollars and a few silver shillings; with this he intended to wander out into the world. But first he went to the churchyard, to his father's grave, to say a prayer, and to bid him "farewell."

Out in the field where he was walking, all the flowers stood fresh and beautiful in the warm sunshine; and they nodded in the wind just as if they would have said, "Welcome to the green-wood! Is it not fine here?" But John turned back once more to look at the old church, in which he had been christened when he was a little child, and where he had been every Sunday with his father, at the service, and had sung his psalm; then, high up in one of the openings of the tower he saw the ringer standing in his little pointed red cap, shading his face with his bent arm, to keep the sun from shining in his eyes. John nodded a farewell to him, and the little ringer waved his red cap, laid his hand on his heart, and kissed his hand to John a great many times, to show that he wished the traveller well and hoped he would have a prosperous journey.

John thought what a number of fine things he would get to see in the great splendid world; and he went on farther—farther than he had ever been before. He did not know the places at all through which he came, nor the people whom he met. Now he was far away in a strange region.

The first night he was obliged to lie down on a haystack in the field to sleep, for he had no other bed. But that was very nice he thought; the King could not be better off. There was the whole field, with the brook, the haystack, and the blue sky above it,—that was certainly a beautiful sleeping room. The green grass with the little red and white flowers was the carpet; the elder-bushes and the wild-rose hedges were garlands of flowers; and for a wash-hand basin he had the whole brook, with the clear fresh water; and the rushes bowed before him and wished him "good evening" and "good morning." The moon was certainly a great night-lamp, high up, under the blue ceiling: and that lamp would never set fire to the curtains with its light:—John could sleep quite safely; and he did so, and never woke until the sun rose and all the little birds were singing around, "Good morning! Good morning! Are you not up yet?"

The bells were ringing for church; it was Sunday. The people went to hear the preacher, and John followed them and sang a psalm, and heard God's word. It seemed to him just as if he was in his own church, where he had been christened, and had sung psalms with his father.

Out in the churchyard were many graves, and on some of them the grass grew high. Then he thought of his father's grave, which would at last look like these, as he could not weed it and adorn it. So he sat down and plucked up the long grass, set up the wooden crosses which had fallen down, and put back in their places the wreath which the wind had blown away from the graves; for he thought, "Perhaps some one will do the same to my father's grave as I cannot do it!"

Outside the churchyard gate stood an old beggar, leaning on his crutch. John gave him the silver shillings which he had, and then went away, happy and cheerful, into the wide world. Towards evening the weather became terribly bad. He made haste to get under shelter,—but dark night soon came on; then at last he came to a little church, which lay quite solitary on a small hill.

"Here I will sit down in a corner," said he, and went in. "I am quite tired and require a little rest." Then he sat down, folded his hands, and said his evening prayer; and before he was aware of it he was asleep and dreaming, while it thundered and lightened without.

When he woke it was midnight; but the bad weather had passed by, and the moon shone in upon him through the windows. In the midst of the church stood an open coffin, with a dead man in it who had not yet been buried. John was not at all timid, for he had a good conscience; and he knew very well that the dead do not harm any one. The living, who do evil, are bad men. Two such living bad men stood close by the dead man, who had been placed here in the church till he should be buried. They had an evil design against him, and would not let him rest quietly in his coffin, but were going to throw him out before the church door, the poor dead man!

"Why will you do that?" asked John. "That is bad and wicked. Let him rest, for mercy's sake." "Nonsense!" replied the two bad men. "He has cheated us. He owes us money and could not pay it, and now he's dead into the bargain, and we shall not get a penny! So we mean to revenge ourselves famously; he shall lie like a dog outside the church door!"

"I have not more than fifty dollars," cried John. "That is my whole inheritance; but I will gladly give it you, if you will honestly promise me to leave the poor dead man in peace. I shall manage to get on without the money; I have hearty strong limbs, and Heaven will always help me!"

"Yes," said these ugly men, "if you will pay his debt we will do nothing to him, you may depend upon that!" And then they took the money he gave them, laughed aloud at his good nature, and went their way. But he laid the corpse out again in the coffin, and folded its hands, took leave of it, and went away contentedly through the great forest.

All around, wherever the moon could shine through, between the trees, he saw the graceful little elves playing merrily. They did not let him disturb them; they knew that he was a good innocent man; and it is only the bad people who never get to see the elves. Some of them were not larger than a finger's breadth, and had fastened up their long yellow hair with golden combs; they were rocking themselves, two and two, on the great dewdrops that lay on the leaves and on the high grass; sometimes the drop rolled away, and then they fell down between the long grass-stalks, and that occasioned much laughter and noise among the other little creatures! It was charming. They sang, and John recognized quite plainly the pretty songs which he had learned as a little boy. Great coloured spiders, with silver crowns on their heads, had to spin long hanging bridges and palaces from hedge to hedge; and as the tiny dewdrops fell on these they looked like gleaming glass in the moonshine. This continued until the sun rose. Then the little elves crept into the flower buds, and the wind caught their bridges and palaces, which flew through the air in the shape of spiders' webs.

John had just come out of the wood, when a strong man's voice called out behind him, "Halloo, comrade, whither are you journeying?" "Into the wide world!" he replied; "I have neither father nor mother, and am but a poor lad. But Providence will help me."

"I am going out into the wide world too," said the strange man. "Shall we two keep one another company?"

"Yes, certainly," said John; and so they went on together. Soon they became very fond of each other, for they were both good men. But John saw that the stranger was much more clever than himself. He had travelled through almost the whole world, and knew how to tell of almost everything that existed.

The sun already stood high, when they seated themselves under a great tree to eat their breakfast; and just then an old woman came up. Oh, she was very old, and walked quite bent, leaning upon a crutch-stick; upon her back she carried a bundle of firewood which she had collected in the forest. Her apron was untied, and John saw that three great stalks of fern and some willow twigs looked out from within it. When she was close to them, her foot slipped; she fell, and gave a loud scream, for she had broken her leg, the poor old woman!

John directly proposed that they should carry the old woman home to her dwelling; but the stranger opened his knapsack, took out a little box, and said that he had a salve here which would immediately make her leg whole and strong, so that she could walk home herself as if she had never broken her leg at all. But for that he required that she should give him the three rods which she carried in her apron.

"That would be paying well!" said the old woman; and she nodded her head in a strange way. She did not like to give away the rods; but then it was not agreeable to lie there with a broken leg. So she gave him the wands; and as soon as he had only rubbed the ointment on her leg, the old mother arose, and walked much better than before. Such was the power of this ointment. But then, it was not to be bought at the chemist's.

"What do you want with the rods?" John asked his travelling companion. "They are three capital fern brooms," replied he. "I like those very much, for I am a whimsical fellow!" and they went on a good way.

"See how the sky is becoming overcast!" said John, pointing straight before them. "Those are terribly thick clouds." "No!" replied his travelling companion, "those are not clouds, they are mountains—the great glorious mountains, on which one gets quite up over the clouds, and into the free air! Believe me, it is delicious! To-morrow we shall certainly be far out into the world."

But that was not so near as it looked; they had to walk for a whole day before they came to the mountains, where the black woods grew straight up towards heaven, and there were stones almost as big as a whole town. It might certainly be hard work to get quite across there; and for that reason John and his comrade went into the inn to rest themselves well, and gather strength for the morrow's journey.

Down in the great common room in the inn many guests were

assembled; for a man was there exhibiting a puppet-show. He had just put up his little theatre, and the people were sitting round to see the play. Quite in front a fat butcher had taken his seat in the very best place; his great bull-dog, who looked very much inclined to bite, sat at his side, and made big eyes, as all the rest were doing too.

Now the play began; and it was a very nice play, with a king and a queen in it; they sat upon a beautiful throne, and had gold crowns on their heads, and long trains to their clothes, for their means admitted of that. The prettiest of wooden dolls with glass eyes and great moustaches stood at all the doors and opened and shut them so that fresh air might come into the room. It was a very pleasant play, and not at all mournful. But goodness knows what the big bull-dog can have been thinking of,—just as the queen stood up and was walking across the boards, as the fat butcher did not hold him, he made a spring upon the stage, and seized the queen round her slender waist so that it cracked again. It was quite terrible!

The poor man who managed the play, was very much frightened and quite sorrowful about his queen! For she was the daintiest doll he possessed, and now the ugly bull-dog had bitten off her head. But afterwards when the people went away, the stranger said that he would put her to rights again; and then he brought out his little box, and rubbed the doll with the ointment with which he had cured the old woman when she broke her leg. As soon as the doll had been rubbed, she was whole again; yes, she could even move all her limbs by herself; it was no longer necessary to pull her by her string. The doll was like a living person, only that she could not speak. The man who had the little puppet-show, was very glad, now he had not to hold this doll any more. She could dance by herself; and none of the others could do that.

When night came on, and all the people in the inn had gone to bed, there was some one who sighed so fearfully, and went on doing it so long, that they all got up to see who this could be. The man who had shown the play went to his little theatre, for it was there that somebody was sighing. All the wooden dolls lay mixed together, the king and all his followers; and it was they who sighed so pitiably, and stared with their glass eyes; for they wished to be rubbed a little as the queen had been, so that they might be able to move by themselves. The queen at once sank on her knees and stretched forth her beautiful crown while she begged: "Take this from me, but rub my husband and my courtiers!" Then the poor man, the proprietor of the theatre and the dolls, could not refrain from weeping, for he was really sorry for them. He immediately promised the travelling companion that he would give him all the money he should receive the next evening for the representation, if the latter would only anoint four or five of his dolls. But the comrade said, he did not require anything at all but the sword the man wore by his side; and on receiving this he anointed six of the dolls, who immediately began to dance so gracefully that all the girls, the living human girls, fell a dancing too. The coachman and the cook danced, the waiter and the chambermaid, and all the strangers, and the fire shovel and tongs: but these latter fell down, just as they made their first leaps. Yes, it was a merry night!

Next morning John went away from them all with his travelling companion, up on to the high mountains, and through the great pine woods. They came so high up that the church steeples under them looked at last like little blue berries among all the green; and they could see very far, many many miles away, where they had never been. So much splendour in the lovely world John had never seen at one time before. And the sun shone warm in the fresh blue air, and among the mountains he could hear the huntsmen blowing their horns so gaily and sweetly that tears came into his eyes, and he could not help calling out: "How kind has Heaven been to us all, to give us all the splendour that is in this world!"

The travelling companion also stood there with folded hands, and looked over the forest and the towns into the warm sunshine. At the same time there arose lovely sounds over their heads; they looked up, and a great white swan was soaring in the air and singing as they had never heard a bird sing till then! But the song became weaker and weaker; he bowed his head and sank quite slowly down at their feet, where he lay dead, the beautiful bird!

"Two such splendid wings," said the travelling companion, "so white and large, as those which the bird has, are worth money; I will take them with me. Do you see that it was good I got a sabre?" And so, with one blow, he cut off both the wings of the dead swan; for he wanted to keep them.

They now travelled for many many miles over the mountains, till at last they saw a great town before them with hundreds of towers which glittered like silver in the sun. In the midst of the town was a splendid marble palace, roofed with pure red gold. And there the King lived.

John and the travelling companion would not go into the town at once but remained in the inn outside the town, that they might dress themselves; for they wished to look nice when they came out into the streets. The host told them that the King was a very good man, who never did harm to any one; but his daughter, yes, goodness preserve us! she was a bad Princess. She possessed beauty enough,—no one could be so pretty and so charming as she was,—but of what use was that? She was a wicked witch, through whose fault many gallant Princes had lost their lives. She had given permission to all men to seek her hand. Any one might come, be he prince or beggar: it was all the same to her. He had only to guess three things she had just thought of, and about which she questioned him. If he could do that, she would marry him, and he was to be King over the whole country when her father should die; but if he could not guess the three things, she caused him to be hanged, or to have his head cut off! Her father, the old King, was very sorry about it; but he could not forbid her to be so wicked, because he had once said that he would have nothing to do with her lovers; she might do as she liked. Every time a Prince came, and was to guess to gain the Princess, he was unable to do it, and was hanged or lost his head. He had been warned in time, you see, and might have given over his wooing. The old King was so sorry for all this misery and woe, that he used to lie on his knees with all his soldiers for a whole day in every year, praying that the Princess might become good; but she would not, by any means. The old women who drank brandy, used to colour it quite black before they drank it, they were in such deep mourning—and they certainly could not do more.

"The ugly Princess!" said John. "She ought really to have the rod, that would do her good. If I were only the old King she should be punished!"

Then they heard the people outside shouting "Hurrah!" The Princess came by; and she was really so beautiful, that all the people forgot how wicked she was, and that is why they cried "Hurrah!" Twelve beautiful virgins all in white silk gowns, and each with a golden tulip in her hand, rode on coal-black steeds at her side. The Princess herself

John and his companion see the princess riding by

had a snow-white horse, decked with diamonds and rubies. Her riding-habit was all of cloth of gold, and the whip she held in her hand looked like a sunbeam, the golden crown on her head was just like little stars out of the sky, and her mantle was sewn together out of more than a thousand beautiful butterflies' wings. In spite of this she herself was much more lovely than all her clothes.

When John saw her, his face became as red as a drop of blood, and he could hardly utter a word. The princess looked just like the beautiful lady with the golden crown, of whom he had dreamt on the night when his father died. He found her so enchanting that he could not help loving her greatly. It could not be true that she was a wicked witch who caused people to be hanged or beheaded if they could not guess the riddles she put to them. "Every one has permission to aspire to her hand, even the poorest beggar. I will really go to the castle, for I cannot help doing it!" They all told him not to attempt it, for certainly he would fare as all the rest had done. His travelling companion too, tried to dissuade him; but John thought it would end well. He brushed his shoes and his coat, washed his face and his hands, combed his nice fair hair, and then went quite alone into the town and to the palace.

"Come in!" said the old King, when John knocked at the door. John opened it, and the old King came towards him, in a dressing-gown and embroidered slippers; he had the crown on his head, and the sceptre in one hand, and the orb in the other. "Wait a little!" said he and put the orb under his arm, so that he could reach out his hand to John. But as soon as he learned that his visitor was a suitor, he began to weep so violently that both the sceptre and the orb fell to the ground, and he was obliged to wipe his eyes with his dressing-gown. Poor old King!

"Give it up!" said he. "You will fare badly, as all the others have done. Well, you shall see!" Then he led him out into the Princess's pleasure garden. There was a terrible sight! In every tree there hung three or four king's sons, who had wooed the Princess, but had not been able to guess the riddles she proposed to them. Each time that the breeze blew, all the skeletons rattled, so that the little birds were frightened and never dared to come into the garden. All the flowers were tied up to human bones, and in the flower-pots stood skulls and grinned. That was certainly a strange garden for a Princess.

"Here you see it"—said the old King. "It will chance to you as it has chanced to all these whom you see here. Therefore you had better give it up. You will really make me unhappy, for I take these things very much to heart!" John kissed the good old King's hand, and said it would go well, for that he was quite enchanted with the beautiful Princess.

Then the Princess herself came riding into the court-yard, with all her ladies; and they went out to her and wished her good morning. She was beautiful to look at, and she gave John her hand. And he cared much more for her than before. She could certainly not be a wicked witch, as the people asserted. Then they betook themselves to the hall, and the little pages waited upon them with preserves and gingerbread nuts. But the old King was quite sorrowful; he could not eat anything at all. Besides, the gingerbread nuts were too hard for him.

It was settled that John should come to the palace again the next morning; then the judges and the whole council would be assembled, and would hear how he succeeded with his answers. If it went well, he should come twice more; but no one had yet come who had succeeded in guessing right the first time; and if he did not manage better than they, he must die.

John was not at all anxious as to how he should fare. On the contrary, he was merry, thought only of the beautiful Princess, and felt quite certain that he should be helped. But how, he did not know; and preferred not to think of it. He danced along, on the road, returning to the inn, where his travelling companion was waiting for him.

John could not leave off telling how polite the Princess had been to him, and how beautiful she was. He declared he already longed for the next day, when he was to go into the palace and try his luck in guessing.

But the travelling companion shook his head and was quite downcast. "I am so fond of you!" said he. "We might have been together a long time yet, and now I am already to lose you! You poor dear John! I should like to cry, but I will not disturb your merriment on the last evening, perhaps, we shall ever spend together. We will be merry, very merry! To-morrow, when you are gone, I can weep undisturbed."

All the people in the town had heard directly that a new suitor for the Princess had arrived; and there was great sorrow on that account. The theatre remained closed; the women who sold cakes tied bits of crape round their sugar-men, and the King and the priests were on their knees in the churches. There was great lamentation; for John would not, they all thought, fare better than the other suitors had fared.

Towards evening the travelling companion mixed a great bowl of punch, and said to John, "Now we will be very merry, and drink to the health of the Princess." But when John had drunk two glasses, he became so sleepy, that he found it impossible to keep his eyes open; he sank into a deep sleep. The travelling companion lifted him very gently from his chair, and laid him in the bed; and when it grew to be dark night, he took the two great wings which he had cut off the swan, and bound them to his own shoulders. Then he put in his pocket the longest of the rods he had received from the old woman who had fallen and broken her leg; and he opened the window and flew away over the town, straight towards the palace, where he seated himself in a corner under the window which looked into the bed-room of the Princess.

All was quiet in the whole town. Now the clock struck a quarter to twelve, the window was opened, and the Princess came out in a long white cloak, and with black wings, and flew away across the town to a great mountain. But the travelling companion made himself invisible so that she could not see him at all, and flew behind her, and whipped the Princess with his rod, so that the blood quite came wherever he struck. Oh, that was a voyage through the air! The wind caught her cloak so that it spread out on all sides, like a great sail, and the moon shone through it.

"How it hails! how it hails!" said the Princess at every blow she got from the rod; and it served her right. At last she arrived at the mountain, and knocked there. There was a rolling like thunder, and the mountain opened, and the Princess went in. The travelling companion followed her, for no one could see him; he was invisible. They went through a great long passage, where the walls shone in quite a peculiar way; there were more than a thousand glowing spiders, running up and down the walls and gleaming like fire. Then they came into a great hall, built of silver and gold; flowers as big as sunflowers, red and blue, shone on the walls; but no one could pluck these flowers, for the stems were ugly poisonous snakes, and the flowers were streams of fire burning out of their mouths. The whole ceiling was covered with shining glow-worms and sky-blue bats, flapping their thin wings. It looked quite terrific! In the middle of the floor was a throne carried by four skeleton horses, with harness of fiery red spiders; the throne itself was of milk-white glass, and the cushions were little black mice, biting each other's tails. Above it was a canopy of pink spider's web, trimmed with the prettiest little green flies which gleamed like jewels. On the throne sat an old magician with a crown on his ugly head and a sceptre in his hand. He kissed the Princess on the forehead, made her sit down beside him on the costly throne, and then the music began. Great black grass-hoppers blew on jews'-harps and the owl beat her wings upon her body, because she hadn't a drum. That was a strange concert! Little black goblins with a Jack-o'lantern light on their caps danced about in the hall. But no one could see the travelling companion; he had placed himself just behind the throne and heard and saw everything. The courtiers, who now came in, were very grand and noble; but he who could see it all, knew very well what it all meant. They were nothing more than broomsticks with heads of cabbage on them, which the magician had animated by his power, and to whom he had given embroidered clothes. But that did not matter, for you see they were only wanted for show.

After there had been a little dancing, the Princess told the magician that she had a new suitor, and therefore she inquired of him what she should think of, to ask the suitor when he should come to-morrow to the palace.

"Listen!" said the magician, "I will tell you that; you must choose something very easy, for then he won't think of it. Think of one of your shoes. That he will not guess. Let him have his head cut off; but don't forget when you come to me to-morrow night to bring me his eyes, for I'll eat them."

The Princess curtsied very low, and said she would not forget the eyes. The magician opened the mountain, and she flew home again; but the travelling companion followed her, and beat her again so hard with the rod, that she sighed quite deeply about the heavy hail-storm, and hurried, as much as she could, to get back into the bed-room through the open window. The travelling companion, for his part, flew back to the inn, where John was still asleep, took off his wings, and then lay down upon the bed, for he might well be tired.

It was quite early in the morning when John awoke. The travelling companion also got up and said he had had a wonderful dream in the night, about the Princess and her shoe; and he therefore begged John to ask if the Princess had not thought about her shoe. For it was this he had heard from the magician in the mountain.

"I may just as well ask about that as about anything else," said John. "Perhaps it is quite right, what you have dreamt. But I will bid you farewell; for if I guess wrong, I shall never see you more."

Then they embraced each other, and John went into the town and to the palace. The entire hall was filled with people: the judges sat in their arm-chairs and had eider-down pillows behind their heads, for they had a great deal to think about. The old King stood up and wiped his eyes with a white pocket handkerchief. Now the Princess came in. She was much more beautiful than yesterday, and bowed to all in a very affable manner; but to John she gave her hand and said: "Good morning to you!"

Now John was to guess what she had thought of. Oh, how lovingly she looked at him. But as soon as she heard the single word "shoe!" pronounced, she became as white as chalk in the face, and trembled all over. But that availed her nothing, for John had guessed right!

Wonder! how glad the old King was. He threw a somersault beautiful to behold. And all the people clapped their hands in honour of him and of John, who had guessed right the first time.

The travelling companion was glad too, when he heard how well matters had gone. But John felt very grateful; and he was sure he should receive help the second and third time, as he had been helped the first. The next day he was to guess again.

The evening passed just like that of yesterday. While John slept the travelling companion flew behind the Princess out to the mountain, and beat her even harder than the time before; for now he had taken two rods. No one saw him, and he heard everything. The Princess was to think of her glove; and this he again told to John as if it had been a dream. Thus John could guess well, which caused great rejoicing in the palace. The whole court threw somersaults, just as they had seen the King do the first time. But the Princess lay on the sofa, and would not say a single word. Now the question was, if John could guess properly the third time. If he succeeded, he was to have the beautiful Princess and inherit the whole kingdom after the old King's death. If he failed, he was to lose his life; and the magician would eat his beautiful blue eyes.

That evening John went early to bed, said his prayers, and went to sleep quite quietly. But the travelling companion bound his wings to his back and his sword by his side, and took all three rods with him, and so flew away to the palace.

It was a very dark night. The wind blew so hard that the tiles flew off from the roofs, and the trees in the garden where the skeletons hung bent like reeds before the storm. The lightning flashed out every minute, and the thunder rolled just as if it were one peal lasting the whole night. Now the window opened, and the Princess flew out. She was as pale as death; but she laughed at the bad weather, and declared it was not bad enough yet. And her white cloak fluttered on the wind like a great sail; but the travelling companion beat her with the three rods, so that the blood dripped upon the ground, and at last she could scarcely fly any further. At length, however, she arrived at the mountain.

"It hails and blows!" she said. "I have never been out in such weather."

"One may have too much of a good thing," said the magician. "I shall think of something of which he has never thought, or he must be a greater conjuror than I. But now we will be merry!" And he took the Princess by the hands, and they danced about with all the little goblins and Jack-o'lanterns that were in the room. The red spiders jumped just as merrily up and down the walls; it looked as if fiery flowers were

The death of the magician

spurting out. The owl played the drum, the crickets piped, and the black grasshoppers played on the jew's-harp. It was a merry ball.

When they had danced long enough the Princess was obliged to go home, for she might be missed in the palace. The magician said he would accompany her; then they would have each other's company on the way.

Then they flew away into the bad weather, and the travelling companion broke his three rods across their backs. Never had the magician been out in such a hail-storm. In front of the palace he said good-bye to the Princess, and whispered to her at the same time, "Think of my head!" But the travelling companion heard it; and just at the moment when the Princess slipped through the window into her bedroom, and the magician was about to turn back, he seized him by his long beard and with his sabre cut off the ugly conjuror's head, just by the shoulders, so that the magician did not even see him. The body he threw out into the sea to the fishes; but the head he only dipped into the water, and then tied it in his silk handkerchief, took it with him into the inn, and then lay down to sleep.

Next morning he gave John the handkerchief, and told him not to untie it until the Princess asked him to tell her thoughts.

There were so many people in the great hall of the palace, that they stood as close together as radishes bound together in a bundle. The council sat in the chairs with the soft pillows, and the old King had new clothes on; the golden crown and sceptre had been polished, and everything looked quite stately. But the Princess was quite pale, and had a coal-black dress on, as if she were going to be buried.

"Of what have I thought?" she asked John. And he immediately untied the handkerchief, and was himself quite frightened when he saw the ugly magician's head. All present shuddered; for it was terrible to look upon; but the Princess sat just like a statue, and would not utter a single word. At length she stood up, and gave John her hand, for he had guessed well. She did not look at any one; only sighed aloud and said, "Now you are my Lord! this evening we will hold our wedding!"

"I like that!" cried the old King. "Thus I will have it." All present cried "Hurrah!" The soldiers' band played music in the streets, the bells rang, and the cake-women took off the black crape from their sugar-dolls, for joy now reigned around. Three oxen roasted whole and stuffed with ducks and fowls, were placed in the middle of the market, that every one might cut himself a slice; the fountains ran with the best wine, and whoever bought a penny cake at the baker's, got six biscuits into the bargain, and the biscuits had raisins in them.

In the evening the whole town was illuminated; the soldiers fired off the cannon, and the boys let off crackers; and there was eating and drinking, clinking of glasses, and dancing, in the palace. All the noble gentlemen and pretty ladies danced with each other, and one could hear, a long distance off, how they sang:—

> Here are many pretty girls who all love to dance;
> See, they whirl like spinning-wheels, retire and advance;
> Turn, my pretty maiden, do, till the sole falls from your shoe.

But still the Princess was a witch, and did not like John. That occurred to the travelling companion; and so he gave John three feathers out of the swan's wings and a little bottle with a few drops in it, and told John that he must put a large tub of water before the Princess's bed; and when the Princess was about to get into bed, he should give her a little push, so that she should fall into the tub, and then he must dip her three times, after he had put in the feathers and poured in the drops; she would then lose her magic qualities, and love him very much.

John did all that the travelling companion had advised him to do. The Princess screamed out loudly, while he dipped her under, and struggled under his hands in the form of a great coal-black swan with fiery eyes. When she came up the second time above the water, the swan was white, with the exception of a black ring round her neck. John let the water close for the third time over the bird; and in the same moment it was changed into the beautiful Princess. She was more beautiful even than before, and thanked him with tears in her lovely eyes, that he had freed her from the magic spell.

The next morning the old King came with his whole court, and then there was great congratulation, till late into the day. Last of all came the travelling companion; he had his staff in his hand, and his knapsack on his back. John kissed him many times, and said he must not depart, he must remain with the friend of whose happiness he was the cause. But the travelling companion shook his head, and said mildly and kindly: "No! now my time is up. I have only paid my debt. Do you remember the dead man, whom the bad people wished to injure? You gave all you possessed in order that he might have rest in his grave. I am that man." And in the same moment he vanished.

The wedding festivities lasted a whole month. John and the Princess loved each other truly, and the old King passed many pleasant days, and let their little children ride on his knees, and play with his sceptre. But John became King over the whole country.

THE LITTLE SEA-MAID

Far out in the sea the water is as blue as the petals of the most beautiful corn-flower, and as clear as the purest glass. But it is very deep; deeper than any cable will sound; many steeples must be placed one above the other to reach from the ground to the surface of the water. And down there live the sea-people.

The sea-maid saves the Prince

Now you must not believe there is nothing down there but the naked sand; no,—the strangest plants and flowers grow there, so pliable in their stalks and leaves, that at the least motion of the water they move just as if they had life. All fishes, great and small, glide among the twigs, just as here the birds do in the trees. In the deepest spot of all lies the sea-king's castle; the walls are of coral, and the tall gothic windows of the clearest amber; shells form the roof, and they open and shut according as the water flows. It looks lovely, for in each shell lie gleaming pearls; a single one of these would have great value in a queen's diadem.

The sea-king below there had been a widower for many years, while his old mother kept house for him. She was a clever woman, but proud of her rank; so she wore twelve oysters on her tail, while the other great people were only allowed to wear six. Beyond this she was deserving of great praise, especially because she was very fond of her grand-daughters the little sea-princesses. These were six pretty children; but the youngest was the most beautiful of all. Her skin was as clear and fine as a rose-leaf, her eyes were as blue as the deepest sea; but like all the rest she had no feet; for her body ended in a fish-tail.

All day long they could play in the castle, down in the halls, where living flowers grew out of the walls. The great amber windows were opened, and then the fishes swam into them, just as the swallows fly in to us when we open our windows; but the fishes swam straight up to the princesses, ate out of their hands, and let themselves be stroked.

Outside the castle was a great garden with bright red and dark blue flowers; the fruit glowed like gold, and the flowers like flames of fire; and they continually kept moving their stalks and leaves. The earth itself was the finest sand, but blue as the flame of brimstone. A peculiar blue radiance lay upon everything down there; one would have thought oneself high in the air, with the canopy of heaven above and around, rather than at the bottom of the deep sea. During a calm the sun could be seen; it appeared like a purple flower, from which all light streamed out.

Each of the little princesses had her own little place in the garden, where she might dig and plant at her good pleasure. One gave her flower-bed the form of a whale; another thought it better to make hers like a little sea-woman; but the youngest made hers quite round, like the sun, and had flowers which gleamed red as the sun itself. She was a strange child, quiet and thoughtful; and when the other sisters made a display of the beautiful things they had received out of wrecked ships, she would have nothing beyond the red flowers which resembled the sun, except a pretty marble statue. This was a figure of a charming boy, hewn out of white clear stone, which had sunk down to the bottom of the sea from a wreck. She planted a pink weeping willow beside this statue; the tree grew famously and hung its fresh branches over the statue towards the blue sandy ground, where the shadow showed violet, and moved like the branches themselves; it seemed as if the ends of the branches and the roots were playing together, and wished to kiss each other.

There was no greater pleasure for her, than to hear of the world of men above them. The old grandmother had to tell all she knew of ships and towns, of men and animals. It seemed particularly beautiful to her, that upon the earth the flowers had fragrance; for they had none down at the bottom of the sea; and that the trees were green; and that the fishes whom one saw there among the trees could sing so loud and clear that it was a pleasure to hear them. What the grandmother called fishes were the little birds; the princess could not understand them in any other way, for she had never seen a bird.

"When you have reached your fifteenth year," said the grandmother, "you shall have leave to rise up out of the sea, to sit on the rocks in the moonlight, and to see the great ships sailing by. Then you will see forests and towns!" In the next year, one of the sisters was fifteen years of age, but each of the others was one year younger than the next; so that the youngest had five full years to wait before she could come up from the bottom of the sea, and find how our world looked. But one promised the others to tell what she had seen, and what she had thought the most beautiful on the first day of her visit; for their grandmother could not tell them enough—there was so much about which they wanted information.

No one was more anxious about these things than the youngest, just that one who had the longest time to wait, and who was always quiet and thoughtful. Many a night she stood by the open window and looked up through the dark blue water, at the fishes plashing with their fins and tails. Moon and stars she could see; they certainly shone quite faintly; but through the water they looked much larger than they appear in our eyes. When something like a black cloud passed among them, she knew that it was either a whale swimming over her head, or a ship with many people; they certainly did not think that a pretty little sea-maid was standing down below stretching up her white hands towards the keel of their ship.

Now the eldest princess was fifteen years old, and might mount up to the surface of the sea.

When she came back, she had a hundred things to tell,—but the finest thing, she said, was to lie in the moonshine on a sand-bank in the quiet sea, and to look at the neighbouring coast, with the large town, where the lights twinkle like a hundred stars, and to hear the music, and the noise and clamour of carriages and men, to see the many church steeples, and to hear the sound of the bells. Just because she could not get up to these, she longed for them more than for any thing.

Oh, how the youngest sister listened; and afterwards when she stood at the open window and looked up through the dark blue water, she thought of the great city with all its bustle and noise; and then she thought she could hear the church bells ringing, even down to the depth where she was.

In the following year, the second sister received permission to mount upward through the water and to swim whither she pleased. She rose up just as the sun was setting; and this spectacle, she said, was the most beautiful. The whole sky looked like gold, she said, and as to the clouds, she could not properly describe their beauty. They sailed away over her, red, and violet-coloured,—but far quicker than the clouds there flew, like a long white veil, a flight of wild swans, over the water towards where the sun stood. She swam towards them; but the sun sank, and the roseate hue faded on the sea and in the clouds.

In the following year the next sister went up. She was the boldest of them all: therefore she swam up a broad stream that poured its waters into the sea. She saw glorious green hills clothed with vines: palaces and castles shone forth from amid splendid woods; she heard how all the birds sang; and the sun shone so warm, that she was often obliged to dive under the water to cool her glowing face. In a little bay she found a whole swarm of little mortals. They were quite naked, and splashed about in the water; she wanted to play with them, but they fled in affright and a little black animal came; it was a dog, but she had never seen a dog, and it barked at her so terribly, that she became frightened, and tried to gain the open sea. But she could never forget the glorious woods, the green hills and the pretty children, who could swim in the water though they had not fish-tails.

The fourth sister was not so bold; she remained out in the midst of the wild sea, and declared that just there it was most beautiful. One could see for many miles around, and the sky above looked like a bell of glass. She had seen ships, but only in the far distance; they looked like sea-gulls, and the funny dolphins had thrown somersaults, and the great whales spouted out water from their nostrils, so that it looked like hundreds of fountains all around.

Now came the turn of the fifth sister. Her birthday came in the winter, and so she saw what the others had not seen the first time. The sea looked quite green, and great icebergs were floating about; each one appeared like a pearl, she said, and yet was much taller than the church steeples built by men. They showed themselves in the strangest forms, and shone like diamonds. She had seated herself upon one of the greatest of all, and let the wind play with her long hair; and all the sailing ships tacked about in a very rapid way beyond where she sat but towards evening the sky became covered with clouds, it thundered and lightened, and the black waves lifted the great iceblocks high up, and let them glow in the red glare. On all the ships the sails were reefed, and there was fear and anguish. But she sat quietly upon her floating iceberg, and saw the forked blue flashes dart into the sea.

The first time one of the sisters came up on the surface of the water, each was delighted with the new and beautiful sights they saw; but as they now had permission, as grown-up girls, to go whenever they liked, it became indifferent to them. They wished themselves back again, and after a month had elapsed they said it was best of all down below; for there one felt so comfortably at home.

Many an evening hour the five sisters took one another by the arm and rose up in a row over the water; they had splendid voices, more charming than any mortal could have; and when a storm was approaching, so that they could apprehend that ships would go down, they swam on before the ships, and sang lovely songs, which told how beautiful it was at the bottom of the sea, and exhorted the sailors not to be afraid to come down. But these could not understand the words, and thought it was the storm sighing; and they did not see the splendours below, for if the ships sunk they were drowned, and came as corpses to the sea-king's palace.

When the sisters thus rose up, arm in arm, in the evening time, through the water, the little sister stood all alone looking after them; and she felt as if she must weep; but the sea-maid has no tears, and for this reason she suffers far more.

"Oh, if I were only fifteen years old!" said she. "I know I shall love the world up there very much, and the people who live and dwell there."

At last she was really fifteen years old.

"You see, now, you are grown up,"—said the grandmother, the old dowager. "Come let me adorn you like your other sisters!"—and she put a wreath of white lilies in the little maid's hair, but each flower was half a pearl; and the old lady let eight great oysters attach themselves to the princess's tail, in token of her high rank.

"But that hurts so" said the little sea-maid. "Yes, pride must suffer pain," replied the old lady.

Oh how glad she would have been to shake off all the tokens of rank, and lay aside the heavy wreath; her red flowers in the garden suited her better; but she could not help it. "Farewell!" she said, and then she rose light and clear like a water-bubble, up through the sea.

The sun had just set when she lifted her head above the sea; but all the clouds still shone like roses and gold, and in the pale red sky the evening stars gleamed bright and beautiful. The air was mild and fresh, and the sea quite calm. There lay a great ship with three masts; one single sail only was set, for not a breeze stirred, and around in the shrouds and on the yards sat the sailors. There was music and singing; and as the evening closed in, hundreds of coloured lanterns were lighted up, and looked as if the flags of all nations were waving in the air. The little sea-maid swam straight to the cabin window, and each time the sea lifted her up, she could look through the panes which were clear as crystal, and see many people dressed in their best standing within. But the handsomest of all was the young Prince with the great black eyes; he was certainly not much more than sixteen years old; it was his birthday, and that was the cause of all this feasting. The sailors were dancing upon deck; and when the young Prince came out, more than a hundred rockets rose into the air; they shone like day, so that the little sea-maid was quite startled, and dived under the water; but soon she put out her head again, and then it seemed just as if all the stars of heaven were falling down upon her. She had never seen such fireworks. Great suns spurted fire around, glorious fiery fishes flew into the blue air, and everything was mirrored in the clear blue sea. The ship itself was so brightly lit up, that every little rope could be seen; and the people therefore appeared the more plainly. Oh, how handsome the young Prince was! and he pressed the people's hands, and smiled while the music rang out in the glorious night.

It became late; but the little sea-maid could not turn her eyes from the ship and from the beautiful Prince. The coloured lanterns were extinguished, rockets ceased to fly into the air, and no more cannons were fired; but there was a murmuring and a buzzing deep down in the sea: and she sat on the water, swaying up and down, so that she could look into the cabin. But the ship got more way, one sail after another was spread, and now the waves rose higher; great clouds came up, and in the distance there was lightning. Oh! it was going to be fearful weather; therefore the sailors furled the sails. The great ship flew in swift career over the wild sea; the waters rose up like great black mountains, which wanted to roll over the masts; but like a swan, the ship dived into the valleys between these high waves, and then let itself be lifted on high again. To the little sea-maid this seemed merry sport, but to the sailors it appeared very differently. The ship groaned and creaked; the thick planks were bent by the heavy blows; the sea broke into the ship; the mainmast snapped in two like a thin reed, and the ship lay over on her side, while the water rushed into the hold. Now the little sea-maid saw that the people were in peril; she herself was obliged to take care to avoid the beams and fragments of the ship, which were floating about on the waters. One moment it was so pitch dark, that not a single object could be descried, but when it lightened it became so bright that she could distinguish every one on board. She looked particularly for the young Prince; and when the ship parted she saw him sink into the sea. Now she was very glad, for now he would come down to her. But then she remembered that people could not live in the water, and that when he got down to her father's palace he would certainly be dead. No, he must not die: so she swam about among the beams and planks that strewed the surface, quite forgetting that one of them might have crushed her. Diving down deeply under the water she again rose high up among the waves; and in this way she at last came to the Prince, who could scarcely swim longer in that stormy sea. His arms and legs began to fail him; his beautiful eyes closed, and he would have died had the little sea-maid not come. She held his head up over the water, and then allowed the waves to carry her and him whither they listed.

When the morning came the storm had passed by. Of the ship not a fragment was to be seen. The sun came up red and shining out of the water; it was as if its beams brought back the hue of life to the cheeks of the Prince, but his eyes remained closed. The sea-maid kissed his high fair forehead, and put back his wet hair, and he seemed to her to be like the marble statue in her little garden; she kissed him again and hoped that he might live.

Now she saw in front of her the dry land; high blue mountains, on whose summits the white snow gleamed, as if swans were lying there. Down on the coast were glorious green forests, and a building, she could not tell whether it was a church or a convent, stood there. In its garden grew orange and citron trees, and high palms waved in front of the gate. The sea formed a little bay there; it was quite calm but very deep; straight towards the rock where the fine white sand had been cast up, she swam with the handsome Prince, and laid him upon the sand, taking especial care that his head was raised in the warm sunshine.

Now all the bells rang in the great white building, and many young girls came walking through the garden. Then the little sea-maid swam farther out between some high stones, that stood up out of the water, laid some sea-foam upon her hair and neck so that no one could see her little countenance, and then she watched to see who would come to the poor Prince.

In a short time a young girl went that way. She seemed to be much startled, but only for a moment; then she brought more people, and the sea-maid perceived that the Prince came back to life, and that he smiled at all around him. But he did not cast a smile to her; he did not know that she had saved him,—and she felt very sorrowful; and when he was led away into the great building, she dived mournfully under the water and returned to her father's palace.

She had always been quiet and melancholy, but now she became much more so. Her sisters asked her what she had seen the first time she rose up to the surface, but she would tell them nothing.

Many an evening and many a morning she went up to the place where she had left the Prince. She saw how the fruits of the garden grew ripe and were gathered; she saw how the snow melted on the high mountain; but she did not see the Prince, and so she always returned home more sorrowful still. Then her only comfort was to sit in her little garden, and to wind her arm round the beautiful marble statue that resembled the Prince; but she did not tend her flowers; they grew as if in a wilderness, over the paths, and trailed their long leaves and stalks up into the branches of trees, so that it became quite dark there.

At last she could endure it no longer and told all to one of her sisters, and then the others heard of it too; but nobody knew of it beyond these and a few other sea-maids, who told the secret to their intimate friends. One of these knew who the Prince was; she too had seen the festival on board the ship, and announced whence he came, and where his kingdom lay.

"Come, little sister!" said the other princesses; and linking their arms together, they rose up in a long row out of the sea, at the place where they knew the Prince's palace lay.

This palace was built of a kind of bright yellow stone, with great marble staircases, one of which led directly down into the sea. Over the roof rose splendid gilt cupolas, and between the pillars which surrounded the whole building stood marble statues which looked as if they were alive. Through the clear glass in the high windows one looked into the glorious halls, where costly silk hangings and tapestries were hung up, and all the walls were decked with splendid pictures so that it was a perfect delight to see them. In the midst of the greatest of these halls a great fountain plashed; its jets shot high up towards the glass dome in the ceiling, through which the sun shone down upon the water, and upon the lovely plants growing in the great basin.

Now she knew where he lived; and many an evening and many a night she spent there on the water. She swam far closer to the land than any of the others would have dared to venture; indeed she went quite up the narrow channel under the splendid marble balcony which threw a broad shadow upon the water. Here she sat, and watched the young Prince, who thought himself quite alone in the bright moonlight.

Many an evening she saw him sailing amid the sounds of music, in his costly boat with the waving flags; she peeped up through the green reeds, and when the wind caught her silver-white veil, and any one saw it, he thought it was a white swan spreading out its wings.

Many a night when the fishermen were on the sea with their torches, she heard much good told of the young Prince; and she rejoiced that she had saved his life when he was driven about, half dead, on the billows; she thought how quietly his head had reclined on her bosom, and how heartily she had kissed him; but he knew nothing of it, and could not even dream of her.

More and more she began to love mankind; more and more she wished to be able to wander about among those whose world seemed far larger than her own. For they could fly over the sea in ships, and mount up the high hills far above the clouds; and the lands they possessed stretched out in woods and fields, farther than her eyes could reach. There was much she wished to know, but her sisters could not answer all her questions; therefore she applied to the old grandmother; and the old lady knew the upper world, which she rightly called "the countries above the sea," very well.

"If people are not drowned," asked the little sea-maid, "can they live for ever? Do they not die as we die down here in the sea?"

"Yes," replied the old lady. "They too must die, and their life is even shorter than ours. We can live to be three hundred years old, but when we cease to exist here, we are turned into foam on the surface of the water, and have not even a grave down here among those we love. We have not an immortal soul; we never receive another life; we are like the green seaweed, which when once cut through can never bloom again. Men, on the contrary have a soul, which lives for ever, which lives on after the body has become dust: it mounts up through the clear air, up to all the shining stars! As we rise up out of the waters and behold all the lands of the earth, so they rise up at unknown glorious places which we can never see."

"Why did we not receive an immortal soul?" asked the little sea-maid sorrowfully. "I would gladly give all the hundreds of years I have to live, to be a human being only for one day, and to have a hope of partaking the heavenly kingdom." "You must not think of that," replied the old lady. "We feel ourselves far more happy and far better than mankind yonder."

"Then I am to die and be cast as foam upon the sea, not hearing the music of the waves, nor seeing the pretty flowers and the red sun? Can I not do anything to win an immortal soul?"

"No!" answered the grandmother. "Only if a man were to love you so that you should be more to him than father or mother; if he should cling to you with his every thought, and with all his love, and let the priest lay his right hand in yours with a promise of faithfulness here and in all eternity, then his soul would be imparted to your body, and you would receive a share of the happiness of mankind. He would give a soul to you, and yet retain his own. But that can never come to pass. What is considered beautiful here in the sea,—the fish-tail—they would consider ugly on the earth; they don't understand it; there one must have two clumsy supports they call legs, to be called beautiful." Then the little sea-maid sighed, and looked mournfully upon her fish-tail.

"Let us be glad!" said the old lady. "Let us dance and leap in the three hundred years we have to live. That is certainly long enough; after that we can rest ourselves all the better. This evening we shall have a court ball."

It was a splendid sight, such as is never seen on earth. The walls and the ceiling of the great dancing saloon were of thick but transparent glass. Several hundreds of huge shells, pink and grass-green, stood on each side in rows, filled with a blue fire which lit up the whole hall and shone through the walls, so that the sea without was quite lit up; one could see all the innumerable fishes, great and small, swimming towards the glass walls; of some the scales gleamed with purple, while in others they shone like silver and gold, through the midst of the hall flowed a broad stream, and on this the sea-men and sea-women danced to their own charming songs. Such beautiful voices the people of the earth have not. The little sea-maid sang the most sweetly of all, and the whole court applauded with hands and tails, and for a moment she felt gay in her heart, for she knew she had the loveliest voice of all in the sea or on the earth. But soon she thought again of the world above her; she could not forget the charming Prince, or her sorrow at not having an immortal soul, like his. Therefore she crept out of her father's palace, and while everything within was joy and gladness, she sat melancholy in her little garden. Then she heard the bugle horn sounding through the waters, and thought, "Now he is certainly sailing above, he on whom my wishes hang, and in whose hand I should like to lay my life's happiness. I will dare everything to win him and an immortal soul. While my sisters dance yonder in my father's palace, I will go to the sea-witch of whom I have always been so much afraid; perhaps she can counsel and help me."

Now the little sea-maid went out of her garden to the foaming whirlpools behind which the sorceress dwelt. She had never travelled that way before; no flowers grew there, no sea-grass,—only the naked grey sand stretched out towards the whirlpools, where the water rushed round like roaring mill-wheels, and tore down everything it seized into the deep. Through the midst of these rushing whirlpools she was obliged to pass to get into the domain of the witch; and for a long way there was no other road except one which led over warm gushing mud; this the witch called her turf-moor. Behind it lay her house in the midst of a singular forest, in which all the trees and bushes were polypes,—half animals, half plants. They looked like hundred-headed snakes growing up out of the earth. All the branches were long slimy arms, with fingers like supple worms; and they moved limb by limb from the root to the farthest point; all that they could seize on in the water they held fast and did not let it go. The little sea-maid stopped in front of them quite frightened; her heart beat with fear, and she was nearly turning back; but then she thought of the Prince and of the human soul, and her courage came back again. She bound her long flying hair close around her head, so that the polypes might not seize it. She put her hands together on her breast and then shot forward as a fish shoots through the water, among the ugly polypes which stretched out their supple arms and fingers after her. She saw that each of them held something it had seized, with hundreds of little arms, like strong iron bands. People who had perished at sea and had sunk deep down, looked forth as white skeletons from among the polypes' arms, ships' oars and chests they also held fast, and skeletons of land animals, and a little sea-woman whom they had caught and strangled; and this seemed the most terrible of all to our little princess.

Now she came to a great marshy place in the wood, whereby fat water-snakes rolled about, showing their ugly cream-coloured bodies. In the midst of this marsh was a house built of white bones of ship-wrecked men; there sat the sea-witch feeding a toad out of her mouth, just as a person might feed a little canary-bird with sugar. She called the ugly fat water-snakes her little chickens and allowed them to crawl upwards and all about her.

"I know what you want," said the sea-witch. "It is stupid of you, but you shall have your way, for it will bring you to grief, my pretty princess. You want to get rid of your fish-tail, and to have two supports instead of it, like those the people of the earth walk with, so that the young Prince may fall in love with you, and you may get an immortal soul." And with this the witch laughed loudly and disagreeably, so that the toad and the water-snakes tumbled down to the ground where they crawled about. "You come just in time," said the witch, "after to-morrow at sun-rise, I could not help you until another year had gone by. I will prepare a draught for you, with which you must swim to land to-morrow before the sun rises, and seat yourself there and drink it; then your tail will shrivel up, and become what the people of the earth call legs, but it will hurt you—it will seem as if you were cut with a sharp sword. All who see you will declare you to be the prettiest human being they ever beheld. You will keep your graceful walk; no dancer will be able to move so lightly as you; but every step you take will be as if you trod upon sharp knives, and as if your blood must flow. If you will bear all this, I can help you."

"Yes!" said the little sea-maid, with a trembling voice; and she thought of the Prince and of the immortal soul.

"But, remember," said the witch, "when you have once received a human form, you can never be a sea-maid again; you can never return through the water to your sisters, or to your father's palace; and if you do not win the Prince's love, so that he forgets father and mother for your sake, is attached to you heart and soul, and tells the priest to join your hands, you will not receive an immortal soul. On the first morn-ing after he has married another, your heart will break, and you will become foam on the water."

"I will do it,"—said the little sea-maid; but she became as pale as death.

"But you must pay me, too," said the witch; "and it is not a trifle that I ask. You have the finest voice of all here at the bottom of the water; with that you think to enchant him—but this voice you must give to me. The best thing you possess I will have for my costly draught! I must give you my own blood in it, so that the draught may be sharp as a two-edged sword."

"But if you take away my voice," said the little sea-maid, "what will remain to me?"

"Your beautiful form," replied the witch; "your graceful walk and your speaking eyes; with those you can take captive a human heart. Well, have you lost your courage? Put out your little tongue, and then I will cut it off by way of payment, and you shall have the strong draught."

"It shall be so,"—said the little sea-maid.

And the witch put on her pot to brew the draught.

"Cleanliness is a good thing," said she; and she cleaned out the pot with the snakes, which she tied up in a big knot; then she scratched herself, and let her black blood drop into it. The steam rose up in the strangest forms, enough to frighten the beholder. Every moment the witch threw something else into the pot; and when it boiled thoroughly, there was a sound like the weeping of a crocodile. At last the draught was ready. It looked like the purest water.

"There you have it,"—said the witch; and she cut off the little sea-maid's tongue, so that now the Princess was dumb, and could neither sing nor speak.

She could see her father's palace. The torches were extinguished in the great hall. All were certainly sleeping within, but she did not dare go to them, now that she was dumb, and was about to quit them for ever. She felt as if her heart would burst with sorrow. She crept into the garden, took a flower from each bed of her sisters, blew a thousand kisses towards the palace, and rose up through the dark blue sea.

The sun had not yet risen, when she beheld the Prince's castle, and mounted the splendid marble staircase. The moon shone beautifully clear. The little sea-maid drank the burning sharp draught, and it seemed as if a two-edged sword went through her delicate body. She fell down in a swoon, and lay as if she were dead. When the sun shone out over the sea she woke, and felt a sharp pain; but just before her stood the handsome young Prince. He fixed his coal-black eyes upon her, so that she cast down her own, and then she perceived that her fish-tail was gone, and that she had the prettiest pair of white feet a little girl could have. But she had no clothes; so she shrouded herself in her long hair. The Prince asked how she came there; and she looked at him mildly, but very mournfully, with her dark blue eyes, for she could not speak. Then he took her by the hand, and led her into the castle. Each step she took was, as the witch had told her, as if she had been treading on pointed needles and knives; but she bore it gladly. At the Prince's hand she moved on, light as a soap-bubble, and he, like all the rest, was astonished at her graceful swaying movements.

She now received splendid clothes of silk and muslin. In the castle she was the most beautiful creature there; but she was dumb, and could neither sing nor speak. Lovely slaves, dressed in silk and gold, stepped forward, and sang before the Prince and his royal parents; one sang more charmingly than all the rest, and the Prince smiled at her and clapped his hands. Then the little sea-maid became sad; she knew that she herself had sung far more sweetly, and thought, "Oh! he should only know that I have given away my voice for ever to be with him."

Now the slaves danced pretty waving dances to the loveliest music; then the little sea-maid lifted her beautiful white arms, stood on the tips of her toes, and glided dancing over the floor as no one had yet danced. At each movement her beauty became more apparent, and her eyes spoke more directly to the heart than the songs of the slaves.

All were delighted, and especially the Prince, who called her his little foundling; and she danced more and more, though each time she touched the earth it seemed as if she was treading on sharp knives. The Prince said that she should always remain with him, and she received permission to sleep on a velvet cushion before his door.

He had a page's dress made for her, that she might accompany him on horseback. They rode through the blooming woods, where the green boughs swept their shoulders, and the little birds sang in the fresh leaves. She climbed with the Prince up the high mountains, and although her delicate feet bled, that even the others could see it, she

The sea-maid dancing before the Prince

laughed at it herself, and followed him, until they saw the clouds sailing beneath them, like a flock of birds travelling to distant lands.

At home in the Prince's castle, when the others slept at night, she went out on the broad marble steps. It cooled her burning feet to stand in the cold sea water, and then she thought of the dear ones in the deep.

Once, in the night-time, her sisters came arm in arm; sadly they sang, as they floated above the water, and she beckoned to them, and they recognized her, and told her how she had grieved them all. Then she visited them every night; and once she saw in the distance her old grandmother, who had not been above the surface for many years, and the sea-king with his crown on his head. They stretched out their hands towards her, but did not venture so near the land as her sisters.

Day by day the Prince grew more fond of her. He loved her as one loves a dear good child, but it never came into his head to make her his wife; and yet she must become his wife, or she would not receive an immortal soul, and would have to become foam on the sea on his marriage morning.

"Do you not love me best of them all?" the eyes of the little sea-maid seemed to say, when he took her in his arms and kissed her fair forehead.

"Yes, you are the dearest to me!" said the Prince; "for you have the best heart of them all. You are the most devoted to me, and are like a young girl whom I once saw, but whom I certainly shall not find again. I was on a ship which was wrecked. The waves threw me ashore near a holy temple, where several young girls performed the service. The youngest of them found me by the shore, and saved my life. I only saw her twice; she was the only one in the world I could love; but you chase her picture out of my mind, you are so like her—she belongs to the holy temple, and therefore my good fortune has sent you to me—we will never part!"

"Ah! he does not know that I saved his life," thought the little sea-maid. "I carried him over the sea," thought the little sea-maid; "I carried him over the sea to the wood, where the temple stands. I sat here under the foam, and looked to see if any one would come. I saw the beautiful girl whom he loves better than me," and the sea-maid sighed deeply—she could not weep. "The maiden belongs to the holy temple, he said; she will never come out into the world—they will meet no more. I am with him, and see him every day; I will cherish him, love him, give up my life for him."

But now they said that the Prince was to marry; and that the beautiful daughter of a neighbouring King was to be his wife, and that was why such a beautiful ship was being prepared. The story was, that the Prince travelled to visit the land of the neighbouring King, but it was done that he might see the King's daughter. A great company was to go with him. The little sea-maid shook her head and smiled; she knew the Prince's thoughts far better than any of the others. "I must travel," he had said to her; "I must see the beautiful Princess—my parents desire it, but they do not wish to compel me to bring her home as my bride. I cannot love her. She is not like the beautiful maiden in the temple, whom you resemble. If I were to choose a bride, I would rather choose you, my dumb foundling, with the speaking eyes"—and he kissed her red lips, and played with her long hair, so that she dreamed of happiness and of an immortal soul.

"You are not afraid of the sea, my dumb child?" said he, when they stood on the superb ship, which was to carry him to the country of the neighbouring King; and he told her of storm and calm, of strange fishes in the deep, and of what the divers had seen there. And she smiled at his tales; but she knew better than any one what happened at the bottom of the sea.

In the moonlight night, when all were asleep, except the steersman who stood by the helm, she sat on the side of the ship gazing down through the clear water. She fancied she saw her father's palace. High on the battlements stood her old grandmother, with the silver crown on her head, and looked through the rushing tide up to the vessel's keel. Then her sisters came forth over the water, and looked mournfully at her, and wrung their white hands. She beckoned to them, smiled, and wished to tell them that she was well and happy; but the cabin-boy approached her, and her sisters dived down, so that he thought the white objects he had seen were foam on the surface of the water.

The next morning the ship sailed into the harbour of the neighbouring King's splendid city. All the church-bells sounded, and from the high towers the trumpets were blown, while the soldiers stood there with flying colours and flashing bayonets. Each day brought some festivity with it; balls and entertainments followed one another; but the Princess was not yet there. People said she was being educated in a holy temple, far away; and there she was learning every royal virtue. At last she arrived.

The little sea-maid was anxious to see the beauty of the Princess, and was obliged to acknowledge it. A more lovely apparition she had never beheld. The Princess's skin was pure and clear, and behind the long dark eyelashes there smiled a pair of faithful dark blue eyes.

"You are the lady who saved me when I lay like a corpse upon the shore!" said the Prince; and he folded his blushing bride to his heart. "Oh! I am too, too happy!" he cried to the little sea-maid. "The best hope I could have is fulfilled. You will rejoice at my happiness, for you are the most devoted to me of them all!" And the little sea-maid kissed his hand; and it seemed already to her as if her heart was broken, for his wedding-morning was to bring death to her, and change her into foam on the sea.

All the church-bells were ringing—the heralds rode about the streets announcing the betrothal. On every altar fragrant oil was burning in gorgeous lamps of silver. The priests swang their censers, and bride and bridegroom laid hand in hand, and received the bishop's blessing. The little sea-maid was dressed in cloth of gold, and held up the bride's train; but her ears heard nothing of the festive music, her eye marked not the holy ceremony; she thought of the night of her death, and of all that she had lost in this world.

On the same evening the bride and bridegroom went on board the ship; the cannon roared, all the flags waved; in the mist of the ship a costly tent of gold and purple, with the most beautiful cushions, had been set up; there the married pair were to sleep in the cool still night.

The sails swelled in the wind, and the ship glided smoothly and lightly over the clear sea. When it grew dark coloured lamps were lighted, and the sailors danced merry dances on deck. The little sea-maid thought of the first time when she had risen up out of the sea, and beheld a similar scene of splendour and joy; and she joined in the whirling dance, and flitted on as the swallow flits away when he is pursued; and all shouted and admired her, for she had danced so prettily. Her delicate feet were cut as if with knives; but she did not feel it, for her heart was wounded far more painfully. She knew this was the last evening on which she should see him, for whom she had left her friends and her home, and had given up her beautiful voice, and had suffered unheard-of pains every day, while he was utterly unconscious of all. It was the last evening she should breathe the same air with him, and behold the starry sky and the deep sea; and everlasting night without thought or dream awaited her, for she had no soul and could win none. And everything was merriment and gladness on the ship till past midnight—and she laughed and danced with thoughts of death in her heart. The Prince kissed his beautiful bride, and she played with his raven hair; and hand in hand they went to rest in the splendid tent.

It became quiet on the ship; only the helmsman stood by the helm, and the little sea-maid leaned her white arms upon the bulwark and gazed out towards the east for the morning dawn—the first ray, she knew, would kill her. Then she saw her sisters rising out of the flood— they were pale, like herself; their long beautiful hair no longer waved in the wind—it had been cut off.

"We have given it to the witch, that we might bring you help, so that you may not die to-night. She has given us a knife; here it is—look! how sharp! Before the sun rises you must thrust it into the heart of the Prince; and when the warm blood falls upon your feet they will grow together again into a fish-tail, and you will become a sea-maid again, and come back to us, and live your three hundred years before you become dead salt sea-foam. Make haste! He or you must die before the sun rises! Our old grandmother mourns so that her white hair has fallen off, as ours did under the witch's scissors. Kill the Prince and come back! Make haste! Do you see that red streak in the sky? In a few minutes the sun will rise, and you must die!" And they gave a very mournful sigh, and vanished beneath the waves.

The little sea-maid drew back the purple curtain from the tent, and saw the beautiful bride lying with her head on the Prince's breast; and she bent down and kissed his brow, and gazed up to the sky where the morning red was gleaming brighter and brighter; then she looked at the sharp knife, and again fixed her eyes upon the Prince, who in his sleep murmured his bride's name. She only was in his thoughts, and the knife trembled in the sea-maid's hands. But then she flung it far away into the waves—they gleamed red where it fell, and it seemed as if drops of blood spurted up out of the water. Once more she looked with half-extinguished eyes upon the Prince; then she threw herself from the ship into the sea, and felt her frame resolving into foam.

Now the sun rose up out of the sea. The rays fell mild and warm upon the cold sea-foam, and the little sea-maid felt nothing of death. She saw the bright sun; and over her sailed hundreds of glorious ethereal beings—she could see them through the white sails of the ship and the red clouds of the sky—their speech was melody, but of such a spiritual kind that no human ear could hear it, just as no human eye could see them; without wings they floated through the air. The little sea-maid found that she had a frame like these, and was rising more and more out of the foam.

"Whither am I going?" she asked; and her voice sounded like that of the other beings, so spiritual, that no earthly music could be compared to it.

"To the daughters of the air!" replied the others. "A sea-maid has no immortal soul, and can never gain one, except she win the love of a mortal. Her eternal existence depends upon the power of another. The daughters of the air have likewise no immortal soul, but they can make themselves one, through good deeds. We fly to the hot countries, where the close pestilent air kills men; there we bring coolness. We disperse the fragrance of the flowers through the air, and spread refreshment and health. After we have striven for three hundred years to accomplish all the good we can bring about we receive an immortal soul, and take part in the eternal happiness of men. You poor little sea-maid have striven with your whole heart after the goal we pursue; you have suffered and endured; you have by good works raised yourself to the world of spirits, and can gain an immortal soul after three hundred years."

And the little sea-maid lifted her glorified eyes towards God's sun, and for the first time she felt them fill with tears. On the ship there was again life and noise. She saw the Prince and his bride searching for her; then they looked mournfully at the pearly foam, as if they knew that she had thrown herself into the waves. Invisible, she kissed the forehead of the bride, fanned the Prince, and mounted with the other children of the air on the rosy cloud which floated through the ether.

After three hundred years we shall thus float into Paradise!

"And we may even get there sooner!" whispered a daughter of the air. "Invisible we float into the houses of men where children are; and for every day on which we find a good child that brings joy to its parents and deserves their love, our time of probation is shortened. The child does not know when we fly through the room; and when we smile with joy at the child's conduct, a year is counted off from the three hundred; but when we see a naughty or a wicked child, we shed tears of grief; and for every tear a day is added to our time of trial."

THE EMPEROR'S NEW CLOTHES

Many years ago there lived an Emperor, who cared so enormously for new clothes that he spent all his money upon them, that he might be very fine. He did not care about his soldiers, and did not care about the theatre, and only liked to drive out and show his new clothes. He had a coat for every hour of the day; and just as they say of a king, "He is in council," one always said of him, "The Emperor is in the wardrobe."

In the great city in which he lived, it was very merry; every day a number of strangers arrived there. One day two cheats came; they gave themselves out as weavers, and declared that they could weave the finest stuff any one could imagine. Not only were the colours and patterns, they said, uncommonly beautiful, but the clothes made of the stuff possessed the wonderful quality that they became invisible to any one who was unfit for the office he held, or was incorrigibly stupid.

"Those would be capital clothes!" thought the Emperor. "If I wore those, I should be able to find out what men in my empire are not fit for the places they have; I could distinguish the clever from the stupid. Yes, the stuff must be woven for me directly!"

And he gave the two cheats a great deal of cash in hand, that they might begin their work.

As for them, they put up two looms and pretended to be working; but they had nothing at all on their looms. They at once demanded the finest silk and the costliest gold; this they put into their own pockets, and worked at the empty looms till late into the night.

"I should like to know how far they have got on with the stuff," thought the Emperor. But he felt quite uncomfortable when he thought that those who were not fit for their offices could not see it. He believed, indeed, that he had nothing to fear for himself, but yet he preferred first to send some one else to see how matters stood. All the people in the whole city knew what peculiar power the stuff possessed, and all were anxious to see how bad or how stupid their neighbours were.

"I will send my old honest Minister to the weavers," thought the Emperor. "He can judge best how the stuff looks, for he has sense, and no one understands his office better than he!"

Now the good old Minister went out into the hall where the two cheats sat working at the empty looms.

"Mercy preserve us!" thought the old Minister, and he opened his eyes wide. "I cannot see anything at all!" But he did not say this.

Both the cheats begged him to be kind enough to come nearer, and asked if he did not approve of the colours and the pattern. Then they pointed to the empty loom, and the poor old Minister went on opening his eyes; but he could see nothing, for there was nothing to see.

"Mercy!" thought he, "can I indeed be so stupid? I never thought that, and not a soul must know it. Am I not fit for my office? No! it will never do for me to tell that I could not see the stuff."

"Do you say nothing to it?" said one of the weavers. "Oh, it is charming,—quite enchanting!" answered the old Minister, as he peered through his spectacles. "What a pattern, and what colours! Yes, I shall tell the Emperor that I am very much pleased with it."

"Well, we are glad of that," said both the weavers; and then they named the colours, and explained the strange pattern. The old Minister listened attentively, that he might be able to repeat it when the Emperor came. And he did so.

Now the cheats asked for more money, and more silk and gold, which they declared they wanted for weaving. They put all into their own pockets, and not a thread was put upon the loom; but they continued as before, to work at the empty frames.

The Emperor soon sent again, despatching another honest statesman, to see how the weaving was going on, and if the stuff would soon be ready. He fared just like the first; he looked and looked, but as there was nothing to be seen but the empty looms he could see nothing.

"Is not that a pretty piece of stuff?" asked the two cheats; and they displayed and explained the handsome pattern which was not there at all.

"I am not stupid!" thought the man,—"it must be my good office, for which I am not fit. It is funny enough, but I must not let it be noticed." And so he praised the stuff which he did not see, and expressed his pleasure at the beautiful colours and the charming pattern. "Yes! it is enchanting"—he said to the Emperor.

All the people in the town were talking of the gorgeous stuff. The Emperor wished to see it himself, while it was still upon the loom. With a whole crowd of chosen men, among whom were also the two

honest statesmen who had already been there, he went to the two
cunning cheats, who were now weaving with might and main without
fibre or thread.

"Is that not splendid?" said the two old statesmen, who had already
been there once. "Does not your Majesty remark the pattern—the colours?" And then they pointed to the empty loom, for they thought that
the others could see the stuff.

"What's this?" thought the Emperor. "I can see nothing at all! That is
terrible. Am I stupid? Am I not fit to be Emperor? That would be the
most dreadful thing that could happen to me." "Oh, it's very pretty!"
he said aloud. "It has our exalted approbation." And he nodded in a

The Emperor inspecting the invisible stuff

contented way, and gazed at the empty loom, for he would not say that he saw nothing. The whole suite whom he had with him looked and looked, and saw nothing, any more than the rest; but, like the Emperor, they said "That is pretty!" and counselled him to wear these new splendid clothes for the first time at the great procession that was going to take place. "It is splendid, tasteful, excellent!" went from mouth to mouth. On all sides there seemed to be general rejoicing, and the Emperor gave the cheats the title "Imperial Court Weavers."

The whole night before the morning on which the procession was to take place the cheats were up, and had lighted more than sixteen candles. The people could see that they were hard at work, completing the Emperor's new clothes. They pretended to take the stuff down from the loom; they made cuts in the air with great scissors, they sewed with needles without thread, and at last they said, "Now the clothes are ready!"

The Emperor came himself with his noblest cavaliers; and the two cheats lifted up one arm as if they were holding something, and said, "See, here are the trousers! here is the coat! here is the cloak!" and so on. "It is as light as a spider's web; one would think one had nothing on; but that is just the beauty of it."

"Yes!" said all the cavaliers; but they could not see anything, for nothing was there.

"Does your Imperial Majesty please to condescend to undress?" said the cheats, "then we will put you on the new clothes here in front of the great mirror."

The Emperor took off his clothes, and the cheats pretended to put on him each new garment as it was ready; and the Emperor turned round and round before the mirror.

"Oh, how well they look! how capitally they fit!" said all. "What a pattern! what colours! That is a splendid dress!"

"They are standing outside with the canopy which is to be borne above your Majesty in the procession!" announced the head master of the ceremonies.

"Well, I am ready"—replied the Emperor. "Does it not suit me well?" And then he turned again to the mirror, for he wanted it to appear as if he contemplated his adornment with great interest.

The chamberlains, who were to carry the train, stooped down with their hands towards the floor, just as if they were picking up the mantle; then they pretended to be holding something up in the air. They did not dare to let it be noticed that they saw nothing.

So the Emperor went in procession under the rich canopy, and every one in the streets said, "How incomparable are the Emperor's new clothes; what a train he has to his mantle; how it fits him!" No one would let it be perceived that he could see nothing, for that would have shown that he was not fit for his office, or was very stupid. No clothes of the Emperor's had ever had such a success as these.

"But he has nothing on!" a little child cried out at last.

"Just hear what that innocent says!" said the father; and one whispered to another what the child had said.

"But he has nothing on!" said the whole people at length. That touched the Emperor, for it seemed to him that they were right; but he thought within himself, "I must go through with the procession." And the chamberlains held on tighter than ever, and carried the train which did not exist at all.

THE GOLOSHES OF FORTUNE

I A BEGINNING

In a house in Copenhagen, not far from the King's New Market, a company—a very large company—had assembled, to receive invitations again from those who were invited. One half of the company already sat at the card-tables, the other half awaited the result of the hostess's question, "What shall we do now?" They had progressed so far, and the entertainment began to make some degree of progress. Among other subjects the conversation turned upon the Middle Ages. Some considered that period much more interesting than our own times: yes, Councillor Knap defended this view so zealously that the lady of the house went over at once to his side; and both exclaimed against Oersted's Treatise in the Almanac on old and modern times, in which the chief advantage is given to our own day. The Councillor considered the times of the Danish King Hans as the noblest and happiest age.

The two waiting-maids

While the conversation takes this turn, only interrupted for a moment by the arrival of a newspaper, which contained nothing worth reading, we will betake ourselves to the antechamber, where the cloaks, sticks, and goloshes had found a place. Here sat two maids—an old one and a young one. One would have thought they had come to escort their mistresses home; but on looking at them more closely, the observer could see that they were not ordinary servants: their shapes were too graceful for that, their complexions too delicate, and the cut of their dresses too uncommon. They were two fairies. The younger was not Fortune, but a lady's-maid of one of the ladies of the bed-chamber of Fortune, who carry about the more trifling gifts of Fortune. The older one looked somewhat more gloomy—she was Care, who always goes herself in her own exalted person to perform her business, for thus she knows that her business is well done.

They were telling each other where they had been that day. The messenger of Fortune had only transacted a few unimportant affairs, as, for instance, she had preserved a new bonnet from a shower of rain, had procured an honest man a bow from a titled Nobody, and so on; but what she had still to relate was something quite extraordinary.

"I can likewise tell," said she, "that to-day is my birthday; and in honour of it a pair of goloshes has been entrusted to me, which I am to bring to the human race. These goloshes have the property that every one who puts them on is at once transported to the time and place in which he likes best to be—every wish in reference to time, place, and circumstance is at once fulfilled; and so for once man can be happy here below!"

"Believe me," said Care, "he will be very unhappy, and will bless the moment when he can get rid of the goloshes again."

"What are you thinking of?" retorted the other. "Now I shall put them at the door. Somebody will take them by mistake, and become the happy one!"

You see, that was the dialogue they held.

II   WHAT HAPPENED TO THE COUNCILLOR

It was late. Councillor Knap, lost in contemplation of the times of King Hans, wished to go home; and fate willed that instead of his own goloshes he should put on those of Fortune, and thus went out into East Street. But by the power of the goloshes he had been put back three hundred years—into the days of King Hans; and therefore he put his foot into mud and mire in the street, because in those days there was not any pavement in the streets.

"Why, it is horrible—how dirty it is here!" said the Councillor. "The good pavement is gone, and all the lamps are put out."

The moon did not yet stand high enough to give much light, and the air was tolerably thick, so that all objects seemed to melt together in the darkness. At the next corner a lamp hung before a picture of the Madonna, but the light it gave was as good as none; he only noticed it when he stood just under it, and his eyes fell upon the painted figures.

"That is probably a museum of art," thought he, "where they have forgotten to take down the sign."

A couple of men in the costume of those past days went by him.

"How they look!" he said. "They must come from a masquerade."

Suddenly, there was a sound of drums and fifes, and torches gleamed brightly. The Councillor started. And now he saw a strange procession go past. First came a whole troop of drummers, beating their instruments very dexterously; they were followed by men-at-arms, with long-bows and cross-bows. The chief man in the procession was a clerical lord. The astonished Councillor asked what was the meaning of this, and who the man might be.

"That is the Bishop of Zealand!"

"What in the world has come to the Bishop!" said the Councillor, with a sigh, and shook his head. "This could not possibly be the Bishop!" Ruminating on this, and without looking to the right or to the left, the Councillor went through the East Street and over the High-bridge Place. The bridge which led to the Palace Square was not to be found; he perceived the shore of a shallow water, and at length encountered two people, who sat in a boat.

"Does the gentleman wish to be ferried over to the Holm?" they asked.

"To the Holm!" repeated the Councillor, who did not know, you see, in what period he was. "I want to go to Christian's Haven and to Little Turf Street."

The men started at him.

"Pray tell me where the bridge is?" said he. "It is shameful that no lanterns are lighted here; and it is as muddy, too, as if one were walking in a marsh." But the longer he talked with the boatmen the less could he understand them. "I don't understand your Bornholm talk," he at last cried, angrily, and turned his back upon them. He could not find the bridge, nor was there any paling. "It is quite scandalous how things look here!" he said—never had he thought his own times so miserable as this evening. "I think it will be best if I take a cab"—thought he. But where were the cabs?—not one was to be seen. "I shall have to go back to the King's New Market, where there are many carriages standing, otherwise I shall never get as far as Christian's Haven."

Now he went towards East Street, and had almost gone through it when the moon burst forth. "What in the world have they been erecting here?" he exclaimed, when he saw the East Gate, which in those days stood at the end of East Street. In the meantime, however, he found a passage open, and through this he came out upon our New Market; but it was a broad meadow. Single bushes stood forth, and across the meadow ran a great canal or stream. A few miserable wooden booths for Dutch skippers were erected on the opposite shore.

"Either I behold a *fata morgana*, or I am tipsy,"—sighed the Councillor. "What can that be, what can that be?"

He turned back, in the full persuasion that he must be ill. In walking up the street he looked more closely at the houses; most of them were built of laths, and many were only thatched with straw.

"No, I don't feel well at all!" he lamented. "And yet I only drank one glass of punch! But I cannot stand that; and besides, it was very foolish to give us punch and warm salmon. I shall mention that to our hostess— the agent's lady. Suppose I go back, and say how I feel. But that looks ridiculous, and it is a question if they will be up still." He looked for the house, but could not find it.

"That is dreadful!" he cried, "I don't know East Street again. Not one shop is to be seen; old, miserable, tumble-down huts are all I see, as if I were at Roeskilde or Ringstedt. Oh, I am ill! It's no use to make ceremony. But where in all the world is the agent's house? It is no longer the same; but within there are people up still. I certainly must be ill!"

He now reached a half-open door, where the light shone through a chink. It was a tavern of that date—a kind of beerhouse. The room had the appearance of a Dutch wineshop; a number of people, consisting of seamen, citizens of Copenhagen, and a few scholars, sat in deep conversation over their jugs, and paid little attention to the new comer.

"I beg pardon," said the Councillor to the hostess, "but I felt very unwell; would you let them get me a fly to go to Christian's Haven?"

The woman looked at him and shook her head; then she spoke to him in German.

The Councillor now supposed that she did not understand Danish, so he repeated his wish in the German language. This, and his costume, convinced the woman that he was a foreigner. She soon understood that he felt unwell, and therefore brought him a jug of water. It certainly tasted a little of seawater, though it had been taken from the spring outside.

The Councillor leaned his head on his hand, drew a deep breath, and thought of all the strange things that were happening about him.

"Is that to-day's number of the *Day*?" he asked, quite mechanically, for he saw that the woman was putting away a large sheet of paper.

She did not understand what he meant, but handed him the leaf; it

The Councillor is alarmed

was a wood-cut, representing a strange appearance in the air which had been seen in the city of Cologne.

"That is very old!" said the Councillor, and became quite cheerful at sight of this antiquity. "How did you come by this strange leaf? That is very interesting, although the whole thing is a fable. Now-a-days, these appearances are explained to be northern lights that have been seen; probably they arise from electricity."

Those who sat nearest to him and heard his speech, looked at him in surprise, and one of them rose, took off his hat respectfully, and said, with a very grave face,—"You must certainly be a very learned man, sir!"

"Oh, no!" replied the Councillor, "I can only say a word or two about things one ought to understand."

"*Modestia* is a beautiful virtue,"—said the man. "Moreover, I must say to your speech, '*mihi secus videtur,*' yet I will gladly suspend my *judicium.*"

"May I ask with whom I have the pleasure of speaking?" asked the Councillor.

"I am a bachelor of theology," replied the man.

This answer sufficed for the Councillor; the title corresponded with the garb. "Certainly," he thought, "this must be an old village school-master, a queer character, such as one finds sometimes over in Jutland."

"This is certainly not a *locus docendi,*" began the man, "but I beg you to take the trouble to speak. You are doubtless well read in the ancients?"

"Oh, yes!" replied the Councillor. "I am fond of reading useful old books; and am fond of the modern ones, too, with the exception of the 'Every-day Stories,' of which we have enough, in all conscience."

"Every-day Stories?" said the bachelor, inquiringly.

"Yes, I mean the new romances we have now."

"Oh!" said the man with a smile, "they are very witty and are much read at court. The King is especially partial to the romance by Messieurs Iffven and Gaudian, which talks about King Arthur and his knights of the round table. He has jested about it with his noble lords."

"That I have certainly not yet read," said the Councillor, "that must be quite a new book published by Heiberg."

"No," retorted the man "it is not published by Heiberg, but by Godfrey von Gehmen.[1]

"Indeed, is he the author?" asked the Councillor. "That is a very old name; was not that the name of about the first printer who appeared in Denmark?" "Why, he is our first printer," replied the man.

So far it had gone well. But now one of the men began to speak of a pestilence which he said had been raging a few years ago; he meant the plague of 1484. The Councillor supposed that he meant the cholera, and so the conversation went on tolerably. The freebooters' war of 1490 was so recent that it could not escape mention. The English pirates had taken ships from the very wharves, said the man; and the

---

[1] The first printer and publisher in Denmark, under King Hans.

Councillor who was well acquainted with the events of 1801 joined in manfully against the English. The rest of the talk, however, did not pass over so well; every moment there was a contradiction. The good bachelor was terribly ignorant, and the simplest assertions of the Councillor seemed to him too bold or too fantastic. They looked at each other, and when it became too bad, the bachelor spoke Latin, in the hope that he would be better understood; but it was no use.

"How are you now?" asked the hostess; and she plucked the Councillor by the sleeve. Now his recollection came back; in the course of the conversation he had forgotten everything that had happened.

"Good heavens! where am I?" he said; and he felt dizzy when he thought of it. "We'll drink claret, mead, and Bremen beer," cried one of the guests, "and you shall drink with us."

Two girls came in. One of them had on a cap of two colours. They poured out drink and bowed; the Councillor felt a cold shudder running all down his back. "What's that!—what's that!" he cried; but he was obliged to drink with them. They took possession of the good man quite politely. He was in despair, and when one said that he was tipsy, he felt not the slightest doubt regarding the truth of the statement, and only begged them to procure him a droschky. Now they thought he was speaking Muscovite.

Never had he been in such rude vulgar company. "One would think the country was falling back into heathenism," was his reflection. "This is the most terrible moment of my life." But at the same time the idea occurred to him to bend down under the table and then to creep to the door. He did so; but just as he had reached the entry the others discovered his intention. They seized him by the feet; and now the goloshes, to his great good fortune, came off, and—the whole enchantment vanished.

The Councillor saw quite plainly, in front of him, a lamp burning, and behind it a great building; everything looked familiar and splendid. It was East Street, as we know it now; he lay with his legs turned towards a porch, and opposite to him sat the watchman asleep.

"Good heavens! Have I been lying here in the street, dreaming?" he exclaimed. "Yes, this is East Street sure enough! how splendidly bright and gay! It is terrible; what an effect that one glass of punch must have had on me?"

Two minutes afterwards he was sitting in a fly which drove him out to Christian's Haven. He thought of the terror and anxiety he had undergone, and praised from his heart the happy present, our own time, which, with all its shortcomings, was far better than the period in which he had been placed a short time before.

III THE WATCHMAN'S ADVENTURES

"On my word, yonder lies a pair of goloshes!" said the watchman. "They must certainly belong to the lieutenant who lives upstairs. They're lying close to the door."

The honest man would gladly have rung and delivered them, for upstairs there was still a light burning; but he did not wish to disturb the other people in the house, and so he let it alone.

"It must be very warm to have a pair of such things on," said he. "How nice and soft the leather is!" They fitted his feet very well. "How droll it is in the world! Now, he might lie down in his warm bed, and yet he does not! There he's pacing up and down the room! He is a happy man! He has neither wife nor children, and every evening he's at a party! Oh I wish I were he, then I should be a happy man!"

As he uttered the wish, the goloshes he had put on produced their effect, and the watchman was transported into the body and being of the lieutenant. Then he stood up in the room and held a little pink paper in his fingers, on which was a poem, a poem written by the lieutenant himself. For who is there who has not once in his life had a poetic moment?—and at such a moment, if one writes down one's thoughts, there is poetry.

Yes, people write poetry when they are in love; but a prudent man does not print such poems. The lieutenant was in love—and poor—that's a triangle, or so to speak, the half of the broken square of happiness. The lieutenant felt that very keenly, and so he laid his head against the window-frame and sighed a deep sigh.

"The poor watchman in the street yonder is far happier than I. He does not know what I call want. He has a home, a wife, and children who weep at his sorrow and rejoice at his joy. Oh! I should be happier than I am, could I change my being for his, and pass through life with his humble desires and hopes. Yes, he is happier than I!"

In that same moment the watchman became a watchman again; for through the power of the goloshes of fortune he had assumed the personality of the lieutenant; but then we know he felt far less content, and preferred to be just what he had despised a short time before. So the watchman became a watchman again.

"That was an ugly dream!" said he, "but droll enough. It seemed to me that I was the lieutenant up yonder, and that it was not pleasant at all. I was without the wife and the boys, who are now ready to half stifle me with kisses."

He sat down again and nodded. The dream would not go quite out of his thoughts. He had the goloshes still on his feet. A falling star glided down along the horizon.

"There went one!" said he. "But for all that, there are enough left. I should like to look at those things a little nearer, especially the moon, for that won't vanish under one's hands. The student for whom my wife washes says that when we die we fly from one star to another. That's not true—but it would be very nice. If I could only make a little spring up there, then my body might lie here on the stairs for all I care."

Now there are certain assertions we should be very cautious of making in this world; but doubly careful when we have goloshes of fortune on our feet. Just hear what happened to the watchman.

So far as we are concerned, we all understand the rapidity of despatch by steam; we have tried it either in railways, or in steamers across the sea. But this speed is as the crawling of the sloth or the march of the snail in comparison with the swiftness with which light travels. That flies nineteen million times quicker. Death is an electric shock we receive in our hearts; and on the wings of electricity the liberated soul flies away. The sunlight requires eight minutes and a few seconds for a journey of more than ninety-five millions of miles; on the wings of electric power the soul requires only a few moments to accomplish the same flight. The space between the orbs of the universe is, for her, not greater than, for us, the distances between the houses of our friends dwelling in the same town and even living close together. Yet this electric shock costs us the use of the body here below, unless, like the watchman, we have the magic goloshes on.

In a few seconds the watchman had traversed the distance of 260,000 miles to the moon, which body, as we know, consists of a much lighter material than that of our earth, and is, as we should say, soft as new-fallen snow. He found himself on one of the many ring-mountains with which we are familiar from Dr. Mâdler's great map of the moon. Within the ring a great bowl-shaped hollow went down to the depth of a couple of miles. At the base of the hollow lay a town, of whose appearance we can only form an idea by pouring the white of an egg into a glass of water; the substance here was just as soft as white of egg, and formed similar towers and cupolas, and terraces like sails, transparent and floating in the thin air. Our earth hung over his head like a great dark-red ball.

He immediately became aware of a number of beings, who were certainly what we call "men"—but their appearance was very different to ours. If they had been put up in a row and painted, one would have said, "That's a beautiful arabesque!" They had also a language, but no one could expect that the soul of the watchman should understand it. But the watchman's soul did understand it, for our souls have far greater abilities than we suppose. Does not its wonderful dramatic talent show itself in our dreams? Then every one of our acquaintances appears speaking in his own character, and with his own voice, in a way that not one of us could imitate in our waking hours.—How does our soul bring back to us people of whom we have not thought for many years? Suddenly they come into our souls with their smallest peculiarities about them. In fact, it is a fearful thing, that memory which our souls possess; it can reproduce every sin, every bad thought; and then, it may be asked, shall we be able to give an account of every idle word that has been in our hearts and on our lips?

Thus the watchman's soul understood the language of the people in the moon very well. They disputed about this earth, and doubted if it could be inhabited; the air, they asserted, must be too thick for a sensible moon-man to live there. They considered that the moon alone was peopled; for that, they said, was the real body in which the old-world people dwelt.

They also talked of politics; but let us go down to the East Street, and see how it fared with the body of the watchman.

He sat lifeless upon the stairs. His pike had fallen out of his hand, and his eyes stared up at the moon, which his honest body was wondering about.

"What's o'clock, watchman?" asked a passer-by. But the man who didn't answer was the watchman. Then the passengers tweaked him quite gently by the nose, and then he lost his balance. There lay the body stretched out at full length—the man was dead. All his comrades were very much frightened; dead he was, and dead he remained. It was reported, and it was discussed, and in the morning the body was carried out to the hospital.

That would be a pretty jest for the soul if it should chance to come back, and probably seek its body in the East Street and not find it. Most likely it would go first to the police and afterwards to the address-office, that inquiries might be made from thence respecting the missing goods; and then it would wander out to the hospital. But we may console ourselves with the idea that the soul is most clever when it acts upon its own account; it is the body that makes it stupid.

As we have said, the watchman's body was taken to the hospital, and brought into the washing-room; and naturally enough the first thing they did here was to pull off the goloshes; and then the soul had to come back. It took its way directly towards the body, and in a few seconds there was life in the man. He declared that this had been the most terrible night of his life; he would not have such feelings again, not for a shilling; but now it was past and over.

The same day he was allowed to leave; but the goloshes remained at the hospital.

IV A GREAT MOMENT—A VERY UNUSUAL JOURNEY

Every one who belongs to Copenhagen knows the look of the entrance to the Frederick's Hospital in Copenhagen; but as perhaps a few will read this story who do not belong to Copenhagen it becomes necessary to give a short description of it.

The hospital is separated from the street by a tolerably high railing, in which the thick iron rails stand so far apart that certain very thin inmates are said to have squeezed between them, and thus paid their little visits outside the premises. The part of the body most difficult to get through was the head; and here, as it often happens in the world, small heads were the most fortunate. This will be sufficient as an introduction.

One of the young volunteers, of whom one could only say in one sense that he had a great head, had the watch that evening. The rain was pouring down; but in spite of this obstacle he wanted to go out, only for a quarter of an hour. It was needless, he thought, to tell the porter of his wish, especially if he could slip through between the rails. There lay the goloshes which the watchman had forgotten. It never occurred to him in the least that they were goloshes of fortune. They could do him very good service in this rainy weather—and he pulled them on. Now the question was whether he could squeeze through the bars; till now he had never tried it. There he stood.

"I wish to goodness I had my head outside!" cried he; and immediately, though his head was very thick and big, it glided easily and quickly through. The goloshes must have understood it well; but now the body was to slip through also, and that could not be done.

"I'm too fat!" said he. "I thought my head was the thickest. I shan't get through."

Now he wanted to pull his head back quickly, but he could not manage it. He could move his neck, but that was all. His first feeling was one of anger; and then his spirits sank down to zero. The goloshes of fortune had placed him in this terrible condition; and, unfortunately, it never occurred to him to wish himself free. No, instead of wishing he only strove, and could not stir from the spot. The rain poured down; not a creature was to be seen in the street; he could not reach the gate-bell; and how was he to get loose? He foresaw that he should have to remain here until the morning, and then they would have to send for a blacksmith, to file through the iron bars. But such a business is not to be done quickly. The whole charity school would be upon its legs; the whole sailors' quarter close by would come up and see him standing in the pillory,—and a fine crowd there would be. "Hu!" he cried, "the blood's rising to my head, and I shall go mad! Yes, I'm going mad. Oh, that I were but free, and then most likely it would pass over."

That's what he ought to have said at first. The moment he had uttered the thought his head was free; and now he rushed in, quite dazed with the fright the goloshes of fortune had given him. But we must not think that the whole affair was over now; there was much worse to come yet.

The night passed away, and the following day too; and nobody sent for the goloshes. In the evening a display of oratory was to take place in an amateur theatre in a distant street. The house was crammed; and among the audience was the volunteer from the hospital, who appeared to have forgotten his adventure of the previous evening. He had the goloshes on; for they had not been sent for; and as it was dirty in the streets, they might do him good service. A new piece was recited; it was called "My Aunt's Spectacles:" these were spectacles which, when any one put them on in a great assembly of people, made all present look like cards, so that one could prophecy from them all that would happen in the coming year.

The idea struck him; he would have liked to possess such a pair of spectacles. If they were used rightly, they would perhaps enable the wearer to look into people's hearts; and that, he thought, would be more interesting, than to see what was going to happen in the next year; for future events would be known in time, but the people's thoughts never. "Now I'll think of the row of ladies and gentlemen on the first bench; if one could look directly into their hearts;—yes, that must be a hollow, a sort of shop! How my eyes would wander about in that shop! At every lady's, yonder, I should doubtless find a great milliner's warehouse; with this one here the shop is empty, but it would do no harm to have it cleaned out. But would there really be such shops? Ah, yes!" he continued, sighing, "I know one in which all the goods are first-rate, but there's a servant in it already; that's the only drawback in the whole shop! From one and another the word would be 'Please to step in!' Oh, that I might only step in, like a neat little thought, and slip through the hearts!"

That was the word of command for the goloshes. The volunteer shrivelled up, and began to take a very remarkable journey through the hearts of the first row of spectators. The first heart through which he passed was that of a lady; but he immediately fancied himself in the Orthopaedic Institute, in the room where the plaster casts of deformed limbs are kept hanging against the walls; the only difference was, that these casts were formed in the Institute when the patients came in, but here in the heart they were formed and preserved after the good persons had gone away. For they were casts of female friends, whose bodily and mental faults were preserved here.

Quickly he had passed into another female heart. But this seemed to him like a great holy church; the white dove of innocence fluttered over the high altar. Gladly would he have sunk down on his knees, but he was obliged to go away into the next heart. Still, however, he heard the tones of the organ, and it seemed to him that he himself had become another and a better man. He felt himself not unworthy to enter into the next sanctuary, which showed itself in the form of a poor garret, containing a sick mother. But through the window the warm sun in, and two sky-blue birds sang full of child-like joy, while the sick mother prayed for a blessing on her daughter.

Now he crept on his hands and knees through an overfilled butcher's shop. There was meat, and nothing but meat, wherever he went. It was the heart of a rich respectable man, whose name is certainly to be found in the address book.

Now he was in the heart of this man's wife; this heart was an old dilapidated pigeon-house. The husband's portrait was used as a weather-cock; it stood in connection with the doors, and these doors opened and shut according as the husband turned.

Then he came into a cabinet of mirrors, such as we find in the castle of Rosenburg. But the mirrors magnified in a great degree. In the middle of the floor sat, like a grand lama, the insignificant I of the proprietor, astonished in the contemplation of his own greatness.

Then he fancied himself transported into a narrow needle-case full of pointed needles; and he thought "this must decidedly be the heart of an old maid!" But that was not the case. It was a young officer, wearing several orders, and of whom one said, "He's a man of intellect and heart."

Quite confused was the poor volunteer when he emerged from the heart of the last person in the first row; he could not arrange his thoughts, and fancied it must be his powerful imagination which had run away with him.

"Gracious powers!" he sighed, "I must certainly have a great tendency to go mad. It is also unconscionably hot in here, the blood is rising to my head!" And now he remembered the great event of the last evening, how his head had been caught between the iron rails of the hospital. "That's where I must have caught it," thought he. "I must do something at once. A Russian bath might be very good. I wish I were lying on the highest board in the bath-house."

And there he lay on the highest board in the vapour bath; but he was lying there in all his clothes, in boots and goloshes; the hot drops from the ceiling were falling on his face.

"Hi!" he cried, and jumped down, to take a plunge bath. The attendant uttered a loud cry, on seeing a person there with all his clothes on. The volunteer had, however, enough presence of mind to whisper to him, "It's for a wager!" But the first thing he did when he got into his own room was to put a big blister on the nape of his neck, and another on his back, that they might draw out his madness.

Next morning he had a very sore back; and that was all he had got by the goloshes of fortune.

V THE TRANSFORMATION OF THE COPYING CLERK

The watchman, whom we surely have not yet forgotten, in the mean time thought of the goloshes, which he had found and brought to the hospital. He took them away: but as neither the lieutenant nor any one in the street would own them, they were taken to the police-office.

"They look exactly like my own goloshes," said one of the copying gentlemen, as he looked at the unowned articles and put them beside his own. "More than a shoemaker's eye is required, to distinguish them from one another!"

"Mr. Copying Clerk!" said a servant, coming in with some papers. The copying clerk turned and spoke to the man; when he had done this, he turned to look at the goloshes again; he was in great doubt if the right-hand or the left-hand pair belonged to him.

"It must be those that are wet!" he thought. Now here he thought wrong, for these were the goloshes of fortune; but why should not the police be sometimes mistaken? He put them on, thrust his papers into his pocket, and put a few manuscripts under his arm, for they were to be read at home, and abstracts to be made from them; but now it was Sunday morning, and the weather was fine. "A walk to Fredericksburg would do me good," said he, and he went out accordingly.

There could not be a quieter, steadier person than this young man. We grant him his little walk with all our hearts; it will certainly do him good after so much sitting. At first he only walked like a vegetating creature, so the goloshes had no opportunity of displaying their magic power.

In the avenue he met an acquaintance, one of our younger poets, who told him that he was going to start, next day, on a summer trip.

"Are you going away again already?" asked the copying clerk. "What a happy, free man you are: You can fly wherever you like; we others have a chain to our foot."

"But it is fastened to the bread-tree!" replied the poet. "You need not be anxious for the morrow; and when you grow old, you get a pension."

"But you are better off after all," said the copying clerk. "It must be a pleasure to sit and write poetry. Every body says agreeable things to you, and then you are your own master. Ah, you should just try it, poring over the frivolous affairs in the court."

The poet shook his head; the copying clerk shook his head also; each retained his own opinion; and thus they parted.

"They are a strange race, these poets!" thought the copying clerk. "I should like to try and enter into such a nature; to become a poet myself. I am certain I should not write such complaining verses as the rest. What a splendid spring day for a poet! The air is so remarkably clear, the clouds are so beautiful, and the green smells so sweet. For many years, I have not felt as I feel at this moment."

We already notice that he has become a poet. To point this out would, in most cases, be what the Germans call "mawkish;" it is a foolish fancy, to imagine a poet different from other people; for among the latter there may be natures more poetical than those of many an acknowledged poet. The difference is only that the poet has a better spiritual memory; his ears hold fast the feeling and the idea until they are embodied clearly and firmly in words, and the others cannot do that. But the transition from an every-day nature to that of a poet is always a transition, and as such it must be noticed in the copying clerk.

"What glorious fragrance!" he cried. "How it reminds me of the violets at Aunt Lora's! Yes, that was when I was a little boy. I have not thought of that for a long time. The good old lady! She lies yonder, by the canal. She always had a twig or a couple of green shoots in the water, let the winter be as severe as it might. The violets bloomed, while I had to put warm farthings against the frozen window panes to make peep-holes. That was a pretty view. Out in the canal the ships were frozen in, and deserted by the whole crew; a screaming crow was the only living creature left. Then, when the spring breezes blew, it all became lively; the ice was sawn asunder amid shouting and cheers, the ships were tarred and rigged, and then they sailed away to strange lands. I remained here, and must always remain, and sit at the police-office, and let others take passports for abroad. That's my fate. Oh, yes!" and he sighed deeply. Suddenly he paused, "Good Heaven, what is come to me? I never thought or felt as I do now. It must be the Spring air; it is just as dizzying as it is charming!" He felt in his pockets for his papers. "These will give me something else to think of," said he, and let his eyes wander over the first leaf. There he read: "*Dame Sigbirth; an original tragedy in five acts*. What is that? And it is my own hand. Have I written this tragedy? *The Intrigue on the Promenade; or, the Day of Penance.—Vaudeville*. But where did I get that from? It must have been put into my pocket. Here is a letter. Yes, it was from the manager of the theatre; the pieces were rejected, and the letter is not at all politely worded. H'm! H'm!" said the copying clerk, and he sat down upon a bench; his thoughts were elastic; his head was quite soft. Involuntarily he grasped one of the nearest flowers; it was a common little daisy. What the botanists require several lectures to explain to us, this flower told in a minute. It told the glory of its birth; it told of the strength of the sunlight which spread out the delicate leaves and made them give out fragrance. Then he thought of the battles of life, which likewise awaken feelings in our breasts. Air and light are the lovers of the flower, but light is the favoured one. Towards the light it turned and, only when the light vanished, the flower rolled her leaves together and slept in the embrace of the air.

"It is light that adorns me!" said the flower.

"But the air allows you to breathe,—" whispered the poet's voice.

Just by him stood a boy, knocking with his stick upon the marshy ground. The drops of water spurted up among the green twigs, and the copying clerk thought of the millions of infusoria which were cast up on high with the drops, which was the same to them, in proportion to their size, as it would be to us if we were hurled high over the region of clouds. And the copying clerk thought of this, and of the great change which had taken place within him; he smiled. "I sleep and dream! It is wonderful, though, how naturally one can dream, and yet know all the time that it is a dream. I should like to be able to remember it all clearly to-morrow, when I wake. I seem to myself quite unusually excited. What a clear appreciation I have of everything, and how free I feel! But I am certain that if I remember anything of it to-morrow, it will be nonsense. That has often been so with me before! It is with all the clever famous things one says and hears in dreams, as with the money of the elves under the earth; when one receives it, it is rich and beautiful, but looked at by daylight, it is nothing but stones and dried leaves. Ah!" he sighed, quite plaintively, and gazed at the chirping birds, as they sprung merrily from bough to bough, "they are much better off than I. Flying is a noble art. Happy he who is born with wings. Yes, if I could change myself into anything it should be into a lark."

In a moment his coat-tails and sleeves grew together and formed wings; his clothes became feathers, and his goloshes claws. He noticed it quite plainly and laughed inwardly. "Well, now I can see that I am dreaming, but so wildly I have never dreamed before." And he flew up into the green boughs and sung; but there was no poetry in the song, for the poetic nature was gone. The goloshes, like every one who wished to do any business thoroughly, could only do one thing at a time. He wished to be a poet; and he became one. Then he wished to be a little bird; and in changing thus, the former peculiarity was lost.

"That is charming!" he said. "In the daytime I sit in the police-office among the driest of law papers; at night I can dream that I am flying about, as a lark in the Fredericksburg garden. One could really write quite a popular comedy upon it."

Now he flew down into the grass, turned his head in every direction, and beat with his beak upon the bending stalks of grass, which, in proportion to his size, seemed to him as long as palm branches of Northern Africa.

It was only for a moment; and then all around him became as the blackest night. It seemed to him that some immense substance was cast over him; it was a great cap, which a sailor-boy threw over the bird. A hand came in and seized the copying clerk by the back and wings in a way that made him whistle. In his first terror he cried aloud: "The impudent rascal! I am copying clerk at the police office!" But that sounded to the boy only like "piep, piep," and he tapped the bird on the beak and wandered on with him.

In the alley the boy met with two other boys who belonged to the educated classes, socially speaking; but, according to abilities, they ranked in the lowest class in the school. These bought the bird for a few Danish shillings; and so the copying clerk was carried back to Copenhagen.

"It's a good thing that I am dreaming," he said, "or I should become really angry. First I was a poet, and now I'm a lark! Yes, it must have been the poetic nature which transformed me into that little creature. It is a miserable state of things, especially when one falls into the hands of boys. I should like to know what the end of it will be!"

The boys carried him into a very elegant room. A stout smiling lady received them. But she was not at all gratified to see the common field-bird, as she called the lark, coming in too. Only for one day she would consent to it; but they must put the bird in the empty cage which stood by the window. "Perhaps that will please Polly!" she added, and laughed at a great parrot swinging himself proudly in his ring in the handsome brass cage. "It's Polly's birthday," she said, simply, "so the little field-bird shall congratulate him."

Polly did not answer a single word; he only swung proudly to and fro. But a pretty canary bird, who had been brought here last summer out of his warm fragrant fatherland, began to sing loudly.

"Screamer!" said the lady; and she threw a white handkerchief over the cage.

"Piep, piep!" sighed he. "Here's a terrible snowstorm." And thus sighing he was silent.

The copying clerk, or as the lady called him, the field-bird, was placed in a little cage close to the canary, and not far from the parrot. The only human words which Polly could say, and which often sounded very comically, were "Come, let's be men now!" Everything else that he screamed out was just as unintelligible as the song of the canary bird, except for the copying clerk, who was now also a bird, and who understood his comrades very well.

"I flew under the green palm tree and the blossoming almond tree!" sang the canary. "I flew with my brothers and sisters over the beautiful flowers and over the bright sea, where the plants waved in the depths. I also saw many beautiful parrots, who told the merriest stories."

"Those were wild birds,"—replied the parrot. "They had no education. Let us be men now! Why don't you laugh? If the lady and all the strangers could laugh at it, so can you. It is a great fault to have no taste for what is pleasant. No, let us be men now."

"Do you remember the pretty girls who danced under the tents spread out beneath the blooming trees? Do you remember the sweet fruits and the cooling juice in the wild plants?"

"Oh, yes!" replied the parrot; "but here I am far better off. I have good care and genteel treatment. I know I've a good head, and I don't ask for more. Let us be men now. You are what they call a poetic soul. I have thorough knowledge and wit. You have genius, but no prudence. You mount up into those high natural notes of yours, and then you get covered up. That is never done to me; no, no, for I cost them a little more. I make an impression with my beak, and can cast wit round me. Now let us be men!"

"O my poor blooming fatherland!" sang the canary. "I will praise thy dark green trees and thy quiet bays, where the branches kiss the clear watery mirror; I'll sing of the joy of all my shining brothers and sisters, where the plants grow by the desert springs."

"Now pray leave off these dismal tones," cried the parrot. "Sing something at which one can laugh! Laughter is the sign of the highest mental development. Look if a dog or a horse can laugh! No; they can cry—but laughter—that is given to men alone. Ho, ho, ho!" screamed Polly, and finished the jest with "Let us be men now."

"You little grey Northern bird," said the canary—"so you have also become a prisoner. It is certainly cold in your woods, but still liberty is there. Fly out! They have forgotten to close your cage; the upper window is open. Fly, fly!"

Instinctively the copying clerk obeyed, and flew forth from his prison. At the same moment the half-opened door of the next room creaked, and stealthily with fierce sparkling eyes, the house cat crept in, and made chase upon him. The canary fluttered in its cage, the parrot flapped its wings, and cried "Let us be men now." The copying clerk felt mortally afraid, and flew through the window, away over the houses and streets; at last he was obliged to rest a little.

The house opposite had a home-like look; one of the windows stood open, and he flew in. It was his own room; he perched upon the table.

"Let us be men now," he broke out, involuntarily imitating the parrot; and in the same moment he was restored to the form of the copying clerk; but he was sitting on the table.

"Heaven preserve me!" he cried. "How could I have come here and fallen so soundly asleep. That was an unquiet dream, too, that I had. The whole thing was great nonsense."

VI THE BEST THAT THE GOLOSHES BROUGHT

On the following day, quite early in the morning, as the clerk still lay in bed, there came a tapping at his door; it was his neighbour who lodged on the same floor, a young theologian; and he came in.

"Lend me your goloshes,"—said he. "It is very wet in the garden, but the sun shines gloriously; I should like to smoke a pipe down there."

He put on the goloshes, and was soon in the garden, which contained a plum tree and an apple tree. Even a little garden like this is highly prized in the midst of great cities.

The theologian wandered up and down the path; it was only six o'clock, and a post-horn sounded out in the street.

"Oh, travelling, travelling!" he cried out, "that's the greatest happiness in all the world. That's the highest goal of my wishes. Then this disquietude that I feel would be stilled. But it would have to be far away. I should like to see beautiful Switzerland, to travel through Italy, to—"

Yes, it was a good thing that the goloshes took effect immediately, for he might have gone too far even for himself, and for us others too. He was travelling; he was in the midst of Switzerland, packed tightly with eight others in the interior of a diligence. He had a headache, and a weary feeling in his neck, and his feet had gone to sleep, for they were swollen by the heavy boots he had on. He was hovering in a condition between sleeping and waking. In his right-hand pocket he had his letter of credit, in his left-hand pocket his passport, and a few louis d'or were sewn into a little bag he wore on his breast. Whenever he dozed off, he dreamed he had lost one or other of these possessions; and then he would start up in a feverish way, and the first movement his hand made was to describe a triangle from left to right, and towards his breast, to feel whether he still possessed them or not. Umbrellas, hats, and walking-sticks swang in the net over him, and almost took away the prospect, which was impressive enough; he glanced out at it, and his heart sang what one poet at least, whom we know, has sung in Switzerland, but has not yet printed:

> 'Tis a prospect as fine as heart can desire,
>   Before me Mont Blanc the rough;
> 'Tis pleasant to tarry here and admire,
>   If only you've money enough.

Great, grave, and dark was all nature around him. The pine woods looked like little mosses upon the high rocks whose summits were lost in cloudy mists; and then it began to snow, and the wind blew cold.

"Hu!" he sighed; "if we were only on the other side of the Alps, then it would be summer, and I should have got money on my letter of credit; my anxiety about this prevents me from enjoying Switzerland. Oh! if I were only at the other side."

And then he was on the other side, in the midst of Italy, between Florence and Rome. The Lake Thrasymene lay spread out in the evening light like flaming gold, among the dark blue hills. Here, where Hannibal beat Flaminius, the grape-vines held each other by their green fingers; pretty half-naked children were keeping a herd of coal-black pigs under a clump of fragrant laurels, by the wayside. If we could reproduce this scene accurately, all would cry, "Glorious Italy!" But neither the theologian nor any of his travelling companions in the carriage of the vetturino thought this.

Poisonous flies and gnats flew into the carriage by thousands. In vain they beat the air frantically with a myrtle branch,—the flies stung them nevertheless. There was not one person in the carriage whose face was not swollen and covered with stings. The poor horses looked miserable, the flies tormented them woefully, and it only mended the matter for a moment when the coachman dismounted and scraped them clean from the insects that sat upon them in great swarms. Now the sun sank down; a short but icy coldness pervaded all nature; it was like the cold air of a funeral vault after the sultry summer day; and all around, the hills and clouds put on that remarkable green tone which we notice on some old pictures, and consider unnatural unless we have ourselves witnessed a similar play of colour. It was a glorious spectacle; but the stomachs of all were empty and their bodies exhausted, and every wish of the heart turned towards a resting-place for the night; but how would that be won? To descry this resting-place all eyes were turned more eagerly to the road than towards the beautiful nature.

The way now led through an olive wood; he could have fancied himself passing between knotty willow trunks at home. Here, by the solitary inn, a dozen crippled beggars had taken up their positions; the quickest among them looked, to quote an expression of Marryat's, like the eldest son of Famine, who had just come of age. The others were either blind or had withered legs, so that they crept about on their hands, or they had withered arms with fingerless hands. This was misery in rags indeed. "Eccellenza, miserabili!" they sighed, and stretched forth their diseased limbs. The hostess herself, in untidy hair, and dressed in a dirty blouse, received her guests. The doors were tied up with string; the floor of the room was of brick, and half of it was grubbed up; bats flew about under the roof, and the smell within—

"Yes, lay the table down in the stable!" said one of the travellers.

"There, at least, one knows what one's breathing."

The windows were opened, so that a little fresh air might find its way in; but quicker than the air came the withered arms and the continual whining, "Miserabili, Eccellenza!" On the walls were many inscriptions; half of them were against "la bella Italia!"

The supper was served. It consisted of a watery soup, seasoned with pepper and rancid oil. This last dainty played a chief part in the salad; musty eggs and roasted cock's-combs were the best dishes. Even the wine had a strange taste; it was dreadful mixture.

At night the boxes were placed against the doors. One of the travellers kept watch while the rest slept. The theologian was the sentry. Oh! how close it was in there. The heat oppressed him, the gnats buzzed and stung, and the miserabili outside moaned in their dreams.

"Yes, travelling would be all very well," said the theologian, "if one had no body! If the body could rest, and the mind fly! Wherever I go, I find a want that oppresses my heart; it is something better than the present moment that I desire. Yes, something better—the best; but what is that, and where is it? In my own heart I know very well what I want; I want to attain to a happy goal, the happiest of all!"

And so soon as the word was spoken he found himself at home. The long white curtains hung down from the windows, and in the middle of the room stood the black coffin; in this he was lying in the quiet sleep of death; his wish was fulfilled, his body was at rest, and his spirit roaming. "Esteem no man happy who is not yet in his grave,"—were the words of Solon; here their force was proved anew.

Every corpse is a sphynx of immortality; the sphynx here, also, in the black sarcophagus answered, what the living man had laid down two days before:—

> Thou strong stern Death! Thy silence waketh fear,
> Thou leavest mould'ring gravestones for thy traces—
> Shall not the soul see Jacob's ladder here?
> No resurrection-type but churchyard grasses?
> The deepest woes escape the world's dull eye,
> Thou that alone on duty's path hast sped,
> Heavier those duties on thy heart would lie
> Than lies the earth now, on thy coffined head.

Two forms were moving to and fro in the room. We know them both. They were the *Fairy of Care* and the *Ambassadress of Happiness*. They bent down over the dead man.

"Do you see?" said Care. "What happiness have your goloshes brought to men?"

"They have at least brought a permanent benefit to him who slumbers here,"—replied Happiness.

"Oh, no!" said Care. "He went away of himself, he was not summoned. His spirit was not strong enough to lift the treasures which he had been destined to lift. I will do him a favour."

And she drew the goloshes from his feet; then the sleep of death was ended, and the awakened man raised himself up. Care vanished, and with her the goloshes disappeared too; doubtless she looked upon them as her property.

THE DAISY

Now you shall hear!

Out in the country, close by the road-side, there was a country-house; you yourself have certainly once seen it. Before it is a little garden with flowers and a paling, which is painted. Close by it, by the ditch, in the midst of the most beautiful green grass, grew a little daisy. The sun shone as warmly and as brightly upon it as on the great splendid garden flowers, and so it grew from hour to hour. One morning it stood full-blown, with its little, shining white leaves, spreading like rays round the little yellow sun in the centre. It never thought that no man would notice it down in the grass, and that it was a poor despised floweret; no, it was very merry, and turned to the warm sun, looked up at it, and listened to the lark carolling high in the air.

The little daisy was as happy as if it were a great holiday, and yet it was only a Monday. All the children were at school; while they sat on their benches learning, it sat on its little green stalk and learned also from the warm sun, and from all around, how good God is; and the daisy was very glad that every thing it silently felt was sung so loudly and charmingly by the lark. And the daisy looked up with a kind of respect to the happy bird, who could sing and fly; but it was not at all sorrowful because it could not fly and sing also. "I can see and hear," it thought; "the sun shines on me, and the forest kisses me. Oh! how richly have I been gifted!"

Within the palings stood many stiff, aristocratic flowers—the less scent they had the more they flaunted. The peonies blew themselves out to be greater than the roses, but size will not do it; the tulips had the most splendid colours; and they knew that, and held themselves bolt upright, that they might be seen more plainly. They did not notice the little daisy outside there, but the daisy looked at them the more and thought, "How rich and beautiful they are! Yes, the pretty bird flies across to them and visits them. I am glad that I stand so near them, for at any rate I can enjoy the sight of their splendour!" And just as she thought that, "keevit"—down came flying the lark, but not down to the peonies and tulips,—no, down into the grass to the lowly daisy, which started so with joy that it did not know what to think.

The little bird danced round about it and sang:—"Oh! how soft the grass is; and see what a lovely little flower, with gold in its heart and silver on its dress." For the yellow point in the daisy looked like gold and the little leaves around it shone silvery white.

How happy was the little daisy—no one can conceive how happy! The bird kissed it with his beak, sang to it, and then flew up again into the blue air. A quarter of an hour passed, at, least before the daisy could recover itself. Half ashamed, and yet inwardly rejoiced, it looked at the other flowers in the garden, for they had seen the honour and happiness it had gained, and must understand what a joy it was. But the tulips stood up twice as stiff as before, and they looked quite peaky in the face and quite red, for they had been vexed. The peonies were quite wrong-headed; it was well that they could not speak, or the daisy would have received a good scolding. The poor little flower could see very well that they were not in a good humour, and that hurt it sensibly. At this moment there came into the garden a girl with a great sharp shining knife; she went straight up to the tulips and cut off one after another of them. "Oh!" sighed the little daisy, "this is dreadful; now it is all over with them." Then the girl went away with the tulips. The daisy was glad to stand out in the grass, and to be only a poor little flower; it felt very grateful, and when the sun went down it folded its leaves and went to sleep, and dreamed all night long about the sun and the little bird.

Next morning, when the flower again happily stretched out all its white leaves, like little arms, towards the air and the light, it recognized the voice of the bird, but the song he was singing sounded mournfully. Yes, the poor lark had good reason to be sad: he was caught, and now sat in a cage close by the open window. He sang of free and happy roaming, sang of the young green corn in the fields, and of the glorious journey he might make on his wings high through the air. The poor lark was not in good spirits, for there he sat a prisoner in a cage.

The little daisy wished very much to help him. But what was it to do? Yes, that was difficult to make out. It quite forgot how everything was beautiful around, how warm the sun shone, and how splendidly white its own leaves were. Ah! it could think only of the imprisoned bird, and how it was powerless to do anything for him.

Just then two little boys came out of the garden. One of them carried

The little boys cut the turf with the daisy on it

in his hand the knife which the girl had used to cut off the tulips. They went straight up to the little daisy, which could not at all make out what they wanted.

"Here we may cut a capital piece of turf for the lark,"—said one of the boys; and he began to cut off a square patch round about the daisy, so that the flower remained standing in its piece of grass.

"Tear off the flower!" said the other boy; and the daisy trembled with fear, for to be torn off would be to lose its life; and now it wanted particularly to live, as it was to be given with the piece of turf to the captive lark.

"No, let it stay!" said the other boy, "it makes such a nice ornament." And so it remained, and was put into the lark's cage. But the poor bird complained aloud of his lost liberty, and beat his wings against the wires of his prison; and the little daisy could not speak, could say no consoling word to him, gladly as it would have done so. And thus the whole morning passed.

"Here is no water,"—said the captive lark. "They are all gone out, and have forgotten to give me anything to drink. My throat is dry and burning. It is like fire and ice within me, and the air is so close. Oh! I must die; I must leave the warm sunshine, the fresh green, and all the splendour that God has created!" And then he thrust his beak into the cool turf to refresh himself a little with it. Then the bird's eye fell upon the daisy, and he nodded to it, and kissed it with his beak, and said:— "You also must wither in here, you poor little flower. They have given you to me with the little patch of green grass on which you grow, instead of the whole world which was mine out there! Every little blade of grass shall be a great tree for me, and every one of your fragrant leaves a great flower. Ah! you only tell me how much I have lost."

"If I could only comfort him,"—thought the little daisy. It could not stir a leaf; but the scent which streamed forth from its delicate leaves was far stronger than is generally found in these flowers; the bird also noticed that, and though he was fainting with thirst, and in his pain plucked up the green blades of grass, he did not touch the flower.

The evening came, and yet nobody appeared to bring the poor bird a drop of water. Then he stretched out his pretty wings and beat the air frantically with them; his song changed to a mournful piping, his little head sank down towards the flower, and the bird's heart broke with want and yearning. Then the flower could not fold its leaves, as it had done on the previous evening, and sleep; it drooped, sorrowful and sick, towards the earth.

Not till the next morning did the boys come; and when they found the bird dead they wept—wept many tears, and dug him a neat grave, which they adorned with leaves of flowers. The bird's corpse was put into a pretty red box, for he was to be royally buried—the poor bird! While he was alive and sang they forgot him, and let him sit in his cage and suffer want; but now that he was dead he had adornment and many tears.

But the patch of turf with the daisy on it was thrown out into the high-road; no one thought of the flower that had felt the most for the little bird, and would have been so glad to console him!

THE HARDY TIN SOLDIER

There were once five and twenty tin soldiers; they were all brothers, for they had all been born of one old tin spoon. They shouldered their muskets, and looked straight before them—their uniform was red and blue, and very splendid. The first thing they had heard in the world, when the lid was taken off their box, had been the words "Tin soldiers!" These words were uttered by a little boy, clapping his hands—the soldiers had been given to him, for it was his birthday; and now he put them upon the table. Each soldier was exactly like the rest; but one of them had been cast last of all, and there had not been enough tin to finish him; but he stood as firmly upon his one leg as the others on their two; and it was just this soldier who became remarkable.

On the table on which they had been placed stood many other playthings, but the toy that attracted most attention was a neat castle of card-board. Through the little windows one could see straight into the hall. Before the castle some little trees were placed round a little looking-glass, which was to represent a clear lake. Waxen swans swam on this lake, and were mirrored in it. This was all very pretty; but the prettiest of all was a little lady, who stood at the open door of the castle; she was also cut out in paper, but she had a dress of the clearest gauze, and a little narrow blue ribbon over her shoulders, that looked like a scarf; and in the middle of this ribbon was a shining tinsel rose as big as her whole face. The little lady stretched out both her arms, for she was a dancer; and then she lifted one leg so high that the tin soldier could not see it at all, and thought that, like himself, she had but one leg.

"That would be a wife for me," thought he; "but she is very grand. She lives in a castle, and I have only a box, and there are five and twenty of us in that. It is no place for her. But I must try to make acquaintance with her." And then he lay down at full length behind a snuff-box, which was on the table; there he could easily watch the little dainty lady, who continued to stand on one leg without losing her balance.

When the evening came, all the other tin soldiers were put into their box, and the people in the house went to bed. Now the toys began to play at "visiting," and at "war," and "giving balls." The tin soldiers rattled in their box, for they wanted to join, but could not lift the lid. The nutcracker threw somersaults, and the pencil amused itself on the table; there was so much noise that the canary woke up, and began to speak too, and even in verse. The only two who did not stir from their places were the tin soldier and the dancing lady; she stood straight up on the point of one of her toes, and stretched out both her arms; and he was just as enduring on his one leg; and he never turned his eyes away from her.

Now the clock struck twelve—and "bounce!—" the lid flew off the snuff-box; but there was not snuff in it, but a little black goblin: you see it was a trick.

"Tin soldier!" said the goblin, "don't stare at things that don't concern you."

But the tin soldier pretended not to hear him.

"Just you wait till to-morrow!" said the goblin.

But when the morning came, and the children got up, the tin soldier was placed in the window; and whether it was the goblin or the draught that did it, all at once the window flew open, and the soldier fell head over heels out of the third story. That was a terrible passage! He put his leg straight up, and stuck with his helmet downwards, and his bayonet between the paving stones.

The servant-maid and the little boy came down directly to look for him, but though they almost trod upon him they could not see him. If the soldier had cried out "Here I am!" they would have found him; but he did not think it fitting to call out loudly, because he was in uniform.

Now it began to rain; the drops soon fell thicker, and at last it came down in a complete stream. When the rain was past, two street boys came by.

"Just look!" said one of them, "there lies a tin soldier. He must come out and ride in the boat."

The birthday present of tin soldiers

And they made a boat out of a newspaper, and put the tin soldier in the middle of it; and so he sailed down the gutter, and the two boys ran beside him and clapped their hands. Goodness preserve us! How the waves rose in that gutter, and how fast the stream ran! But then it had been a heavy rain! The paper boat rocked up and down, and sometimes turned round so rapidly, that the tin soldier trembled; but he remained firm, and never changed countenance, and looked straight before him, and shouldered his musket.

All at once the boat went into a long drain, and it became as dark as if he had been in his box.

"Where am I going now?" he thought. "Yes, yes, that's the goblin's fault. Ah! if the little lady only sat here with me in the boat, it might be twice as dark for what I cared."

Suddenly there came a great water-rat, which lived under the drain.

"Have you a passport?" said the rat. "Give me your passport!"

But the tin soldier kept silence, and held his musket tighter than ever.

The boat went on, but the rat came after it. Hu! how he gnashed his teeth, and called out to the bits of straw and wood, "Hold him, hold him, he hasn't paid toll—he hasn't shown his passport!"

But the stream became stronger and stronger. The tin soldier could see the bright daylight where the arch ended; but he heard a roaring noise, which might well frighten a bolder man. Only think.—Just where the tunnel ended, the drain ran into a great canal; and for him that would have been as dangerous as for us to be carried down a great waterfall.

Now he was already so near it that he could not stop. The boat was carried out, the poor tin soldier stiffening himself as much as he could; and no one could say that he moved an eyelid. The boat whirled round three or four times, and was full of water to the very edge—it must sink. The tin soldier stood up to his neck in water, and the boat sank deeper and deeper, and the paper was loosened more and more; and now the water closed over the soldier's head. Then he thought of the pretty little dancer, and how he should never see her again; and it sounded in the soldier's ears—

Farewell, farewell, thou warrior brave,
For this day thou must die!

And now the paper parted, and the tin soldier fell out; but at that moment he was snapped up by a great fish.

Oh! how dark it was in the fish's body! It was darker yet than in the drain-tunnel; and then it was very narrow, too. But the tin soldier remained unmoved, and lay at full length shouldering his musket.

The fish swam to and fro; he made the most wonderful movements, and then became quite still. At last something flashed through him like lightning. The daylight shone quite clear, and a voice said aloud, "The tin soldier." The fish had been caught, carried to market, bought, and taken into the kitchen, where the cook cut him open with a large knife.

She seized the soldier round the body with both her hands, and carried him into the room, where all were anxious to see the remarkable man, who had travelled about in the inside of a fish; but the tin soldier was not at all proud. They placed him on the table, and there—no, what curious things may happen in the world! The tin soldier was in the very room in which he had been before; he saw the same children, and the same toys stood on the table; and there was the pretty castle with the graceful little dancer. She was still balancing herself on one leg, and held the other extended in the air. She was hardy too. That moved the tin soldier; he was very nearly weeping tin tears, but that would not have been proper. He looked at her, but they said nothing to each other.

Then one of the little boys took the tin soldier and flung him into the stove. He gave no reason for doing this. It must have been the fault of the goblin in the snuff-box.

The tin soldier stood there quite illuminated, and felt a heat that was terrible; but whether this heat proceeded from the real fire or from love, he did not know. The colours had quite gone off from him; but whether that had happened on the journey, or had been caused by grief, no one could say. He looked at the little lady, she looked at him, and he felt that he was melting; but he still stood firm, shouldering his musket. Then suddenly the door flew open, and the draught of air caught the dancer, and she flew like a sylph just into the stove to the tin soldier, and flashed up in a flame, and she was gone. Then the tin soldier melted down into a lump, and when the servant-maid took the ashes out next day, she found him in the shape of a little tin heart. But of the dancer nothing remained but the tinsel rose, and that was burnt as black as a coal.

THE WILD SWANS

Far away where the swallows fly when our winter comes on, lived a King who had eleven sons, and one daughter named Eliza. The eleven brothers were Princes, and went to school each with a star on his breast and his sword by his side. They wrote with pencils of diamond upon slates of gold, and learned by heart just as well as they read; one could see directly that they were Princes. The sister Eliza sat upon a little stool of plateglass, and had a picture-book which had been bought for the price of half a kingdom.

Oh, the children were particularly well off; but it was not always to remain so.

Their father, who was King of the whole country, married a bad Queen who did not love the poor children at all. On the very first day they could notice this. In the whole palace there was great feasting, and the children were playing there. Then guests came; but instead of the children receiving, as they had been accustomed to do, all the spare cake and all the roasted apples, they only had some sand given them in a teacup, and were told that they might make believe that was something.

The next week the Queen took the little sister Eliza into the country to a peasant and his wife; and but a short time had elapsed before she told the King so many falsehoods about the poor Princes that he did not trouble himself any more about them.

"Fly out into the world and get your own living!" said the wicked Queen. "Fly, like great birds without a voice." But she could not make it so bad for them as she had intended, for they became eleven magnificent wild swans. With a strange cry they flew out of the palace windows, far over the park and into the wood.

It was yet quite early morning, when they came by the place where their sister Eliza lay in the peasant's room, asleep. Here they hovered over the roof, turned their long necks and flapped their wings; but no one heard or saw it. They were obliged to fly on, high up towards the clouds, far away into the wide world; there they flew into a great dark wood, which stretched away to the sea-shore.

Poor little Eliza stood in the peasant's room and played with a green leaf; for she had no other playthings. And she pricked a hole in the leaf, and looked through it up at the sun, and it seemed to her that she saw her brothers' clear eyes; each time the warm sun shone upon her cheeks she thought of all the kisses they had given her.

Each day passed just like the rest. When the wind swept through the great rose hedges outside the house, it seemed to whisper to them, "What can be more beautiful than you?" But the roses shook their heads and answered, "Eliza!" And when the old woman sat in front of her door on Sunday and read in her hymn-book, the wind turned the leaves and said to the book, "Who can be more pious than you?" and the hymn-book said "Eliza!" And what the rose-bushes and the hymn-book said was the simple truth.

When she was fifteen years old, she was to go home. And when the Queen saw how beautiful she was, she became spiteful and filled with hatred towards her. She would have been glad to change her into a wild swan, like her brothers; but she did not dare to do so at once, because the King wished to see his daughter.

Early in the morning the Queen went into the bath, which was built of white marble, and decked with soft cushions, and the most splendid tapestry; and she took three toads and kissed them, and said to the first, "Sit upon Eliza's head when she comes into the bath, that she may become as stupid as you." "Seat yourself upon her forehead," she said to the second, "that she may become as ugly as you, and her father may not know her." "Rest on her heart," she whispered to the third, "that she may receive an evil mind and suffer pain from it." Then she put the toads into the clear water, which at once assumed a green colour; and calling Eliza, caused her to undress and step into the water. And while

Eliza looking out for her brothers, the wild swans

Eliza dived, one of the toads sat upon her hair, and the second on her forehead, and the third on her heart; but she did not seem to notice it; and as soon as she rose three red poppies were floating on the water. If the creatures had not been poisonous, and if the witch had not kissed them, they would have been changed into red roses. But at any rate they became flowers, because they had rested on the girl's head, and forehead, and heart. She was too good and innocent for sorcery to have power over her.

When the wicked Queen saw that, she rubbed Eliza with walnut juice, so that the girl became dark brown, and smeared a hurtful ointment on her face and let her beautiful hair hang in confusion. It was quite impossible to recognize the pretty Eliza.

When her father saw her he was much shocked, and declared this was not his daughter. No one but the yard-dog and the swallows would recognize her; but they were poor animals who had nothing to say.

Then poor Eliza wept, and thought of her eleven brothers, who were all away. Sorrowfully she crept out of the castle, and walked all day over field and moor till she came into the great wood. She did not know whither she wished to go, only she felt very downcast, and longed for her brothers; they had certainly been, like herself, thrust forth into the world, and she would seek for them and find them.

She had been only a short time in the wood, when the night fell; she quite lost the path; therefore she lay down upon the soft moss, prayed her evening prayer, and leaned her head against the stump of a tree. Deep silence reigned around; the air was mild, and in the grass and in the moss, gleamed like a green fire hundreds of glow-worms; when she lightly touched one of the twigs with her hand, the shining insects fell down upon her like shooting stars.

The whole night long she dreamed of her brothers; they were children again playing together, writing with their diamond pencils upon their golden slates, and looking at the beautiful picture-book which had cost half a kingdom. But on the slates they were not writing as they had been accustomed to do, lines and letters, but the brave deeds they had done, and all they had seen and experienced; and in the picture-book everything was alive; the birds sang, and the people went out of the book and spoke with Eliza and her brothers. But when the leaf was turned, they jumped back again directly, so that there should be no confusion.

When she awoke, the sun was already standing high. She could certainly not see it; for the lofty trees spread their branches far and wide above her. But the rays played there above like a gauzy veil, there was a fragrance from the fresh verdure, and the birds almost perched upon her shoulders. She heard the plashing of water; it was from a number of springs all flowing into a lake which had the most delightful sandy bottom. It was surrounded by thick growing bushes, but at one part the stags had made a large opening, and here Eliza went down to the water. The lake was so clear, that if the wind had not stirred the branches and the bushes, so that they moved, one would have thought they were painted upon the depths of the lake; so clearly was every leaf mirrored, whether the sun shone upon it or whether it lay in shadow.

When Eliza saw her own face she was terrified—so brown and ugly was she; but when she wetted her little hand and rubbed her eyes and her forehead, the white skin gleamed forth again. Then she undressed and went down into the fresh water; a more beautiful King's daughter than she was could not be found in the world. And when she had dressed herself again, and plaited her long hair, she went to the bubbling spring, drank out of her hollow hand, and then wandered far into the wood, not knowing whither she went. She thought of her dear brothers, and thought that Heaven would certainly not forsake her. It is God who lets the wild apples grow, to satisfy the hungry. He showed her a wild apple-tree, with the boughs bending under the weight of the fruit. Here she held her midday meal, placed props under the boughs, and then went into the darkest part of the forest. There it was so still that she could hear her own footsteps, as well as the rustling of every dry leaf which bent under her feet. Not one bird was to be seen, not one ray of sunlight could find its way through the great dark boughs of the trees; the lofty trunks stood so close together that when she looked before her it appeared as though she were surrounded by sets of palings one behind the other. Oh, here was a solitude such as she had never before known!

The night came on quite dark! Not a single glow-worm now gleamed in the grass. Sorrowfully she lay down to sleep. Then it seemed to her as if the branches of the trees parted above her head, and mild eyes of angels looked down upon her from on high.

When the morning came she did not know if it had really been so, or if she had dreamt it.

She went a few steps forward, and then she met an old woman with berries in her basket, and the old woman gave her a few of them. Eliza asked, if the dame had not seen eleven Princes riding through the wood.

"No,"—replied the old woman, "but yesterday I saw eleven swans swimming in the river close by, with golden crowns on their heads."

And she led Eliza a short distance further to a declivity, and at the foot of the slope a little river wound its way. The trees on its margin stretched their long leafy branches across towards each other; and where their natural growth would not allow them to come together, the roots had been torn out of the ground, and hung, intermingled with the branches, over the water.

Eliza said farewell to the old woman, and went beside the river to the place where the stream flowed out to the great open shore.

The whole glorious sea lay before the young girl's eyes; but not one sail appeared on its surface, and not a boat was to be seen. How was she to proceed? She looked at the innumerable little pebbles on the shore; the water had worn them all round. Glass, iron, stones, everything that was there had received its shape from the water, which was much softer than even her delicate hand. "It rolls on unweariedly; and thus what is hard becomes smooth. I will be just as unwearied. Thanks for your lesson, you clear rolling waves; my heart tells me that one day you will lead me to my dear brothers."

On the foam-covered sea-grass lay eleven white swan feathers—she collected them into a bunch. Drops of water were upon them, whether they were dewdrops or tears nobody could fell. Solitary it was there on the strand, but she did not feel it; for the sea showed continual change— more in a few hours than the lovely lakes can produce in a whole year. Then a great black cloud came, it seemed as if the sea would say, "I can look angry, too;" and then the wind blew and the waves turned the white side outwards. But when the clouds gleamed red, and the winds slept, the sea looked like a rose-leaf; sometimes it became green, some-times white. But however quietly it might rest, there was still a slight motion on the shore; the water rose gently like the breast of a sleeping child.

When the sun was just about to set, Eliza saw eleven wild swans, with crowns on their heads, flying towards the land: they swept along one after the other, so that they looked like a long white band. Then Eliza descended the slope, and hid herself behind a bush. The swans alighted near her, and flapped their great white wings.

So soon as the sun had disappeared beneath the water the swans' feathers fell off, and eleven handsome Princes, Eliza's brothers, stood there. She uttered a loud cry;—for although they were greatly altered, she knew and felt that it must be they. And she sprang into their arms, and called them by their names; and the Princes felt supremely happy when they saw their little sister again; and they knew her, though she was now tall and beautiful. They smiled and wept; and soon they understood how bad their stepmother had been to them all.

"We brothers," said the eldest, "fly about as wild swans, so long as the sun is in the sky; directly it sinks down we receive our human form again. Therefore we must always take care that we have a resting-place for our feet when the sun sets; for if at that moment we were flying up towards the clouds, we should sink down into the deep as men. We do not dwell here; there lies a land just as fair as this beyond the sea. But the way thither is long; we must cross the great sea, and on our path there is no island where we could pass the night, only a little rock stands forth in the midst of the waves; it is but just large enough that we can rest upon it, close to each other.

If the sea is rough, the foam spurts far over us, but we thank God for the rock. There we pass the night in our human form; but for this rock we could never visit our beloved native land, for we require two of the longest days in the year for our journey. Only once in each year is it granted to us to visit our home. For eleven days we may stay here, and fly over the great wood from whence we can see the palace in which we were born, and in which our father lives, and the high church tower, beneath whose shade our mother lies buried. Here it seems to us as though the bushes and trees were our relatives; here the wild horses career across the steppe, as we have seen them do in our childhood; here the charcoal-burner sings the old songs, to which we danced as

Eliza and her brothers, the swans

children; here is our fatherland; hither we feel ourselves drawn, and here we have found you, our dear little sister. Two days more we may stay here; then we must away across the sea, to a glorious land, but which is not our native land. How can we bear you away? We have neither ship nor boat."

"In what way can I release you?" asked the sister; and they conversed nearly the whole night, only slumbering for a few hours.

She was awakened by the rustling of the swans' wings above her head. Her brothers were again enchanted, and they flew in wide circles and at last far away; but one of them, the youngest, remained behind; and the swan laid his head in her lap, and she stroked his wings; and the whole day they remained together. Towards evening the others came back and when the sun had gone down, they stood there in their own shapes.

"To-morrow we fly far away from here, and cannot come back until a whole year has gone by. But we cannot leave you thus! Have you courage to come with us? My arm is strong enough to carry you in the wood; and should not all our wings be strong enough to fly with you over the sea?"

"Yes, take me with you,"—said Eliza.

The whole night they were occupied weaving a net of the pliable willow bark and tough reeds; and it was great and strong. On this net Eliza lay down; and when the sun rose and her brothers were changed into wild swans, they seized the net with their beaks, and flew with their beloved sister who was still asleep, high up towards the clouds. The sunbeams fell exactly upon her face; so one of the swans flew over her head, that his broad wings might overshadow her.

They were far away from the shore when Eliza awoke; she was still dreaming, so strange did it appear to her to be carried high through the air and over the sea. By her side lay a branch with beautiful ripe berries and a bundle of sweet-tasting roots. The youngest of the brothers had collected them, and placed them there for her. She smiled at him thankfully, for she recognized him; he it was who flew over her and shaded her with his wings.

They were so high that the greatest ship they descried beneath them seemed like a white seagull lying upon the waters. A great cloud stood behind them. It was a perfect mountain; and upon it Eliza saw her own shadow and those of the eleven swans; there they flew on, gigantic in size. Here was a picture, a more splendid one than she had ever yet seen. But as the sun rose higher and the cloud was left farther behind them, the floating shadowy image vanished away.

The whole day they flew onward through the air, like a whirring arrow; but their flight was slower than it was wont to be, for they had their sister to carry. Bad weather came on; the evening drew near; Eliza looked anxiously at the setting sun, for the lonely rock in the ocean could not be seen. It seemed to her as if the swans beat the air more strongly with their wings. Alas, she was the cause that they did not advance fast enough. When the sun went down, they must become men and fall into the sea and drown. Then she prayed a prayer from the depths of her heart; but still she could descry no rock. The dark cloud came nearer in a great black threatening body, rolling forward like a mass of lead, and the lightening burst forth, flash upon flash.

Now the sun just touched the margin of the sea. Eliza's heart trembled; then the swans darted downwards, so swiftly that she thought they were falling, but they paused again. The sun was half hidden below the water; and now for the first time she saw the little rock beneath her. It looked no larger than a seal might look, thrusting his head forth from the water. The sun sank very fast; at last it appeared only like a star; and then her foot touched the firm land. The sun was extinguished like the last spark in a piece of burnt paper; her brothers were standing around her, arm in arm, but there was not more than just enough room for her and for them. The sea beat against the rock and went over her like small rain; the sky glowed in continual fire, and peal on peal the thunder rolled; but sister and brothers held each other by the hand, and sang psalms from which they gained comfort and courage.

In the morning twilight the air was pure and calm; so soon as the sun rose the swans flew away with Eliza from the island. The sea still ran high; and when they soared up aloft, the white foam looked like millions of white swans swimming upon the water.

When the sun mounted higher Eliza saw before her, half floating in the air, a mountainous country with shining masses of ice on its water, and in the midst of it rose a castle, apparently a mile long, with row above row of lofty columns; while beneath the palm-woods waved, and bright flowers as large as mill-wheels. She asked if this was the country to which they were bound; but the swans shook their heads, for what she beheld was the gorgeous, ever changing palace of Fata Morgana; and into this they might bring no human being. As Eliza gazed at it, mountains, woods and castle fell down, and twenty proud churches, all nearly alike, with high towers and pointed windows, stood before them. She fancied she heard the organs sounding, but it was the sea she heard. When she was quite near the churches, they changed to a fleet sailing beneath her; but when she looked down it was only a sea-mist gliding over the ocean. Thus she had a continual change before her eyes, till at last she saw the real land to which they were bound. There arose the most glorious blue mountains with cedar forests, cities and palaces. Long before the sun went down, she sat on the rock in front of a great cave overgrown with delicate green trailing plants, looking like embroidered carpets.

"Now we shall see what you will dream of here to-night," said the youngest brother; and he showed her bed-chamber.

"Heaven grant that I may dream of a way to release you,"—she replied. And this thought possessed her mightily; and she prayed ardently for help; yes, even in her sleep she continued to pray. Then it seemed to her as if she were flying high in the air to the cloudy palace of Fata Morgana; and the fairy came out to meet her, beautiful and radiant; and yet the fairy was quite like the old woman who had given her berries in the wood, and had told her of the swans with golden crowns on their heads.

"Your brothers can be released,"—said she. "But have you courage and perseverance? Certainly, water is softer than your delicate hands, and yet it changes the shape of stones; but it feels not the pain that your fingers will feel; it has no heart, and cannot suffer the agony and torment you will have to endure. Do you see the stinging nettle which I hold in my hand? Many of the same kind grow around the cave in which you sleep; those only, and those that grow upon churchyard graves are serviceable, remember that. Those you must pluck though they will burn your hands into blisters. Break these nettles to pieces with your feet, and you will have flax; of this you must plait and weave eleven shirts of mail with long sleeves; throw these over the eleven swans and the charm will be broken. But recollect well, from the moment you begin this work until it is finished, even though it should take years to accomplish, you must not speak. The first word you utter will pierce your brothers' hearts like a deadly dagger. Their lives hang on your tongue. Remember all this!"

And she touched her hand with the nettle; it was like a burning fire:

and Eliza woke with the smart. It was broad daylight; and close by the spot where she had slept lay a nettle like the one she had seen in her dream. She fell on her knees, and prayed gratefully, and went forth from the cave to begin her work.

With her delicate hands she groped among the ugly nettles. These stung like fire, burning great blisters in her arms and hands; but she thought she would bear it gladly, if she could only release her dear brothers. Then she bruised every nettle with her bare feet and plaited the green flax.

When the sun had set, her brothers came; and they were frightened when they found her dumb. They thought it was some new sorcery of the wicked stepmother's; but when they saw her hands, they understood what she was doing for their sake, and the youngest brother wept. And where his tears dropped she felt no more pain, and the burning blisters vanished.

She passed the night at her work; for she could not sleep till she had delivered her dear brothers. The whole of the following day while the swans were away, she sat in solitude; but never had time flown so quickly with her as now. One shirt of mail was already finished, and now she began the second.

Then a hunting horn sounded among the hills, and she was struck with fear. The noise came nearer and nearer; she heard the barking dogs; and timidly she fled into the cave, bound into a bundle the nettles she had collected and prepared, and sat upon the bundle.

Immediately a great dog came bounding out of the ravine; and then another, and another: they barked loudly, ran back, and then came again. Only a few minutes had gone before all the huntsmen stood before the cave, and the handsomest of them was the King of the country. He came forward to Eliza, for he had never seen a more beautiful maiden.

"How did you come hither, you delightful child?" he asked. Eliza shook her head, for she might not speak; it would cost her brothers their deliverance and their lives. And she hid her hands under her apron, so that the King might not see what she was suffering.

"Come with me!" said he. "You cannot stop here. If you are as good as you are beautiful, I will dress you in velvet and in silk, and place the golden crown on your head, and you shall dwell in my richest castle, and rule." And then he lifted her on his horse. She wept and wrung her hands; but the king said, "I only wish for your happiness; one day you will thank me for this,"—and then he galloped away among the mountains, with her on his horse; and the hunters galloped at their heels.

When the sun went down, the fair regal city lay before them, with its churches and cupolas; and the King led her into the castle, where great fountains plashed in the lofty marble halls, and where walls and ceilings were covered with glorious pictures. But she had no eyes for all this; she only wept and mourned. Passively she let the women put royal robes upon her, and weave pearls in her hair, and draw dainty gloves over her blistered fingers.

When she stood there in full array, she was dazzlingly beautiful, so that the Court bowed deeper than ever. And the King chose her for his bride, though the Archbishop shook his head, and whispered that the beauteous fresh maid was certainly a witch, who blinded the eyes and led astray the heart of the King.

But the King gave no ear to this, but ordered that the music should sound, and the costliest dishes should be served, and the most beautiful maidens should dance before them. And she was led through fragrant gardens into gorgeous halls; but never a smile came upon her lips or shone in her eyes; there she stood, a picture of grief. Then the King opened a little chamber close by, where she was to sleep. This chamber was decked with splendid green tapestry, and completely resembled the cave in which she had been. On the floor lay the bundle of flax which she had prepared from the nettles, and under the ceiling hung the shirt of mail she had completed. All these things one of the huntsmen had taken with him as curiosities.

"Here you may dream yourself back in your former home,"—said the King. "Here is the work which occupied you there; now, in the midst of all your splendour, it will amuse you to think of that time."

When Eliza saw this that lay so near her heart, a smile played round her mouth, and the crimson blood came back into her cheeks. She thought of her brothers' deliverance, and kissed the King's hand; and he pressed her to his heart, and caused the marriage-feast to be announced by all the church-bells. The beautiful dumb girl out of the wood became the Queen of the country.

Then the Archbishop whispered evil words into the King's ear; but they did not sink into the King's heart. The marriage was to take place; the Archbishop himself was obliged to place the crown on her head, and with wicked spite he pressed the narrow circlet so tightly upon her brow that it pained her. But a heavier ring lay close around her heart—sorrow for her brothers—she did not feel the bodily pain. Her mouth was dumb, for a single word would cost her brothers their lives; but her eyes glowed with love for the kind, handsome King, who did everything to rejoice her. She loved him with her whole heart, more and more every day. Oh, that she had been able to confide in him, and to tell him of her grief! But she was compelled to be dumb, and to finish her work in silence. Therefore at night she crept away from his side, and went quietly into the little chamber which was decorated like the cave, and wove one shirt of mail after another. But when she began the seventh she had no flax left.

She knew that in the churchyard nettles were growing that she could use; but she must pluck them herself, and how was she to go out there?

"Oh, what is the pain in my fingers to the torment my heart endures?" thought she. "I must venture it, help will not be denied me!" With a trembling heart, as though the deed she purposed doing had been evil, she crept into the garden in the moonlight night, and went through the lanes and through the deserted streets to the churchyard. There, on one of the broadest tombstones, she saw sitting a circle of lamias. These hideous wretches took off their ragged garments, as if they were going to bathe; then with their skinny fingers they clawed upon the fresh graves, and with fiendish greed they snatched up the corpses and ate the flesh. Eliza was obliged to pass close by them, and they fastened their evil glances upon her; but she prayed silently, and collected the burning nettles, and carried them into the castle.

Only one person had seen her, and that was the Archbishop. He was awake while others slept. Now he felt sure his opinion was correct, that all was not as it should be with the Queen; she was a witch, and thus she had bewitched the King and the whole people.

In secret he told the King what he had seen, and what he feared, and when the hard words came from his tongue, the pictures of saints in the cathedral shook their heads, as though they could have said, "It is not so! Eliza is innocent!" And the Archbishop interpreted this differently; he thought they were bearing witness against her, and shaking their heads at her sinfulness. Then two heavy tears rolled down the King's cheeks; he went home with doubt in his heart, and at night pretended to be asleep; but no quiet sleep came upon his eyes, for he noticed that Eliza got up. Every night she did this, and each time he followed her silently, and saw how she disappeared in her chamber.

From day to day his face became darker. Eliza saw it, but did not understand the reason; but it frightened her—and what did she not suffer in her heart for her brothers? Her hot tears flowed upon the royal velvet and purple; they lay there like sparkling diamonds, and all who saw the splendour wished they were Queens. In the meantime she had almost finished her work. Only one shirt of mail was still to be completed; but she had no flax left, and not a single nettle. Once more, for the last time, she must therefore go to the churchyard, only to pluck a few handfuls. She thought with terror of this solitary wandering, and of the horrible lamias; but her will was firm as her trust in Providence.

Eliza went; but the King and the Archbishop followed her. They saw her vanish into the churchyard through the wicket-gate; and when they drew near, the lamias were sitting upon the gravestones, as Eliza had seen them; and the King turned aside, for he fancied her among them, whose head had rested against his breast that very evening.

"The people must condemn her,"—said he. And the people condemned her to suffer death by fire.

Out of the gorgeous regal halls, she was led into a dark damp cell, where the wind whistled through the grated window; instead of velvet and silk they gave her the bundle of nettles which she had collected; on this she could lay her head; and the hard burning coats of mail which she had woven were to be her coverlet. But nothing could have been given her that she liked better. She resumed her work and prayed. Without, the street-boys were singing jeering songs about her; and not a soul comforted her with a kind word.

But towards evening there came the whirring of swan's wings close by the grating—it was the youngest of her brothers. He had found his sister, and she sobbed aloud with joy, though she knew that the approaching night would probably be the last she had to live. But now the work was almost finished, and her brothers were here.

Now came the Archbishop, to be with her in her last hour, for he had promised the King to do so. And she shook her head, and with looks and gestures she begged him to depart; for in this night she must finish her work or else all would be in vain, all her tears, her pain and her sleepless nights. The Archbishop withdrew uttering evil words against her; but poor Eliza knew she was innocent, and continued her work.

It was still twilight; not till an hour afterwards would the sun rise,— and the eleven brothers stood at the castle-gate, and demanded to be brought before the King. That could not be, they were told, for it was still almost night, the King was asleep, and might not be disturbed. They begged, they threatened, the sentries came, yes, even the King himself came out, and asked what was the meaning of this?—At that moment the sun rose, and no more were the brothers to be seen; but eleven wild swans flew away over the castle.

All the people came flocking out at the town-gate, for they wanted to see the witch burnt. The old horse drew the cart on which she sat. They had put upon her a garment of coarse sackcloth. Her lovely hair hung loose about her beautiful head; her cheeks were as pale as death, and her lips moved silently, while her fingers were engaged with the green flax. Even on the way to death she did not interrupt the work she had begun; the ten shirts of mail lay at her feet, and she wrought at the eleventh. The mob derided her.

Eliza carried on a cart to be executed

"Look at the red witch, how she mutters? She has no hymn-book in her hand; no, there she sits with her ugly sorcery—tear it in a thousand pieces."

And all pressed upon her, and wanted to tear up the shirts of mail; then eleven wild swans came flying up, and sat round about her on the cart, and beat with their wings; and the mob gave way terrified.

"That is a sign from heaven! She is certainly innocent!" whispered many. But they did not dare say it aloud.

Now the executioner seized her by the hand; then she hastily threw the eleven shirts over the swans, and immediately eleven handsome princes stood there. But the youngest had a swan's wing instead of an arm, for a sleeve was wanting to his shirt—she had not finished it.

"Now I may speak!" she said. "I am innocent!"

And the people who saw what happened, bowed before her as before a saint; but she sank lifeless in her brother's arms, such an effect had suspense, anguish, and pain upon her.

"Yes, she is innocent,"—said the eldest brother—and now he told everything that had taken place; and while he spoke a fragrance arose as of millions of roses; for every piece of faggot in the pile had taken root, and was sending forth shoots; and a fragrant hedge stood there, tall and great, covered with red roses, and at the top a flower, white and shining, gleaming like a star. This flower the King plucked and placed in Eliza's bosom; and she awoke with peace and happiness in her heart.

And all the church-bells rang of themselves, and the birds came in great flocks. And back to the castle such a marriage procession was held as no King had ever yet seen.

THE LOVELIEST ROSE IN THE WORLD

Once there reigned a Queen, in whose garden were found the most glorious flowers at all seasons, and from all the lands in the world; but especially she loved roses, and therefore she possessed the most various kinds of this flower, from the wild dog-rose, with the apple-scented green leaves, to the most splendid Provence rose; they grew against the earth walls, wound themselves round pillars and window frames, into the passages and all along the ceiling in all the halls, and the roses were various in fragrance, form, and colour.

But care and sorrow dwelt in these halls; the Queen lay upon a sickbed, and the doctors declared that she must die.

"There is still one thing that can save her," said the wisest of them. "Bring her the loveliest rose in the world, the one which is the expression of the brightest and purest love; for if that is brought before her eyes, ere they close, she will not die!"

And young and old came from every side with roses, the loveliest that bloomed in each garden; but they were not the right sort. The flower was to be brought out of the garden of Love; but what rose was it there that expressed the highest and purest love?

And the poets sang of the loveliest rose in the world, and each one named his own, and intelligence was sent far round in the land to every heart that beat with love; to every class and condition, and to every age.

"No one has till now named the flower,"—said the wise man. "No one has pointed out the place where it bloomed in its splendour. They are not the roses from the coffin of Romeo and Juliet, or from the Walburg's grave, though these roses will be ever fragrant in song, they are not the roses that sprouted forth from Winkelried's blood-stained lances, from the blood that flows in a sacred cause from the breast of the hero who dies for his country; though no death is sweeter than this, and no rose redder than the blood that flows then. Nor is it that wondrous flower, to cherish which man devotes, in a quiet chamber, many a sleepless night and much of his fresh life—the magic flower of Science."

"I know where it blooms," said a happy mother, who came with her pretty child to the bedside of the queen. "I know where the loveliest rose of the world is found! The rose that is the expression of the highest and purest love springs from the blooming cheeks of my sweet child when, strengthened by sleep, it opens its eyes and smiles at me with all its affection!"

"Lovely is this rose; but there is still a lovelier,"—said the wise man.

"Yes; a far lovelier one," said one of the women. "I have seen it and a loftier, purer rose does not bloom. I saw it on the cheeks of the Queen. She had taken off her golden crown, and in the long dreary night she was carrying her sick child in her arms; she wept, kissed it, and prayed for her child as a mother prays in the hour of her anguish!"

The wise man visits the sick Queen

Holy and wonderful in its might is the white rose of grief; but it is not the one we seek.

"No, the loveliest rose of the world, I saw at the altar of the Lord," said the good old bishop. "I saw it shine as if an angel's face had appeared. The young maiden went to the Lord's Table, and renewed the promise made at her baptism, and roses were blushing, and pale roses shining on their fresh cheeks; a young girl stood there; she looked with all the purity and love of her young spirit up to heaven; that was the expression of the highest and the purest love."

"May she be blessed!" said the wise man, "but not one of you has yet named to me the loveliest rose of the world."

Then there came into the room a child, the Queen's little son; tears stood in his eyes and glistened on his cheeks; he carried a great open book, and the binding was of velvet, with great silver clasps.

"Mother!" cried the little boy, "only hear what I have read." And the child sat by the bedside, and read from the book of Him who suffered death on the Cross to save men, and even those who were not yet born."

"Greater love there is not—"

And a roseate hue spread over the cheeks of the Queen, and her eyes gleamed, for she saw that from the leaves of the book there bloomed the loveliest rose, that sprang from the blood of Christ shed on the Cross.

"I see it," she said, "he who beholds this, the loveliest rose on earth, shall never die."

THE GARDEN OF PARADISE

Once there was a king's son. No one had so many beautiful books as he, everything that had happened in this world he could read there, and could see pictures of all, in lovely copper-plates. Of every people and of every land he could get intelligence; but there was not a word to tell where the Garden of Paradise could be found; and it was just that of which he thought most.

His grandmother had told him, when he was quite little, but was to begin to go to school, that every flower in this Paradise Garden was a delicate cake, and the pistils contained the choicest wine; on one of the flowers history was written, on another geography or tables; so that one had only to eat cake, and one knew a lesson; and the more one ate, the more history, geography or tables did one learn.

At that time he believed this. But when he became a bigger boy, and learned more and became wiser, he understood well that the splendour in the Garden of Paradise must be of quite a different kind.

Oh, why did Eve pluck from the tree of knowledge? Why did Adam eat the forbidden fruit? If I had been he, it would never have happened—Then sin would never have come into the world!"

That he said then, and he still said it when he was seventeen years old. The Garden of Paradise filled all his thoughts.

One day he walked in the wood. He was walking quite alone, for that was his greatest pleasure. The evening came, and the clouds gathered together; rain streamed down as if the sky were one single river from which the water was pouring; it was as dark as it usually is at night in the deepest well. Often he slipped on the smooth grass; often he fell over the smooth stones which peered up out of the wet rocky ground.

Everything was soaked with water and there was not a dry thread on the poor Prince. He was obliged to climb over great blocks of stone, where the water spirted from the thick moss. He was nearly fainting. Then he heard a strange rushing, and saw before him a great illuminated cave. In the midst of it burned a fire, so large that a stag might have been roasted at it. And this was in fact being done. A glorious deer, had been stuck, horns and all, upon a spit, and was turning slowly between two felled pine trunks. An elderly woman, large and strongly built, looking like a disguised man, sat by the fire, into which she threw one piece of wood after another.

"Come nearer!" said she. "Sit down by the fire and dry your clothes."

"There's a great draught here!" said the Prince; and he sat down on the ground. "That will be worse when my sons come home,"—replied the woman. "You are here in the Cavern of the Winds; my sons are the four winds of the world; can you understand that?"

"Where are your sons?" asked the Prince. "It is difficult to answer when stupid questions are asked,"—said the woman. "My sons do business on their own account. They play at shuttlecock with the clouds up yonder in the King's hall,"—and she pointed upwards.

"Oh indeed!" said the Prince. "But you speak rather gruffy, by the way, and are not so mild as the women I generally see about me."

"Yes, they have most likely nothing else to do! I must be hard, if I want to keep my sons in order; but I must be hard, if I can do it, though they are obstinate fellows. Do you see the four sacks hanging here by the wall? They are just as frightened of those, as you used to be of the rod stuck behind the glass. I can bend the lads together, I tell you, and then I pop them into the bag; we don't make any ceremony. There they sit, and may not wander about again, until I think fit to allow them. But here comes one of them!"

It was the North-wind, who came in with piercing cold; great hail-stones skipped about on the floor, and snow-flakes fluttered about. He was dressed in a jacket and trousers of bearskin; a cap of sealskin was drawn down over his ears; long icicles hung on his beard, and one hail-stone after another rolled down from the collar of his jacket.

"Do not go to the fire directly,"—said the prince. "You might get your hands and face frost-bitten."

"Frost-bitten?" repeated the North-wind, and he laughed aloud.

"Cold is exactly what rejoices me most! But what kind of little tailor art thou? How did you find your way into the Cavern of the Winds?"

"He is my guest," interposed the old woman, "and if you're not satisfied with this explanation, you may go into the sack;—do you understand me?"

You see that was the right way; and now the North-wind told whence he came, and where he had been for almost a month.

"I came from the Polar Sea," said he; "I have been in the bear's icy land with the walrus hunters. I sat and slept on the helm, when they went away from the North Cape; and when I awoke now and then, the storm-bird flew round my legs. That's a comical bird! He gives a sharp clap with his wings, and then holds them quite still and shoots along in full career."

"Don't be too long-winded,"—said the Mother of the Winds. "So you came to the Bear's Island?"

"It is beautiful there! There's a floor for dancing on, as flat as a plate. Half-thawed snow, with a little moss, sharp stones and skeletons of walruses and polar bears lay around, and likewise gigantic arms and legs of a rusty green colour. One would have thought the sun had never shone there. I blew a little upon the mist, so that one could see the hut; it was a house built of wreck-wood, and covered with walrus skins, the fleshy side turned outwards. It was full of red and green; on the roof sat a live polar bear who was growling. I went to the shore to look after the bird's nests, and saw the unfledged nestlings screaming and opening their beaks; then I blew down into their thousand throats, and taught them to shut their mouths. Farther on the walruses were splashing like great maggots with pig's heads and teeth an ell long!"

"You tell your story well, my son," said the old lady. "My mouth waters when I hear you!"

"Then the hunting began! The harpoon was hurled into the walrus's breast, so that a smoking stream of blood spurted like a fountain over the ice. When I thought of my sport, I blew, and let my sailing ships, the big icebergs, crush the boats between them. Ho! how the people whistled and how they cried! But I whistled louder than they. They were obliged to throw the dead walruses and their chests and tackle out upon the ice; I shook the snow-flakes over them, and let them drive

The East-wind telling his story

south in their crushed boats with their booty to taste salt water. They'll never come to Bear's Island again!"

"Then you have done a wicked thing!" said the Mother of the Winds.

"What good I have done others may tell," replied he. "But here comes a brother from the west. I like him best of all; he tastes of the sea, and brings a delicious coolness with him."

"Is that Little Zephyr?" asked the Prince. "Yes, certainly, that is Zephyr,"—replied the old woman. "But he is not little. Years ago he was a pretty boy, but that's past now."

He looked like a wild man, but he had a broad-brimmed hat on, to save his face. In his hand he held a club of mahogany, hewn in the American mahogany forests. It was no trifle.

"Where do you come from?" said his mother. "Out of the forest wilderness,"—said he "where the water-snake lies in the wet grass, and people don't seem to be wanted."

"What were you doing there?"

"I looked into the deepest river, and watched how it rushed down from the rocks, and turned to spray, and shot up towards the clouds to carry the rainbow. I saw the wild buffalo swimming in the stream, but the stream carried him away. He drifted with the flock of wild ducks that flew up where the water fell down in a cataract. The buffalo had to go down it; that pleased me; and I blew a storm, so that ancient trees were split up into splinters!"

"And have you done nothing else?" asked the old dame.

"I have thrown somersaults in the Savannahs; I have stroked the wild horses and shaken the cocoa-nut palms. Yes, yes, I have stories to tell! But one must not tell all one knows. You know that, old lady." And he kissed his mother so roughly, that she almost tumbled over. He was a terribly wild young fellow!

Now came the South-wind with a turban on, and a flying Bedouin's cloak.

"It's terribly cold, out here!" cried he, and threw some more wood on the fire. "One can feel that the North-wind came first."

"It's so hot that one could roast a Polar bear here," said the North-wind.

"You're a Polar bear yourself,"—retorted the South-wind.

"Do you want to be put in the sack?" asked the old dame. "Sit upon the stone yonder, and tell me where you have been."

"In Africa, mother,"—he answered. "I was out hunting the lion with the Hottentots in the land of the Kaffirs. Grass grows there in the plains, green as an olive. There the ostrich ran races with me; but I am swifter than he. I came into the desert where the yellow sand lies; it looks there like the bottom of the sea. I met a caravan. The people were killing their last camel to get water to drink; but it was very little they got. The sun burned above, and the sand below. The outspread deserts had no bounds. Then I rolled in the fine loose sand, and whirled it up in great pillars. That was a dance! You should have seen how the dromedary stood there terrified, and the merchant drew the caftan over his head. He threw himself down before me, as before Allah, his God. Now they are buried; a pyramid of sand covers them all. When I some day blow that away, the sun will bleach the white bones; then travellers may see that men have been there before them. Otherwise, one would not believe that, in the desert!"

"So you have done nothing but evil!" exclaimed the mother, "March into the sack!" And before he was aware, she had seized the South-wind round the body and popped him into the bag. He rolled about on the floor; but she sat down on the sack, and then he had to keep quiet.

"Those are lively boys of yours,"—said the Prince.

"Yes," she replied, and I know how to punish them! Here comes the fourth!"

That was the East-wind, who came dressed like a Chinaman. "Oh! do you come from that region?" said his mother. "I thought you had been in the Garden of Paradise!"

"I don't fly there till to-morrow!" said the East-wind. "It will be a hundred years to-morrow since I was there! I come from China now, where I danced round the porcelain tower till all the bells jingled again! In the streets the officials were being thrashed; the bamboos were broken upon their shoulders, yet they were high people, from the first to the ninth grade. They cried, 'Many thanks, my paternal benefactor!' But it didn't come from their hearts; and I rang the bells and sang 'Tsing, tsang, tsu!'"

"You are foolish!" said the old dame. "It is a good thing that you are going into the Garden of Paradise to-morrow; that always helps your education. Drink bravely out of the spring of Wisdom, and bring home a little bottle full for me."

"That I will do!" said the East-wind. "But why have you clapped my brother South in the bag? Out with him! He shall tell me about the Phoenix bird; for about that bird the Princess in the Garden of Paradise always wants to hear, when I pay my visit every hundreth year. Open the sack, then you shall be my sweetest of mothers, and I will give you two pocketfuls of tea, green and fresh, as I plucked it at the place where it grew!"

"Well, for the sake of tea, and because you are my darling boy, I will open the sack."

She did so, and the South-wind crept out; but he looked quite down-cast, because the strange Prince had seen his disgrace.

"There you have a palm leaf for the Princess,"—said the South-wind.

"This palm leaf was given me by the bird Phoenix, the only one who is in the world. With his beak he has scratched upon it a description of all the hundred years he has lived. Now she may read herself how the phoenix bird set fire to her nest, and sat upon it, and was burned to death like a Hindoo's widow. How the dry branches burst into flame; the old phoenix turned to ashes; but her egg lay red hot in the fire; it burst with a great bang, and the young one flew out. Now this young one is ruler over all the birds, and the only phoenix in the world. It has bitten a hole in the palm leaf I have given you; that is a greeting to the Princess."

"Let us have something to eat," said the Mother of the Winds. And now they all sat down to eat of the roasted deer. The Prince sat beside the East-wind, and they soon became good friends.

"Just tell me," said the Prince, "what Princess is that, about whom there is so much talk here; and where does the Garden of Paradise lie?"

"Ho, ho!" said the East-wind, "do you want to go there? Well then, fly to-morrow with me! But I must however tell you that no man has been there since the time of Adam and Eve. You have read of them in your Bible histories?"

"Yes," said the Prince.

"When they were driven away, the Garden of Paradise sank into the earth; but it kept its warm sunshine, its mild air, and all its splendour. The Queen of the Fairies lives there; there lies the Island of Happiness, where death never comes, and where it is beautiful. Sit upon my back to-morrow, and I will take you with me; I think it can very well be done. But now leave off talking, for I want to sleep." And then they all went to rest.

In the early morning the Prince awoke, and was not a little aston-ished to find himself high above the clouds. He was sitting on the back of the East-wind, who was faithfully holding him; they were so high in the air, that woods and fields, rivers and lakes, looked as if they were painted on a map below them.

"Good morning!" said the East-wind. "You might very well sleep a little longer, for there is not much to be seen on the flat country under us, unless you care to count the churches. They stand like dots of chalk on the green carpet."

What he called green carpet was field and meadow.

"It was rude of me not to say good-bye to your mother and your brothers," said the Prince.

"When one is asleep one must be excused,"—replied the East-wind. And then they flew on faster than ever. One could hear it in the tops of the trees, for when they passed over them the leaves and twigs rustled; one could hear it on the sea and on the lakes, for when they flew by the water rose higher, and the great ships bowed themselves towards the water like swimming swans.

Towards evening, when it became dark, the great towns looked charming, for lights were burning below, here and there; it was just as when one has lighted a piece of paper, and sees all the little sparks which vanish one after another. And the Prince clapped his hands; but the East-wind begged him to let that be, and rather to hold fast; otherwise he might easily fall down, and get caught on a church spire.

The eagle in the dark woods flew lightly; but the East-wind flew more lightly still. The Cossack on his little horse skimmed swiftly over the surface of the earth; but the Prince skimmed more swiftly still.

"Now you can see the Himalaya!" said the East-wind. "That is the highest mountain range in Asia. Now we shall soon get to the Garden of Paradise."

Then they turned more to the south, and soon the air was fragrant with flowers and spices; figs and pomegranates grew wild, and the wild vine bore clusters of red and purple grapes. Here both alighted and stretched themselves on the soft grass, where the flowers nodded to the wind, as though they would have said "Welcome!"

"Are we now in the Garden of Paradise?" asked the Prince.

"Not at all,"—replied the East-wind. "But we shall soon get there. Do you see the rocky wall yonder, and the great cave, where the vines cluster like a broad green curtain? Through that we shall pass. Wrap yourself in your cloak. Here the sun scorches you. A step further and it will be icy cold. The bird which hovers past the cave has one wing in the region of summer, and the other in the wintry cold."

"So this is the way to the garden of Paradise,"—observed the Prince.

They went into the cave. Ugh! but it was icy cold there. Yet this did not last long. The East-wind spread out his wings, and they gleamed like the brightest fire. What a cave was that! Great blocks of stone from which water dripped down, hung over them in the strangest shapes; sometimes it was so narrow that they had to creep on their hands and knees, sometimes as lofty and broad as in the open air. The place looked like a number of mortuary chapels, with dumb organ pipes, the organs themselves being petrified.

"We are going through the way of Death to the Garden of Paradise, are we not?" inquired the Prince.

The East-wind answered not a syllable; but he pointed forward to where a lovely blue light gleamed upon them. The stone blocks over their heads became more and more like a mist, and at last looked like a white cloud in the moonlight. Now they were in a deliciously mild air, fresh as on the hills, fragrant as among the roses of the valley. There ran a river, clear as the air itself; and the fishes were like silver and gold; purple eels, flashing out blue sparks at every moment, played in the water below; and the broad water-plant leaves shone in the colours of the rainbow; the flower itself was an orange-coloured burning flame, which gave nourishment to the water, as the oil to the burning lamp; a bridge of marble, strong indeed, but so lightly built that it looked as if made of lace and glass beads, led them across the water to the Island of Happiness, where the Garden of Paradise bloomed.

Were they palm trees that grew here, or gigantic water-plants? Such verdant mighty trees the Prince had never beheld; the most wonderful climbing plants hung there in long festoons, as one only sees them illuminated in gold and colours on the margins of gold missal-books, or twined among the initial letters. Here were the strangest groupings of birds, flowers, and twining lines. Close by, in the grass, stood a flock of peacocks with their starry shining trains outspread.

Yes, it was really so! But when the Prince touched these, he found they were not birds, but plants; they were great burdocks, which shone like the peacock's gorgeous train. The lion and the tiger sprang to and fro like agile cats among the green bushes which were fragrant as the blossom of the olive-tree; and the lions and the tiger were tame. The wild wood-pigeon shone like the most beautiful pearl, and beat her wings against the lion's mane; and the antelope, usually so timid, stood by nodding its head, as if it wished to play too.

Now came the Fairy of Paradise. Her garb shone like the sun, and her countenance was cheerful like that of a happy mother when she is well pleased with her child. She was young and beautiful, and was followed by a number of pretty maidens, each with a gleaming star in her hair. The East-wind gave her the written leaf from the phoenix bird; and her eyes shone with pleasure.

She took the Prince by the hand, and led him into her palace, where the walls had the colour of a splendid tulip leaf when it is held up in the sunlight. The ceiling was a great sparkling flower, and the more one looked up at it, the deeper did its cup appear. The Prince stepped to the window, and looked through one of the panes. Here he saw the tree of knowledge with the serpent; and Adam and Eve were standing close by.

"Were they not driven out?" he asked.

And the Fairy smiled, and explained to him that Time had burnt in the picture upon that pane—but not, as people are accustomed to see pictures.—No, there was life in it; the leaves of the trees moved; men came and went, as in a dissolving view. And he looked through another pane, and there was Jacob's dream, with the ladder reaching up into heaven, and the angels with great wings were ascending and descending. Yes, everything that had happened in the world lived and moved in the glass panes; such cunning pictures only Time could burn in.

The Fairy smiled, and led him into a great lofty hall, whose walls appeared transparent. Here were portraits, and each face looked fairer than the last. There were to be seen millions of happy ones who smiled and sang, so that it flowed together into a melody; the uppermost were so small that they looked like the smallest rosebud, when it is drawn as a point, upon paper. And in the midst of the hall stood a great tree with rich pendent boughs; golden apples, great and small, hung like oranges among the leaves. That was the tree of knowledge, of whose fruit Adam and Eve had eaten. From each leaf fell a shining red dewdrop; it was as though the tree wept tears of blood.

"Let us now get into the boat," said the Fairy, "then we will enjoy some refreshment on the heaving waters. The boat rocks, yet does not quit its station; but all the lands of the earth will glide past in our sight."

And it was wonderful to behold how the whole coast moved. There came the lofty snow-covered Alps, with clouds and black pine trees; the horn sounded with its melancholy note, and the shepherd trolled his merry song in the valley. Then the banana trees bent their long hanging branches over the boat; coal-black swans swam on the water, and the strangest animals and flowers showed themselves upon the shore. That was New Holland, the fifth great division of the world, which glided past with a background of blue hills. They heard the song of the priests, and saw the savages dancing to the sound of drums and of bone trumpets. Egypt's pyramids, towering aloft to the clouds, overturned pillars and sphynxes, half buried in the sand, sailed past likewise. The northern lights shone over the extinct volcanoes of the pole; it was a firework that no one could imitate. The Prince was quite happy; and he saw a hundred times more than we can relate here.

"And can I always stay here?" asked he.

"That depends upon yourself," answered the fairy. "If you do not, like Adam, yield to the temptation to do what is forbidden, you may always remain here."

"I shall not touch the apples on the tree of knowledge!" said the Prince. "Here are thousands of fruits, just as beautiful as those."

"Search your own heart, and if you are not strong enough, go away with the East-wind that brought you hither. He is going to fly back and will not show himself here again for a hundred years; the time will pass for you in this place, as if it were a hundred hours, but it is a long time for the temptation of sin. Every evening, when I leave you, I shall have to call to you 'Come with me!' and I shall have to beckon to you with my hand. But stay where you are; do not go with me, or your longing will become greater with every step. You will then come into the hall, where the tree of knowledge grows; I sleep under its fragrant pendent boughs; you will bend over me, and I must smile, but if you press a kiss upon my mouth, the Paradise will sink deep into the earth, and be lost for you. The keen wind of the desert will rush around you, the cold rain drop upon your head. Sorrow and woe will be your portion."

"I shall stay here!" said the Prince. And the East-wind kissed him on the forehead and said: "Be strong, and we shall meet here again in a hundred years! Farewell, farewell!" And the East-wind spread out his broad wings, and they flashed like sheet-lightning in harvest time, or like the northern light in the cold winter.

"Farewell! farewell!" sounded from among the flowers and the trees. Storks and pelicans flew away in rows like fluttering ribands, and bore him company to the boundary of the garden.

"Now we will begin our dances!" cried the Fairy. "At the end, when I dance with you, when the sea goes down, you will see me beckon to you; you will hear me call to you: 'Come with me;' but do not obey. For a hundred years I must repeat this every evening; every time, when the trial is past, you will gain more strength; at last you will not think of it at all. This evening is the first time; and now I have warned you!"

And the Fairy led him into a great hall of white transparent lilies; the yellow stamens in each flower formed a little golden harp, which sounded like stringed instrument and flute. The most beautiful maidens, floating and slender, clad in gauzy mist, glided by in the dance, and sang of the happiness of living, and declared that they would never die, and that the Garden of Paradise would bloom for ever.

And the sun went down. The whole sky shone like gold, which gave to the lilies the hue of the most glorious roses; and the prince drank of the foaming wine which the maidens poured out to him, and felt a happiness he had never yet known. He saw how the back ground of the hall opened, and the tree of knowledge stood in a glory which blinded his eyes; the singing there was soft and lovely as the voice of his mother, and it was as though she sang:—"My child! my beloved child!"

Then the Fairy beckoned to him, and called out so persuasively, "Come with me! Come with me!"—And he rushed towards her, forgetting getting his promise, forgetting it the very first evening; and still she beckoned and smiled. The fragrance, the delicious fragrance around became stronger, the harps sounded far more lovely, and it seemed as though the millions of smiling heads in the hall, where the tree grew, nodded and sang—"One must know everything—man is the lord of the Earth." And they were no longer drops of blood, that the tree of knowledge wept; they were red shining stars which he seemed to see. "Come, come!" the quivering voice still cried, and at every step the Prince's cheeks burned more hotly, and his blood flowed more rapidly. "I must!" said he. "It is no sin, it cannot be one! Why not follow beauty and joy? I only want to see her asleep; there will be nothing lost, if I only refrain from kissing her; and I will not kiss her; I am strong, and have a resolute will!"

And the Fairy threw off her shining cloak, and bent back the branches, and in another moment she was hidden among them.

"I have not yet sinned," said the Prince, "and I will not;" and he pushed the boughs aside. There she slept already, beautiful as only a Fairy in the Garden of Paradise can be. She smiled in her dreams, and he bent over her, and saw tears quivering beneath her eyelids!"

"Do you weep for me?" he whispered. "Weep not, thou glorious woman! Now only I understand the bliss of Paradise! It streams through my blood, through my thoughts; the power of the angel and of increasing life I feel in my mortal body! May it be always right for me; one moment like this is wealth enough!" and he kissed the tears from her eyes; his mouth touched hers.

Then there resounded a clap of thunder so loud and dreadful that no one had ever heard the like, and everything fell down; and the beautiful Fairy, and the charming Paradise sank down, deeper and deeper. The Prince saw it vanish in the black night; like a little bright star it gleamed out of the far distance; a deadly chill ran through his frame; he closed his eyes and lay for a long time as one dead.

The cold rain fell upon his face, the keen wind roared round his head, then his senses returned to him. "What have I done?" he sighed. "I have sinned, like Adam,—sinned, so that Paradise has sunk deep down!" And he opened his eyes,—and the star in the distance—the star that gleamed like the Paradise that had sunk down, was the morning star in the sky.

He stood up, and found himself in the great forest, close by the Cavern of the Winds, and the Mother of the Winds sat by his side; she looked angry, and raised her arm in the air.

"The very first evening!" said she. "I thought it! Yes, if you were my son, you would have to go into the sack!"

"Yes, he shall go in there!" said Death. He was a strong old man, with a scythe in his hand, and with great black wings. "Yes, he shall be laid in his coffin; but not yet, I only register him and let him wander awhile in the world and expiate his sins, and grow better. But one day I shall come. When he least expects it, I shall clap him in the black coffin, put him on my head, and fly up towards the star. There, too, blooms the Garden of Paradise, and if he is good and pious, he will go in there; but if his thoughts are evil, and his heart still full of sin, he will sink with his coffin deeper than Paradise has sunk, and only every thousandth year I shall fetch him, that he may sink deeper, or that he may attain to the star—the shining star up yonder!"

A GREAT GRIEF

This story really consists of two parts; the first part might be left out, but it gives us a few particulars, and these are useful.

We are staying in the country at a gentleman's seat, where it happened that the master was absent for a few days. In the meantime there arrived from the next town a lady; she had a pug dog with her, and came, she said, to dispose of shares in her tanyard. She had her papers with her, and we advised her to put them in an envelope, and to write thereon the address of the proprietor of the estate, "General War-Commissary Knight," &c.

She listened to us attentively, seized the pen, paused, and begged us to repeat the direction slowly. We complied, and she wrote; but in the midst of the "General War . . ." she stuck fast, sighed deeply, and said, "I am only a woman!" Her Puggie had seated itself on the ground while she wrote, and growled; for the dog had come with her for amusement and for the sake of its health; and then the bare floor ought not to be offered to a visitor. His outward appearance was characterized by a snub nose, and a very fat back.

"He doesn't bite!" said the lady, "He has no teeth. He is like one of the family, faithful and grumpy, but the latter is my grandchildren's fault for they have teased him; they play at wedding, and want to give him the part of the bridesmaid, and that's too much for him, poor old fellow."

And she delivered her papers, and took Puggie upon her arm; and this is the first part of the story, which might have been left out.

"PUGGIE DIED." That's the second part.

It was about a week afterwards we arrived in the town, and put up at the inn. Our windows looked into the courtyard, which was divided into two parts by a partition of planks; in one half were many skins and hides, raw and tanned. Here was all the apparatus necessary to carry on

Waiting to see Puggie's grave

a tannery, and it belonged to the widow. Puggie had died in the morning, and was to be buried in this part of the yard; the grandchildren of the widow (that is of the tanner's widow, for Puggie had never been married) filled up the grave, and it was a beautiful grave; it must have been quite pleasant to lie there.

The grave was bordered with pieces of flower-pots, and strewn over with sand; quite at the top they had stuck up half a beer bottle, with the neck upwards, and that was not at all allegorical.

The children danced round the grave, and the eldest of the boys among them, a practical youngster of seven years, made the proposition that there should be an exhibition of Puggie's burial place for all who lived in the lane; the price of admission was to be a trouser button, for every boy would be sure to have one, and each might also give one for a little girl; this proposal was adopted by acclamation.

And all the children out of the lane—yes, even out of the little lane at the back—flocked to the place, and each gave a button; many were noticed to go about on that afternoon with only one brace; but then they had seen Puggie's grave, and the sight was worth much more.

But in front of the tanyard, close to the entrance, stood a little girl clothed in rags, very pretty to look at, with curly hair, and eyes so blue and clear that it was a pleasure to look into them; the child said not a word, nor did she cry; but each time the little door was opened she gave a long, long look into the yard. She had not a button,—that she knew right well, and therefore she remained standing sorrowfully outside, till all the others had seen the grave, and had gone away; then she sat down, held her little brown hands before her eyes, and burst into tears; this girl alone had not seen Puggie's grave. It was a grief, as great to her as any grown person can experience.

We saw this from above; and looked at from above, how many a grief of our own and of others can make us smile! That is the story, and whoever does not understand it may go and purchase a share in the tanyard from the widow.

THE SWAN'S NEST

Between the Baltic and the North Sea there lies an old swan's nest, wherein swans are born and have been born, that shall never die.

In olden times a flock of swans flew over the Alps to the green plains around Milan, where it was delightful to dwell; this flight of swans men called "*the Lombards*."

Another flock, with shining plumage and honest eyes, soared southward to Byzantium; the swans established themselves there by the Emperor's throne, and spread their wings over him as shields to protect him. They received the name of *Varangians*.

On the coast of France there sounded a cry of fear, for the blood-stained swans that came from the north, with fire under their wings; and the people prayed, "Heaven deliver us from the wild *Northmen*."

On the fresh sward of England stood the Danish swan by the open sea-shore, with the crown of three kingdoms on his head; and he stretched out his golden sceptre over the land. The heathens on the Pomeranian coast bent the knee, and the Danish swans came with the banner of the cross and with the drawn sword.

"That was in the very old times," you say.

In later days, two mighty swans have been seen to fly from the nest. A

The northern swans flying forth

light shone far through the air, far over the lands of the earth; the swan, with the strong beating of his wings, scattered the twilight mists, and the starry sky was seen, and it was as if it came nearer to the earth. That was the swan *Tycho Brahe*.

"Yes, then," you say, "but in our own days!"

We have seen swan after swan soar by in glorious flight. One let his pinions glide over the strings of the golden harp, and it resounded through the north; Norway's mountains seemed to rise higher in the sunlight of former days;—there was a rustling among the pine trees and the birches; the gods of the North, the heroes and the noble women showed themselves in the dark forest depths.

We have seen a swan beat with his wings upon the marble crag, so that it burst, and the forms of beauty imprisoned in the stone stepped out to the sunny day, and men in the lands round about lifted up their heads to behold these mighty forms.

We have seen a third swan spinning the thread of thought that is fastened from country to country round the world, so that the word may fly with lightning speed from land to land.

And our Lord loves the old swan's nest between the Baltic and the

Northern Sea. And when the mighty birds came soaring through the air to destroy it, even the callow young stand round in a circle on the margin of the nest, and though their breasts may be struck so that their blood flows they bear it, and strike with their wings and their claws.

Centuries will pass by, swans will fly forth from the nest, men will see them and hear them in the world, before it shall be said in spirit and in truth, "This is the last swan—the last song from the swan's nest."

HOLGER DANSKE

"In Denmark there lies a castle named Kronenburg. It lies close by the Oer Sound, where the ships pass through by hundreds every day, English, Russian, and likewise Prussian ships. And they salute the old castle with cannons: 'Boom!' And the castle answers with a 'Boom!' for that's what the cannons say instead of 'Good day,' and 'Thank you!' In winter no ships sail there; for the whole sea is covered with ice quite across to the Swedish coast; but it has quite the look of a high road;—there wave the Danish flag and the Swedish flag, and Danes and Swedes say 'Good day!' and 'Thank you!' to each other, not with cannons, but with a friendly grasp of the hand; and one gets white bread and biscuits from the other—for strange fare tastes best. But the most beautiful of all is the old Kronenburg; and here it is that Holger Danske sits in the deep dark cellar, where nobody goes. He is clad in iron and steel, and leans his head on his strong arm; his long beard hangs down over the marble table, and has grown into it; he sleeps and dreams, but in his dreams he sees everything that happens up here in Denmark. Every Christmas eve comes an angel, and tells him that what he has dreamed is right, and that he may go to sleep in quiet, for that Denmark is not yet in any real danger; but when once such a danger comes, then old Holger Danske will rouse himself, so that the table shall burst when he draws out his beard! Then he will come forth and strike, so that it shall be heard in all the countries of the world."

An old grandfather sat and told his little grandson all this about Holger Danske; and the little boy knew that what his grandfather told him was true. And while the old man sat and told his story, he carved at

Holger Danske

an image which was to represent Holger Danske, and to be fastened to the prow of a ship; for the old grandfather was a carver of figure-heads, that is, one who cuts out the figures fastened to the front of ships, and from which every ship is named. And here he had cut out Holger Danske, who stood there proudly with his long beard, and held the broad battle-sword in one hand, while with the other he leaned upon the Danish arms.

And the old grandfather told so much about distinguished men and women, that it appeared at last to the little grandson as if he knew as much as Holger Danske himself, who after all could only dream; and when the little fellow was in his bed, he thought so much of it, that he actually pressed his chin against the coverlet, and fancied he had a long beard that had grown fast to it.

But the old grandfather remained sitting at his work, and carved away at the last part of it; and this was the Danish coat of arms. When he had done, he looked at the whole, and thought of all he had read and heard, and that he had told this evening to the little boy; and he nodded, and wiped his spectacles, and put them on again, and said: "Yes, in my time Holger Danske will probably not come; but the boy in the bed yonder may get to see him, and be there when the push really comes." And the old grandfather nodded; and the more he looked at Holger Danske the more plain did it become to him that it was a good image he had carved; it seemed really to gain colour, and the armour appeared to gleam like iron and steel; the hearts in the Danish arms became redder and redder, and the lions with the golden crowns on their heads leaped up.[1]

"That's the most beautiful coat-of-arms there is in the world!" said the old man. "The lions are strength, and the heart is gentleness and love!" And he looked at the uppermost lion, and thought of King Canute, who bound great England to the throne of Denmark; and he looked at the second lion, and thought of Waldemar, who united Denmark and conquered the Wendish lands; and he glanced at the third lion, and remembered Margaret, who united Denmark, Sweden, and Norway. But while he looked at the red hearts, they gleamed more brightly than before; they became flames, and his heart followed each of them.

The first heart led him into a dark narrow prison; there sat a prisoner, a beautiful woman, the daughter of Christian the Fourth, Eleanor Ulfeld;[2] and the flame, which was shaped like a rose, attached itself to her bosom and blossomed, so that it became one with the heart of her, the noblest and best of all Danish women.

And his spirit followed the second flame, which led him out upon the sea, where the cannons thundered, and the ships lay shrouded in

[1] The Danish arms consist of three lions between nine hearts.
[2] This highly gifted Princess was the wife of Corfitz Ulfeld, who was accused of high treason. Her only crime was the most faithful love to her unhappy consort; but she was compelled to pass twenty-two years in a horrible dungeon, until her persecutor, Queen Sophia Amelia, was dead.

smoke; and the flame fastened itself in the shape of a riband of honour on the breast of Hvitfeld, as he blew himself and his ship into the air, that he might save the fleet.[3]

And the third flame led him to the wretched huts of Greenland, where the preacher Hans Egede[4] wrought, with love in every word and deed; the flame was a star on his breast, another heart in the Danish arms.

And the spirit of the old grandfather flew on before the waving flames, for his spirit knew whither the flames desired to go. In the humble room of the peasant woman stood Frederick the Sixth, writing his name with chalk on the beam;[5] the flame trembled on his breast, and trembled in his heart; in the peasant's lowly room his heart too became a heart in the Danish arms. And the old grandfather dried his eyes, for he had known King Frederick with the silvery locks, and the honest blue eyes, and had lived for him; he folded his hands, and looked in silence straight before him. Then came the daughter-in-law of the old grandfather, and said that it was late; he ought now to rest, and the supper-table was spread.

"But it is beautiful, what you have done, grandfather!" said she. "Holger Danske, and all our old coat-of-arms! It seems to me just as if I had seen that face before!"

"No, that can scarcely be," replied the old grandfather; "but I have seen it, and I have tried to carve it in wood as I have kept it in my memory. It was when the English lay in front of the wharf, on the

[3] In the naval battle in Kjoge bay between the Danes and the Swedes, in 1710, Hvitfeld's ship, the *Danebrog*, took fire. To save the town of Kjoge, and the Danish fleet which was being driven by the wind towards his vessel, he blew himself and his whole crew into the air.

[4] Hans Egede went to Greenland in 1721 and toiled there during fifteen years among incredible hardships and privations; not only did he spread Christianity, but exhibited in himself a remarkable example of a Christian man.

[5] On a journey on the west coast of Jutland, the King visited an old woman. When he had already quitted her house, the woman ran after him, and begged him, as a remembrance, to write his name upon a beam; the King turned back, and complied. During his whole lifetime he felt and worked for the peasant class. Therefore the Danish peasants begged to be allowed to carry his coffin to the royal vault at Roeskilde, four Danish miles from Copenhagen.

Danish second of April,[6] when we showed that we were old Danes. In the Denmark, on board which I was, in Steen Bille's squadron, I had a man at my side—it seemed as if the bullets were afraid of him! Merrily he sang old songs, and shot and fought as if he were something more than a man. I remember his face yet; but whence he came, and whither he went, I know not—nobody knows. I have often thought, he might have been old Holger Danske himself, who had swum down from the Kronenburg, and aided us in the hour of danger; that was my idea, and there stands his picture."

And the statue threw its great shadow up against the wall, and even over part of the ceiling; it looked as though the real Holger Danske were standing behind it, for the shadow moved; but this might have been because the flame of the candle did not burn steadily. And the daughter-in-law kissed the old grandfather, and led him to the great arm-chair by the table; and she and her husband, who was the son of the old man, and father of the little boy in the bed, sat and ate their supper; and the grandfather spoke of the Danish lions and of the Danish hearts, of strength and of gentleness; and quite clearly did he explain that there was another strength besides the power that lies in the sword; and he pointed to the shelf on which were the old books, where stood the plays of Holberg, which had been read so often; for they were very amusing; one could almost fancy one recognized the people of bygone days in them.

"See, he knew how to strike too," said the old grandfather; "he scourged the foolishness and prejudice of the people, so long as he could,"—and the grandfather nodded at the mirror, above which stood the Calendar, with the "Round Tower"[7] on it, and said, "Tycho Brahe was also one who used the sword, not to cut into flesh and bone, but to build up a plainer way among all the stars of heaven. And then *he*, whose father belonged to my calling, the son of the old figure-head carver, he whom we have ourselves seen, with his silver hairs and his broad shoulders, he whose name is spoken of in all lands! Yes, he was a sculptor, I am only a carver! Yes, Holger Danske may come in many

[6] On the 2nd of April, 1801, occurred the sanguinary naval battle between the Danes and the English, under Sir Hyde Parker and Nelson.
[7] The astronomical observatory at Copenhagen.

forms, so that one hears in every country in the world of Denmark's strength. Shall we now drink the health of Bertel?"[8]

But the little lad in the bed saw plainly the old Kronenburg with the Oer Sound, the real Holger Danske, who sat deep below with his beard grown through the marble table, dreaming of all that happens up here. Holger Danske also dreamt of the little humble room where the carver sat; he heard all that passed, and nodded in his sleep and said, "Yes, remember me, ye Danish folk; remember me. I shall come in the hour of need."

And without by the Kronenburg shone the bright day, and the wind carried the notes of the hunting-horn over from the neighbouring land: the ships sailed past, and saluted "Boom, Boom!" and from the Kronenburg came the reply, "Boom, Boom!" But Holger Danske did not awake, however loudly they shot, for it was only "Good day," and "Thank you." There must be another kind of shooting before he awakes; but he will awake, for there is faith in Holger Danske.

"IT'S QUITE TRUE!"

"That is a terrible affair," said a hen; and she said it in a quarter of the town where the occurrence had not happened. "That is a terrible affair in the poultry house. I cannot sleep alone to-night! It is quite fortunate that there are many of us on the roost together!" and she told a tale, at which the feathers of the other birds stood on end, and the cock's comb fell down flat. It's quite true!

But we will begin at the beginning; and the beginning begins in a poultry house in another part of the town. The sun went down, and the fowls jumped up on their perch to roost; there was a hen, with white feathers and short legs, who laid her right number of eggs, and was a respectable hen in every way; as she flew up on the roost she pecked herself with her beak, and a little feather fell out.

"There it goes!" said she, "the more I peck myself the handsomer I grow!" and she said it quite merrily, for she was a joker among the

[8] Bertel Thorwaldsen.

hens, though as I have said she was very respectable,—and then she went to sleep.

It was dark all around; hen sat by hen, but the one that sat next to the merry hen did not sleep: she heard and she didn't hear, as one should do in this world if one wishes to live in quiet; but she could not refrain from telling it to her next neighbour—"Did you hear what was said here just now? I name no names; but here is a hen who wants to peck her feathers out to look well! If I were a cock I should despise her."

And just above the hens sat the owl, with her husband and her little owlets; the family had sharp ears, they all heard every word that the neighbouring hen had spoken, and they rolled their eyes, and the mother owl clapped her wings and said—"Don't listen to it! But I suppose you heard what was said there? I heard it with my own ears, and one must hear much before one's ears fall off! There is one among the fowls who has so completely forgotten what is becoming conduct in a hen that she pulls out all her feathers, and then lets the cock see her."

"*Prenez garde aux enfants*,"—said the father owl. "That's not fit for the children to hear!"

"I'll tell it to the neighbour owl; she's a very proper owl to associate with,"—and she flew away.

The owls tell the pigeons the dreadful news

"Hoo! hoo! to-whoo!" they both screeched in front of the neighbour's dovecot to the doves within. "Have you heard it? Have you heard it? Hoo! hoo! There's a hen who has pulled out all her feathers for the sake of the cock. She'll die with cold, if she's not dead already."

"Coo, coo! Where, where?" cried the pigeons. "In the neighbour's poultry yard. I've as good as seen it myself. It's hardly proper to repeat the story. It's quite true!"

"Believe it! Believe every single word of it!" cooed the pigeons, and they cooed down into their own poultry yard. "There's a hen, and some say that there are two of them, that have plucked out all their feathers that they may not look like the rest, and that they may attract the cock's attention. That's a bold game, for one may catch cold and die of a fever, and they are both dead."

"Wake up! wake up!" crowed the cock, and he flew upon the plank; his eyes were still heavy with sleep; but yet he crowed. "Three hens have died of an unfortunate attachment to a cock. They had plucked out all their feathers. That's a terrible story. I won't keep it to myself; let it travel further."

"Let it travel further!" piped the bats, and the fowls clucked and the cocks crowed. "Let it go further! let it go further!" and so the story travelled from poultry yard to poultry yard, and at last came back to the place from which it had gone forth.

"Five fowls," it was told, "have plucked out all their feathers to show which of them had become thinnest out of love to the cock; and then they had pecked each other, and fallen down dead, to the shame and disgrace of their families and to the great loss of the proprietor!"

And the hen who had lost the little loose feather, of course did not know her own story again; and as she was a very respectable hen, she said, "I despise those fowls; but there are many of that sort. One ought not to hush up such a thing, and I shall do what I can that the story may get into the papers, and then it will be spread over all the country, and that will serve those fowls right, and their families too."

It was put into the newspaper; it was printed, and it's quite true—that one little feather may swell till it becomes five fowls.

THE FLYING TRUNK

There was once a merchant, who was so rich, that he could pave the whole street with gold, and almost have enough left for a little lane. But he did not do that; he knew how to employ his money differently. When he spent a shilling he got back a crown, such a clever merchant was he; and this continued till he died.

His son now got all this money; and he lived merrily, going to the masquerade every evening, making kites out of dollar notes and playing at ducks and drakes on the seacoast with gold pieces instead of pebbles. In this way the money might soon be spent, and indeed it was so. At last he had no more than four shillings left, and no clothes to wear but a pair of slippers and an old dressing-gown. Now his friends did not trouble themselves any more about him as they could not walk with him in the street, but one of them, who was good-natured sent him an old trunk, with the remark "Pack up!" Yes, that was all very well, but he had nothing to pack, therefore he seated himself in the trunk.

That was a wonderful trunk. So soon as any one pressed the lock, the trunk could fly. He pressed it, and, whirr, away flew the trunk with him through the chimney, and over the clouds farther and farther away. But so often as the bottom of the trunk cracked a little he was in great fear lest it might go to pieces, and then he would have flung a fine somersault! In that way he came to the land of the Turks. He hid the trunk in a wood under some dry leaves, and then went into the town. He could do that very well, for among the Turks all the people went dressed like himself in dressing-gown and slippers. Then he met a nurse with a little child. "Hear, you Turkish nurse," he began, "what kind of a great castle is that close by the town, in which the windows are so high up?"

"There dwells the Sultan's daughter!" replied she. "It is prophesied that she would be very unhappy respecting a lover; and therefore nobody may go to her, unless the Sultan and Sultana are there too."

"Thank you!" said the merchant's son; and he went out into the forest, seated himself in his trunk, flew on the roof, and crept through the window into the Princess's room.

She was lying asleep on the sofa; she was so beautiful that the mer-

chant's son was compelled to kiss her. Then she awoke, and was very much startled: but he said he was a Turkish angel who had come down to her through the air; and that pleased her.

They sat down side by side, and he told her stories about her eyes; he told her they were the most glorious dark lakes, and that thoughts were swimming about in them like mermaids. And he told her about her forehead; that it was a snowy mountain with the most splendid halls and pictures. And he told her about the stork who brings the lovely little children.

Yes, those were fine histories! Then he asked the Princess if she would marry him, and she said "Yes," directly.

"But you must come here on Saturday,"—said she. "Then the Sultan and the Sultaness will be here to tea. They will be very proud that I am to marry a Turkish angel. But take care that you know a very pretty story, for both my parents are very fond indeed of stories. My mother likes them highflown and moral, but my father likes them merry, so that one can laugh."

"Yes, I shall bring no marriage gift but a story,"—said he, and so they parted. But the Princess gave him a sabre, the sheath embroidered with gold pieces; and that was very useful to him.

Now he flew away, bought a new dressing-gown, and sat in the forest and made up a story; it was to be ready by Saturday and that was not an easy thing.

By the time he had finished it, Saturday had come. The Sultan and his wife and all the court were at the Princess's to tea. He was received very graciously.

"Will you relate us a story?" said the Sultaness; "one that is deep and edifying."

"Yes, but one that we can laugh at,"—said the Sultan. "Certainly,"—he replied; and began. And now listen well.

There was once a bundle of matches; and these matches were particularly proud of their high descent. Their genealogical tree, that is to say the great fir tree, of which each of them was a little splinter, had been a great old tree out in the forest. The matches now lay between a tinder-box and an old iron pot; and they were telling about the days of their youth. "Yes, when we were upon the green boughs," they said, "then we were really on the green boughs! Every morning and evening there was diamond tea for us, I mean dew; we had sunshine all day long whenever the sun shone, and all the little birds had to tell stories. We could see very well that we were rich, for the other trees were only dressed out in summer, while our family had the means to wear green dresses in the winter as well. But then the woodcutter came, like a great revolution, and our family was broken up. The head of the family got an appointment as main-mast in a first-rate ship, which could sail round the world, if necessary; the other branches went to other places, and now we have the office of kindling a light for the vulgar herd. That's how we grand people came to be in the kitchen."

"My fate was of a different kind,"—said the iron pot which stood next to the matches. "From the beginning, ever since I came into the world, there has been a great deal of scouring and cooking done in me! I look after the practical part, and am the first here in the house. My only pleasure is, to sit in my place after dinner, very clean and neat, and to carry on a sensible conversation with my comrades. But except the waterpot, which sometimes is taken down into the courtyard, we always live within our four walls. Our only newsmonger is the market-basket: but he speaks very uneasily about the government and the people. Yes, the other day there was an old pot that fell down from fright and burst. He's liberal I can tell you!" "Now you're talking too much,"—the tinder-box interrupted, and the steel struck against the flint, so that sparks flew out. "Shall we not have a merry evening?"

"Yes, let us talk about who is the grandest,"—said the matches.

"No, I don't like to talk about myself,"—retorted the pot. "Let us get up an evening entertainment. I will begin. I will tell a story from real life, something that everyone has experienced, so that we can easily imagine the situation, and take pleasure in it. On the Baltic, by the Danish shore—"

"That's a pretty beginning!" cried all the plates. "That will be a story we shall like."

"Yes, it happened to me in my youth, when I lived in a quiet family where the furniture was polished, and the floors scoured and new curtains were put up every fortnight."

"What an interesting way you have of telling a story,"—said the carpet-broom. "One can tell directly that a man is speaking who has been in woman's society. There's something pure runs through it." And the pot went on telling his story, and the end was as good as the beginning.

All the plates rattled with joy, and the carpet-broom brought some green parsley out of the dusthole, and put it like a wreath on the pot, for he knew that it would vex the others. "If I crown him to-day," it thought, "he will crown me to-morrow."

"Now I'll dance," said the firetongs, and they danced. Preserve us! How that implement could lift up one leg! The old chair-cushion burst to see it. "Shall I be crowned too?" thought the tongs; and indeed a wreath was awarded.

"They're only common people after all!" thought the matches.

Now the tea-urn was to sing; but she said she had taken cold, and could not sing unless she felt boiling within. But that was only affectation; she did not want to sing, except when she was in the parlour with the grand people.

In the window sat an old quill pen, with which the maid generally wrote; there was nothing remarkable about this pen, except that it had been dipped too deep into the ink, but she was proud of that. "If the tea-urn won't sing," she said "she may leave it alone. Outside hangs a nightingale in a cage, and he can sing. He hasn't had any education, but this evening we'll say nothing about that."

"I think it very wrong," said the tea-kettle, he was the kitchen singer, and half-brother to the tea-urn, "that that rich and foreign bird should be listened to! Is that patriotic? Let the market-basket decide."

"I am vexed," said the market-basket. "No one can imagine how much I am secretly vexed. Is that a proper way of spending the evening? Would it not be more sensible to put the house in order? Let each one go to his own place, and I would arrange the whole game. That would be quite another thing."

"Yes, let us make a disturbance," cried they all. Then the door opened and the maid came in, and they all stood still; not one stirred. But there was not one pot among them who did not know what he could do, and how grand he was. "Yes, if I had liked," each one thought, "it might have been a very merry evening."

The servant girl took the matches and lighted the fire with them. Mercy! How they sputtered and burst out into flame. "Now everyone can see," thought they, "that we are the first. How we shine! What a light!"—and they burned out.

"That was a capital story," said the Sultaness. "I feel myself quite carried away to the kitchen, to the matches. Yes, now thou shalt marry our daughter."

"Yes, certainly," said the Sultan, "thou shalt marry our daughter on

Monday." And they called him *thou*, because he was to belong to the family.

The wedding was decided on, and on the evening before it the whole city was illuminated. Biscuits and cakes were thrown among the people, the street boys stood on their toes, called "Hurrah!" and whistled on their fingers; it was uncommonly splendid.

"Yes, I shall have to give something as a treat,"—thought the merchant's son. So he bought rockets and crackers, and every imaginable sort of firework; put them all into his trunk, and flew up into the air.

"Crack!" how they went, and how they went off. All the Turks hopped up with such a start that their slippers flew about their ears; such a meteor they had never yet seen. Now they could understand that it must be a Turkish angel who was going to marry the Princess.

What stories people tell! Every one whom he asked about it, had seen it in a separate way; but one and all thought it fine.

"I saw the Turkish angel himself," said one. "He had eyes like glowing stars, and a beard like foaming water." "He flew in a fiery mantle," said another; "the most lovely little cherub peeped forth from among the folds."

Yes, they were wonderful things that he heard; and on the following day he was to be married.

Now he went back into the forest to rest himself in his trunk. But what had become of that? A spark from the fireworks had set fire to it, and the trunk was burnt to ashes. He could not fly any more, and could not get to his bride.

She stood all day on the roof waiting; and most likely she is waiting still. But he wanders through the world telling fairy tales; but they are not so merry as that one he told about the matches.

THE LAST PEARL

We are in a rich, a happy house; all are cheerful and full of joy, master, servants, and friends of the family; for on this day an heir, a son had been born, and mother and child were doing exceedingly well.

The burning lamp in the bed-chamber had been partly shaded, and

The angels discoursing about the child

the windows were guarded by heavy curtains of some costly silken fabric. The carpet was thick, and soft as a mossy lawn, and everything invited to slumber—was charmingly suggestive of repose—and the nurse found that, for she slept; and here she might sleep, for everything was good and blessed. The guardian spirit of the house learned against the head of the bed; over the child at the mother's breast there spread, as it were, a net of shining stars in endless number, and each star was a pearl of happiness. All the good stars of life had brought their gifts to the new-born one; here sparkled health, wealth, fortune, and love—in short, everything that man can wish for on earth.

"Everything has been presented here!" said the guardian spirit.

"No; not everything,"—said a voice near him, the voice of the child's *good angel*.

"One fairy has not yet brought her gift; but she will do so some day, even if years should elapse first, she will bring her gift; the *last pearl* is yet wanting."

"Wanting! Here nothing may be wanting, and if it should be the case, let me go and seek the powerful fairy; let us betake ourselves to her!"

"She comes! She will come some day unsought! Her pearl may not be wanting; it must be there, so that the complete crown may be won."

"Where is she to be found? Where does she dwell? Tell it me, and I will procure the pearl."

"You will do that?" said the good angel of the child. "I will lead you to her directly, wherever she may be. She has no abiding place— sometimes she rules in the Emperor's palace, sometimes you will find her in the peasant's humble cot; she goes by no person without leaving a trace; she brings two gifts to all, be it a world or a trifle! To this child also she must come. You think the time is equally long, but not equally profitable. Come, let us go for this pearl, the last pearl in all this wealth."

And hand in hand they floated towards the spot where the fairy was now lingering.

It was a great house with dark windows, and empty rooms, and a peculiar stillness reigned therein; a whole row of windows had been opened, so that the rough air could penetrate at its pleasure; the long white hanging curtains moved to and fro in the current of wind.

In the middle of the room was placed an open coffin, and in this coffin lay the corpse of a woman, still in the bloom of youth, and very beautiul. Fresh roses were scattered over her, so that only the delicate folded hands, and the noble face, glorified in death by the solemn look of consecration and entrance to the better world were visible.

Around the coffin stood the husband and the children, a whole troop; the youngest child rested on the father's arm, and all bade their mother the last farewell; the husband kissed her hand, the hand which now was as a withered leaf: but which a short time ago had been working and striving in diligent love for them all. Tears of sorrow rolled over their cheeks, and fell in heavy drops to the floor; but not a word was spoken. The silence which reigned here expressed a world of grief. With silent footsteps and with many a sob, they quitted the room.

A burning light stands in the room, and the long red wick peers out high above the flame that flickers in the current of air. Strange men come in, and lay the lid on the coffin over the dead one, and drive the nails firmly in, and the blows of the hammer resound through the house, and echo in the hearts that are bleeding.

"Whither art thou leading me?" asked the guardian spirit. "Here dwells no fairy whose pearl might be counted amongest the best gifts for life!"

"Here she lingers; here in this sacred hour,"—said the angel, and pointed to a corner of the room; and there where in her lifetime the mother had taken her seat amid flowers and pictures; there from whence, like the beneficent fairy of the house, she had greeted husband, children, and friends; from whence, like the sunbeams she had spread joy and cheerfulness, and been the centre and the heart of all. There sat a strange woman, clad in long garments, it was "the Chastened Heart," now mistress and mother here in the dead lady's place. A hot tear rolled down into her lap, and formed itself into a pearl glowing with all the colours of the rainbow; the angel seized it, and the pearl shone like a star of sevenfold radiance.

The pearl of Chastening, the last, which must not be wanting! It heightens the lustre and the meaning of the other pearls. Do you see the sheen of the rainbow—of the bow that unites heaven and earth! A bridge has been built between this world and the heaven beyond. Through the earthly night we gaze upward to the stars, looking for perfection. Contemplate it, the pearl of Chastening, for it hides within itself the wings that shall carry us to the better world.

THE STORKS

On the last house in a little village stood a stork's nest. The mother stork sat in it with her four young ones, who stretched out their heads with the pointed black beaks, for their beaks had not yet turned red. A little way off stood the father stork, all alone, on the ridge of the roof, quite upright and stiff; he had drawn up one of his legs, so as not to be quite idle while he stood sentry. One would have thought he had been carved out of wood, so still did he stand. He thought— "It must look very grand, that my wife has a sentry standing by her nest. They can't tell that it is her husband. They certainly think I have been commanded to stand here. That looks so aristocratic!" and he went on standing on one leg.

Below in the street a whole crowd of children were playing; and when they caught sight of the storks, one of the boldest of the boys, and afterwards all of them, sang the old verse about the storks. But they only sang it just as he could remember it:—

> Stork, stork, fly away;
> Stand not on one leg to-day.
> Thy dear wife is in the nest,
> Where she rocks her young to rest.
>
> The first he will be hanged,
> The second will be hit;
> The third he will be shot,
> And the forth put on the spit.

"Just hear what those boys are saying!" said the little stork-children. "They say we're to be hanged and killed."

"You're not to care for that!" said the mother stork. "Don't listen to it, and then it won't matter."

But the boys went on singing, and pointed at the stork mockingly with their fingers; only one boy, whose name was Peter, declared that it was a sin to make a jest of animals, and he would not join in it at all.

The mother stork comforted her children. "Don't you mind it at all," she said; "see how quiet your father stands, though it's only on one leg."

"We are very much afraid," said the young storks; and they drew their heads far back into the nest.

Now to-day, when the children came out again to play, and saw the storks, they sang their song:—

> The first he will be hanged,
> The second will be hit—

"Shall we be hanged and beaten?" asked the young storks.

"No, certainly not," replied the mother. "You shall learn to fly; I'll exercise you, then we shall fly out into the meadows and pay a visit to

The boys mocking the storks

the frogs; they will bow before us in the water, and sing 'Co-ax, Co-ax,' and then shall eat them up. That will be a real pleasure."

"And what then?" asked the young storks.

"Then all the storks will assemble, all that are here in the whole country, and the autumn exercises begin; then one must fly well, for that is highly important. For whoever cannot fly properly, will be thrust dead by the general's beak; so take care and learn well when the exercising begins."

"But then we shall be killed, as the boys say:—and only listen, now they're singing again."

"Listen to me, and not to them,"—said the mother stork. "After the great review we shall fly away to the warm countries, far away from here over moutains and forests. We shall fly to Egypt, where there are three covered houses of stone, which curl in a point and tower above the clouds; they are called pyramids, and are older than a stork can imagine. There is a river in that country which runs out of its bed; and then all the land is turned to mud. One walks about in the mud, and eats frogs."

"Oh!" cried all the young ones.

"Yes! It is glorious there! One does nothing all day long but eat; and while we are so comfortable over there, here there is not a green leaf on the trees; here it is so cold that that the clouds freeze to pieces, and fall down in little white rags!"

It was the snow that she meant, but she could not explain it in any other way.

"And do the naughty boys freeze to pieces?" asked the young Storks.

"No, they do not freeze to pieces; but they are not far from it, and must sit in the dark room and cower. You, on the other hand, can fly about in foreign lands, where there are flowers, and the sun shines warm."

Now some time had elapsed, and the nestlings had grown so large that they could stand upright in the nest and look far around; and the father stork came every day with delicious frogs, little snakes, and all kinds of stork-dainties as he found them. Oh, it looked funny, when he performed feats before them! He laid his head quite back upon his tail, and clapped with his beak as if he had been a little clapper; and then he told them stories, all about the marshes.

"Listen! Now you must learn to fly!" said the mother stork one day; and all the four young ones had to go out on the ridge of the roof. Oh! How they tottered; how they balanced themselves with their wings! And yet they were nearly falling down.

"Only look at me,"—said the mother. "Thus you must hold your heads! Thus you must pitch your feet! One, two! one, two! That's what will help you on in the world."

Then she flew a little way, and the young ones made a little clumsy leap. Bump! There they lay, for their bodies were too heavy.

"I will not fly!" said one of the young storks, and crept back into the nest; "I don't care about getting to the warm countries."

"Do you want to freeze to death here, when the winter comes? Are the boys to come and hang you, and singe you, and roast you? Now, I'll call them!"

"Oh, no!" cried the young stork, and hopped out on to the roof again, like the rest. On the third day they could actually fly a little, and then they thought they could also soar, and hover in the air. They tried it, but bump! Down they tumbled; and they had to shoot their wings again quickly enough. Now the boys came into the street again, and sang their song:—

Stork, stork, fly away!

"Shall we fly down and pick their eyes out?" asked the young storks.

"No!" replied the mother—"let them alone. Only listen to me, that's far more important. One, two, three! Now we fly round to the right. One, two, three! Now to the left round the chimney! See, that was very good! The last kick with the feet was so neat and correct, that you shall have permission to-morrow to fly with me to the marsh! Several nice stork families go there with their young; show them that mine are the nicest, and that you can start proudly; that looks well, and will get you consideration!"

"But are we not to take revenge on the rude boys?" asked the young storks.

"Let them scream as much as they like! You will fly up to the clouds, and get to the land of the pyramids, when they will have to shiver, and not have a green leaf or a sweet apple."

"Yes, we will revenge ourselves!" they whispered to one another; and then the exercising went on.

Among all the boys down in the street, the one most bent upon singing the teasing song was he who had begun it; and he was quite a little boy. He could hardly be more than six years old. The young storks certainly thought he was a hundred, for he was much bigger than their mother and father; and how should they know how old children and grown-up people can be? Their revenge was to come upon this boy; for it was he who had begun, and he always kept on. The young storks were very angry; and as they grew bigger they were less inclined to bear it,—at last their mother had to promise them that they should be revenged, but not till the last day of their stay.

"We must first see how you behave at the grand review. If you get through badly, so that the General stabs you through the chest with his beak, the boys will be right, at least in one way. Let us see."

"Yes, you shall see!" cried the young storks; and then they took all imaginable pains. They practised every day, and flew so neatly and so lightly that it was a pleasure to see them.

Now the autumn came on; all the storks began to assemble, to fly away to the warm countries while it is winter here. That was a review. They had to fly over forests and villages to show how well they could soar, for it was a long journey they had before them. The young storks did their part so well that they got as a mark, "Remarkably well, with frogs and snakes." That was the highest mark; and they might eat the frogs and snakes; and that is what they did.

"Now we will be revenged!" they said.

"Yes, certainly!" said the mother stork. "What I have thought of will be the best. I know the pond in which all the little mortals lie, till the stork comes and brings them to their parents. The pretty little babies lie there and dream so sweetly as they never dream afterwards. All parents are glad to have such a child, and all children want to have a sister or a brother. Now we fly to the pond, and bring one for each of the children who have not sung the naughty song and laughed at the storks."

"But he who began to sing—that naughty, ugly boy,"—screamed the young storks; "what shall we do with him?"

"There is a little dead child in the pond; one that has dreamed itself to death; we will bring that for him. Then he will cry because we have brought him a little dead brother. But that good boy—you have not forgotten him, the one who said, "It is wrong to laugh at animals!"—for him we will bring a brother and a sister too. And as his name is Peter, all of you shall be called Peter too!"

And it was done as she said; all the storks were named Peter, and so they are all called even now.

THE METAL PIG

In the city of Florence, not far from the *Piazza del Granduca*, there runs a little cross street, I think it is called *Porta Rosa*. In this street, in front of a kind of market-hall where vegetables are sold, there lies a pig artistically fashioned of metal. The fresh clear water pours from the jaws of the creature, which has become a blackish-green from age; only the snout shines as if it had been polished, and indeed it has been, by many hundreds of children and lazzaroni, who seize it with their hands, and place their mouths close to the mouth of the animal, to drink. It is a perfect picture to see the well-shaped creature clasped by a half-naked boy, who lays his red lips against its jaws.

Every one who comes to Florence can easily find the place; he need only ask the first beggar he meets for the metal pig, and he will find it.

It was late on a winter evening. The mountains were covered with snow; but the moon shone, and moonlight in Italy is just as good as the light of a murky northern winter's day; nay, it is better, for the air shines and lifts us up, while in the north the cold grey leaden covering seems to press us downwards to the earth,—the cold damp earth, which will once press down our coffin.

In the garden of the grand duke's palace, under a penthouse roof, where a thousand roses bloom in winter, a little ragged boy had been sitting all day long, a boy who might serve as a type of Italy, pretty and smiling, and yet suffering. He was hungry and thirsty, but no one gave him anything; and when it became dark, and the garden was to be closed the porter turned him out. Long he stood musing on the bridge that spans the Arno, and looked at the stars, whose light glittered in the water between him and the splendid marble bridge *Della Trinità*.

He took the way towards the metal pig, half knelt down, clasped his arms round it, put his mouth against its shining snout, and drank the fresh water in deep draughts. Close by lay a few leaves of salad and one or two chestnuts; these were his supper. No one was in the street but himself; it belonged to him alone, and he boldly sat down on the pig's back, bent forward, so that his curly head rested on the head of the animal, and before he was aware he fell asleep.

It was midnight:—the metal pig stirred, and he heard it say quite

The metal pig

distinctly, "You little boy, hold tight, for now I am going to run," and away it ran with him; this was a wonderful ride. First they got to the *Piazza del Granduca*, and the metal horse which carries the duke's statue neighed aloud; the painted coats-of-arms on the old council horse looked like transparent pictures, and Michael Angelo's "David" swang his sling: there was a strange life stirring among them. The metal groups representing persons, and the rape of the Sabines, stood there as if they were alive, a cry of mortal fear escaped them, and resounded over the splendid square.

By the *Palazzo degli Uffizi*, in the arcade, where the nobility assemble for the Carnival amusements, the metal pig stopped. "Hold tight," said the creature, "for now we are going up-stairs." The little boy spoke not a word, for he was half frightened, half delighted.

They came into a long gallery where the boy had already been. The walls shone with pictures; here stood statues and busts, all in the most charming light, as if it had been broad day: but the most beautiful of all was when the door of a side-room opened; the little boy could remember the splendour that was there, but on this night everything shone in the most glorious colours.

Here stood a beautiful woman, as radiant in beauty as nature and the greatest master of sculpture could make her; she moved her graceful limbs, dolphins sprang at her feet, and immortality shone out of her eyes. The world calls her the Venus de Medici. By her side are statues in which the spirit of life has been breathed into the stone; they are handsome unclothed men—one was sharpening a sword and was called the grinder; the wrestling gladiators formed another group; and the sword was sharpened, and they strove for the goddess of beauty.

The boy was dazzled by all this pomp; the walls gleamed with bright colours, everything was life and movement.

What splendour, what beauty shone from hall to hall; and the little boy saw everything plainly, for the metal pig went step by step from one picture to another, through all this scene of magnificence. Each fresh glory effaced the last;—one picture only fixed itself firmly in his soul, especially through the very happy children introduced into it; for these the little boy had greeted in the daylight.

Many persons pass by this picture with indifference; and yet it contains a treasure of poetry. It represents the Saviour descending into hell. But these are not the damned whom the spectator sees around him, they are heathen. The Florentine Angiolo Bronzino painted this picture. Most beautiful is the expression on the faces of the children, the full confidence that they will get to heaven; two little beings are already embracing; and one little one stretches out his hand towards another who stands below him, and points to himself as if he were saying, "I am going to heaven!" The older people stand uncertain, hoping, but bowing in humble adoration before the Lord Jesus. The boy's eyes rested longer on this picture than on any other. The metal pig stood still before it. A low sigh was heard; did it come from the picture or from the animal? The boy lifted up his hands towards the smiling children; then the pig ran away with him, away through the open vestibule. "Thanks and blessings to you, you dear thing!" said the little boy, and caressed the metal pig, as it sprang down the steps with him.

"Thanks and blessings to yourself," replied the metal pig. "I have helped you, and you have helped me, for only with an innocent child on my back do I receive power to run! Yes, you see, I may even step into the rays of the lamp, in front of the picture of the madonna, only I mayn't go into the church. But from without, when you are with me, I may look in through the open door. Do not get down from my back; if you do so, I shall lie dead as you see me in the daytime at the *Porta Rosa*."

"I will stay with you, my dear creature!" cried the child; so they went in hot haste through the streets of Florence, out into the place before the church *Santa Croce*.

The folding doors flew open and lights gleamed out from the altar through the church on the deserted square.

A wonderful blaze of light streamed forth from a monument in the left aisle, and a thousand moving stars seemed to form a glory round it. A coat of arms shone upon the grave, a red ladder in a blue field seemed to glow like fire; it was the grave of Galilei. The monument is unadorned, but the red ladder is a significant emblem, as if it were that of art, for here the way always leads up a burning ladder, towards heaven. The prophets of mind soar upwards towards heaven, like Elias of old.

To the right, in the aisle of the church, every statue on the richly carved sarcophagi seemed endowed with life. Here stood Michael Angelo, there Dante with the laurel wreath round his brow, Alfieri and Machiavelli; for here the great men, the pride of Italy, rest side by side.[1] It is a glorious church, far more beautiful than the marble cathedral of Florence, though not so large.

It seemed as if the marble vestments stirred, as if the great forms raised their heads higher and looked up, amid song and music, to the bright altar glowing with colour, where the white-clad boys swing the golden censers; and the strong fragrance streamed out of the church into the open square.

The boy stretched forth his hand towards the gleaming light; and in a moment the metal pig resumed its headlong career; he was obliged to cling tightly, and the wind whistled about his ears, he heard the church-door creak on its hinges as it closed; but at the same moment

[1] Opposite to the grave of Galilei is the tomb of Michael Angelo. On the monument his bust is displayed, with three figures, representing Sculpture, Painting and Architecture. Close by is a monument to Dante, whose corpse is interred at Ravenna; on this monument Italy is represented pointing to a colossal statue of the poet, while Poetry weeps over his loss. A few paces farther on is Alfieri's monument, adorned with laurel, the lyre, and dramatic masks: Italy weeps at his grave. Machiavelli here close the series of celebrated men.

his senses seemed to desert him—he felt a cold shudder pass over him, and awoke.

It was morning; and he was still sitting on the metal pig, which stood, where it always stood on the *Porta Rosa*, and he had slipped half off its back.

Fear and trembling filled the soul of the boy at the thought of her whom he called mother, and who had yesterday sent him forth to bring money; for he had none, and was hungry and thirsty. Once more he clasped his arms round the neck of his metal horse, kissed its lips, and nodded farewell to it. Then he wandered away into one of the narrowest streets where there was scarcely room for a laden ass. A great iron-clamped door stood ajar; he passed through it, and climbed up a brick stair with dirty walls and a rope for a balustrade, till he came to an open gallery hung with rags; from here a flight of stairs led down into the court, where there was a fountain, and great iron wires led up to the different stories, and many water buckets hung side by side, and at times the roller creaked, and one of the buckets would dance into the air, swaying so that the water splashed out of it down into the court-yard. A second ruinous brick staircase here led upwards; two Russian sailors were running briskly down, and almost overturned the poor boy. They were going home from their nightly carouse. A large woman no longer young, followed them, "What do you bring home?" she asked the boy.

"Don't be angry;" he pleaded. "I received nothing, nothing at all," and he seized the mother's dress, and would have kissed it. They went into the little room. I will not describe it, but only say that there stood in it an earthen pot with handles, made for holding fire, and called a *marito*. This pot she took in her arms, warmed her fingers and pushed the boy with her elbow. "Certainly you must have brought some money," said she.

The boy wept, and she struck him with her foot so that he cried aloud.

"Will you be silent, or I'll break your screaming head!" and she brandished the fire-pot which she held in her hand; the boy crouched down to the earth with a scream of terror. Then a neighbour stepped in, also with a *marito* in her arms. "Felicita," she said, "what are you doing to the child?"

"The child is mine,"—retorted Felicita. "I can murder him if I like, and you, too, Giannina,"—and she swung her fire-pot. The other lifted up her's in self-defence, and the two pots clashed together with such fury that fragments, fire and ashes flew about the room: but at the same moment the boy rushed out at the door, sped across the court-yard, and fled from the house. The poor child ran till he was quite out of breath; he stopped by the church whose great doors had opened to him the previous night, and went in. Everything was radiant; the boy knelt down at the first grave on the right hand, the grave of Michael Angelo; and soon he sobbed aloud. People came and went, and Mass was performed; but no one noticed the boy, only an elderly citizen stood still, looked at him, and then went away like the rest.

Hunger and thirst tormented the child; he was quite faint and ill, and he crept into a corner between the marble monuments, and went to sleep. Towards evening he was awakened by a tug at his sleeve; he started up and the same citizen stood before him.

"Are you ill? Where do you live? Have you been here all day?" were three of the many questions the old man asked of him. He answered, and the old man took him into his little house, close by, in a back street. They came into a glover's workshop, where a woman sat sewing busily. A little white Spitz-dog, so closely shaven that his pink skin could be seen, frisked about on the table, and gambolled before the boy.

"Innocent souls make acquaintance," said the woman; and she caressed the boy and the dog. The good people gave the child food and drink, and said he should be permitted to stay the night with them; and next day Father Giuseppe would speak to his mother. A little simple bed was assigned to him; but for him who had often slept on the hard stones it was a royal couch; and he slept sweetly, and dreamed of the splendid pictures and of the metal pig.

Father Giuseppe went out next morning; the poor child was not glad of this, for he knew that the object of the errand was to send him back to his mother. He wept, and kissed the little merry dog, and the woman nodded approvingly at both.

What news did Father Giuseppe bring home? He spoke a great deal with his wife, and she nodded and stroked the boy's cheek. "He is a capital lad!" said she. "He may become an accomplished glove-maker, like you; and look what delicate fingers he has! Madonna intended him for a glove-maker!"

And the boy stayed in the house, and the woman herself taught him to sew; he ate well, slept well, and became merry, and began to tease Bellissima, as the little dog was called; but the woman grew angry at this, and scolded and threatened him with her finger. This touched the boy's heart, and he sat thoughtful in his little chamber. This chamber looked upon the street in which skins were dried; there were thick bars of iron before his window; he could not sleep, the metal pig was always present in his thoughts, and suddenly he heard outside a pit-pat. That must be the pig! He sprang to the window; but nothing was to be seen, it had passed by already.

"Help the gentleman to carry his box of colours!" said the woman next morning, to the boy, when their young neighbour the artist, passed by carrying a paint-box and a large rolled canvas. The boy took the box and followed the painter; they betook themselves to the gallery, and mounted the same staircase which he remembered well from the night when he had ridden on the metal pig. He recognized the statues and pictures, the beautiful marble Venus, and the Venus that lived in the picture; and again he saw the Madonna, and the Saviour, and St. John.

They stood still before the picture by Bronzino, in which Christ is descending into hell, and the children smiled around him, in the sweet expectation of Heaven; the poor child smiled too, for he felt as if his Heaven were here.

"Go home now!" said the painter, when the boy had stood until the other had set up his easel.

"May I see you paint?" asked the boy. "May I see you put the picture upon this white canvas?"

"I am not going to paint yet," replied the man; and he brought out a piece of white chalk. His hand moved quickly; his eye measured the great picture, and though nothing appeared but a thin line, the figure of the Saviour stood there, as in the coloured picture.

"Why don't you go?" said the painter. And the boy wandered home silently, and seated himself on the table and learned to sew gloves.

But all day long his thoughts were in the picture gallery; and so it came that he pricked his fingers, and was awkward; but he did not tease Bellissima. When evening came, and when the house-door stood open, he crept out, it was cold but starlit, a bright beautiful evening. Away he went through the already deserted streets, and soon came to the metal pig; he bent down on it, kissed its shining mouth, and seated himself on its back. "You happy creature," he said; "how I have longed for you! We must take a ride to-night!"

The metal pig lay motionless, and the fresh stream gushed forth from its mouth. The little boy sat astride on its back: then something tugged at his clothes. He looked down and there was Bellissima,—little smooth-shaven Bellissima, barking as if she would have said, "Here am I too, why are you sitting there?" A fiery dragon could not have terrified the boy so much, as did the little dog in this place. Bellissima in the street, and not *dressed* as the old lady called it! What would be the end of it? The dog never came out in winter, except attired in a little lambskin, which had been cut out and made into a coat for him; it was made to fasten with a red riband round the little dog's neck and body, and was adorned with bows and with bells. The dog almost looked like a little kid, when in winter he got permission to patter out with mistress. Bellissima was outside, and not dressed! What would be the end of it? All his fancies were put to flight; yet the boy kissed the metal pig once more, and then took Bellisima on his arm; the little thing trembled with cold, therefore the boy ran as fast as he could.

"What are you running away with there?" asked two police-soldiers whom he met, and at whom Bellissima barked. "Where have you stolen that pretty dog?" they asked, and they took it away from him.

"Oh, give it back to me!" cried the boy despairingly.

"If you have not stolen him, you may say at home that the dog may be sent for from the watch-house,"—and they told him where the watch-house was, and went away with Bellissima.

Here was a terrible calamity. The boy did not know whether he should jump into the Arno, or go home and confess everything; they would certainly kill him, he thought. "But I will gladly be killed; then I shall die and get to Heaven,"—he reasoned; and he went home, principally with the idea of being killed.

The door was locked, he could not reach the knocker; no one was in the street, but a stone lay there, and with this he thundered at the door.

"Who is there?" cried somebody from within.

"It is I!" said he. "Bellissima is gone. Open the door, and then kill me!"

There was quite a panic; Madame was especially concerned for poor Bellissima. She immediately looked at the wall, where the dog's dress usually hung—and there was the little lambskin.

"Bellissima in the watch-house!" she cried loudly. "You bad boy! How did you entice her out? She'll be frozen, the poor delicate little thing! among those rough soldiers!"

The father was at once despatched—the woman lamented, and the boy wept. All the inhabitants of the house came together, and among the rest, the painter; he took the boy between his knees and questioned him; and in broken sentences he heard the whole story about the metal pig and the gallery, which was certainly rather incomprehensible. The painter consoled the little fellow, and tried to calm the old lady's anger; but she would not be pacified until the father came in with Bellissima, who had been among the soldiers; then there was great rejoicing; and the painter caressed the boy, and gave him a handful of pictures.

Oh, those were capital pieces—such funny heads!—and truly the metal pig was there among them, bodily. Oh, nothing could be more superb! By means of a few strokes it was made to stand there on the paper, and even the house that stood behind it was sketched in.

O! For the ability to draw and paint. He who could do this, could conjure up the whole world around him!

On the first leisure moment of the following day, the little fellow seized the pencil, and on the back of one of the pictures he attempted to copy the drawing of the metal pig;—and he succeeded!—It was certainly rather crooked, rather up and down, one leg thick and another thin; but still it was to be recognized, and he rejoiced himself at it. The pencil would not quite work as it should do, that he could well observe; on the next day a second metal pig was drawn by the side of the first, and this looked a hundred times better; the third was already so good, that everyone could tell what it was meant for.

But the glove-making prospered little, and the orders given in the town were executed but slowly; for the metal pig had taught him, that all pictures may be drawn on paper; and Florence is a picture book for any one who chooses to turn over its pages. On the *Piazza del Trinitá* stands a slender pillar, and upon it the goddess of Justice blindfolded, and with her scales in her hand. Soon she was placed on the paper; and it was the little glove-maker's boy who placed her there. The collection of pictures increased, but as yet it only contained representations of lifeless objects; when one day Bellissima came gambolling before him. "Stand still!" said he, "then you shall be made beautiful and put into my collection!" But Bellissima would not stand still, she had to be bound fast; her head and tail were tied, and she barked and jumped, and the string had to be pulled tight; and then the signora came in.

"You wicked boy! The poor creature!" was all she could utter; and she pushed the boy aside, thrust him away with her foot, forbade him to enter her house again, and called him a most ungrateful good-for-nothing and a wicked boy; and then weeping she kissed her little half-strangled Bellissima.

At this very moment the painter came down-stairs, and here is the turning point of the story.

In the year 1834 there was an exhibition in the Academy of Arts at Florence. Two pictures, placed side by side, collected a number of spectators. The smaller of the two represented a merry little boy who sat drawing, with a little white Spitz-dog, curiously shorn, for his model; but the animal would not stand still, and was therefore bound by a string, fastened to its head and its tail; there was a truth and life in this picture, that interested everyone. The painter was said to be a young Florentine, who had been found in the streets in his childhood, had been brought up by an old glove-maker, and had taught himself to draw. It was further said that a painter, now become famous, had discovered this talent just as the boy was to be sent away for tying up the favourite little dog of Madame, and using it as a model.

The glove-maker's boy had become a great painter, the picture proved this, and still more the larger picture that stood beside it. Here was represented only one figure, a handsome boy, clad in rags, asleep in the streets, and leaning against the metal pig in the *Porta Rosa* street. All the spectators knew the spot. The child's arms rested upon the head of the pig; the little fellow was so fast asleep—the lamp before the picture of the Madonna threw a strong effective light on the pale delicate face of the child—it was a beautiful picture! A great gilt frame surrounded it, and on one corner of the frame a laurel wreath had been hung; but a black band wound unseen among the green leaves, and a streamer of crape hung down from it. For within the last few days the young artist had—died!

GRANDMOTHER

Grandmother is very old; she has many wrinkles, and her hair is quite white; but her eyes, which are like two stars, and even more beautiful, look at you mildly and pleasantly, and it does you good to look into them. And then she can tell the most wonderful stories—and she has a

Grandmother looking at the withered flower

gown, with great flowers worked in it, and it is of heavy silk, and it rustles. Grandmother knows a great deal, for she was alive before father and mother, that's quite certain! Grandmother has a hymn-book, with great silver clasps, and she often reads in that book; in the middle of the book lies a rose, quite flat and dry; it is not as pretty as the roses she has standing in the glass, and yet she smiles at it most pleasantly of all, and tears even come into her eyes. I wonder why grandmother looks at the withered flower in the old book in that way? Do you know? Why, each time that grandmother's tears fall upon the rose its colours become fresh again; the rose swells and fills the whole room with its fragrance; the walls sink as if they were but mist, and all around her is the glorious green wood, where in summer the sunlight streams through the leaves of the trees; and grandmother—why she is young again, a charming maiden with light curls and full blooming cheeks, pretty and graceful, fresh as any rose; but the eyes, the mild blessed eyes, they have been left to grandmother. At her side sits a young man, tall and strong; he gives the rose to her, and she smiles; grandmother cannot smile thus now!— yes, now she smiles! But now he has passed away, and many thoughts and many forms of the past, and the handsome young man is gone, and the rose lies in the hymn-book, and grandmother she sits there again, an old woman, and glances down at the withered rose that lies in the book.

Now grandmother is dead. She had been sitting in her arm-chair, and telling a long, long capital tale; and she said the tale was told now, and she was tired, and she leaned her head back to sleep a while. One could hear her breathing as she slept; but it became quieter and more quiet, and her countenance was full of happiness and peace; it seemed as if a sunshine spread over her features; and she smiled again, and then the people said she was dead.

She was laid in the black coffin; and there she lay shrouded in the white linen folds, looking beautiful and mild; though her eyes were closed; but every wrinkle had vanished, and there was a smile around her mouth; her hair was silver-white and venerable, and we did not feel at all afraid to look at the corpse of her who had been the dear good grandmother. And the hymn-book was placed under her head, for she had wished it so, and the rose was still in the old book; and then they buried grandmother.

On the grave, close by the churchyard wall, they planted a rose tree,— and it was full of roses, and the nightingale flew singing over the flowers and over the grave; in the church the finest psalms sounded from the organ; the psalms that were written in the old book under the dead one's head. The moon shone down upon the grave; but the dead one was not here; every child could go safely, even at night, and pluck a rose there by the churchyard wall. A dead person knows more than all we living ones. The dead know what a terror would come upon us, if the strange thing were to happen, that they appeared among us; the dead are better than we all; the dead return no more. The earth has been heaped over the coffin, and it is earth that lies in the coffin; and the leaves of the hymn-book are dust, and the rose with all its recollections has returned to dust likewise. But above there bloom fresh roses; the nightingale sings and the organ sounds, and the remembrance lives of the old grandmother, with the mild eyes that always looked young. *Eyes can never die!* Ours will once behold grandmother again, young and beautiful, as when for the first time she kissed the fresh red rose that is now dust in the grave.

THE UGLY DUCKLING

It was glorious out in the country. It was summer, and the cornfields were yellow, and the oats were green; the hay had been put up in stacks in the green meadows, and the stork went about on his long red legs, and chattered Egyptian, for this was the language he had learned from his good mother. All around the fields and meadows were great forests, and in the midst of these forests lay deep lakes. Yes, it was really glorious out in the country. In the midst of the sunshine there lay an old farm, surrounded by deep canals; and from the wall down to the water grew great burdocks, so high that little children could stand upright under the loftiest of them. It was just as wild there as in the deepest wood. Here sat a duck upon her nest, for she had to hatch her young ones; but she was almost tired out before the little ones came; and then she so seldom had visitors. The other ducks liked better to swim about in the canals than to run up to sit down under a burdock, and cackle with her.

The duckling teased by the goose

At last one egg shell after another burst open. "Piep! piep!" it cried, and in all the eggs there were little creatures that stuck out their heads.

"Rap, rap!" they said; and they all came rapping out as fast as they could, looking all round them under the green leaves; and the mother let them look as much as they choose, for green is good for the eyes.

"How wide the world is!" said the young ones, for they certainly had much more room now than when they were in the eggs.

"Do you think this is all the world?" asked the mother. "That extends far across the other side of the garden, quite into the parson's field, but I have never been there yet. I hope you are all together,"—she continued, and stood up. "No, I have not all. The largest egg still lies there. How long is that to last? I am really tired of it." And she sat down again.

"Well, how goes it?" asked an old duck, who had come to pay her a visit.

"It lasts a long time with that one egg!" said the duck, who sat there, "It will not burst. Now, only look at the others; are they not the prettiest ducks one could possibly see? They are all like their father; the bad fellow never comes to see me."

"Let me see the egg which will not burst!" said the old visitor. "Believe me, it is a turkey's egg! I was once cheated in that way, and had much anxiety and trouble with the young ones, for they are afraid of the water. I could not get them to venture in. I quacked and clucked, but it was no use. Let me see the egg. Yes, that's a turkey's egg! Let it lie there, and teach the other children to swim."

"I think I will sit on it a little longer,"—said the duck. "I've sat so long now that I can sit a few days more."

"Just as you please,"—said the old duck; and she went away.

At last the great egg burst. "Piep! piep!" said the little one, and crept forth. It was very large, and very ugly. The duck looked at it. "It's a very large duckling," said she; "none of the others looks like that: can it really be a turkey chick? Now we shall soon find it out. It must go into the water, even if I have to thrust it in myself."

The next day the weather was splendidly bright, and the sun shone on all the green trees. The mother duck went down to the water with all her little ones. Splash, she jumped into the water. "Quack, quack!" she said, and one duckling after another plunged in. The water closed over their heads but they came up in an instant, and swam capitally; their legs went of themselves, and there they were all in the water. The ugly grey duckling swam with them.

"No, it's not a turkey,"—said she; "look how well it can use its legs and how upright it holds itself. It is my own child! On the whole it's quite pretty, if one looks at it rightly. Quack! quack! come with me, and I'll lead you out into the great world, and present you in the poultry yard; but keep close to me, so that no one may tread on you, and take care of the cats!"

And so they came into the poultry yard. There was a terrible riot going on in there; for two families were quarrelling about an eel's head, and the cat got it after all.

"See, that's how it goes in the world!" said the mother duck; and she whetted her beak, for she, too, wanted the eel's head. "Only use your legs," she said. "See that you can bustle about, and bow your heads before the old duck yonder. She's the grandest of all here; she's of Spanish blood, that's why she's so fat; and do you see, she has a red rag round her leg; that's something particularly fine, and the greatest distinction a duck can enjoy; it signifies that one does not want to lose her, and that she's to be recognized by man and beast! Shake yourselves—don't turn in your toes; a well-brought-up duck turns its toes quite out, just like father and mother, so! Now bend your necks and say "Rap!"

And they did so; but the other ducks round about looked at them, and said quite boldly, "Look there! Now we're to have these hanging on, as if there were not enough of us already! And fie! How that duckling yonder looks; we won't stand that!" and one duck flew up immediately, and bit it in the neck.

"Let it alone," said the mother; "it does no harm to any one."

"Yes, but it's too large and peculiar," said the duck who had bitten it; "and therefore it must be buffeted."

"Those are pretty children, that the mother has there," said the old duck with the rag round her leg. "They're all pretty but that one; that was a failure; I wish she could alter it."

"That cannot be done, my lady," replied the mother duck: "It is not pretty, but it has a really good disposition, and swims as well as any other; I may even say it swims better; I think it will grow up pretty, and become smaller in time; it has lain too long in the egg, and therefore is not properly shaped!" And then she pinched it in the neck, and smoothed its feathers. "Moreover, it is a drake," she said, "and therefore it is not of so much consequence. I think he will be very strong; he makes his way already."

"The other ducklings are graceful enough," said the old duck; "make yourself at home; and if you find an eel's head, you may bring it me."

And now they were at home. But the poor duckling, which had crept last out of the egg, and looked so ugly, was bitten and pushed and jeered, as much by the duck as by the chickens.

"It is too big!" they all said; and the turkey-cock who had been born with spurs, and therefore thought himself an emperor, blew himself up like a ship in full sail, and bore straight down upon it; then he gobbled, and grew quite red in the face. The poor duckling did not know where it should stand or walk; it was quite melancholy because it looked ugly, and was scoffed at by the whole yard.

So it went on the first day; and afterwards it became worse and worse. The poor duckling was hunted about by every one; even its brothers and sisters were quite angry with it, and said, "If the cat would only catch you, you ugly creature!" and the mother said, "If you were only far away!" And the duck bit it, and the chickens beat it, and the girl who had to feed the poultry kicked at it with her foot.

Then it ran and flew over the fence; the little birds in the bushes flew up in fear.

"That is because I am so ugly!" thought the duckling; and it shut its eyes, but flew on further; thus it came out into the great moor, where the wild ducks lived. Here it lay the whole night long; and it was weary and downcast.

Towards morning the wild ducks flew up, and looked at their new companion. "What sort of a one are you?" they asked; and the duckling turned in every direction, and bowed as well as it could. "You are remarkably ugly" said the wild ducks. "But that is very indifferent to us; so long as you do not marry into our family."

Poor thing! It certainly did not think of marrying, and only hoped to obtain leave to lie among the reeds and drink some of the swamp-water.

Thus it lay two whole days; then came thither two wild geese, or, properly speaking, two wild ganders. It was not long since each had crept out of an egg, and that's why they were so saucy.

"Listen, comrade," said one of them. "You're so ugly that I like you. Will you go with us, and become a bird of passage? Near here, in another moor, there are a few sweet lovely wild geese, all unmarried, and all able to say 'Rap!' You've a chance of making your fortune, ugly as you are!"

"Piff! paff!" sounded through the air; and the two ganders fell down dead in the swamp, and the water became blood-red. "Piff! paff!" it sounded again; and whole flocks of wild geese rose up from the reeds. And then there was another report. A great hunt was going on. The hunters were lying in wait all round the moor; and some were even sitting up in the branches of the trees, which spread far over the reeds. The blue smoke rose up like clouds among the dark trees, and was wafted far away across the water; and the hunting-dogs came "splash, splash!" into the swamp, and the rushes and reeds bent down on every side. That was a fright for the poor duckling! It turned its head, and put it under its wing; but at that moment a frightful great dog stood close by the duckling. His tongue hung far out of his mouth and his eyes gleamed horrible and ugly; he thrust out his nose close against the duckling, showed his sharp teeth, and—splash, splash—on he went, without seizing it.

"Oh, Heaven be thanked!" sighed the duckling. "I am so ugly, that even the dog does not like to bite me!"

And so it lay quite quiet, while the shots rattled through the reeds, and gun after gun was fired. At last, late in the day, silence was restored; but the poor duckling did not dare to rise up; it waited several hours before it looked round, and then hastened away out of the moor as fast as it could. It ran on over field and meadow; there was such a storm raging that it was difficult to get from one place to another.

Towards evening the duck came to a little miserable peasant's hut.

This hut was so dilapidated that it did not know on which side it should fall; and that's why it remained standing. The storm whistled round the duckling in such a way that the poor creature was obliged to sit down, to stand against it; and the tempest grew worse and worse. Then the duckling noticed that one of the hinges of the door had given way, and the door hung so slanting, that the duckling could slip through the crack into the room: and it did so.

Here lived a woman, with her tom-cat and her hen. And the tom-cat, whom she called Sonnie, could arch his back and purr, he could even give out sparks; but for that one had to stroke his fur the wrong way. The hen had quite little short legs, and therefore she was called Chickabiddy-shortshanks; she laid good eggs, and the woman loved her as her own child.

In the morning the strange duckling was at once noticed, and the tom-cat began to purr, and the hen to cluck. "What's this?" said the woman, and looked all round; but she could not see well, and therefore she thought the duckling was a fat duck that had strayed. "This is a rare prize!" she said. "Now I shall have duck's eggs. I hope it is not a drake. We must try that."

And so the duckling was admitted on trial for three weeks; but no eggs came. And the tom-cat was master of the house, and the hen was the lady, and always said "We and the world!" for she thought they were half the world, and by far the better half. The duckling thought one might have a different opinion, but the hen would not allow it.

"Can you lay eggs?" she asked. "No—" "Then you'll have the goodness to hold your tongue," and the tom-cat said, "Can you curve your back, and purr, and give out sparks?" "No." "Then you cannot have any opinion of your own, when sensible people are speaking!"

And the duckling sat in a corner and was melancholy; then the fresh air and the sunshine streamed in; and it was seized with such a strange longing to swim on the water, that it could not help telling the hen of it.

"What are you thinking of?" cried the hen. "You have nothing to do, that's why you have these fancies. Purr, or lay eggs, and they will pass over."

"But it is so charming to swim on the water!" said the duckling, "So refreshing to let it close above one's head, and to dive down to the bottom."

"Yes, that must be a mighty pleasure, truly,"—quoth the hen. "I fancy you must have gone crazy. Ask the cat about it,—he's the cleverest animal I know,—ask him if he likes to swim on the water, or to dive down: I won't speak about myself. Ask our mistress, the old woman; no one in the world is cleverer than she! Do you think she has any desire to swim, and to let the water close above her head?"

"You don't understand me," said the duckling.

"We don't understand you? Then pray who is to understand you? You surely don't pretend to be cleverer than the tom-cat and the woman—I won't say anything of myself! Don't be conceited, child! And be grateful for all the kindness you have received! Did you not get into a warm room, and have you not fallen into company from which you may learn something? But you are a chatterer, and it is not pleasant to associate with you! You may believe me, I speak for your good. I tell you disagreeable things, and by that one may always know one's true friends! Only take care that you learn to lay eggs, or to purr, and give out sparks!"

"I think I will go out into the wide world!" said the duckling.

"Yes, do go,"—replied the hen.

And the duckling went away. It swam on the water, and dived, but it was slighted by every creature because of its ugliness.

Now came the autumn. The leaves in the forest turned yellow and brown; the wind caught them, so that they danced about; and up in the air it was very cold. The clouds hung low, heavy with hail and snow-flakes, and on the fence stood the raven, crying "Croak, croak!" for mere cold; yes, it was enough to make one feel cold to think of this. The poor little duckling certainly had not a good time. One evening—the sun was just setting in his beauty—there came a whole flock of great handsome brids out of the bushes; they were dazzlingly white, with long flexible necks; they were swans. They uttered a very peculiar cry, spread forth their glorious great wings, and flew away from that cold region to warmer lands, to fair open lakes! They mounted so high, so high, and the ugly little duckling felt quite strangely, as it watched them. It turned round and round in the water, like a wheel, stretched out its neck towards them, and uttered such a strange loud cry as frightened itself. Oh! It could not forget those beautiful, happy birds; and so soon as it could see them no longer, it dived down to the very bottom, and when it came up again, it was quite beside itself. It knew not the name of those birds, and knew not whither they were flying; but it loved them more than it had ever loved any one. It was not at all envious of them. How could it think of wishing to possess such loveli-ness as they had? It would have been glad if only the ducks would have endured its company—the poor ugly creature!

And the winter grew cold, very cold! The duckling was forced to swim about in the water, to prevent the surface from freezing entirely but every night the hole in which it swam about became smaller and smaller. It froze so hard, that the icy covering crackled again; and the duckling was obliged to use its legs continually to prevent the hole from freezing up. At last it became exhausted, and lay quite still, and thus froze fast into the ice.

Early in the morning a peasant passed by; when he saw what had happened, he took his wooden shoe, broke the ice-crust to pieces, and carried the duckling home to his wife. Then it came to itself again. The children wanted to play with it; but the duckling thought they would do it an injury; and in its terror fluttered up into the milk-pan so that the milk spurted down into the room. The woman clasped her hands, at which the duckling flew down into the butter-tub, and then into the meal-barrel and out again. How it looked then! The woman screamed, and struck at it with the fire-tongs; the children tumbled over one another, in their efforts to catch the duckling; and they laughed and screamed finely! Happily the door stood open, and the poor creature was able to slip out between the shrubs into the newly fallen snow; and there it lay quite exhausted.

But it would be too melancholy, if I were to tell all the misery and care which the duckling had to endure in the hard winter. It lay out on the moor among the reeds, when the sun began to shine again, and the larks to sing; it was a beautiful spring.

Then all at once the duckling could flap its wings; they beat the air more strongly than before and bore it strongly away;—and before it well knew how all this happened, it found itself in a great garden, where the elder trees smelt sweet, and bent their long green branches down to the canals that wound through the region. Oh, here it was so beautiful, such a gladness of spring! And from the thicket came three glorious white swans; they rustled their wings, and swam lightly on the waters. The duckling knew the splendid creatures, and felt oppressed by a peculiar sadness.

"I will fly away to them, to the royal birds!—And they will kill me, because, I that am so ugly, dare to approach them. But it is of no consequence! Better to be killed by them, than to be pursued by ducks, and beaten by fowls, and pushed about by the girl who takes care of the poultry yard, and to suffer hunger in winter!" And it flew out into the water, and swam towards the beautiful swans; these looked at it, and came sailing down upon it with outspread wings. "Kill me!" said the poor creature, and bent its head down upon the water, expecting nothing but death. But what was this, that it saw in the clear water? It beheld its own image; and lo, it was no longer a clumsy dark-grey bird, ugly and hateful to look at—but a swan.

It matters nothing if one is born in a duck-yard, if one has only lain in a swan's egg.

The four swans

It felt quite glad at all the need and misfortune it had suffered, now it realized its happiness in all the splendour that surrounded it. And the great swans swam round it, and stroked it with their beaks.

Into the garden came little children who threw bread and corn into the water; and the youngest cried, "There is a new one!" and the other children shouted joyously, "Yes, a new one had arrived!" And they clapped their hands and danced about, and ran to their father and mother; and bread and cake were thrown into the water; and they all said: "The new one is the most beautiful of all! So young and handsome!" And the old swans bowed their heads before him.

Then he felt quite ashamed; and hid his head under his wings, for he did not know what to do; he was so happy, and yet not at all proud. He thought how he had been persecuted and despised; and now he heard them saying that he was the most beautiful of all birds. Even the alder-tree bent its branches straight down into the water before him, and the sun shone warm and mild! Then his wings rustled, he lifted his slender neck, and cried rejoicingly from the depths of his heart, "I never dreamed of so much happiness, when I was still the ugly duckling!"

A PICTURE FROM THE FORTRESS WALL

It is autumn; we stand on the fortress wall and look out over the sea; we look at the numerous ships, and at the Swedish coast on the other side of the Sound, which rises far above the mirror of waters in the evening glow; behind us the wood stands sharply out; mighty trees surround us, the yellow leaves flutter down from the branches; below at the foot of the wall stands gloomy houses fenced in with palisades;

The prisoner

in these it is very narrow and dismal, but still more dismal is it behind the grated loopholes in the wall, for there sit the prisoners, the worst criminals.

A ray of the sinking sun shoots into the bare cell of one of the captives. The sun shines upon the good and the evil. The dark stubborn criminal throws an impatient look at the cold ray. A little bird flies towards the grating. The bird twitters to the wicked as to the just. He only utters his short, "tweet, tweet;" but he perches on the grating, claps his wings, pecks a feather from one of them, puffs himself out, and sets his feather on end on his neck and breast, and the bad, chained man looks at him; a milder expression comes in to the criminal's hard face; in his breast there swells up a thought—a thought he himself cannot rightly analyse; but the thought has to do with the sunbeam, with the scent of violets which grow luxuriantly in spring at the foot of the wall. Now the horns of the chasseur soldiers sound merry and full. The little bird starts, and flies away; the sunbeam gradually vanishes, and again it is dark in the room, and dark in the heart of the bad man; but still the sun has shone into that heart, and the twittering of the bird has touched it!

Sound on ye glorious strains of the hunting horn! Continue to sound, for the evening is mild, and the surface of the sea smooth as a mirror, heaves slowly and gently.

THE SHEPHERDESS AND THE CHIMNEY-SWEEPER

Have you ever seen a very old wooden cupboard, quite black with age, and ornamented with carved foliage and arabesques? Just such a cupboard stood in a parlour: it had been a legacy from the great-grandmother, and was covered from top to bottom with carved roses and tulips. There were the quaintest flourishes upon it, and from among these peered forth little stags' heads with antlers. In the middle of the cupboard door an entire figure of a man had been cut out; he was certainly ridiculous to look at, and he grinned; for you could not call it laughing: he had goat's legs, little horns on his head, and a long ears. The children in the room always called him the Billygoat-legs-Major-and-Lieutenant-General-War-Commandet-Sergeant; that was a difficult name to pronounce, and there are not many who obtain this title! But it was something to have cut him out. And there he was! He was always looking at the table under the mirror, for on this table stood a lovely little Shepherdess made of china. Her shoes were gilt, her dress was adorned with a red rose, and besides this she had a golden hat, and a shepherd's crook; she was very lovely. Close by her stood a little Chimney-sweeper, black as a coal, and also made of porcelain; he was as clean and neat as any other man, for it was only make-believe that he was a sweep; the china-workers might just as well have made a prince of him, if they had been so minded.

There he stood very nattily with his ladder, and with a face as white and pink as a girl's; and that was really a fault, for he ought to have been a little black. He stood quite close to the Shepherdess; they had both been placed where they stood; but as they had been placed there they had become engaged to each other. They suited each other well. Both were young people, both made of the same kind of china, and both were brittle.

Close to them stood another figure, three times greater than they. This was an old Chinaman, who could nod. He was also of porcelain, and declared himself to be the grandfather of the little shepherdess; but he could not prove his relationship. He declared he had authority over her, and that therefore he had nodded to Mr. Billygoat-legs-Lieutenant-and-Major-General-War-Commander-Sergeant, who was wooing her for his wife.

"Then you will get a husband," said the old Chinaman, "a man who I verily believe is made of mahogany. He can make you Billygoat-legs-Lieutenant-and-Major-General-War-Commander-Sergeant's lady; he has the whole cupboard full of sliver plate which he hoards up in secret drawers."

"I won't go into the dark cupboard!" said the little Shepherdess. "I have heard tell that he has eleven porcelain wives in there."

"Then you may become the twelfth!" cried the Chinaman. "This night, so soon as it rattles in the old cupboard, you shall be married as true as I am an old Chinaman!" and with that he nodded his head and fell asleep. But the little Shepherdess wept and looked at her heart's

The old Chinaman and the young couple

beloved the porcelain Chimney-sweeper. "I should like to beg of you," said she, "to go out with me into the wide world; for we cannot remain here."

"I'll do whatever you like!" replied the little Chimney-sweep. "Let us start directly! I think I can keep you by exercising my profession."

"If we were only safely down from the table," said she. "I shall not be happy, until we are out in the wide world." And he comforted her, and showed her how she must place her little foot upon the carved corners and the gilded foliage at the foot of the table; he brought his ladder too, to help her, and they were soon together upon the floor. But when they looked up at the old cupboard there was great commotion within; all carved stags were stretching out their heads, rearing up their antlers, and turning their necks; and the Billygoat-legs-Lieutenant-and-Major-General-War-Commander-Sergeant sprung high in the air, and called across to the old Chinaman: "Now they're running away! Now they're running away."

Then they were a little frightened, and jumped quickly into the drawer of the window-seat. Here were three or four packs of cards which were not complete, and a little puppet show, which had been built up as well as it could be done. There plays were acted, and all the ladies, diamonds, clubs, hearts and spades sat in the first row, fanning themselves; and behind them stood all the knaves, showing that they had a head above and below, as is usual in playing cards. The play was about two people who were not to be married to each other, and the Shepherdess wept, because it was just like her own history.

"I cannot bear this!" said she. "I must go out of the drawer." But when they arrived on the floor, and looked up at the drawer the old Chinaman was awake and was shaking over his whole body—for below he was all one lump.

"Now the old Chinaman's coming!" cried the little Shepherdess; and she fell down upon her porcelain knee, so startled was she.

"I have an idea," said the Chimney-sweeper. "Shall we creep into the great pot-pourri vase, which stands in the corner? Then we can lie on roses and lavender, and throw salt in his eyes, if he comes."

"That will be of no use," she replied. "Besides, I know that the old Chinaman and the pot-pourri vase were once engaged to each other, and a kind of liking always remains when people have stood in such a position to each other. No, there's nothing left for us but to go out into the wide world!"

"Have you really courage, to go into the wide world with me?" asked the Chimney-sweeper. "Have you considered how wide the world is, and that we can never come back here again?" "I have,"— replied she. And the Chimney-sweeper looked fondly at her, and said, "My way is through the chimney, if you have really courage to creep with me through the stove, through the iron fire-box as well as up the pipe! Then we can get out into the chimney, and I know how to find my way through there. We'll mount so high that they can't catch us, and quite at the top there's a hole that leads out into the wide world." And he led her to the door of the stove.

"It looks very black there," said she, but still she went with him, through the box and through the pipe where it was pitch-dark night.

"Now we are in the chimney," said he, "and look, look! Up yonder a beautiful star is shining."

And it was a real star in the sky, which shone straight down upon them, as if it would show them the way. And they clambered and crept; it was a frightful way, and terribly steep; but he supported her and helped her up; he held her, and showed her the best places where she could place her little porcelain feet; and thus they reached the edge of the chimney, and upon that they sat down; for they were desperately tired, as they might well be.

The sky with all its stars was high above, and all the roofs of the town deep below them. They looked far around; far, far out into the world. The poor Shepherdess had never thought of it as it really was; she leant her little head against the Chimney-sweeper, then she wept so bitterly, that the gold ran down off her girdle.

"That is too much," she said. "I cannot bear that. The world is too large. If I were only back on the table, below the mirror. I shall never be happy until I am there again. Now I have followed you out into the wide world, you may accompany me back again, if you really love me."

And the Chimney-sweeper spoke sensibly to her, spoke of the old Chinaman and of the Billygoat-legs-Lieutenant-and-Major-General-War-Commander-Sergeant; but she sobbed bitterly and kissed her little Chimney-sweeper, so that he could not help giving way to her, though it was foolish.

And so with much labour they climbed down the chimney again. And they crept through the pipe and the fire-box! That was not pleasant at all. And there they stood in the dark store; there they listened behind the door, to find out what was going on in the room. Then it was quite quiet; they looked in, ah! There lay the old Chinaman in the middle of the floor. He had fallen down from the table, as he was pursuing them, and now he lay broken into three pieces; his back had come off, all in one piece, and his head had rolled into a corner. The Billygoat-legs-Lieutenant-and-Major-General-War-Commander-Sergeant stood where he had always stood, considering.

"That is terrible!" said the little Shepherdess. "The old grandfather has fallen to pieces, and it is our fault. I shall never survive it!" and then she wrung her little hands.

"He can be mended! He can be mended," said the Chimney-sweeper. Don't be so violent; if they glue his back together, and give him a good rivet in his neck he will be as good as new, and may say many a disagreeable thing to us yet." "Do you think so?" cried she, but they climbed back upon the table where they used to stand.

"You see we have come to this," said the Chimney-sweeper, "we might have saved ourselves all the trouble we have had." "If the old grandfather was only riveted," said the Shepherdess. "I wonder if that is dear?" And he was really riveted. The family had his back cemented and a great rivet was passed through his neck; he was as good as new; only he could no longer nod.

"It seems you have become proud, since you fell to pieces?" said the Billygoat-legs-Lieutenant-and-Major-General-War-Commander-Sergeant. "I don't think you have any reason to give yourselves such airs. Am I to have her, or am I not?"

And the Chimney-sweeper and the little Shepherdess looked at the old Chinaman most piteously; for they were afraid he might nod. But he could not do that; and it was irksome to him, to tell a stranger that he always had a rivet in his neck. And so the porcelain people remained together, and loved one another until they broke.

The party of toys

THE MONEY-PIG

In the nursery a number of toys lay strewn about; high up, on the wardrobe, stood the money-box made of clay and purchased of the potter, and it was the shape of a little pig; of course the pig had a slit in its back, and this slit had been so enlarged with a knife that whole dollar pieces could slip through; and indeed, two such had slipped into the box, beside a number of pence. The money-pig was stuffed so full that it could no longer rattle, and that is the highest point of perfection a money-pig can attain. There it stood upon the cupboard, high and lofty, looking down upon everything else in the room; it knew very well that what it had in its stomach would have bought all the toys, and that's what we call having self-respect.

The others thought of that too, even if they did not exactly express it, for there were many other things to speak of. One of the drawers was half pulled out, and there lay a great handsome doll, though she was somewhat old, and her neck had been mended. She looked out and said, "Now we'll play at men and women, for that is always something!" and now there was a general uproar, and even the framed prints on the walls turned round and showed that there was a wrong side to them; but they did not do it to protest against the proposal.

It was late at night; the moon shone through the window frames and afforded the cheapest light. The game was now to begin, and all, even the children's go-cart, which certainly belonged to the coarser play-things, were invited to take part in the sport.

"Each one has his own peculiar value!" said the go-cart, "we cannot all be noblemen! There must be some who do the work, as the saying is. The money-pig was the only one who received a written invitation, for he was of high standing, and they were afraid he would not accept the verbal message. Indeed, he did not answer to say whether he would come, nor did he come; if he was to take a part, he must enjoy the sport from his own home; they were to arrange accordingly, and so they did.

The little toy theatre was now put up in such a way that the money-pig could look directly in; they wanted to begin with a comedy, and afterwards there was to be a tea party, and a discussion for mental improvement, and with this latter part they began immediately. The rocking horse spoke of training and race; the go-cart of railways and steam power, for all this belonged to their profession, and it was quite right they should talk of it. The clock talked politics—ticks—ticks, and knew what was the time of day, though it was whispered he did not go correctly; the bamboo cane stood there, stiff and proud, for he was conceited about his brass ferule and his silver top, for being thus bound above and below; on the sofa lay two worked cushions, pretty and stupid, and now the play began.

All sat and looked on, and it was requested the audience should applaud, and crack and stamp according as they were gratified. But the riding whip said he never cracked for old people, only for young ones who were not yet married. "I crack for everything," said the cracker, and these were the thoughts they had while the play went on. The piece was worthless, but it was well played; all the characters turned their painted side to the audience, for they were so made that they should only be looked at from that side, and not from the other; and all played wonderfully well, coming out quite beyond the lamps, because the wires were a little too long, but that only made them come out the more. The darned doll was quite exhausted with excitement—so thoroughly exhausted that she burst at the darned place in her neck, and the money-pig was so enchanted in his way that he formed the resolution to do something for one of the players, and to remember him in his will as the one who should be buried with him in the family vault, when matters were so far advanced.

It was true enjoyment; such true enjoyment that they quite gave up the thoughts of tea, and only carried out the idea of mental recreation; that's what they called playing at men and women, and there was nothing wrong in it, for they were only playing; and each one thought of himself and of what the money-pig might think; and the money-pig thought farthest of all, for he thought of making his will and of his burial, and when might this come to pass! Certainly far sooner than was expected. Crack! It fell down from the cupboard; fell on the ground, and was broken to pieces; and the pennies hopped and danced in comical style; the little ones turned round like tops, and the bigger ones rolled away, particularly the one great silver dollar, who wanted to go out into the world. And he came out into the world, and they all succeeded in doing so; and the pieces of the money-pig were put into the dust-bin; but the next day a new money-pig was standing on the cupboard; it had not yet a farthing in its stomach, and therefore could not rattle, and in this it was like the other—and that was a beginning—and with that we will make an end.

THE RED SHOES

There was once a little girl; a very nice pretty little girl. But in summer she had to go barefoot, because she was poor, and in winter she wore thick wooden shoes, so that her little instep became quite red, altogether red.

In the middle of the village lived an old shoemaker's wife; she sat, and sewed, as well as she could, a pair of little shoes, of old strips of red cloth; they were clumsy enough, but well meant, and the little girl was to have them. The little girl's name was Karen.

On the day when her mother was buried she received the red shoes and wore them for the first time. They were certainly not suited for mourning; but she had no others, and therefore thrust her little bare feet into them and walked behind the plain deal coffin.

Suddenly a great carriage came by; and in the carriage sat an old lady; she looked at the little girl and felt pity for her, and said to the clergyman, "Give me the little girl, and I will provide for her."

Karen thought this was for the sake of the shoes; but the old lady declared they were hideous; and they were burned. But Karen herself was clothed neatly and properly; she was taught to read and to sew, and the people said she was agreeable. But her mirror said, "You are much more than agreeable; you are beautiful!"

Once the Queen travelled through the country, and had her little daughter with her; and the daughter was a Princess. And the people flocked towards the castle, and Karen too was among them; and the little Princess stood in a fine white dress at a window, and let herself be gazed at. She had neither train nor golden crown; but she wore splendid red morocco shoes; they were certainly far handsomer than those the shoemaker's wife had made for little Karen. Nothing in the world can compare with red shoes!

Now Karen was old enough to be confirmed; new clothes were made for her, and she was to have new shoes. The rich shoemaker in the town took the measure of her little feet; this was done in his own house, in his little room, and there stood great glass cases with neat shoes and shining boots. It had quite a charming appearance, but the old lady could not see well, and therefore took no pleasure in it. Among the shoes stood a red pair, just like those which the Princess had worn. How beautiful they were! The shoemaker also said they had been made for a Count's child, but they had not fitted.

"That must be patent leather," observed the old lady. "The shoes shine so!"

"Yes, they shine!" replied Karen; and they fitted her, and were bought. But the old lady did not know that they were red; for she would never have allowed Karen to go to her confirmation in red shoes; and that is what Karen did.

Every one was looking at her shoes. And when she went across the church porch, towards the door of the choir, it seemed to her as if the old pictures on the tombstones, the portraits of clergymen and clergymen's wives in their stiff collars and long black garments fixed their eyes upon her red shoes. And she thought of her shoes only, when the priest laid his hand on her head, and spoke holy words. And the organ pealed solemnly, the children sang with their fresh sweet voices, and the old precentor sang too; but Karen thought only of her red shoes.

In the afternoon the old lady was informed by every one that the shoes were red; and she said it was naughty and unsuitable and that when Karen went to church in future, she should always go in black shoes, even if they were old.

Next Sunday was Sacrament Sunday. And Karen looked at the black shoes, and looked at the red ones,—looked at them again—and put on the red ones.

Karen and the old soldier

The sun shone gloriously; Karen and the old lady went along the footpath through the fields, and it was rather dusty.

By the church door stood an old invalid soldier with a crutch and a long beard; the beard was rather red than white, for it was red altogether; and he bowed down almost to the ground, and asked the old lady if he might dust her shoes. And Karen also stretched out her little foot. "Look, what pretty dancing-shoes!" said the old soldier. "Fit tightly when you dance!" And he tapped the soles with his hand. And the old lady gave the soldier an alms, and went into the church with Karen.

And every one in the church looked at Karen's red shoes, and all the pictures looked at them. And while Karen knelt in the church she only thought of her red shoes; and she forgot to sing her psalm, and forgot to say her prayer.

Now all the people went out of church; and the old lady stepped into her carriage. Karen lifted up her foot to step in too; then the old soldier said: "Look, what beautiful dancing-shoes!" And Karen could not resist; she was obliged to dance a few steps; and when she once began, her legs went on dancing. It was just as though the shoes had received power over her. She danced round the corner of the church, she could not help it; the coachman was obliged to run behind her and seize her; he lifted her into the carriage, but her feet went on dancing, so that she kicked the good old lady violently. At last they took off her shoes, and her legs became quiet.

At home the shoes were put away in a cupboard; but Karen could not resist looking at them.

Now the old lady became very ill; and it was said she would not recover. She had to be nursed and waited on; and this was no one's duty so much as Karen's. But there was to be a great ball in the town; and Karen was invited. She looked at the old lady who could not recover; she looked at the red shoes, and thought there would be no harm in it—she put on the red shoes, and that she might very well do;—but they went to the ball and began to dance.

But when she wished to go to the right hand, the shoes danced to the left, and when she wanted to go upstairs the shoes danced downwards, down into the street and out at the town-gate. She danced and was obliged to dance, straight out into the dark wood.

There was something glistening up among the trees, and she thought it was the moon, for she saw a face. But it was the old soldier with the red beard; he sat and nodded, and said: "Look, what beautiful dancing-shoes!"

Then she was frightened, and wanted to throw away the red shoes; but they clung fast to her. And she tore off her stockings; but the shoes had grown fast to her feet. And she danced and was compelled to go dancing over field and meadow, in rain and sunshine, by night and by day; but it was most dreadful at night.

She danced out into the open churchyard; but the dead there do not dance; they have far better things to do. She wished to sit down on the poor man's grave, where the bitter fern grows; but there was no peace nor rest for her. And when she danced towards the open church door, she saw there an angel in long white garments, with wings that reached from his shoulders to his feet; his countenance was serious and stern, and in his hand he held a sword that was broad and gleaming.

"Thou shalt dance!" he said,—"dance on thy red shoes, till thou art pale and cold, and till thy skin shrivels to a skeleton. Thou shalt dance from door to door; and where proud, haughty children dwell, shalt thou knock, that they may hear thee, and be afraid of thee! Thou shalt dance, dance!"

"Mercy!" cried Karen. But she did not hear what the angel answered, for the shoes carried her away, carried her through the door on to the field, over stock and stone, and she was always obliged to dance.

One morning she danced past a door, which she knew well; there was a sound of psalm-singing within; a coffin was carried out, adorned with flowers. Then she knew that the old lady was dead, and she felt that she was deserted by all, and condemned by the angel of heaven.

She danced, and was compelled to dance—to dance in the dark night. The shoes carried her on over thorn and brier; she scratched herself till she bled; she danced away across the heath to a little lonely house. Here she knew the executioner dwelt; and she tapped with her fingers on the panes and called, "Come out, come out! I cannot come in, for I must dance!"

And the executioner said, "You probably don't know who I am? I cut off the bad people's heads with my axe, and mark how my axe rings!"

"Do not strike off my head!" said Karen, "for if you do, I cannot repent of my sin. But strike off my feet with the red shoes!"

And then she confessed all her sin, and the executioner cut off her feet with the red shoes; but the shoes danced away with the little feet over the fields and into the deep forest.

And he cut her a pair of wooden feet, with crutches, and taught her a psalm, which the criminals always sing, and she kissed the hand that had held the axe, and went away across the heath.

"Now I have suffered enough for the red shoes," said she. "Now I will go into the church, that they may see me!" And she went quickly towards the church door; but when she came there, the red shoes danced before her, so that she was frightened and turned back.

The whole week through she was sorrowful, and wept many bitter tears; but when Sunday came, she said: "Now I have suffered and striven enough! I think that I am just as good as many of those who sit in the church and carry their heads high!" And then she went boldly on; but she did not get further than the churchyard-gate before she saw the red shoes dancing along before her; then she was seized with terror, and turned back, and repented her sin right heartily.

And she went to the parsonage, and begged to be taken there as a servant; she promised to be industrious, and to do all she could; she did not care for wages, and only wished to be under a roof and with good people. The clergyman's wife pitied her, and took her into her service. And she was industrious and thoughtful. Silently she sat and listened when in the evening the pastor read the Bible aloud. All the little ones were very fond of her; but when they spoke of dress and splendour and beauty she would shake her head.

Next Sunday they all went to church, and she was asked if she wished to go too; but she looked sadly, with tears in her eyes, at her crutches. And then the others went to hear God's word; but she went alone into her little room, which was only large enough to contain her bed and a chair. And here she sat with her hymn-book; and as she read it with a pious mind, the wind bore the notes of the organ over to her from the church; and she lifted up her face, wet with tears, and said, "Oh Lord, help me!"

Then the sun shone so brightly; and before her stood the angel in the white garments, the same she had seen that night at the church door. But he no longer grasped the sharp sword; he held a green branch covered with roses; and he touched the ceiling, and it rose up high; and wherever he touched it, a golden star gleamed forth; and he touched the walls, and they spread forth widely, and she saw the organ which was pealing forth sound; and she saw the old pictures of clergymen and their wives; and the congregation sat in the decorated seats, and sang from their hymn-books. The church had come to the poor girl in her narrow room, or her chamber had become a church. She sat in the chair with the rest of the clergyman's people; and when they had finished the psalm, and looked up, they nodded and said, "That was right, that you came here, Karen!"

"It was mercy!" said she.

And the organ sounded, and the children's voices singing in chorus sounded so sweet and lovely! The clear sunshine streamed so warm through the window upon the chair, in which Karen sat; her heart became so filled with sunshine, peace, and joy, that it broke; her soul flew on the sunbeams to Heaven; and there was nobody who asked after the RED SHOES!

THE WICKED PRINCE

There was once a wicked Prince. His aim and object was to conquer all the countries in the world, and to inspire all men with fear; he went about with fire and sword, and his soldiers trampled down the corn in the fields, and set fire to the peasants' houses, so that the red flames licked the leaves from the trees, and the fruit hung burnt on the black charred branches. With her naked baby in her arms, many a poor mother took refuge behind the still smoking walls of her burnt house; but here even the soldiers sought for their victims, and if they found them, it was new food for their demoniac fury; evil spirits could not have raged worse than did these soldiers; but the Prince thought their deeds were right, and that it must be so. Every day his power increased; his name was feared by all, and fortune accompanied him in all his actions. From conquered countries he brought vast treasures home; in his capital an amount of wealth was heaped, unequalled in any other

The priests exhorting the wicked Prince

place. And he caused gorgeous palaces, churches, and halls to be built, and every one who saw those great buildings and these vast treasures cried out respectfully, "What a great Prince!" They thought not of the misery he had brought upon other lands and cities; they heard not all the sighs and all the mournings that arose from among the ruins of demolished towns.

The Prince looked upon his gold, and upon his mighty buildings, and his thoughts were like those of the crowd, "What a great Prince am I; but," so his thought ran on, "I must have more, far more! No power may be equal to mine, much less exceed it!" And he made war upon all his neighbours, and overcame them all. The conquered kings he caused to be bound with fetters of gold to his chariot, and thus he drove through the streets of his capital; when he banqueted, those kings were compelled to kneel at his feet, and at the feet of his courtiers, and receive the broken pieces which were thrown to them from the table.

At last the Prince caused his own statue to be set up in the open squares and in the royal palaces, and he even wished to place it in the churches before the altars; but here the priests stood up against him, and said, "Prince thou art mighty, but Heaven is mightier, and we dare not fulfil thy commands."

"Good, then," said the Prince, "I will vanquish Heaven likewise." And in his pride and impious haughtiness he caused a costly ship to be built, in which he could sail through the air; it was gay and glaring to behold, like the tail of a peacock, and studded and covered with thousands of eyes; but each eye was the muzzle of gun. The Prince sat in the midst of the ship, and needed only to press on a spring, and a thousand bullets flew out on all sides, while the gun barrels were re-loaded immediately. Hundreds of eagles were harnessed in front of the ship, and with the speed of an arrow, they flew upwards towards the sun. How deep the earth lay below them! With its mountains and forests it seemed but a field through which the plough had drawn its furrows, and along which the green bank rose covered with turf; soon it appeared only like a flat map with indistinct lines, and at last it lay completely hidden in mist and cloud. Ever higher flew the eagles, up into the air; then one of the innumerable angels appeared. The wicked Prince hurled thousands of bullets against him; but the bullets sprang back from the angel's shining pinions, and fell down like common hailstones; but a drop of blood, one single drop, fell from one of the white wing feathers, and this drop fell upon the ship in which the Prince sat, and burnt its way deep into the ship, and weighing like a thousand hundred weight of lead dragged down the ship in headlong fall towards the earth; the strongest pinions of the engles broke, the wind roared round the Prince's head, and the clouds aroused—formed from the smoke of burned cities—drew themselves together in threatening shapes like huge sea crabs, stretching forth their claws and nippers towards him, and piled themselves up in great overshadowing rocks, with crushing fragments rolling down them, and then to fiery dragons, till the Prince lay half dead in the ship, which at last was caught with a terrible shock in the thick branches of a forest.

"I will conquer Heaven," said the Prince. "I have sworn it, and my will must to be done!" And for seven years he caused his men to work at making ships for sailing through the air, and had thunderbolts made of the hardest steel, for he wished to storm the fortress of heaven; but of all his dominions he gathered armies together, so that when they were drawn up in rank and file they covered a space of several miles. The armies went on board the ships, and the Prince approached his own vessel; then there was sent out against him a swarm of gnats, a single little swarm of gnats. The swarm buzzed round the Prince, and stung his face and hands; raging with anger he drew his sword, and struck all round him; but he only struck the empty air, for he could not hit the gnats. Then he commanded his people to bring costly hangings, and to wrap them around him, so that no gnat might further sting him, and the servants did as he commanded them. But a single gnat had attached itself to the inner side of the hangings, and crept into the ear of the Prince, and stung him; it burned like fire, and the poison penetrated to his brain: like a madman he tore the hangings from his body and hurled them far away, tore his clothes and danced about naked before the eyes of his rude, savage soldiers, who now jeered at the mad Prince, who wanted to overcome Heaven, and who himself was conquered by one single little gnat.

CHILDREN'S PRATTLE

At the rich merchant's there was a children's party; rich people's children and grand people's children were there. The merchant was a learned man; he had once gone through the college examination, for his honest father had kept him to this, his father who had at first only been a cattle dealer, but always an honest and industrious man; the trade had brought money, and the merchant had managed to increase the store. Clever he was, and he had also a heart, but there was less said of his heart than of his money. At the merchant's, grand people went in and out; people of blood, as it is called, and people of intellect, and people who had both of these, and people who had neither. Now there was a children's party there, and children's prattle, and children speak frankly from the heart. Among the rest there was a beautiful little girl, and the little one was terribly proud, but the servants had taught her that, not her parents, who were far too sensible people. Her father was a groom of the bed-chamber, and that is a very grand office, and she knew it.

"I am a child of the bed-chamber," she said. Now she might just as well have been a child of the cellar, for nobody can help his birth; and then she told the other children that she was "well born," and said that no one who was not well born could get on far in the world; it was of no use to read and to be industrious, if one was not well born one could not achieve anything.

"And those whose names end with 'sen,'" said she, "they cannot be anything at all! One must put one's arms akimbo and make the elbows quite pointed, and keep them at a great distance, these "sen! sen!" And she struck out her pretty little arms, and made the elbows quite pointed, to show how it was to be done, and her little arms were very pretty. She was a sweet little girl.

But the little daughter of the merchant became very angry at this speech, for her father's name was Petersen, and she knew that the name ended in "sen," and therefore she said, as proudly as ever she could—

"But my papa can buy a hundred dollars' worth of bon-bons, and strow them to the children! Can your papa do that?"

"Yes, but my papa," said an author's little daughter, "my papa can put your papa and everybody's papa into the newspaper. All people are afraid of him, my mamma says, for it is my father who rules in the paper."

And the little maiden looked exceeding proud, as though she had been a real princess, who is expected to look proud.

But outside, at the door which was ajar, stood a poor boy, peeping through the crack of the door. He was of such lowly station that he was not even allowed to enter the room. He had turned the spit for the cook, and she had allowed him to stand behind the door, and to look at the well-dressed children who were making a merry day within, and for him that was great deal.

"Oh! To be one of them," thought he, and then he heard what was said, which was certainly calculated to make him very unhappy. His parents at home had not a penny to spare to buy a newspaper, much less could they write one; and what was worst of all, his father's name, and consequently his own, ended completely in "sen," and so he could not turn out well. That was terrible. But after all he had been born, and very well born as it seemed to him; that could not be otherwise.

And that is what was done on that evening.

The poor child at the door

Many years have elapsed since then, and in the course of years children become grown-up persons.

In the town stood a splendid house; it was filled with all kinds of beautiful objects and treasures, and all people wished to see it, even people who dwelt out of town came in to see it. Which of the children of whom we have told might call this house his own? To know that is very easy. No, no; it is not so very easy. The house belonged to the poor little boy who had stood on that night behind the door, and he had become something great, although his name ended in "sen,"— Thorwaldsen.

And the three other children! The children of blood and of money, and of spiritual pride—well, they had nothing wherewith to reproach each other—they turned out well enough, for they had been well dowered by nature—and what they had thought and spoken on that evening long ago was mere children's prattle.

Ole Luk-Oie's visit

OLE LUK-OIE

There's nobody in the whole world who knows so many stories as Ole Luk-Oie. He can tell capital histories.

Towards evening, when the children still sit nicely at table, or upon their stools, Ole Luk-Oie comes. He comes up the stairs quite softly for he walks in his socks; he opens the doors noiselessly, *and whisk!* he squirts sweet milk into the children's eyes, a small, small stream, but enough to prevent them from keeping their eyes open—and thus they cannot see him. He creeps just among them, and blows softly upon their necks; and this makes their heads heavy. Yes, but it doesn't hurt them, for Old Luk-Oie is very fond of the children; he only wants them to be quiet, and that they are not, until they are taken to bed; they are to be quiet that he may tell them stories.

When the children sleep, Ole Luk-Oie sits down upon their bed. He is well dressed, his coat is of silk; but it is impossible to say of what colour, for it shines red, green, and blue, according as he turns. Under each arm he carries an umbrella, the one, with pictures on it, he spreads over the good children, and then they dream all night the most glorious stories; but on his other umbrella nothing at all is painted. This he spreads over the naughty children, and these sleep in a dull way, and when they awake in the morning they have not dreamt of anything at all.

Now we shall hear how Old Luk-Oie, every evening through one whole week, came to a little boy named Hjalmar, and what he told him. There are seven stories; for there are seven days in the week.

MONDAY

"Listen," said Ole Luk-Oie in the evening, when he had put Hjalmar to bed; "now I'll clear up!" And all the flowers in the flower-pots became great trees, stretching out their long branches under the ceiling of the room and along the walls, so that the whole room looked like a beauteous bower; and all the twigs were covered with flowers, and each flower was more beautiful than a rose, and smelt sweet, and one wanted to eat it, it was sweeter than jam! The fruit gleamed like gold, and there were cakes bursting with mere raisins. It was incomparably beautiful! But at the same time a terrible wail sounded from the table-drawer, where Hjalmar's school-book lay.

"Whatever can that be?" said Ole Luk-Oie; and he went to the table, and opened the drawer. It was the slate which was suffering from convulsions, for a wrong number had got into the sum, so that it was nearly falling in pieces; the slate pencil tugged and jumped at its string, as if it had been a little dog who wanted to help the sum; but he could not. And thus there was a great lamentation in Hjalmar's copy book; it was quite terrible to hear. On each page the great letters stood in a row one underneath the other, and each with a little one at its side; that was the copy; and next to these were a few more letters which thought they looked just like the first; and these Hjalmar had written; but they lay down just as if they had tumbled over the pencil lines on which they were to stand.

See, this is how you should hold yourselves," said the copy. "Look, sloping in this way, with a powerful swing!" "Oh, we should be very glad to do that," replied Hjalmar's letters—"but we cannot; we are too weakly!"

"Then you must take medicine," said Ole Luk-Oie. "Oh no," cried they, and they immediately stood up so gracefully, that it was beautiful to behold.

"Yes, now we cannot tell any stories," said Ole Luk-Oie, "now I must exercise them. One, two; one, two!" and thus he exercised the letters; and they stood quite slender, and as beautiful as any copy can be. But when Ole Luk-Oie went away, and Hjalmar looked at them next morning, they were as weak and miserable as ever.

TUESDAY

As soon as Hjalmar was in bed, Ole Luk-Oie touched all the furniture in the room with his little magic squirt, and they immediately began to converse together, and each one spoke of itself with the exception of the spitoon, which stood silent, and was vexed that they should be so vain as to speak only of themselves, and think only of themselves, without any regard for him who stood so modestly in the corner for everyone's use.

Over the chest of drawers hung a great picture in a gilt frame—it was a landscape; one saw therein large old trees, flowers in the grass, and a broad river which flowed round about a forest, past many castles, and far out into the wild ocean.

Ole Luk-Oie touched the painting with his magic squirt, and the birds in it began to sing, the branches of the trees stirred, and the clouds began to move across it: one could see their shadows glide over the landscape.

Now Ole Luk-Oie lifted little Hjalmar up to the frame, and put the boy's feet into the picture, just in the high grass; and there he stood; and the sun shone upon him through the branches of the trees. He ran to the water and seated himself in a little boat which lay there; it was painted red and white, the sails gleamed like silver, and six swans, each with a gold circlet round its neck and a bright blue star on its forehead drew the boat past the great wood, where the trees tell of robbers and witches, and the flowers of the graceful little elves, and of what the butterflies have told them.

Gorgeous fishes, with scales like silver and gold, swam after their boat; sometimes they gave a spring, so that it splashed in the water, and birds, blue and red, little and great, flew after them in two long rows; the gnats danced, and the cockchafers said, "Boom! Boom!" they all wanted to follow Hjalmar, and each one had a story to tell.

That was a pleasure voyage. Sometimes the forest was thick and dark, sometimes like a glorious garden full of sunlight and flowers; and there were great palaces of glass and of marble; on the balconies stood princesses, and these were all little girls whom Hjalmar knew well,—he had already played with them. Each one stretched forth her hand, and held out the prettiest sugar heart which ever a cake-woman could sell; and Hjalmar took hold of each sugar heart as he passed by, and the princess held fast, so that each of them got a piece; she the smaller share, and Hjalmar the larger. At each palace little princes stood sentry. They shouldered golden swords, and caused raisins and tin soldiers to shower down: one could see that they were real princes. Sometimes Hjalmar sailed through forests, sometimes through great halls or through the midst of a town. He also came to the town where his nurse lived, who had carried him in her arms when he was quite a little boy, and who had always been so kind to him; and she nodded and beckoned, and sang the pretty verse she had made herself and had sent to Hjalmar.

> I've loved thee, and kissed thee, Hjalmar, dear boy;
>   I've watched thee waking and sleeping;
> May the good Lord guard thee in sorrow, in joy,
>   And have thee in His keeping.

And all the birds sang too, the flowers danced on their stalks, and the old trees nodded, just as if Ole Luk-Oie had been telling stories to them also.

WEDNESDAY

How the rain was streaming down without. Hjalmar could hear it in his sleep; and when Ole Luk-Oie opened a window, the water stood quite up to the window-sill: there was quite a lake outside, and a noble ship lay close by the house.

"If thou wilt sail with me, little Hjalmar," said Ole Luk-Oie, thou canst voyage to-night to foreign climes, and be back again to-morrow. And Hjalmar suddenly stood in his Sunday clothes upon the glorious ship, and immediately the weather became fine, and they sailed through the streets, and steered round by the church; and now everything was one great wild ocean. They sailed on, until no land was longer to be seen, and they saw a number of storks, who also came from their home, and were travelling towards the hot countries; these storks flew in a row, one behind the other, and they had already flown far—far! One of them was so weary, that his wings would scarcely carry him farther; he was the very last in the row, and soon remained a great way behind the rest; at last he sank, with outspread wings, deeper and deeper; he gave a few more strokes with his pinions, but it was no use; now he touched the rigging of the ship with his feet, then he glided down from the sail, and "bump!" he stood upon the deck.

Now the cabin-boy took him and put him into the hencoop with the fowls, ducks and turkeys; the poor stork stood among them quite embarrassed.

"Just look at the fellow!" said all the fowls.

And the turkey-cock swelled himself up as much as ever he could, and asked the stork who he was; and the ducks walked backwards and quacked to each other "quackery, quackery." And the stork told them of hot Africa, of the pyramids, and of the ostrich, which runs like a wild horse through the desert; but the ducks did not understand what he said, and they said to one another, "We're all of the same opinion, namely, that he's stupid."

"Yes, certainly he's stupid," said the turkey-cock; and then he gobbled. Then the stork was quite silent, and thought of his Africa.

"Those are wonderful thin legs of yours," said the turkey-cock. "Pray how much do they cost a yard?"

"Quack, quack, quack," grinned all the ducks; but the stork

pretended not to hear it at all. "You may just as well laugh too," said the turkey-cock to him, "for that was very wittily said. Or was it perhaps too high for you? Yes, yes, he isn't very penetrating. Let us continue to be interesting among ourselves!" and then he gobbled, and the ducks quacked. "Gick, gack, gick, gack!" It was terrible how they made fun among themselves.

But Hjalmar went to the hencoop, opened the back-door, and called to the stork; and the stork hopped out to him to the deck. Now he had rested, and it seemed as if he nodded at Hjalmar, to thank him. Then he spread his wings, and flew away to the warm countries; but the fowls clucked, and the ducks quacked, and the turkey-cock became fiery red in the face.

"To-morrow we shall make songs of you!" said Hjalmar, and so saying he awoke, and was lying in his linen bed. It was a wonderful journey, that Ole Luk-Oie had caused him to take this night.

THURSDAY

"I tell you what," said Ole Luk-Oie. "You must not be frightened. Here you shall see a little mouse," and he held out his hand with the pretty little creature in it. "It has come to invite you to a wedding. There are two little mice here who are going to enter into the marriage state to-night. They live under the floor of your mother's store-closet; that is said to be a charming dwelling place!"

But how can I get through the little mouse-hole in the floor?" asked Hjalmar.

"Let me manage that," replied Ole Luk-Oie. "I will make you small." And he touched Hjalmar with his magic squirt, and the boy began to shrink and shrink, until he was not so long as a finger. "Now you may borrow the uniform of a tin soldier; I think it would fit you, and it looks well to wear a uniform, when one is in society." "Yes, certainly," said Hjalmar; and in a moment he was dressed like the spiciest of tin soldiers.

"Will your honour not be kind enough to take a seat in your mamma's thimble?" asked the mouse. "Then I shall have the honour of drawing you."

"Will the young lady really take so much trouble?" cried Hjalmar;

and thus they drove to the mouse's wedding. First they came into a long passage beneath the boards, which was only just so high that they could drive through it in the thimble; and the whole passage was lit up with rotten-wood.

"Is there not a delicious smell here?", observed the mouse. "The entire road has been greased with bacon-rinds; and there can be nothing more exquisite."

Now they came into the festive hall. On the right hand stood all the little lady-mice; and they whispered and giggled as if they were making fun of each other. On the left stood all the gentleman-mice, stroking their whiskers with their forepaws; and in the centre of the hall the bridegroom and bride might be seen, standing in a hollow cheese-rind, and kissing each other terribly before all the guests; for this was the betrothal, and the marriage was to follow immediately.

More and more strangers kept flocking in. One mouse was nearly treading another to death; and the happy couple had stationed themselves just in the doorway, so that one could neither come in nor go out. Like the passage the room had been greased with bacon-rinds, and that was the entire banquet; but for the dessert a pea was produced, in which a mouse belonging to the family had bitten the name of the betrothed pair, that is to say the first letter of the name; that was something quite out of the common way.

All the mice said that it was a beautiful wedding, and that the entertainment had been very agreeable. And then Hjalmar drove home again; he had really been in grand company; but he had been obliged to crawl, to make himself little, and to put on a tin soldier's uniform.

FRIDAY

"It is wonderful how many grown-up people there are, who would be glad to have me!" said Ole Luk-Oie; "especially those who have done something wrong. 'Good little Ole,' they say to me, 'we cannot close our eyes, and so we lie all night, and see our evil deeds, which sit on the bedstead like ugly little goblins, and throw hot water over us; will you not come and drive them away, so that we may have a good sleep?'—and then they sigh deeply—'we would really be glad to pay for it. Good night, Ole; the money lies on the window-sill.' But I do nothing for money"—says Ole Luk-Oie.

"What shall we do this evening?" asked Hjalmar.

"I don't know if you care to go to another wedding to-night. It is of a different kind than that of yesterday. Your sister's great doll, that looks like a man, and is called Hermann, is going to marry the doll Bertha. Moreover, it is the dolls' birthday, and therefore they will receive very many presents."

"Yes, I know that," replied Hjalmar. "Whenever the dolls want new clothes my sister lets them keep their birthday or celebrate a wedding; that has certainly happened a hundred times already."

"Yes, but to-night is the hundred and first wedding; and when number one hundred and one is past, it is all over; and that is why it will be so splendid. Only look!"

And Hjalmar looked at the table. There stood the little cardboard house with the windows illuminated, and in front of it all the tin soldiers were presenting arms. The bride and bridegroom sat quite thoughtful, and with good reason, on the floor, leaning against a leg of the table. And Ole Luk-Oie, dressed in the grandmother's black gown, married them to each other. When the ceremony was over, all the pieces of furniture struck up the following beautiful song, which the pencil had written for them. It was sung to the melody of the soldiers' tattoo:—

Let the song swell like the rushing wind,
In honour of those who this day are joined,
Although they stand here so stiff and blind,
Because they are both of a leathery kind.
Hurrah! hurrah! Though they're deaf and blind,
Let the song swell like the rushing wind!

And now they received presents—but they had declined to accept provisions of any kind, for they intended to live on love.

"Shall we now go into a summer lodging, or start on a journey?" asked the bridegroom. And the swallow, who was a great traveller, and the old yard-hen, who had brought up five broods of chickens, were consulted on the subject. And the swallow told of the beautiful warm climes, where the grapes hung in ripe heavy clusters, where the air is mild, and the mountains glow with colours here unknown.

"But you have not our brown cole there!" objected the hen. "I was once in the country, with my children in one summer that lasted five weeks, there was a sand-pit, in which we could walk about and scratch; and we had the entrée to a garden where brown cole grew; it was so hot there, that one could scarcely breathe; and then we have not all the poisonous animals that infest these warm countries of yours, and we are free from robbers! He is a villain who does not consider our country the most beautiful—he certainly does not deserve to be here!" And then the hen wept, and went on: "I have also travelled. I rode in a coop above twelve miles! And there is no pleasure at all in travelling!"

"Yes, the hen is a sensible woman!" said the doll Bertha. "I don't think anything of travelling among mountains, for you only have to go up, and then down again. No, we will go into the sand-pit beyond the gate, and walk about in the cabbage-garden." And so it was settled.

SATURDAY

"Am I to hear some stories now?" asked little Hjalmar, so soon as Ole Luk-Oie had set him to sleep.

"This evening we have no time for that," replied Ole Luk-Oie; and he spread his finest umbrella over the lad. "Only look at these Chinamen!" And the whole umbrella looked like a great China dish, with blue trees and pointed bridges with little Chinamen upon them, who stood there nodding their heads. "We must have the whole world prettily decked out for to-morrow morning," said Ole Luk-Oie, "for that will be a holiday, it will be Sunday. I will go to the church steeples to see that the little church goblins are polishing the bells, that they may sound sweetly. I will go out into the field, and see if the breezes are blowing the dust from the grass and leaves; and what is the greatest work of all, I will bring down all the stars, to polish them. I take them in my apron; but first each one must be numbered, and the holes, in which they are placed up there, must be numbered likewise, so that they may be placed in the same grooves again; otherwise they would not sit fast, and we should have too many shooting stars; for one after another would fall down."

"Hark ye, do you know, Mr. Ole Luk-Oie!" said an old portrait which hung on the wall where Hjalmar slept, "I am Hjalmar's great-grandfather; I thank you for telling the boy stories; but you must not confuse his ideas. The stars cannot come down and be polished! The stars are world-orbs, just like our own earth, and that is just the good thing about them."

"I thank you, old great-grandfather," said Ole Luk-Oie, "I thank you! You are the head of the family. You are the ancestral head; but I am older than you! I am an old heathen: the Romans and Greeks called me the Dream-God! I have been in the noblest houses, and am admitted there still! I know how to act with great people and with small! Now you may tell your story!" and Ole Luk-Oie took his umbrella, and went away.

"Well, well! May one not even give an opinion now-a-days?" grumbled the old portrait. And Hjalmar awoke.

SUNDAY

"Good evening!" said Ole Luk-Oie—and Hjalmar nodded, and then ran and turned his great-grandfather's portrait against the wall, that it might not interrupt them, as it had done yesterday.

"Now you must tell me stories; about the five green peas that lived in one shell, and about the cock's foot that paid court to the hen's foot, and of the darning-needle who gave herself such airs because she thought herself a working needle."

"There may be too much of a good thing!" said Ole Luk-Oie. "You know that I prefer showing you something. I will show you my brother. His name, like mine, is Ole Luk-Oie, but he never comes to anyone more than once; and he takes him, to whom he comes, upon his horse, and tells him stories. He only knows two. One of these is so exceedingly beautiful, that no one in the world can imagine it, and the other so horrible and dreadful, that it cannot be described." And then Ole Luk-Oie lifted little Hjalmar up to the window, and said, "There you will see my brother, the other Ole Luk-Oie. They also call him Death! Do you see, he does not look so terrible as they make him in the picture-books, where he is only a skeleton. No, that is silver embroidery that he has on his coat; that is a splendid hussar's uniform;

a mantle of black velvet flies behind him over the horse. See how he gallops along!"

And Hjalmar saw how this Ole Luk-Oie rode away, and took young people as well as old upon his horse. Some of them he put before him, and some behind; but he always asked first—"How stands it with the mark-book?" "Well,"—they all replied. "Yes, let me see it myself," he said; and then each one had to show him the book; and those who had "very well," and "remarkably well," written in their books, were placed in front of his horse, and a lovely story was told to them; while those who had "middling," or "tolerably well," had to sit up behind, and heard a very terrible story indeed. They trembled and wept, and wanted to jump off the horse, but this they could not do, for they had all, as it were, grown fast to it.

"But death is a most splendid Ole Luk-Oie," said Hjalmar, "I am not afraid of him!" "Nor need you be," replied Ole Luk-Oie, "but see that you have a good mark-book!"

"Yes, that is improving!" muttered the great-grandfather's picture. "It is of some use giving one's opinion." And now he was satisfied.

You see, that is the story of Ole Luk-Oie; and now, he may tell you more himself, this evening!

THE STORY OF A MOTHER

A mother sat by her little child; she was very sorrowful, and feared that it would die. Its little face was pale, and its eyes were closed. The child drew its breath with difficulty, and sometimes so deeply, as if it were sighing; and then the mother looked more sorrowfully than before on the little creature.

Then there was a knock at the door, and a poor old man came in, wrapped up in something that looked like a great horse-cloth, for that keeps warm, and he required it; for it was cold winter. Without, every-thing was covered with ice and snow, and the wind blew so sharply that it cut one's face.

And as the old man trembled with cold, and the child was quiet for a moment, the mother went and put some beer in the stove in a little pot, to warm it for him. The old man sat down and rocked the cradle, and the mother seated herself on an old chair by him, looked at her sick child, that drew its breath so painfully, and seized the little hand.

"You think I shall keep it, do you not?" she asked. "The good God will not take it from me!"

And the old man—he was *Death*—nodded in such a strange way, that it might just as well mean *yes* as *no*. And the mother cast down her eyes, and tears rolled down her cheeks. Her head became heavy; for three days and three nights she had not closed her eyes; and now she slept, but only for a minute; then she started up and shivered with cold. "What is that?" she asked, and looked round on all sides; but the old man was gone, and her little child was gone; he had taken it with him. And there in the corner the old clock was humming and whirring; the heavy leaden weight ran down to the floor—plump—and the clock stopped.

But the poor mother rushed out of the house crying for her child.

Out in the snow sat a woman in long black garments, and she said, "Death has been with you in your room; I saw him hasten away with your child; he strides faster than the wind, and never brings back what he has taken away."

"Only tell me which way he has gone,"—said the mother. "Tell me the way, and I will find him."

"I know him;" said the woman in the black garments, "but before I tell you, you must sing me all the songs that you have sung to your child. I love those songs; I have heard them before; I am Night, and I saw your tears when you sang them."

"I will sing them all, all!" said the mother. "But do not detain me, that I may overtake him, and find my child."

But Night sat dumb and still. Then the mother wrung her hands, and sang and wept. And there were many songs but yet more tears. And then Night said, "Go to the right into the dark fir-wood; for I saw Death take that path with your little child."

Deep in the forest there was a cross road, and she did not know which way to take. There stood a blackthorn bush, with not a leaf nor a blossom upon it; for it was in the cold winter time, and icicles hung from the twigs.

"Have you not seen Death go by, with my little child." "Yes," replied the bush, "but I shall not tell you which way he went, unless you warm me on your bosom. I'm freezing to death here, I'm turning to ice."

And she pressed the blackthorn bush to her bosom, quite close that it might be well warmed. And the thorns pierced into her flesh, and her blood oozed out in great drops. But the blackthorn shot out fresh green leaves, and blossomed in the dark winter night; so warm is the heart of a sorrowing mother! And the blackthorn bush told her the way that she should go.

Then she came to a great lake on which there were neither ships nor boats. The lake was not frozen enough to carry her, nor sufficiently open to allow her to wade through, and yet she must cross it if she was to find her child. Then she laid herself down to drink the lake; and that was impossible for any one to do. But the sorrowing mother thought that perhaps a miracle might be wrought.

"No, that can never succeed," said the lake. "Let us rather see how we can agree. I'm fond of collecting pearls, and your eyes are the two clearest I have ever seen; if you will weep them out into me I will carry you over into the great greenhouse where Death lives, and cultivates flowers and trees; each of these is a human life."

"Oh, what would I not give to get my child!" said the afflicted mother, and she wept yet more, and her eyes fell into the depths of the lake, and became two costly pearls. But the lake lifted her up, as if she sat in a swing, and she was wafted to the opposite shore, where stood a wonderful house, miles in length. One could not tell if it was a mountain, containing forests and caves, or a place that had been built. But the poor mother could not see it, for she had wept her eyes out.

"Where shall I find Death, who went away with my little child?" she asked.

"He has not arrived here yet," said an old grey-haired woman, who was going about and watching the hothouse of Death. "How have you found your way here, and who helped you?"

"The good God has helped me," she replied. "He is merciful, and you will be merciful too. Where shall I find my little child?"

"I do not know it," said the old woman, "and you cannot see. Many flowers and trees have faded this night, and Death will soon come and transplant them. You know very well that every human being has his tree of life or his flower of life, just as each is arranged. They look like

The mother watching her sick child

other plants; but their hearts beat. Children's hearts can beat too! Think of this, perhaps you may recognize the beating of your child's heart. But what will you *give* me if I tell you what more you must do?"

"I have nothing more to give," said the afflicted mother. "But I will go for you to the ends of the earth."

"I have nothing for you to do there," said the old woman, "but you can give me your long black hair. You must know yourself that it is beautiful, and it pleases me! You can take my white hair for it, and that is always something."

"Do you ask for nothing more?" asked she. "I will give you that gladly," and she gave her beautiful hair, and received in exchange the old woman's white hair.

And then they went into the great hothouse of Death, where flowers and trees were growing marvellously intertwined. There stood fine hyacinths under glass bells; some quite fresh, others somewhat sickly, water-snakes were twining about them, and black crabs clung tightly to the stalks. There stood gallant palm trees, oaks, and plantains, and parsley and blooming thyme. Each tree and flower had its name; each was a human life; the people were still alive, one in China, another in Greenland, scattered about in the world. There were great trees thrust into little pots, so that they stood quite crowded, and were nearly bursting the pots; there was also many a little weakly flower in rich earth, with moss round about it, cared for and tended. But the sorrowful mother bent down over all the smallest plants, and heard the human heart beating in each, and out of millions she recognized that of her child.

"That is it!" she cried, and stretched out her hand over a little crocus-flower, which hung down quite sick and pale.

"Do not touch the flower," said the old dame. "But place yourself here, and when Death comes—I expect him every minute—then don't let him pull up the plant, but threaten him that you will do the same to the other plants, then he'll be frightened. He has to account for them all; not one may be pulled up till he receives commission from Heaven."

And all at once there was an icy cold rush through the hall, and the blind mother felt that Death was arriving.

"How did you find your way hither?" said he. "How have you been able to come quicker than I." "I am a mother," she answered.

And Death stretched out his long hand towards the little delicate flower; but she kept her hands tight about it, and held it fast; and yet she was full of anxious care lest she should touch one of the leaves. Then Death breathed upon her hands, and she felt that his breath was colder than the icy wind; and her hands sank down powerless.

"You can do nothing against me," said Death. "But the merciful God can," she replied.

"I only do what He commands," said Death. "I am his gardener. I take all his trees and flowers and transplant them into the great Paradise gardens, in the unknown land. But how they will flourish there, and how it is there, I may not tell you." "Give me back my child," said the mother; and she wept and implored. All at once she grasped two pretty flowers with her two hands, and called to Death, "I'll tear off all your flowers, for I am in despair!"

"Do not touch them," said Death. "You say you are so unhappy, and now you would make another mother just as unhappy?" "Another mother?" said the poor woman; and she let the flowers go.

"There are your eyes for you," said Death. "I have fished them up out of the lake; they gleamed up quite brightly. I did not know that they were yours. Take them back, they are clearer now than before, and then look down into the deep well close by. I will tell you the names of the two flowers you wanted to pull up, and you will see what you were about to frustrate and destroy."

And she looked down into the well, and it was a happiness to see how one of them became a blessing to the world, how much joy and gladness she diffused around her. And the woman looked at the life of the other, and it was made up of care and poverty, misery and woe.

"Both are the will of God!" said Death.

"Which of them is the flower of misfortune, and which the blessed one?" she asked.

"That I may not tell you," answered Death; "but this much you shall hear, that one of these two flowers is that of your child. It was the fate of your child that you saw, the future of your own child!"

Then the mother screamed aloud for terror. "Which of them belongs to my child? Tell me that! Release the innocent child! Let my child free from all that misery! Rather carry it away! Carry it into God's kingdom! Forget my tears, forget my entreaties, and all that I have done!"

"I do not understand you!" said Death. "Will you have your child back, or shall I carry it to that place that you know not?"

Then the mother wrung her hands, and fell on her knees, and prayed to the good God. "Hear me not when I pray against Thy will, which is at all times the best! Hear me not! Hear me not!" And she let her head sink down on her bosom.

And Death went away with her child into the unknown land.

THE LOVERS

A whip-top and a little ball were together in a drawer among some other toys; and the top said to the ball: "Shall we not be bridegroom and bride, as we live together in the same box?" But the ball, which had a coat of morocco leather, and was just as conceited as any fine lady, would make no answer to such a proposal.

Next day the little boy came to whom the toys belonged: he painted the top red and yellow, and hammered a brass nail into it; and it looked splendid, when the top turned round!

"Look at me!" he cried to the little ball, "What do you say now? Shall we not be engaged to each other? We suit one another so well! You jump, and I dance! No one could be happier than we two should be."

"Indeed? Do you think so?" replied the little ball. "Perhaps you do not know that my papa and my mamma were morocco slippers, and that I have a Spanish cork inside me?"

"Yes, but I am made of mahogany," said the top; "and the mayor himself turned me. He has a turning-lathe of his own, and it amused him greatly."

"Can I depend upon that?" asked the little ball.

"May I never be whipped again, if it is not true!" replied the top.

"You can speak well for yourself," observed the ball. "But I cannot grant your request. I am as good as engaged to a swallow; every time I leap up into the air, he puts his head out of his nest and says, 'Will you?' And now I have silently said 'Yes,' and that is as good as half engaged—but I promise I will never forget you!"

"Yes, that will be much good!" said the top. And they spoke no more to each other.

Next day, the ball was taken out by the boy. The top saw how it flew high into the air, like a bird; at last one could no longer see it. Each time

The maid finds the whip-top

it came back again, but gave a high leap when it touched the earth, and that was done either from its longing to mount up again, or because it had a Spanish cork in its body. But the ninth time the little ball remained absent, and did not come back again; and the boy sought and sought, but it was gone.

"I know very well where it is!" sighed the top. "It is in the swallow's nest, and has married the swallow!"

The more the top thought of this, the more it longed for the ball. Just because it could not get the ball, its love increased; and the fact that the ball had chosen another, formed a peculiar feature in the case. So the top danced round and hummed, but always thought of the little ball, which became more and more beautiful in his fancy. Thus several years went by, and now it was an old love.

And the top was no longer young! But one day he was gilt all over; never had he looked so handsome; he was now a golden top, and sprang till he hummed again. Yes, that was something worth seeing! But all at once he sprang too high, and—he was gone!

They looked and looked, even in the cellar, but he was not to be found. Where could he be?

He had jumped into the dust-box, where all kinds of things were lying: cabbage-stalks, sweepings, and dust, that had fallen down from the roof.

"Here's a nice place to lie in! The gilding will soon leave me here. Among what a rabble have I alighted!" And then he looked sideways at a long leafless cabbage-stump, and at a curious round thing that looked like an old apple; but it was not an apple it was an old ball, which had lain for years in the gutter on the roof, and was quite saturated with water.

"Thank goodness, here comes one of us, with whom one can talk!" said the little ball, and looked at the gilt top. "I am really morocco worked by maidens' hands, and have a Spanish cork within me; but no one would think it, to look at me. I was very nearly marrying a swallow but I fell into the gutter on the roof, and have lain there full five years and become quite wet through. You may believe me, that's a long time for a young girl."

But the top said nothing. He thought of his old love, and the more he heard, the clearer it became to him that this was she.

Then came the servant-girl, and wanted to turn out the dust-box. "Aha, there's a gilt top!" she cried.

And so the top was brought again to notice and honour, but nothing was heard of the little ball. And the top spoke no more of his old love; for that dies away, when the beloved object has lain for five years in a roof-gutter, and got wet through; yes, one does not know her again when one meets her in the dust-box.

THE OLD STREET LAMP

Did you ever hear the story of the old street lamp? It is not very remarkable, but it may be listened to for once in a way.

It was a very honest old lamp, that had done its work for many, many years, but which was now to be pensioned off. It hung for the last time to its post, and gave light to the street. It felt as an old dancer at the theatre, who is dancing for the last time, and who to-morrow will sit forgotten in her garret. The lamp was in great fear about the morrow, for it knew that it was to appear in the council-house, and to be inspected by the mayor and the council, to see if it were fit for further service or not.

And then it was to be decided, whether it was to show its light in future for the inhabitants of some suburb, or in the country in some manufactory; perhaps it would have to go at once into an iron-foundry to be melted down. In this last case anything might be made of it; but the question whether it would remember, in its new state, that it had been a street lamp, troubled it terribly. Whatever might happen, this much was certain, that it would be separated from the watchman and his wife, whom it had got to look upon as quite belonging to its family. When the lamp had been hung up for the first time the watchman was a young sturdy man; it happened to be the very evening on which he entered on his office. Yes, that was certainly a long time ago, when it first became a lamp, and he a watchman. The wife was a little proud in those days. Only in the evening when she went by, she deigned to glance at the lamp; in the daytime never. But now, in these latter years, when all three, the watchman, his wife, and the lamp, had grown old, the wife had also tended it, cleaned it, and provided it with oil. The two old people were thoroughly honest; never had they cheated the lamp of a single drop of the oil provided for it.

It was the lamp's last night in the street; and to-morrow it was to go to the council-house;—those were two dark thoughts! No wonder, that it did not burn brightly. But many other thoughts passed through its brain. On what a number of events had it shone—how much it had seen! Perhaps as much as the mayor and the whole council had beheld. But it did not give utterance to these thoughts, for it was a good honest old lamp, that would not willingly hurt any one, and least of all those in authority. Many things passed through its mind, and at times its light flashed up. In such moments it had a feeling, that it, too, would be remembered. "There was that handsome young man—it is certainly a long while ago—he had a letter, on pink paper with a gilt edge. It was so prettily written, as if by a lady's hand. Twice he read it, and kissed it, and looked up to me with eyes, which said plainly, 'I am the happiest of men!' Only he and I know what was written in this first letter from his true love. Yes! I remember another pair of eyes. It is wonderful how our thoughts fly about! There was a funeral procession in the street; the young beautiful lady lay in the decorated hearse, in a coffin adorned with flowers and wreaths; and a number of torches quite darkened my light. The people stood in crowds by the houses; and all followed the procession. But when the torches had passed from before my face, and I looked round, a single person stood leaning against my post, weeping. I shall never forget the mournful eyes that looked up to me!" This and similar thoughts occupied the old street lantern which shone to-night for the last time.

The sentry, relieved from his post, at least, knows who is to succeed him and may whisper a few words to him; but the lamp did not know its successor: and yet it might have given a few useful hints with respect to rain and fog, and some information as to how far the rays of the moon lit up the pavement, from what direction the wind usually came, and much more of the same kind.

On the bridge of the gutter stood three persons who wished to introduce themselves to the lamp; for they thought the lamp itself could appoint its successor. The first was a herring's head, that could gleam with light in the darkness. He thought it would be a great saving of oil if they put him up on the post. Number two was a piece of rotten wood, which also glimmers in the dark. He conceived himself descended from an old stem, once the pride of the forest. The third person was a glow-worm. Where this one had come from, the lamp could not imagine; but there it was, and it could give light. But the rotten wood and the herring's head swore by all that was good, that it only gave light at certain times, and could not be brought into competition with themselves.

The old lamp declared that not one of them gave sufficient light, to fill the office of a street lamp; but not one of them would believe this. When they heard that the lamp had not the office to give away, they were very glad of it; and declared that the lamp was too decrepid to make a good choice.

At the same moment the wind came careering from the corner of the street, and blew through the air-holes of the old street lamp. "What's this I hear?" he asked. "You are to go away to-morrow? Do I see you for the last time? Then I must make you a present at parting. I will blow into your brain-box in such a way, that you shall be able in future not only to remember everything you have seen and heard, but that you shall have such light within you as shall enable you to see all that is read of or spoken of in your presence."

"Yes, that is really much, very much!" said the old lamp. "I thank you heartily. I only hope I shall not be melted down."

"That is not likely to happen at once!" said the wind. "Now I will blow a memory into you; if you receive several presents of this kind, you may pass your old days very agreeably."

"If I am only not melted down!" said the lamp again. "Or should I retain my memory even in that case?"

"Be sensible, old lamp," said the wind; and he blew, and at that moment the moon stepped forth from behind the clouds.

"What will you give the old lamp?" asked the wind.

"I'll give nothing," replied the moon. "I am on the wane, and the lamps never lighted me; but on the contrary I've often given light for the lamps." And with these words the moon hid herself again behind the clouds, to be safe from further importunity.

A drop now fell upon the lamp, as if from the roof; but the drop explained that it came from the clouds, and was a present—perhaps the best present possible. "I shall penetrate you so completely that you shall receive the faculty, if you wish it, to turn into rust in one night, and to crumble into dust."

The lamp considered this a bad present, and the wind thought so too.

"Does no one give more? Does no one give more?" it blew as loud as it could.

Then a bright shooting star fell down, forming a long bright stripe.

"What was that?" cried the herring's head. "Did not a star fall? I

really think it went into the lamp! Certainly if such high-born person-
ages try for this office, we may say good-night and betake ourselves
home."

And so they did, all three. But the old lamp shed a marvellously
strong light around. "That was a glorious present," it said. "The bright
stars which I have always admired and which shine as I could never
shine though I shone with all my might, have noticed me, a poor old
lamp, and have sent me a present, by giving me the faculty that all I
remember and see so clearly, as if it stood before me, shall also be seen
by all whom I love. And in this lies the true pleasure; for joy that we
cannot share with others is only half enjoyed."

"That sentiment does honour to your heart," said the wind. "But for
that wax-lights are necessary. If these are not lit up in you, your rare
faculties will be of no use to others. Look you, the stars did not think of
that; they take you and every other light for wax. But I will go down."
And he went down.

"Good heavens! Wax light!" exclaimed the lamp. "I never had those
till now, nor am I likely to get them! If I am only not melted down!"

The next day.—Yes, it will be best that we pass over the next day.—The
next evening the lamp was resting in a grandfather's chair. And guess
where! In the watchman's dwelling. He had begged as a favour of the
mayor and the council, that he might keep the street lamp, in consideration of his long and faithful service—for he himself had put up and lit
the lantern for the first time on the first day of entering on his duties
four-and-twenty years ago. He looked upon it as his child, for he had
no other; and the lamp was given to him.

Now it lay in the great arm-chair, by the warm stove. It seemed as if
the lamp had grown bigger, now that it occupied the chair all alone.

The old people sat at supper, and looked kindly at the old lamp, to
whom they would willingly have granted a place at their table.

Their dwelling was certainly only a cellar two yards below the foot-
way; and one had to cross a stone passage to get into the room. But
within it was very comfortable and warm; and strips of list had been
nailed to the door. Everything looked clean and neat, and there were
curtains round the bed and the little windows. On the window-sill
stood two curious flower-pots, which sailor Christian had brought
home from the East or West Indies. They were only of clay, and

represented two elephants. The backs of these creatures had been cut off; and instead of them there bloomed from within the earth with which one elephant was filled, some very excellent chives,—and that was the kitchen garden; out of the other grew a great geranium,—and that was the flower garden. On the wall hung a great coloured print representing the Congress of Vienna. There you had all the kings and emperors at once. A clock with heavy weights went "tick, tick!" and in fact, it always went too fast; but the old people declared this was far better than if it went too slow. They ate their supper, and the street lamp lay, as I have said, in the arm-chair close beside the stove. It seemed to the lamp as if the whole world had been turned round. But when the old watchman looked at it, and spoke of all that they two had gone through, in rain and in fog, in the bright short nights of summer, and in the long winter nights, when the snow beat down, and one longed to be at home in the cellar,—then the old lamp found its wits again. It saw everything as clearly as if it was happening then; yes, the wind had kindled a capital light for it.

The old people were very active and industrious; not a single hour was wasted in idleness. On Sunday afternoon some book or other was brought out; generally a book of travels. And the old man read aloud about Africa, about the great woods, with elephants running about wild; and the old woman listened intently, and looked furtively at the clay elephants which served for flower-pots.

"I can almost imagine it to myself!" said she. And the lamp wished particularly that a wax candle had been there, and could be lighted up in it; for then the old woman would be able to see everything to the smallest detail, just as the lamp saw it—the tall trees with great branches all entwined, the naked black men on horseback, and whole droves of elephants crashing through the reeds with their broad clumsy feet.

"Of what use are all my faculties if I can't obtain a wax light?" sighed the lamp. "They have only oil and tallow candles,—and that's not enough!"

One day a great number of wax candle ends came down into the cellar; the larger pieces were burned, and the smaller ones the old woman used for waxing her thread. So there were wax candles enough; but no one thought of putting a little piece into the lamp.

"Here I stand with my rare faculties!" thought the lamp. "I carry

The old street lamp in good quarters

everything within me, and cannot let them partake of it; they don't know that I am able to cover these white walls with the most gorgeous tapestry, to change them into noble forests, and all that they can possibly wish."

The lamp, however, was kept neat and clean, and stood all shining in a corner, where it caught the eyes of all. Strangers considered it a bit of old rubbish; but the old people did not care for that; they loved the lamp.

One day—it was the old watchman's birthday—the old woman approached the lantern, smiling to herself, and said:—"I'll make an illumination to-day, in honour of my old man!" And the lamp rattled its metal cover, for it thought—"Well, at last there will be a light within me!" But only oil was produced, and no wax light appeared. The lamp burned throughout the whole evening, but now understood, only too well, that the gift of the stars would be a hidden treasure for all its life. Then it had a dream—for one possessing its rare faculties, to dream was not difficult. It seemed as if the old people were dead, and that itself had been taken to the iron foundry to be melted down. It felt as much alarmed as on that day when it was to appear in the council-house to be inspected by the mayor and council. But though the power had been given it to fall into rust and dust at will, it did not use this power. It was put into the furnace and turned into an iron candlestick, as fair a candlestick as you would desire,—one on which wax lights were to be burned. It had received the form of an angel, holding a great nosegay; and the wax light was to be placed in the middle of the nosegay.

The candlestick had a place assigned to it on a green writing table. The room was very comfortable; many books stood round about the walls, which were hung with beautiful pictures; it belonged to a poet. Everything that he wrote or composed showed itself round about him. Nature appeared sometimes in thick dark forests, sometimes in beautiful meadows, where the storks strutted about, sometimes again in a ship sailing on the foaming ocean, or in the blue sky with all its stars.

"What faculties lie hidden in me!" said the old lamp, when it awoke. "I could almost wish to be melted down! But no! that must not be, so long as the old people live! They love me for myself; they have cleaned me, and brought me oil. I am as well off now, as the whole congress, in looking at which they also take pleasure."

And from that time it enjoyed more inward peace; and the honest old street lamp had well deserved to enjoy it.

TWO BROTHERS

On one of the Danish Islands where old Thingstones, the seats of justice of our forefathers, are found in the fields, and great trees tower in the beechwoods, there lies a little town, whose low houses are covered with red tiles. In one of these houses wondrous things were brewed over glowing coals on the open hearth, there was a boiling in glasses, a mixing and a distilling, and herbs were cut up, and bruised in mortars, and an elderly man attended to all this.

"One must only do the right thing," said he, "yes, the right thing; one must learn the truth about every created particle, and keep close to this truth."

In the room with the good housewife sat her two sons, still small; but with grown-up thoughts. The mother had always spoken to them of right and justice, and had exhorted them to hold truth fast, declaring that it was as the countenance of the Almighty in this world.

The elder of the boys looked roguish and enterprising; it was his

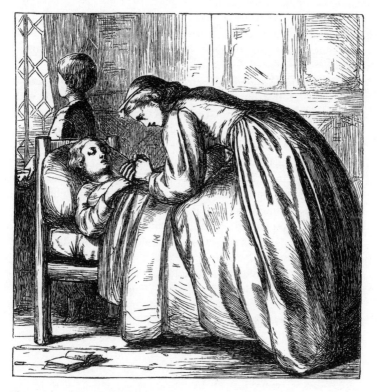

The two brothers in their bedroom

delight to read of the forces of nature, of the sun and of the stars; no fairy tale pleased him so much as these. O! How glorious it must be, he thought, to go out on voyages of discovery, or to find out how the wings of birds could be imitated, and then to fly through the air; yes, to find that out would be the right thing; father was right, and mother was right, truth keeps the world together.

The younger brother was quieter, and quite lost himself in books. When he read of Jacob clothing himself in sheepskins to be like Esau, and to cheat his brother of his birthright, his little fist would clench in anger against the deceiver; when he read of tyrants and of all the wickedness and wrong that is in the world, the tears stood in his eyes, and he was quite filled with the thought of the right and truth which must and will at last be triumphant. One evening he already lay in bed; but the curtains were not yet drawn close, and the light streamed in upon him; he had taken the book with him to bed, because he wanted to finish reading the story of Solon.

And his thoughts lifted and carried him away marvellously, and it seemed to him that his bed became a ship, careering onward with swelling sails. Did he dream? Or what was happening to him? It glided onward over the rolling waters and the great ocean of time, and he heard the voice of Solon. In a strange tongue, and yet intelligible to him, he heard the Danish motto, "With law the land is ruled."

And the genius of the human race stood in the humble room, and bent down over the bed, and printed a kiss on the boy's forehead. "Be thou strong in fame, and strong in the battle of life! With the truth in thy breast fly thou towards the land of truth!"

The elder brother was not yet in bed; he stood at the window gazing out at the mists that rose from the meadows; they were not elves dancing there, as the old muse had told him; he knew better; they were vapours, warmer than the air, and that consequently mounted. A shooting star gleamed athwart the sky, and the thoughts of the boy were roused from the mists of the earth to the shining meteor. The stars of heaven twinkled, and golden threads seemed to hang from them down upon the earth.

"Fly with me," it sang and sounded in the boy's heart, and the mighty genius, swifter than the bird, than the arrow, than anything that flies with earthly means, carried him aloft to the region where rays stretching from star to star bind the heavenly bodies to each other—our earth revolved in the thin air—the cities on its surface seemed quite close together, and through the sphere it sounded: "What is near, what is far, when the mighty genius of mind lifts them up?"

And again the boy stood at the window and gazed forth, and the younger brother lay in his bed, and their mother called them by their names, "Anders Sandoe" and "Hans Christian!"

Denmark knows them; the world knows them—the two brothers Oersted.

THE BELL

At evening, in the narrow streets of the great city, when the sun went down and the clouds shone like gold among the chimneys, there was frequently heard, sometimes by one, and sometimes by another, a strange tone, like the sound of a church bell; but it was only heard for a moment at a time, for in the streets there was a continual rattle of carriages, and endless cries of men and women—and that is a sad interruption. Then people said, "Now the evening bell sounds, now the sun is setting!"

Those who were walking outside the city, where the houses stood farther from each other, with gardens and little fields between, saw the evening sky looking still more glorious, and heard the sound of the bell far more clearly. It was as though the tones came from a church, deep in the still quiet, fragrant wood, and people looked in that direction and became quite meditative.

Now a certain time passed—and one said to another, "Is there not a church out yonder in the wood? That bell has a peculiarly beautiful sound! Shall we not go out and look at it more closely?" And rich people drove out, and poor people walked; but the way seemed marvellously long to them, and when they came to a number of willow trees that grew on the margin of the forest, they sat down and looked up to the long branches, and thought they were now really in the green wood. The pastrycook from the town came there too, and pitched his tent; but another pastrycook came and hung up a bell just over his own

The Prince goes in search of the bell

tent, in fact a bell that had been tarred so as to resist the rain—but it had no clapper. And when the people went home again, they declared the whole affair had been very romantic, and that meant much more than merely that they had taken tea. Three persons declared that they had penetrated into the wood to where it ended; and that they had always heard the strange sound of bells, but it had appeared to them as if it came from the town. One of the three wrote a song about it, and said, that the sound was like the song of a mother singing to a dear good child; no melody could be more beautiful than the sound of that bell.

The Emperor of that country was also informed of it, and promised that the person who could really find out whence the sound came, should have the title of "Bell-finder"—even if it should turn out not to be a bell.

Many went to the forest, on account of the good entertainment there; but there was only one, who came back with a kind of explanation. No one had penetrated deep enough into the wood, nor had he; but he said that the sound came from a very great owl in a hollow tree; it was an owl of wisdom, that kept knocking its head continually against the tree, but whether the sound came from the owl's head, or from the trunk of the tree, he could not say with certainty. He was invested with the title "Bell-finder," and every year wrote a short treatise upon the owl; and people were just as wise after reading his works as they were before.

On a certain day a confirmation was held. The clergymen had spoken well and impressively, and the candidates for confirmation were quite moved. It was an important day for them; for from being children, they became grown-up people, and the childish soul was as it were to be transferred to a more sensible person. The sun shone gloriously, the confirmed children marched out of the town, and from the wood the great mysterious bell sounded with peculiar strength. They at once wished to go out to it, and all felt this wish, except three. One of these desired to go home to try on her ball-dress; the second was a poor boy, who had borrowed the coat and boots in which he was confirmed, from the son of his landlord, and he had to give them back at an appointed time; the third said he never went to a strange place unless his parents went with him, that he had always been an obedient son, and would continue to be so, even after he was confirmed, and they were not to laugh at him! But they did laugh at him, nevertheless.

So these three did not go, but the others trotted on. The sun shone, and the birds sang, and the young people sang too, and held each other by the hand, for they had not yet received any office and were all alike before Heaven on that day. But two of the smallest soon became weary and returned to the town, and two little girls sat down to bind wreaths and did not go with the rest. And when the others came to the willow trees where the pastrycook lived, they said: "Well, now we are out here, the bell does not really exist, it is only an imaginary thing."

Then suddenly the bell began to ring in the forest, with such a deep and solemn sound, that four or five determined to go still deeper into the wood. The leaves hung very close, it was really difficult to get forward; lilies of the valley and anemones grew thick, and blooming convolvolus and blackberry bushes stretched in long garlands from tree to tree, where the nightingales sang and the sunbeams played. It was splendid; but the path was not practicable for girls, they would have torn their clothes. There lay great blocks of stone covered with mosses of all colours; the fresh spring-water gushed forth, and it sounded strangely, almost like, "luck, luck."

"That cannot be the bell!" said one of the party, and he laid himself down and listened. "That should be properly studied!" and he remained there and let the others go on.

They came to a house built of the bark of trees, and of twigs, a great tree laden with wild apples, stretched out its branches over the dwelling, as though it would pour its whole blessing upon the roof, which was covered with blooming roses, the long branches turned about the gables, and from the gable hung a little bell. Could that be the bell they had heard? They all agreed that it was, except one; this dissentient said that the bell was too small, and too delicate to be heard at such a distance, and that they were quite different sounds that had so deeply moved the human heart. He who spoke thus was a King's son, and the others declared that a person of that kind always wanted to be wiser than every one else.

Therefore they let him go alone, and as he went, his mind was more and more impressed with the solitude of the forest, but still he heard the little bell, at which the others were rejoicing; and sometimes, when the wind carried towards him sounds from the pastrycook's abode, he could hear how the party there were singing at their tea. But the deep tones of the bell sounded louder still; sometimes it was as if an organ were playing to it; the sound came from the left, the side in which the heart is placed.

Now there was a rustling in the bushes, and a little boy stood before the Prince, a boy with wooden shoes, and such a short jacket, that one could plainly see what long wrists he had. They knew one another; the boy was the youngster who had been confirmed that day, and had not been able to come with the rest, because he had to go home and give up the borrowed coat and boots to his landlord's son. This he had done, and had then wandered away alone in his poor clothes and his wooden shoes, for the bell sounded so invitingly he had been obliged to come out.

"We can go together!" said the Prince. But the poor lad in the wooden shoes was quite embarrassed. He pulled at the short sleeves of his jacket and said he was afraid he could not come quickly enough; besides he thought the bell must be sought on the right hand, for there the place was great and glorious.

"But then we shall not meet at all!" said the Prince, and he nodded to the poor boy who went away into the deepest, deepest part of the forest, where the thorns tore his shabby garments and scratched his face, his feet and his hands. The Prince also had two or three brave rents, but the sun shone bright on his path; and it is he whom we will follow, for he was a brisk companion.

"I must and will find the bell!" said he, "though I have to go to the end of the world."

Ugly apes sat up in the trees, and grinned and showed their teeth. "Shall we beat him?" said they. "Shall we smash him? He's a King's son!"

But he went contentedly further and further into the forest, where the most wonderful trees grew; there stood white star-lilies with blood-red stamens, sky-blue tulips that glittered in the breeze, and apple-trees whose apples looked completely like great shining soap-bubbles; only think how those trees must have gleamed in the sun-beams! All around lay the most beautiful green meadows, where hart and hind played in the grass, and noble oaks and beech trees grew there; and when the bark of any tree split, grass and long climbing plants grew out of the rifts; there were also great wooded tracts with quiet lakes, on which white swans floated, and flapped their wings. The Prince often stood still and listened, often he thought that the bell sounded upwards to him from one of the deep lakes; but soon he noticed that the sound did not come from thence, but that the bell was sounding deeper in the wood.

Now the sun went down. The sky shone red as fire; it became quite quiet in the forest, and he sank on his knees, sang his evening hymn, and said, "I shall never find what I seek! Now the sun is going down, and the night, the dark night is coming. But perhaps I can once more see the round sun, before he disappears beneath the horizon; I will climb upon the rocks, for they are higher than the highest trees."

And he seized hold of roots and climbing plants, and clambered up the wet stones, where the water-snakes writhed and the toads seemed to be barking at him; but he managed to climb up, before the sun which he could see from this elevation, had quite set. Oh, what splendour! The sea, the great glorious sea, which rolled its great billows towards the shore, lay stretched out before him, and the sun stood aloft like a great flaming altar, there where sea and sky met; everything melted together in glowing colours; the wood sang, and his heart sang too. All nature was a great holy church, in which trees and floating clouds were the pillars and beams, flowers and grass the velvet carpet, and the heavens themselves the vaulted roof. The red colours faded up there, when the sun sank to rest; but millions of stars were lighted up; diamond lamps glittered, and the Prince stretched forth his arms towards heaven, towards the sea, and towards the forest. Suddenly there came from the right hand, the poor lad who had been confirmed, with his short jacket and his wooden shoes; he had arrived here at the same time, and had come his own way. And they ran to meet each other and each took the other's hand, in the great temple of nature and of poetry. And above them sounded the invisible holy bell; and blessed spirits surrounded them and floated over them singing a rejoicing song of Praise!

The old pensioner

BY THE ALMSHOUSE WINDOW

Near the grass-covered rampart which encircles Copenhagen lies a great red house; balsams and other flowers greet us from the long rows of windows in the house, whose interior is sufficiently poverty-stricken; and poor and old are the people who inhabit it. The building is the Warton Almshouse.

Look! At the window there leans an old maid; she plucks the withered leaf from the balsam and looks at the grass-covered rampart,

on which many children are playing. What is the old maid thinking of?
A whole life-drama is unfolding itself before her inward gaze.

The poor little children, how happy they are, how merrily they play
and romp together! What red cheeks and what angels' eyes! But they
have no shoes nor stockings. They danced on the green rampart, just on
the place where, according to the old story, the ground always sank in,
and where a sportive frolicsome child had been lured by means of
flowers, toys, and sweetmeats into an open grave ready dug for it, and
which was afterwards closed over the child;—and from that moment,
the old story says, the ground gave way no longer, the mound remained
firm and fast, and was quickly covered with fine green turf. The little
people who now play on that spot, know nothing of the old tale, else
would they fancy they heard the child crying deep below the earth, and
the dewdrops on each blade of grass would be to them tears of woe.
Nor do they know anything of the Danish King, who here, in the face
of the coming foe, took an oath before all his trembling courtiers, that
he would hold out with the citizens of his capital, and die here in his
nest;—they knew nothing of the men who had fought here, or of the
women who from here had drenched with boiling water the enemy,
clad in white, and 'biding in the snow to surprise the city.

No! The poor little ones are playing with light childish spirits. Play
on, play on, thou little maiden! Soon the years will come—yes, those
glorious years. The priestly hands have been laid on the candidates for
confirmation; hand in hand they walk on the green rampart; thou hast
a white frock on, it has cost thy mother much labour, and yet it is only
cut down for thee out of an old larger dress! You will also wear a red
shawl; and what if it hang too far down? People will only see how
large, how very large it is. You are thinking of your dress, and of the
Giver of all Good; so glorious is it to wander on the green rampart.

And the years roll by; they have no lack of dark days, but you have
your cheerful young spirit, and you have gained a friend, you know not
how. You met, oh, how often! You walk together on the rampart in the
fresh spring, on the high days and holidays, when all the world comes
out to walk on the ramparts, and all the bells of the church steeples
seem to be singing a song of praise for the coming spring.

Scarcely have the violets come forth;—but there on the rampart, just
opposite the beautiful castle of Rosenberg, there is a tree bright with

the first green buds. Every year this tree sends forth fresh green shoots;—alas, it is not so with the human heart! Dark mists, more in number than those that cover the northern skies, cloud the human heart. Poor child—thy friend's bridal chamber is a black coffin, and thou becomest an old maid. From the almshouse window behind the balsams thou shalt look on the merry children at play, and shalt see thy own history renewed.

And that is the life-drama that passes before the old maid, while she looks out upon the rampart, the green sunny rampart, where the children with their red cheeks and bare shoeless feet are rejoicing merrily, like the other free little birds.

LITTLE TUK

Yes, that was little Tuk. His name was not really Tuk; but when he could not speak plainly, he used to call himself so. It was to mean "Charley," and it does very well, if one only knows it. Now, he was to take care of his little sister Gustava, who was much smaller than he, and at the same time he was to learn his lesson; but these two things would not suit well together. The poor boy sat there with his little sister on his lap, and sung her all kinds of songs that he knew, and every now and then he gave a glance at her geography book, that lay open before him; by to-morrow morning he was to know all the towns in Zealand by heart, and to know everything about them that one can well know.

Now his mother came home, for she had been out, and took little Gustava in her arms. Tuk ran quickly to the window, and read so zealously that he had almost read his eyes out, for it became darker and darker; but his mother had no money to buy candles.

"There goes the old washerwoman out of the lane yonder!" said his mother, as she looked out of the window. "The poor woman can hardly drag herself along, and now she is to carry the pail of water from the well. Be a good boy, Tuk, and run across, and help the old woman. Won't you?"

And Tuk ran across quickly, and helped her; but when he came back into the room, it had become quite dark. There was nothing said about a candle, and now he was to go to bed, and his bed was an old settle! There he lay, and thought of his geography lesson, and of Zealand, and of all the master had said. He ought certainly to have read it again, but he could not do that. So he put the geography book under his pillow, because he had heard that this is a very good way to learn one's lesson; but one cannot depend upon it. There he lay, and thought and thought; and all at once he fancied some one kissed him upon his eyes and mouth. He slept, and yet he did not sleep; it was just as if the old washerwoman were looking at him with her kind eyes, and saying, "It would be a great pity if you did not know your lesson to-morrow. You have helped me, therefore now I will help you; and Providence will help us both!"

And all at once the book began to crawl—crawl—about under Tuk's pillow.

"Kikeliki! Put! put!" It was a hen that came crawling up, and she came from Kjöge. "I'm a Kjöge-hen!"[1] she said, and then she told him how many inhabitants were in the town, and about the battle that had been fought there, though that was really hardly worth mentioning. "Kribli, kribli; plumps!" Something fell down: it was a wooden bird, the parrot from the shooting match at Prästoôe. He said that there were just as many inhabitants yonder as he had nails in his body; and he was very proud. "Thorwaldsen lived close to me.[2] Plumps! Here I lie very comfortably."

But now little Tuk no longer lay in bed; on a sudden he was on horseback. Gallop, gallop; hop, hop; and so he went on. A splendidly attired knight, with glowing plume, held him on the front of his saddle, and so they were riding on through the wood of the old town of Wordingborg, and that was a great and very busy town. On the king's castle rose high towers, and the radiance of lights streamed from every window; within was song and dancing, and King Waldemar and the young gaily dressed maids of honour danced together. Now, the morning came on, and so soon as the sun appeared the whole city and the king's castle suddenly sank down, one tower falling after another; and at last only one remained standing on the hill, where the castle had

---

[1] Kjöge, a little town on Kjöge-bay. Lifting up children by putting the two hands to the sides of their heads, is called "showing them Kjöge-hens."

[2] Prastoe, a still smaller town. A few hundred paces from it lies the estate of Nysoe, where Thorwaldsen usually lived while he was in Denmark, and where he executed many immortal works.

formerly been;[3] and the town was very small and poor, and the school-boys came with their books under their arms, and said, "Two thousand inhabitants;" but that was not true, for the town had not so many.

And little Tuk lay in his bed, as if he dreamed, and yet as if he did not dream; but some one stood close beside him.

"Little Tuk, little Tuk!" said the voice. It was a seaman, quite a little personage, as small as if he had been a cadet; but he was not a cadet. "I'm to bring you a greeting from Corsör;[4] that is a town which is just in good progress—a lively town that has streamers and mail-coaches. In times past they used always to call it ugly, but that is now no longer true." "I lie by the seashore," said Corsör. "I have high-roads and pleasure gardens; and I gave birth to a poet, who was witty and enter-taining, and that cannot be said of all of them. I wanted once to fit out a ship that was to sail round the world; but I did not do that, though I might have done it. But I smell deliciously, for close to my gates the loveliest roses bloom!"

Little Tuk looked, and it seemed red and green before his eyes; but when the confusion of colour had a little passed by, it changed all at once into a wooded declivity close by a bay, and high above it stood a glorious old church with two high-pointed towers. Out of this hill flowed springs of water in thick columns, so that there was a continual splashing, and close by sat an old king with a golden crown upon his white head: that was King Hroar of the springs, close by the town of Roeskilde, as it is now called. And up the hill into the old church went all the Kings and Queens of Denmark, hand-in-hand, all with golden crowns; and the organ played, and the springs plashed. Little Tuk saw all and heard all. "Don't forget the towns,"[5] said King Hroar.

[3] Wordingborg, in King Waldemar's time a considerable town, now a place of no importance. Only a lonely tower and a few remains of a wall show where the castle once stood.

[4] Corsör, on the Great Belt, used to be called the most tiresome of Danish towns before the establishment of steamers; for in those days travellers had often to wait there for a favourable wind. The poet Baggesen was born here.

[5] Roeskilde (Roesquelle, *Rose-spring*, falsely called Rothschild), once the capital of Den-mark. The town took its name from King Hroar and from the many springs in the vicinity. In the beautiful cathedral most of the Kings and Queens of Denmark are buried. In Roeskilde the Danish estates used to assemble.

Little Tuk's marvellous ride

At once everything had vanished, and whither? It seemed to him like turning a leaf in a book. And now stood there an old peasant woman, who came from Soröe, where grass grows on the market-place; she had an apron of grey cotton thrown over her head and shoulders, and the apron was very wet; it must have been raining. "Yes, that it has!" said she; and she knew many pretty things out of Holberg's plays, and about Waldemar and Absalom. But all at once she cowered down, and wagged her head as if she were about to spring. "Koax!" said she; "it is wet, it is wet. There is a very agreeable death-silence in Soröe!"[16] Now she changed all at once to a frog. "Koax!"— and then she became an old woman again. "One must dress according to the weather," she said. "It is wet, it is wet! My town is just like a bottle; one goes in at the cork, and one must come out again at the rock. In old times I had capital fish, and now I've fresh red-cheeked boys in the bottom of the bottle, and they learn wisdom—Hebrew, Greek, Koax!" That sounded just like the croak of the frogs, or the sound of some one marching across the moor in great boots; always the same note, so monotonous and wearisome that little Tuk fairly fell asleep, and that could not hurt him at all.

But even in this sleep came a dream, or whatever it was. His little sister Gustava with the blue eyes, and the fair curly hair was all at once a tall, slender maiden, and, without having wings, she could fly; and now they flew over Zealand, over the green forests and the blue lakes.

"Do you hear the cock crow, little Tuk? Kikelike! The fowls are flying up out of Kjöge! You shall have a poultry yard—a great, great poultry yard! You shall not suffer hunger nor need; and you shall hit the bird, as the saying is; you shall become a rich and happy man. Your house shall rise up like King Waldemar's tower, and shall be richly adorned with marble statues, like those from Prästöe. You understand me well. Your name shall travel with fame round the whole world, like the ship that was to sail from Corsör, and in Roeskilde." "Don't forget the towns," said King Hroar. "You will speak well and sensibly, little Tuk; and when at last you descend to your grave, you shall sleep peacefully—"

"As if I lay in Soröe," said Tuk, and he awoke. It was bright morning, and he could not remember his dream. But that was not necessary, for one must not know what is to happen.

Now he sprang quickly out of his bed, and read his book, and all at once he knew his whole lesson. The old washerwoman, too, put her head in at the door, nodded to him in a friendly way, and said, "Thank you, you good child, for your help. May your beautiful dreams come true!"

Little Tuk did not know at all what he had dreamt, but there was One above who knew it.

---

[16] Soröe, a very quiet little town, in the a fine situation, surrounded by forests and lakes. Holberg, after Molière of Denmark, here founded a noble academy. The poets Hanch and Ingman were professors here.

THE DARNING-NEEDLE

There was once a darning-needle, who thought herself so fine, she imagined she was an embroidering needle.

"Take care, and mind you hold me tight!" she said to the fingers which took her out. "Don't let me fall! If I fall on the ground, I shall certainly never be found again, for I am so fine!"

"That's as it may be," said the fingers; and they grasped her round the body.

"See, I'm coming with a train!" said the darning-needle, and she drew a long thread after her; but there was no knot in this thread. The fingers pointed the needle just at the cook's slipper, in which the upper leather had burst, and was to be sewn together.

"That's vulgar work!" said the darning-needle. "I shall never get through. I'm breaking, I'm breaking!" and she really broke. "Did I not say so!" said the darning-needle, "I'm too fine!"

"Now it's quite useless!" said the fingers, but they were obliged to hold her fast, all the same; for the cook dropped some sealing-wax upon the needle, and pinned her handkerchief together with it, in front.

"So, now I'm a breast-pin!" said the darning-needle. "I knew very well, that I should come to honour; when one is something, one comes to something!" and she laughed quietly to herself; one can never see when a darning-needle laughs. There she sat, as proud as in a state coach, and looked all about her.

"May I be permitted to ask if you are of gold?" she inquired of the pin, her neighbour. "You have a very pretty appearance, and a peculiar head, but it is only little. You must take pains to grow, for it's not everyone that has sealing-wax dropped upon him!" And the darning-needle drew herself up so proudly, that she fell out of the handkerchief, right into the sink, which the cook was rinsing out.

"Now we're going on a journey!" said the darning-needle. "If I only don't get lost!" But she really was lost.

"I'm too fine for this world," she observed, as she lay in the gutter.

"But I know who I am, and there's always something in that!" So the darning-needle kept her proud behaviour, and did not lose her good humour.

And things of many kinds swam over her, chips and straws and pieces of old newspapers. "Only look how they sail!" said the darning-needle. "They don't know what is under them! I'm here, I remain firmly here. See, there goes a chip thinking of nothing in the world but of himself, of a 'chip!' There's a straw going by now! How he turns, how he twirls about! Don't think only of yourself, you might easily run up against a stone. There swims a bit of newspaper! What's written upon it has long been forgotten, and yet it gives itself airs! I sit quietly and patiently here. I know who I am, and I shall remain what I am."

One day something lay close beside her, that glittered splendidly; then the darning-needle believed that it was a diamond: but it was a bit of broken bottle; and because it shone the darning-needle spoke to it, introducing herself as a breast-pin.

"I suppose you are a diamond?" she observed. "Why, yes, something of that kind," and then each believed the other to be a very valuable thing; and they began speaking about the world, and how very conceited it was.

"I have been in a lady's box,"—said the darning-needle; "and this lady was a cook. She had five fingers on each hand, and I never saw anything so conceited as those five fingers! And yet they were only there that they might take me out of the box, and put me back into the box."

"Were they of good birth?" asked the bit of bottle.

"No, indeed!"—replied the darning-needle,—"but very haughty. There were five brothers, all of the finger family. They kept very proudly together, though they were of different lengths,—the outermost, the thumbling, was short and fat; he walked out in front of the ranks, and only had one joint in his back, and could only make a single bow; but he said that if he were hacked off from a man, that man was useless for service in war. Dainty-mouth, the second finger, thrusts himself into sweet and sour, pointed to sun and moon, and gave the impression, when they wrote. Longman, the third, looked at all the others over his shoulder. Goldborder, the fourth, went about with a golden bell round his waist, and little Playmandil nothing at all, and

The cook with the darning-needle

was proud of it. There was nothing but bragging among them, and therefore I went away."

"And now we sit here and glitter!" said the bit of bottle.

At that moment more water came into the gutter, so that it overflowed, and the bit of bottle was carried away.

"So he was disposed of,"—observed the darning-needle. "I remain here, I am too fine. But that's my pride, and my pride is honourable!" And proudly she sat there, and had many great thoughts.

"I could almost believe I had been born of a sunbeam, I'm so fine. It really appears to me as if the sunbeams were always seeking for me under the water. Ah! I'm so fine that my mother cannot find me. If I had my old eye, which broke off, I think I should cry—but no; I should not do that; it's not genteel to cry!"

One day a couple of street boys lay grubbing in the gutter, where they sometimes found old nails, farthings, and similar treasures. It was dirty work, but they took great delight in it.

"Oh!"—cried one, who had pricked himself with the darning-needle—"there's a fellow for you!"

"I'm not a fellow, I'm a young lady!" said the darning-needle; but nobody listened to her. The sealing-wax had come off, and she had turned black; but black makes one look slender, and she thought herself finer even than before.

"Here comes an egg-shell, sailing along!" said the boys, and they stuck the darning-needle fast in the egg-shell.

"White walls, and black myself, that looks well," remarked the darning-needle; now one can see me! I only hope I shall not be sea-sick!" But she was not sea-sick at all.

"It is good against sea-sickness, if one has a steel stomach, and does not forget that one is a little more than an ordinary person! Now my sea-sickness is over! The finer one is, the more one can bear!"

"Crack!" said the egg-shell; for a hand-barrow went over her.

"Good Heavens, how it crushes one!" said the darning-needle. 'I'm getting sea-sick now,—I'm quite sick." But she was not really sick, though the hand-barrow went over her she lay there at full length, and there she may lie.

THE FIR-TREE

Out in the forest stood a pretty little fir-tree. It had a good place; it could have sunlight, air there was in plenty, and all around grew many larger comrades, pines as well as firs. But the little fir-tree wished ardently to become greater. It did not care for the warm sun and the fresh air, it took no notice of the peasant children, who went about talking together, when they had come out to look for strawberries and raspberries. Often they came with a whole pot full, or had strung

The children and the fir-tree

berries on a straw; then they would sit down by the little fir-tree and say, "How pretty and small that one is!" and the tree did not like to hear that at all.

Next year he had grown a great joint, and the following year he was longer still, for in fir-trees one can always tell by the number of rings they have, how many years they have been growing.

"Oh! If I were only as great a tree as the others," sighed the little fir, "then I would spread my branches far around, and look out with my crown into the wide world. The birds would then build nests in my boughs, and when the wind blew, I could nod just as grandly as the others yonder."

It took no pleasure in the sunshine, in the birds, and in the red clouds that went sailing over him, morning and evening.

When it was winter, and the snow lay all around, white and sparkling, a hare would often come jumping along, and spring right over the little fir-tree, oh! This made him so angry. But two winters went by, and when the third came, the little tree had grown so tall that the hare was obliged to run round it. O! To grow, to grow, and become old; that's the only fine thing in the world, thought the tree.

In the autumn, woodcutters always came and felled a few of the largest trees; that was done this year too, and the little fir-tree that was now quite well-grown shuddered with fear, for the great stately trees fell to the ground with a crash, and their branches were cut off, so that the trees looked quite naked, long and slender,—they could hardly be recognized. But then they were laid upon wagons, and horses dragged them away out of the wood. Where were they going? What destiny awaited them?

In the spring when the swallows and the stork came, the tree asked them, "Do you know where they were taken? Did you not meet them?"

The swallows knew nothing about it, but the stork looked thoughtful, nodded his head and said, "Yes I think so. I met many new ships when I flew out of Egypt; on the ships were stately masts; I fancy that these were the trees. They smelt like fir. I can assure you they're stately—very stately."

"Oh, that I were only big enough to go over the sea! What kind of thing is this sea, and how does it look?"

"It would take too long to explain all that," said the stork; and he went away.

"Rejoice in thy youth," said the sunbeams; "rejoice in thy fresh growth, and in the young life that is within thee."

And the wind kissed the tree, and the dew wept tears upon it; but the fir-tree did not understand that.

When Christmas time approached, quite young trees were felled, sometimes trees which were neither so old nor so large as this fir-tree, that never rested but always wanted to go away. These young trees which were always the most beautiful, kept all their branches; they were put upon wagons, and horses dragged them away out of the wood.

"Where are they going?" asked the fir-tree. "They are not greater than I, indeed one of them was much smaller. Why do they keep all their branches? Whither are they taken?"

"We know that! We know that!" chirped the sparrows. "Yonder in the town, we looked into the windows. We know where they go. Oh! They are dressed up in the greatest pomp and splendour that can be imagined. We have looked into the windows, and have perceived that they are planted in the middle of the warm room, and adorned with the most beautiful things, gilt apples, honey cakes, playthings and many hundreds of candles."

"And then?" asked the fir-tree, and trembled through all its branches. "And then? What happens then?"

"Why, we have not seen anything more. But it was incomparable."

"Perhaps I may be destined to tread this glorious path, one day!" cried the fir-tree rejoicingly. "That is even better than travelling across the sea. How painfully I long for it. If it were only Christmas now. Now I am great and grown up, like the rest who were led away last year. Oh! If I were only on the carriage. If I were only in the warm room, among all the pomp and splendour, and then? Yes, then something even better will come, something far more charming, or else why should they adorn me so? There must be something grander, something greater still to come, but what? Oh! I'm suffering, I'm longing! I don't know myself what is the matter with me!"

"Rejoice in us," said air and sunshine. "Rejoice in thy fresh youth here in the woodland."

But the fir-tree did not rejoice at all, but it grew and grew; winter and summer it stood there, green, dark green. The people who saw it said: "That's a handsome tree!" and at Christmas time it was felled before any one of the others. The axe cut deep into its marrow and the tree fell to the ground with a sigh; it felt a pain, a sensation of faintness, and could not think at all of happiness, for it was sad at parting from its home, from the place where it had grown up; it knew that it should never again see the dear old companions, the little bushes and flowers all around; perhaps not even the birds. The parting was not at all agreeable.

The tree only came to itself when it was unloaded in a yard, with other trees, and heard a man say: "This one is famous; we only want this one!"

Now two servants came in gay liveries, and carried the fir-tree into a large beautiful saloon. All around the walls hung pictures, and by the great stove stood large Chinese vases with lions on the covers; there were rocking-chairs, silken sofas, great tables covered with picture-books, and toys for a hundred times a hundred dollars, at least the children said so. And the fir-tree was put into a great tub filled with sand; but no one could see that it was a tub, for it was hung round with green cloth and stood on a large many-coloured carpet. Oh! How the tree trembled. What was to happen now? The servants, and the young ladies also, decked it out. On one branch they hung little nets, cut out of coloured paper; every net was filled with sweetmeats; golden apples and walnuts hung down as if they grew there, and more than a hundred little candles, red, white, and blue, were fastened to the different boughs. Dolls that looked exactly like real people—the tree had never seen such before—swung among the foliage, and high on the summit of the tree was fixed a tinsel star; it was splendid, particularly splendid.

"This evening," said all: "this evening it will shine."

"Oh!" thought the tree, "that it were evening already. Oh! That the lights may be soon lit up. When may that be done? I wonder if trees will come out of the forest to look at me? Will the sparrows fly against the panes? Shall I grow fast here, and stand adorned in summer and winter?"

Yes, he did not guess badly. But he had a complete back-ache from mere longing, and the back-ache is just as bad for a tree, as the head-ache for a person.

At last the candles were lighted. What a brilliance, what a splendour! The tree trembled so in all its branches, that one of the candles set fire to a green twig, and it was scorched. "Heaven preserve us!" cried the young ladies; and they hastily put the fire out.

Now the tree might not even tremble. Oh! That was terrible. It was so afraid of setting fire to some of its ornaments; it was quite bewildered with all the brilliance. And now the folding doors were thrown open, and a number of children rushed in, as if they would have overturned the whole tree; the older people followed more deliberately. The little ones stood quite silent, but only for a minute; then they shouted till the room rang: they danced gleefully round the tree, and one present after another was plucked from it.

"What are they about?" thought the tree. What's going to be done?" And the candles burned down to the twigs, and as they burned down they were extinguished, and then the children received permission to plunder the tree. Oh! They rushed in upon it, so that every branch cracked again: if it had not been fastened by the top, and by the golden star to the ceiling, it would have fallen down.

The children danced about with their pretty toys. No one looked at the tree except the old man, who came up and peeped among the branches; but only to see if a fig or an apple had not been forgotten.

"A story! a story!" shouted the children; and they drew a little fat man towards the tree; and he sat down just beneath it,—for "then we shall be in the greenwood," said he, "and the tree may have the advantage of listening to my tale. But I can only tell one. Will you hear the story of Ivede-Avede, or of Klumpey-Dumpey, who fell down stairs, and still was raised up to honour, and married the Princess?"

"Ivede-Avede," cried some, "Klumpey-Dumpey," cried others; and there was a great crying and shouting! Only the fir-tree was quite silent, and thought, "Shall I not be in it; shall I have nothing to do in it?" But he had been in the evening's amusement, and had done what was required of him.

And the man told about "Klumpey-Dumpey," who fell down stairs, and yet was raised to honour, and married the Princess. And the children clapped their hands, and cried "Tell another, tell another!" for they wanted to hear about Ivede-Avede; but they only got the story of Klumpey-Dumpey. The fir-tree stood quite silent and thoughtful; never had the birds in the wood told such a story as that. Klumpey-Dumpey fell down stairs, and yet came to honour, and married the Princess! "Yes, so it happens in the world!" thought the fir-tree, and believed it must be true, because that was such a nice man who told it. "Well, who can know? Perhaps I shall fall down stairs too, and marry a Princess!" And it looked forward with pleasure to being adorned again, the next evening, with candles and toys, gold and fruit.

"To-morrow I shall not tremble," it thought. "I will rejoice in all my splendour. To-morrow I shall hear the story of Klumpey-Dumpey again, and perhaps, that of Ivede-Avede too." And the tree stood all night quiet and thoughtful.

In the morning the servants and the chambermaid came in. "Now my splendour will begin afresh," thought the tree. But they dragged him out of the room, and up-stairs to the garret; and here they put him in a dark corner, where no daylight shone. "What's the meaning of this?" thought the tree. "What am I to do here? What is to happen?" and he leant against the wall, and thought, and thought. And he had time enough, for days and nights went by, and nobody came up; and when at length some one came, it was only to put some great boxes in a corner. Now the tree stood quite hidden away; and the supposition was that it was quite forgotten.

"Now it's winter outside," thought the tree. "The earth is hard and covered with snow, and people cannot plant me: therefore I suppose I'm to be sheltered here until spring comes! How considerate that is! How good people are! If it were only not so dark here, and so terribly solitary!—Not even a little hare! That was pretty out there in the wood, when the snow lay thick, and the hare sprang past; yes, even when he jumped over me; but then I did not like it. It is terribly lonely up here!

"Piep, piep!" said a little mouse, and crept forward, and then came another little one. They smelt at the fir-tree, and then slipped among the branches.

"It's horribly cold!" said the little mice, "or else it would be comfortable here! Don't you think so, you old fir-tree?"

"I'm not old at all," said the fir-tree. "There are many much older than I."

"Where do you come from?" asked the mice. "And what do you know?" They were dreadfully inquisitive. "Tell us about the most beautiful spot on earth. Have you been there? Have you been in the store-room, where cheeses lie on the shelves, and hams hang from the ceiling, where one dances on tallow candles, and goes in thin and comes out fat?"

"I don't know that!" replied the tree; "but I know the wood, where the sun shines, and where the birds sing!" and then it told all about its youth; and the little mice had never heard anything of the kind; and they listened and said, "What a number of things you have seen! How happy you have been!"

"I?" said the fir-tree; and it thought about what it had told. "Yes, those were really quite happy times." But then he told of the Christmas-eve, when he had been hung with sweetmeats and candles.

"Oh!" said the little mice, "how happy you have been, you old fir-tree!"

"I'm not old at all!" said the tree. "I only came out of the wood this winter! I'm only rather backward in my growth!"

"What splendid stories you can tell!" said the little mice. And next night they came with four other little mice, to hear what the tree had to relate; and the more it spoke, the more clearly did it remember everything, and thought, "Those were quite merry days! But they may come again. Klumpey-Dumpey fell down stairs; and yet he married the Princess. Perhaps I may marry a princess too!" And then the fir-tree thought of a pretty little birch-tree that grew out in the forest: for the fir-tree, that birch was a real princess.

"Who's Klumpey-Dumpey?" asked the little mice. And then the fir-tree told the whole story. It could remember every single word; and the little mice were ready to leap to the very top of the tree with pleasure. Next night a great many more mice came, and on Sunday two rats even appeared: but these thought the story was not pretty, and the little mice were sorry for that, for now they also did not like it so much as before.

"Do you only know one story?" asked the rats.

"Only that one," replied the tree. I heard that on the happiest evening of my life; I did not think, then, how happy I was."

"That's a very miserable story. Don't you know any about bacon and tallow candles; a store-room story?" "No," said the tree.

"Then we'd rather not hear you," said the rats; and they went back to their own people. The little mice at last stayed away also, and then the tree sighed and said, "It was very nice, when they sat round me, the merry little mice, and listened when I spoke to them. Now that's past too. But I shall remember to be pleased when they take me out." But when did that happen? Why, it was one morning that people came and rummaged in the garret; the boxes were put away, and the tree brought out: they certainly threw him rather roughly on the floor, but a servant dragged him away at once to the stairs, where the daylight shone.

"Now life is beginning again!" thought the tree; it felt the fresh air, and the first sunbeams, and now it was out in the courtyard. Everything passed so quickly, the tree quite forgot to look at itself, there was so much to look at all round. The courtyard was close to a garden, and here everything was blooming; the roses hung fresh and fragrant over the little paling, the linden trees were in blossom, and the swallows cried "Quinze-wit, quinze-wit, my husband's come!" But it was not the fir-tree that they meant.

"Now I shall live!" said the tree rejoicingly, and spread its branches far out; but, alas, they were all withered and yellow; and it lay in the corner, among nettles and weeds. The tinsel star was still upon it, and shone in the bright sunshine.

In the courtyard a couple of the merry children were playing, who had danced round the tree at Christmas time, and had rejoiced over it. One of the youngest ran up, and tore off the golden star.

"Look what is sticking to the ugly old fir-tree," said the child; and he trod upon the branches till they cracked again under his boots.

And the tree looked at all the blooming flowers and the splendour of the garden, and then looked at itself, and wished it had remained in the dark corner of the garret; it thought of its fresh youth in the wood, of the merry Christmas-eve, and of the little mice which had listened so pleasantly to the story of Klumpey-Dumpey.

"Past, past!" said the old tree. "Had I but rejoiced when I could have done so! Past, past!"

And the servant came and chopped the tree into little pieces; a whole bundle lay there; it blazed brightly up under the great brewing copper, and it sighed deeply, and each sigh was like a little shot: and the children who were at play there, ran up and seated themselves at the fire, looked into it, and cried "Puff, puff!" But at each explosion, which was a deep sigh, the tree thought of a summer day in the woods, or of a winter night there, when the stars beamed; he thought of Christmas-eve and of Klumpey-Dumpey, the only story he had ever heard, and knew how to tell; and then the tree was burnt.

The boys played in the garden, and the youngest had on his breast a golden star, which the tree had worn on its happiest evening. Now that was past, and the tree's life was past, and the story is past too,—past, past—and that's the way with all stories.

A ROSE FROM THE GRAVE OF HOMER

All the songs of the East tell of the love of the nightingale to the rose; in the silent starlit nights the winged songster serenades his fragrant flower.

Not far from Smyrna, under the lofty plantains, where the merchant drives his loaded camels, that proudly lift their long necks and tramp over the holy ground, I saw a hedge of roses. Wild pigeons flew among the branches of the high trees, and their wings glistened, while a sunbeam glided over them, as if they were of mother-of-pearl.

The rose-hedge bore a flower, which was the most beautiful among all, and the nightingale sang to her, of his woes;—but the rose was silent; not a dewdrop lay, like a tear of sympathy, upon her leaves,—she bent down over a few great stones.

"Here rests the greatest singer of the world!" said the rose; "over his tomb will I pour out my fragrance, and on it I will let fall my leaves, when the storm tears them off! He who sang of Troy became earth, and from that earth I have sprung! I, a rose from the grave of Homer, am too lofty to bloom for a poor nightingale!"

And the nightingale sang himself to death.

The camel-driver came with his loaded camels and his black slaves; his little son found the dead bird, and buried the little songster in the grave of the great Homer; and the rose trembled in the wind. The evening came, and the rose wrapped her leaves more closely together, and dreamed thus: "It was a fair sunshiny day; a crowd of strangers drew near, for they had undertaken a pilgrimage to the grave of Homer. Among the strangers was a singer from the North, the home of clouds and of the Northern light; he plucked the rose, placed it in a book, and carried it away into another part of the world, to his distant fatherland. The rose faded with grief, and lay in the narrow book, which he opened in his home, saying 'Here is a rose from the grave of Homer.'"

This the flower dreamed; and she awoke and trembled in the wind. A drop of dew fell from the leaves upon the singer's grave. The sun rose, and the rose glowed more beauteous than before; it was a hot day, and she was in her own warm Asia. Then footsteps were heard, and Frank-ish strangers came, such as the rose had seen in her dream, and among

The two friends

the strangers was a poet from the North; he plucked the rose, pressed a kiss upon her fresh mouth, and carried her away to the home of the clouds and of the Northern light.

Like a mummy the flower corpse now rests in his "Iliad;" and as in a dream she hears him open the book and say: "Here is a rose from the grave of Homer."

THE SWINEHERD

There was once a poor Prince, he had a kingdom which was quite small; but still it was large enough that he could marry upon it, and that is what he wanted to do.

Now it was certainly somewhat bold of him to say to the Emperor's daughter, "Will you have me?" But he did not venture it, for his name was famous far and wide, there were hundreds of Princesses who would have been glad to say yes; but did *she* say so? Well, we shall see.

On the grave of the Prince's father there grew a rose-bush, a very beautiful rose-bush. It bloomed only every fifth year, and even then it bore only a single rose, but what a rose that was! It was so sweet that whoever smelt at it forgot all sorrow and trouble. And then he had a nightingale, which could sing as if all possible melodies were collected in its little throat. This rose and this nightingale the Princess was to have, and therefore they were put into great silver vessels and sent to her.

The Emperor caused the presents to be carried before him into the great hall where the Princess was, playing at "visiting," with her maids of honour, and when she saw the great silver vessels with the presents in them, she clapped her hands with joy.

"If it were only a little pussy-cat!" said she. But then came out the rose-bush with the splendid rose.

"Oh! How pretty it is made," said all the court ladies. "It is more than pretty," said the Emperor, "it is charming."

But the Princess felt it, and then she almost began to cry.

"Fie, papa!" she said, "it is not artificial, it's a *natural* rose." "Fie," said all the court ladies, "it's a natural one."

"Let us first see what is in the other vessel before we get angry," said the Emperor, and then the nightingale came out; it sang so beautifully, that they did not at once know what to say against it.

"*Superbe! Charmant!*" said the maids of honour, for they all spoke French as badly as possible.

"How that bird reminds me of the late Emperor's musical snuff box," said an old cavalier. "Yes, it is the same tone, the same expression!" "Yes," said the Emperor, and then he wept like a little child.

"I really hope it is not a natural bird," said the Princess, "yes, it is a natural bird," said they who had brought it. "Then let the bird fly away," said the Princess, and she would by no means allow the Prince to come.

But the Prince was not to be frightened, he stained his face brown and black, drew his hat down over his brows, and knocked at the door. "Good day, Emperor!" he said, "could I not be employed here in the castle?"

"Yes," replied the Emperor, "but there are so many who ask for an appointment, that I do not know if it can be managed; but I'll bear you in mind. But it just occurs to me that I want some one who can keep the pigs, for we have many pigs here, very many."

So the Prince was appointed the Emperor's swineherd. He received a miserable small room down by the pigsty, and here he was obliged to stay; but all day long he sat and worked, and when it was evening he had finished a neat little pot, all around it were bells, and when the pot boiled these bells rang out prettily and played the old melody—

Oh, my darling Augustine,
All is lost, all is lost.

But the cleverest thing about the whole arrangement, was, that by holding one's finger in the smoke, one could at once smell what provisions were being cooked at every hearth in the town. That was quite a different thing to the rose.

Now the Princess came with all her maids of honour, and when she heard the melody, she stood still and looked quite pleased; for she, too, could play "Oh my darling Augustine," on the piano. It was the only thing she could play, but then she played it with one finger.

"Why, that is what I play!" she cried. "He must be an educated swineherd! Harkye, go down and ask the price of the instrument."

So one of the maids of honour had to go down; but first she put on a pair of pattens.

"What do you want for the pot?" inquired the lady. "I want ten kisses from the Princess," replied the swineherd. "Heaven preserve us!" exclaimed the maid of honour. "Well, I won't do it for less," said the swineherd.

"And what did he say?" asked the Princess. "I don't like to repeat it," replied the lady.

"Well, you can whisper it in my ear."

"He is very rude," declared the Princess, and she went away. But when she had gone a little way, the bells sounded so prettily,

Oh, my darling Augustine,
All is lost, all is lost.

"Harkye," said the Princess, "ask him if he will take ten kisses from my maids of honour?"

"I'm much obliged," replied the swineherd—"Ten kisses from the Princess, or I shall keep my pot."

"How tiresome that is!" cried the Princess. "But at least you must stand before me, so that nobody sees it." And the maids of honour stood before her, and spread out their dresses, and then the swineherd received ten kisses, and she received the pot.

Then there was rejoicing! All the evening, and all day long the pot was kept boiling; there was not a kitchen hearth in the whole town, of which they did not know what it had cooked, at the shoemaker's as well as the chamberlain's. The ladies danced with pleasure, and clapped their hands.

"We know who will have sweet soup and pancakes for dinner, we know who has hasty-pudding and cutlets; how interesting that is!"

"Very interesting!" said the head lady-superintendent.

"Yes, but keep counsel, for I'm the Emperor's daughter." "Yes certainly," said all.

The swineherd, that is to say the Prince—but of course they did not know but that he was a regular swineherd, let no day pass by, without doing something, and so he made a rattle; when any person swung this rattle, he could play all the waltzes, hops, and polkas that have been known since the creation of the world.

"But that is *superbe!*" cried the Princess, as she went past. "I have never heard a finer composition. Harkye, go down and ask what the instrument costs; but I give no more kisses."

"He demands a hundred kisses from the Princess," said the maid of of honour, who had gone down to make the inquiry.

"I think he must be mad!" exclaimed the Princess, and she went away, but when she had gone a little distance she stood still. "One must encourage art," she observed. "I am the Emperor's daughter! Tell him he shall receive ten kisses, like last time, and he may take the rest from my maids of honour."

"Ah, but we don't like to do it!" said the maids of honour.

"That's all nonsense!" retorted the Princess, "and if I can allow myself to be kissed, you can too; remember, I give you board and wages;" and so the maids of honour had to go down to him again.

The swineherd receiving payment

"A hundred kisses from the Princess," said he, "or each shall keep his own."

"Stand before me," said she then, and all the maids of honour stood before her, and he kissed the Princess.

"What is that crowd down by the pigsty?" asked the Emperor, who had stepped out to the balcony. He rubbed his eyes, and put on his spectacles. "Why those are the maids of honour, at their tricks, yonder; I shall have to go down to them," and he pulled up his slippers behind, for they were shoes that he had trodden down at heel.

Gracious mercy, how he hurried!

So soon as he came down in the courtyard, he went quite softly, and the maids of honour were too busy counting the kisses, and seeing fair play, to notice the Emperor. Then he stood on tiptoe.

"What's that?" said he, when he saw that there was kissing going on, and he hit them on the head with his slipper, just as the swineherd was taking the eighty-sixth kiss.

"Be off!" said the Emperor, for he was angry; and the Princess and the swineherd were both expelled from his dominions. So there she stood and cried, the rain streamed down, and the swineherd scolded.

"O miserable wretch that I am!" said the Princess; "if I had only taken the handsome Prince! Oh, how unhappy I am!

Then the swineherd went behind a tree, washed the brown and black stain out of his face, threw away the shabby clothes, and stepped forth in his princely attire, so handsome, that the Princess was fain to bow before him.

"I have come to this, that I despise you," said he. "You would not have an honest Prince; you did not value the rose and the nightingale, but for a plaything you kissed the swineherd, and now you have your reward."

And then he went into his kingdom and shut the door in her face. So now she might stand outside and sing—

Oh, my darling Augustine,
   All is lost, all is lost.

ELDER-TREE MOTHER

There was once a little boy who had caught cold; he had gone out and got wet feet; no one could imagine how it had happened, for it was quite dry weather. Now his mother undressed him, put him to bed, and had the tea-urn brought in to make him a good cup of elder-tea, for that warms well! At the same time there also came in at the door the old friendly man who lived all alone at the top of the house, and was very solitary. He had neither wife nor children, but he was very fond of all children, and knew so many stories, that it was quite delightful.

"Now you are to drink your tea," said the mother, "and then perhaps you will hear a story."

"Ah! if one only could tell a new one," said the old man, with a friendly nod. "But where did the little man get his feet wet?" he asked.

"Yes," replied the mother, "no one can tell how that came about."

"Shall I have a story?" asked the boy.

"Yes, if you can tell me at all accurately—for I must know that first— how deep the gutter is in the little street through which you go to school."

"Just half way up to my knee," answered the boy, "that is, if I put my feet in the deep hole."

"You see, that's how we get our feet wet," said the old gentleman. "Now I ought certainly to tell you a story; but I don't know any more."

"You can make up one directly," answered the little boy. "Mother says that everything you look at can be turned into a story, and that you can make a tale of everything you touch."

"Yes, but those stories and tales are worth nothing! No, the real ones come of themselves. They knock at my forehead and say, "Here I am!""

"Will there soon be a knock?" asked the little boy, and the mother laughed and put elder-tea in the pot, and poured hot water upon it.

"A story! A story!"

"Yes, if a story would come of itself; but that kind of thing is grand; it only comes when it's in the humour. Wait!" he cried all at once. "Here we have it. Look you; there's one in the teapot now."

And the little boy looked across at the teapot. The lid raised itself more and more, and the elder flowers came forth from it, white and fresh; they shot forth long fresh branches, even out of the spout they spread abroad in all directions, and became larger and larger; there was the most glorious elder-bush—in fact, quite a great tree. It penetrated even to the bed, and thrust the curtains aside; how fragrant it was, and how it bloomed! And in the midst of the tree sat an old, pleasant-looking woman in a strange dress. It was quite green, like the leaves of the elder-tree, and bordered with great white elder blossoms; one could not at once discern whether this border was of stuff, or of living green and real flowers.

"What is the woman's name?" the little boy asked.

"The Romans and Greeks," replied the old man, "used to call her a

Dryad; but we don't understand that; out in the sailor's suburb we have a better name for her; there she's called Elder-tree Mother, and it is to her you must pay attention; only listen, and look at that glorious elder-tree."

Just such a great blooming tree stands outside; it grew there in the corner of a little poor yard, and under this tree two old people sat one afternoon in the brightest sunshine. It was an old, old sailor, and his old, old wife; they had great-grandchildren, and were soon to celebrate their golden wedding;[1] but they could not quite make out the date, and the elder-tree mother sat in the tree and looked pleased, just as she does here. "I know very well when the golden wedding is to be," said she, but they did not hear it; they were talking of old times.

"Yes, do you remember," said the old seaman, "when we were quite little, and ran about and played together; it was in the very same yard where we are sitting now, and we planted little twigs in the yard, and made a garden."

"Yes," replied the old woman, "I remember it very well; we watered the twigs, and one of them was an elder twig; that struck root, shot out other green twigs, and has become a great tree, under which we old people sit."

"Surely," said he, "and yonder in the corner stood a butt of water; there I swam my boat; I had cut it out myself. How it could sail! But I certainly soon had to sail elsewhere myself."

"But first we went to school and learned something," said she, "and then we were confirmed; we both cried, but in the afternoon we went hand in hand to the round tower, and looked out into the wide world, over Copenhagen and across the water; then we went out to Frie-drichsberg, where the King and Queen were sailing in their splendid boats upon the canals."

"But I was obliged to sail elsewhere, and that for many years, far away on long voyages."

"Yes, I often cried about you," she said, "I thought you were dead and gone, and lying down in the deep waters, rocked by the waves. Many a night I got up to look if the weather-cock was turning. Yes, it

---

[1] The golden wedding is celebrated in several countries of the Continent, by the two wedded pairs who survive to see the fiftieth anniversary of their marriage day.

turned indeed; but you did not come. I remember so clearly how the rain streamed down from the sky; the man with the cart who fetched away the dust came to the place where I was in service. I went down with him to the dustbin, and remained standing in the doorway, what wretched weather it was! And just as I stood there the postman came up and gave me a letter! It was from you! How that letter had travelled about! I tore it open and read; I laughed and wept at once, I was so glad. There it stood written that you were in the warm countries where the coffee beans grow. You told me so much, and I read it all while the rain was streaming down, and I stood by the dustbin. Then somebody came and clasped me round the waist."

The old neighbour visits the little boy

"And you gave him a terrible box on the ear—one that sounded?"

"I did not know that it was you. You had arrived just as quickly as your letter. And you were so handsome; but that you are still. You had a large yellow silk handkerchief in your pocket, and a hat on your head. You were so handsome, and heavens! What weather it was, and how the street looked!"

"Then we were married," said he, "do you remember? And then when our first little boy came, and then Marie, and Niels, and Peter, and Jack, and Christian."

"Yes, and how all of these have grown up to be respectable people, and every one likes them!"

"And their children have had little ones in their turn," said the old sailor. "Yes, those are children's children! They're of the right sort. It was, if I don't mistake, at this season of the year that we were married?"

"Yes; this is the day of your golden wedding," said the Elder-mother, putting out her head just between the two old people, and they thought it was a neighbour nodding to them, and they looked at each other and took hold of one another's hands. Soon afterwards came their children and grandchildren; these knew very well that it was the golden wedding-day; they had already brought their congratulations in the morning, but the old people had forgotten it, while they remembered everything right well that had happened years and years ago. And the elder-tree smelt so sweet, and the sun that was just setting shone just in the faces of the old couple, so that their cheeks looked quite red; and the youngest of their grandchildren danced about them, and cried out quite gleefully that there was to be a feast this evening, for they were to have hot potatoes; and the Elder-mother nodded in the tree, and called out "hurrah!" with all the rest.

"But that was not a story," said the little boy who had heard it told.

"Yes, so you understand it," replied the old man, "but let us ask the Elder-mother about it."

"That was not a story," said the Elder-mother, "but now it comes; but of truth the strangest stories are formed, otherwise my beautiful elder-tree could not have sprouted forth out of the teapot." And then she took the little boy out of bed, and laid him upon her bosom, and the blossoming elder branches wound round them, so that they sat as it were in the thickest arbour, and this arbour flew with them through the air; it was indescribably beautiful. Elder-mother all at once became a young pretty girl; but her dress was still of the green stuff with the white blossoms that Elder-mother had worn; in her bosom she had a real elder blossom, and on her head a wreath of elder flowers; her eyes were so large and blue, they were beautiful to look at! She and the boy were of the same age, and they kissed each other and felt similar joys.

Hand in hand they went forth out of the arbour, and now they stood in the beauteous flower garden of home. The father's staff was tied up near the fresh grass plot, and for the little boy there was life in that staff. As soon as they seated themselves upon it the polished head turned into a noble neighing horse's head, with a flowing mane, and four slender legs shot forth; the creature was strong and spirited, and they rode at a gallop round the grass plat, hurrah! "Now we're going to ride many miles away," said the boy, "we'll ride to the nobleman's estate, where we went last year!" And they rode round and round the glass plot, and the little girl, who, as we know, was no one else but Elder-mother, kept crying out, "Now we're in the country! Do you see the farmhouse, with the great baking oven, standing out of the wall like an enormous egg by the wayside? The elder-tree spreads its branches over it, and the cock walks about, scratching for his hens; look how he struts! Now we are near the church; it lies high upon the hill, under the great oak trees, one of which is half dead. Now we are at the forge, where the fire burns, and the half-clad men beat with their hammers, so that the sparks fly far around. Away, away to the splendid nobleman's seat!" And everything that the little maiden mentioned, as she sat on the stick behind him, that flew past them, and the boy saw it all, though they were only riding round and round the grass plot. Then they played in the side walk, and scratched up the earth to make a little garden, and she took elder flowers out of her hair and planted them, and they grew just like those that the old people had planted, when they were little, as has been already told. They went hand in hand just as the old people had done in their childhood; but not to the high tower, or to the Friedrichsberg garden. No, the little girl took hold of the boy round the body, and then they flew far away in the whole country. And it was spring, and summer came, and autumn, and winter, and thousands of pictures were mirrored in the boy's eyes and heart, and the little maiden was always singing to him. You will never forget that; and throughout their whole journey the elder-tree smelt so sweet, so fragrant; he noticed the roses and the fresh beech trees; but the elder-tree smelt stronger than all, for its flowers hung round the little girl's heart, and he often leaned against them as they flew onward.

"Here it is beautiful in spring!" said the little girl; and they stood in the green beech wood, where the thyme lay spread in fragrance at their feet, and the pale pink anemones looked glorious among the vivid green.

"Oh, that it were always spring, in the merry greenwood!"

"Here it is beautiful in summer!" said she; and they passed by old castles of knightly days, castles whose high walls and pointed turrets were mirrored in the canals, where swans swam about, and looked down the old shady avenues. In the fields the corn waved like a sea, in the ditches yellow and red flowers were growing, and in the hedges wild hops and blooming convolvolus. In the evening the moon rose round and large, and the haystacks in the meadows smelt sweet. "That is never forgotten."

"Here it is beautiful in autumn!" said the little girl; and the sky seemed twice as lofty and twice as blue as before; and the forest was decked in the most gorgeous tints of red, yellow, and green. The hunting dogs raced about; whole flocks of wild ducks flew screaming over the Hun-graves, on which bramble bushes twined over the old stones. The sea was dark blue, and covered with ships with white sails; and in the barns sat old women, girls, and children, picking hops into a large tub; the young people sang songs, and the older ones told tales of magicians and goblins. It could not be finer anywhere.

"Here it is beautiful in winter!" said the little girl; and all the trees were covered with hoar frost, so that they looked like white trees of coral. The snow crumbled beneath one's feet, as if every one had new boots on; and one shooting star after another fell from the sky. In the room the Christmas tree was lighted up, and there were presents, and there was happiness. In the country people's farmhouses the violin sounded, and there were merry games for apples; and even the poorest child said: "It is beautiful in winter!"

Yes, it was beautiful; and the little girl showed the boy everything; and still the blossoming tree smelt sweet, and still waved the red flag with the white cross, the flag under which the old seaman had sailed. The boy became a youth, and was to go out into the wide world, far away to the hot countries where the coffee grows. But when they were to part the little girl took an elder blossom from her breast, and gave it to him to keep. It was laid in his hymn-book, and in the foreign land, when he opened the book, it was always at the place where the flower of remembrance lay; and the more he looked at the flower the fresher it became, so that he seemed, as it were, to breathe the forest air of home; then he plainly saw the little girl, looking out, with her clear blue eyes, from between the petals of the flower, and then she whispered: "Here it is beautiful in spring, summer, autumn, and winter!" and hundreds of pictures glided through his thoughts.

Thus many years went by, and now he was an old man, and sat with his old wife under the blossoming elder-tree; they were holding each other by the hand, just as the great-grandmother and great-grandfather had done outside; and, like these, they spoke of old times and of the golden wedding. The little maiden with the blue eyes and with the elder blossoms in her hair sat up in the tree, and nodded to both of them and said: "To-day is your golden wedding-day!" and then she took two flowers out of her hair and kissed them, and they gleamed first like silver and then like gold, and when she laid them on the heads of the old people each changed into a golden crown. There they both sat, like a King and a Queen, under the fragrant tree which looked quite like an elder-bush, and he told his old wife of the story of the Elder-tree Mother, as it had been told to him when he was quite a little boy, and they both thought that the story in many points resembled their own, and those parts they liked the best.

"Yes, thus it is!" said the little girl in the tree. "Some call me Elder-tree Mother, others the Dryad, but my real name is Remembrance; it is I who sit in the tree that grows on and on, and I can think back and tell stories. Let me see if you have still your power."

And the old man opened his hymn-book; there lay the elder blossom as fresh as if it had only just been placed there, and Remembrance nodded, and the two old people with the golden crowns on their heads sat in the red evening sunlight, and they closed their eyes, and—and—the story was finished.

The little boy lay in his bed and did not know whether he had been dreaming or had heard a tale told; the teapot stood on the table, but no elder-bush was growing out of it, and the old man who had told about it was just going out of the door, and indeed he went.

"How beautiful that was!" said the little boy. "Mother, I have been in the hot countries."

"Yes, I can imagine that!" replied his mother. "When one drinks two cups of hot elder-tea one very often gets into the hot countries!" and she covered him up well, that he might not take cold. "You have slept well while I disputed with him as to whether it was a story or a fairy tale."

"And where is the elder-tree, mother?" asked the little lad.

"She's in the teapot," replied his mother; "and there she may stay."

FIVE OUT OF ONE SHELL

There were five peas in one shell; they were green, and the pod was green, and so they thought all the world was green; and that was just as it should be! The shell grew, and the peas grew; they accommodated themselves to circumstances, sitting all in a row. The sun shone without, and warmed the husk, and the rain made it clear and transparent; it was mild and agreeable in the bright day and in the dark night, just as it should be, and the peas as they sat there became bigger and bigger, and more and more thoughtful, for something they must do.

"Are we to sit here everlastingly?" asked one. "I'm afraid we shall become hard by long sitting. It seems to me, there must be something outside, I have a kind of inkling of it."

And weeks went by; the peas became yellow, and the pod turned yellow. "All the world's turning yellow," said they; and they had a right to say it.

Suddenly they felt a tug at the shell. The shell was torn off, passed through human hands, and glided down into the pocket of a jacket, in company with other full pods. "Now we shall soon be opened!" they said; and that is just what they were waiting for.

"I should like to know who of us will get farthest!" said the smallest of the five. "Yes, now it will soon show itself."

"What is to be, will be," said the biggest. "Crack!" the pod burst, and all the five peas rolled out into the bright sunshine. There they lay in a child's hand; a little boy was clutching them and said they were fine peas for his pea-shooter; and he put one in directly and shot it out.

"Now I'm flying out into the wide world, catch me if you can!" and he was gone. "I," said the second, "I shall fly straight into the sun. That's a shell worth looking at, and one that exactly suits me," and away he went.

"We'll go to sleep wherever we arrive," said the two next, "but we shall roll on all the same." And they certainly rolled and tumbled down on the ground before they got into the pea-shooter; but they were put in for all that. "We shall go farthest," said they.

"What is to happen will happen!" said the last, as he was shot forth out of the pea-shooter; and he flew up against the old board under the garret window, just into a crack which was filled up with moss and soft mould; and the moss closed round him; there he lay, a prisoner indeed, but not forgotten by provident nature.

"What is to happen will happen," said he.

Within, in the little garret, lived a poor woman, who went out in the day, to clean stoves, chop wood small, and to do other hard work of the same kind, for she was strong and industrious too. But she always remained poor; and at home in the garret lay her half-grown only daughter, who was very delicate and weak; for a whole year she had kept her bed, and it seemed as if she could neither live nor die.

"She is going to her little sister," the woman said. "I had only the two children, and it was not an easy thing to provide for both, but the good God provided for one of them by taking her home to Himself; now I should be glad to keep the other that was left to me; but I suppose they are not to remain separated, and my sick girl will go to her sister in heaven."

But the sick girl remained where she was; she lay quiet and patient all day long while her mother went to earn money out of doors. It was spring, and early in the morning, just as the mother was about to go out to work, the sun shone mildly and pleasantly through the little window, and threw its rays across the floor; and the sick girl fixed her eyes on the lowest pane in the window.

"What may that green thing be that looks in at the window? It is moving in the wind."

And the mother stepped to the window, and half opened it. "Oh!" said she "on my word, that is a little pea which has taken root here, and is putting out its little leaves. How can it have got here into the crack? That is a little garden with which you can amuse yourself."

And the sick girl's bed was moved nearer to the window, so that she could see the growing pea; and the mother went forth to her work.

"Mother, I think I shall get well," said the sick child in the evening. "The sun shone in upon me to-day, delightfully warm. The little pea is prospering famously, and I shall prosper too, and get up, and go out into the warm sunshine."

"God grant it!" said the mother, but she did not believe it would be so; but she took care to prop with a little stick the green plant which had given her daughter the pleasant thoughts of life, so that it might not be broken by the wind; she tied a piece of string to the window-sill, and to the upper part of the frame, so that the pea might have something round which it could twine, when it shot up; and it did shoot up indeed, one could see how it grew every day.

"Really, here is a flower coming!" said the woman one day; and now she began to cherish the hope that her sick daughter would recover; she remembered that lately the child had spoken much more cheerfully than before, that in the last few days it had risen up in bed of its own accord and had sat upright, looking with delighted eyes at the little garden in which only one plant grew. A week afterwards the invalid for the first time sat up for a whole hour. Quite happy she sat there in the warm sunshine; the window was opened, and outside, before it stood a pink pea-blossom fully blown. The sick girl bent down, and gently kissed the delicate leaves. This day was like a festival.

"The Heavenly Father himself has planted that pea, and caused it to prosper, to be a joy to you, and to me also, my blessed child!" said the glad mother, and she smiled at the flower, as if it had been a good angel.

But about the other peas! Why, the one who flew out into the wide world, and said, "Catch me if you can," fell into the gutter on the roof, and found a home in a pigeon's crop. The two lazy ones got just as far, for they, too, were eaten up by pigeons, and thus, at any rate they were of some real use; but the fourth who wanted to go up into the sun fell into the sink, and lay there in the dirty water for weeks and weeks and swelled prodigiously.

"How beautifully fat I'm growing!" said the pea. "I shall burst at last; and I don't think any pea can do more than that. I'm the most remarkable of all the five that were in the shell," and the sink said he was right.

But the young girl at the garret window stood there with gleaming eyes, with the roseate hue of health on her cheeks, and folded her thin hands over the pea-blossom, and thanked heaven for it.

"I," said the sink, "stand up for my own pea."

THE SNOW QUEEN

In Seven Stories

FIRST STORY
Which treats of the mirror and fragments

Look you, now we're going to begin. When we are at the end of the story we shall know more than we do now, for he was a bad goblin. He was one of the very worst, for he was a demon. One day he was in very good spirits, for he had made a mirror, which had this peculiarity, that everything good and beautiful that was reflected in it, shrunk together into almost nothing, but that whatever was worthless and looked ugly became prominent and looked worse than ever. The most lovely landscapes seen in this mirror looked like boiled spinach, and the best people became hideous, or stood on their heads and had no bodies; their faces were so distorted as to be unrecognizable, and a single freckle was shown spread out over nose and mouth. That was very amusing, the demon said. When a good pious thought passed through any person's mind these were again shown in the mirror, so that the demon chuckled at his artistic invention. Those who visited the goblin school,—for he kept a goblin school,—declared everywhere that a

The magic mirror

wonder had been wrought. For now, they asserted, one could see, for the first time, how the world, and the people in it really looked. Now they wanted to fly up to heaven, to sneer and scoff at the angels themselves. The higher they flew with the mirror, the more it grinned; they could scarcely hold it fast. They flew higher and higher, and then the mirror trembled so terribly amid its grinning that it fell down out of their hands to the earth, where it was shattered into a hundred million million and more fragments. And now this mirror occasioned much more unhappiness than before; for some of the fragments were scarcely so large as a sandcorn, and these flew about in the world, and whenever they flew into anyone's eye they stuck there, and those people saw everything wrongly, or had only eyes for the bad side of a thing, for every little fragment of the mirror had retained the same power which the whole glass possessed. A few persons even got a fragment of the mirror into their hearts, and that was terrible indeed; for such a heart became a block of ice. A few fragments of the mirror were so large that they were used as window panes; but it was a bad thing to look at one's friends through these panes; other pieces were made into spectacles, and then it went badly when people put on these spectacles to see rightly and to be just; and then the demon laughed till his paunch shook, for it tickled him so. But without, some little fragments of glass still floated about in the air—and now we shall hear.

SECOND STORY
A little boy, and a little girl

In the great town where there are many houses and so many people, that there is not room enough for everyone to have a little garden, and where consequently most persons are compelled to be content with some flowers in flower-pots, were two poor children who possessed a garden somewhat larger than a flower-pot. They were not brother and sister, but they loved each other quite as much as if they had been. Their parents lived just opposite each other in two garrets, there, where the roof of one neighbour's house joined that of another; and where the water-pipe ran between the two houses was a little window; one had only to step across the pipe to get from one window to the other.

The parents of each child had a great box, in which grew kitchen herbs that they used, and a little rose-bush; there was one in each box and they grew famously. Now it occurred to the parents to place the boxes across the pipe, so that they reached from one window to another, and looked quite like two embankments of flowers. Pea plants hung down over the boxes, and the rose-bushes shot forth long twigs, which clustered round the windows and bent down towards each other, it was almost like a triumphal arch of flowers and leaves. As the boxes were very high and the children knew that they might not creep upon them, they often obtained permission to step out upon the roof behind the boxes, and to sit upon their little stools under the roses, and there they could play capitally.

In the winter there was an end of this amusement. The windows were sometimes quite frozen over. But then they warmed copper shillings on the stove, and held the warm coin against the frozen pane; and this made a capital peep-hole, so round, so round, and behind it gleamed a pretty mild eye one at each window; and these eyes belonged to the little boy and the little girl. His name was Kay and her's Gerda.

In the summer they could get to one another at one bound; but in the winter they had to go down and up the long staircase, while the snow was pelting without.

"Those are the white bees swarming," said the old grandmother.

"Have they a Queen-bee?" asked the little boy. For he knew that there is one among the real bees.

"Yes, they have one," replied grandmamma. "She flies there, where they swarm thickest. She is the largest of them all, and never remains quiet upon the earth; she flies up again into the black cloud. Many a midnight she is flying through the streets of the town, and looks in at the windows, and then they freeze in such a strange way, and look like flowers."

"Yes, I've seen that!" cried both the children; and now they knew that it was true.

"Can the Snow Queen come in here?" asked the little girl. "Only let her come," cried the boy; "I'll set her upon the warm stove, and then she'll melt."

But grandmother smoothed his hair, and told some other tales.

In the evening, when little Kay was at home and half undressed, he clambered upon the chair by the window, and looked through the little hole; a few flakes of snow were falling outside, and one of them, the largest of them all, remained lying on the edge of one of the flower-boxes. The snow-flake grew larger and larger, and at last became a maiden clothed in the finest white gauze, put together of millions of starry flakes. She was beautiful and delicate, but of ice—of shining, glittering ice. Yet she was alive; her eyes flashed like two clear stars; but there was no peace or rest in them. She nodded towards the window, and beckoned with her hand. The little boy was frightened, and sprang down from the chair; then it seemed as if a great bird flew by outside, in front of the window.

Next day there was a clear frost, and then the spring came; the sun shone, the green sprouted forth, the swallows built nests, the windows were opened, and the little children again sat in their garden high up in the roof, over all the floors.

How splendidly the roses bloomed this summer! The little girl had learned a psalm, in which mention was made of roses; and, in speaking of roses, she thought of her own; and she sang it to the little boy, and he sang, too,—

The roses will fade and pass away,
But we the Christ-child shall see one day.

And the little ones held each other by the hand, kissed the roses, looked at God's bright sunshine, and spoke to it, as if the Christ-child were there. What splendid summer days those were! How beautiful it was without, among the fresh rose-bushes, which seemed as if they would never leave off blooming!

Kay and Gerda sat and looked at the picture-book of beasts and birds. Then it was while the clock was just striking twelve on the church-tower, that Kay said, "Oh! Something struck my heart and pricked me in the eye."

The little girl fell upon his neck; he blinked his eyes. No, there was nothing at all to be seen.

"I think it is gone," said he; but it was not gone. It was just one of those glass fragments which sprung from the mirror—the magic mirror that we remember well, the ugly glass that made everything great and good which was mirrored in it to seem small and mean; but in which the mean and the wicked things were brought out in relief, and every fault was noticeable at once. Poor little Kay had also received a splinter just in his heart, and that will now soon become like a lump of ice. It did not hurt him now, but the splinter was still there.

"Why do you cry?" he asked. "You look ugly like that. There's nothing the matter with me. Oh, fie!" he suddenly exclaimed, "that rose is worm-eaten, and this one is quite crooked. After all, they're ugly roses. They're like the box in which they stand;" and then he kicked the box with his foot, and tore both the roses off.

"Kay, what are you about?" cried the little girl; and when he noticed her fright he tore off another rose, and then sprang in at his own window, away from little pretty Gerda.

When she afterwards came with her picture-book, he said it was only fit for babies in arms; and when grandmother told stories he always came in with a but; and when he could manage it, he would get

Gerda and Kay

behind her, put on a pair of spectacles, and talk just as she did; he could do that very cleverly, and the people laughed at him. Soon he could mimic the speech and the gait of everybody in the street. Everything that was peculiar or ugly about him Kay could imitate; and people said, "That boy must certainly have a remarkable head." But it was the glass that stuck deep in his heart; so it happened that he even teased little Gerda, who loved him with all her heart.

His games now became quite different to what they had been before; they became quite sensible. One winter's day when it snowed he came out with a great burning glass, held up the blue tail of his coat and let the snow-flakes fall upon it:

"Now look at the glass, Gerda," said he, and every flake of snow was magnified, and looked like a splendid flower, or a star with ten points; it was beautiful to behold. "See how clever that is," said Kay. "That's much more interesting than real flowers, and there is not a single fault in it, they're quite regular, until they begin to melt."

Soon after Kay came in thick gloves, and with his sledge upon his back, he called up to Gerda, "I've got leave to go into the great square, where the other boys play," and he was gone.

In the great square the boldest among the boys often tied their sledges to the country people's carts, and thus rode with them a good way. That went capitally. When they were in the midst of their playing there came a great sledge. It was painted quite white, and in it sat somebody wrapped in a rough white fur, and with a white rough cap on his head. The sledge drove twice round the square, and Kay bound his little sledge to it, and so he drove on with it. It went faster and faster straight into the next street. The man who drove turned round and nodded in a friendly way to Kay; it was as if they knew one another; each time when Kay wanted to cast loose his little sledge, the stranger nodded again, and then Kay remained where he was, and thus they drove out of the town-gate. Then the snow began to fall so rapidly that the boy could not see a hand's breadth before him, but still he drove on. Now he hastily dropped the cord, so as to get loose from the great sledge, but that was no use, his sledge was fast bound to the other, and now they went on like the wind. Then he called out quite loudly, but nobody heard him; and the snow beat down, and the sledge flew onward; every now and then it gave a jump, and they seemed to be flying over hedges and ditches. The boy was quite frightened. He wanted to say his prayer, but could remember nothing but the multi-plication table.

The snow-flakes became larger and larger, at last they looked like great white fowls. All at once they sprang aside and the great sledge stopped, and the person who had driven it rose up. The fur and the cap were made altogether of ice, it was *a lady*, tall and slender, and bril-liantly white; it was the Snow Queen.

"We have driven well!" said she. "But why do you tremble with cold, creep into my fur." And she seated him beside her in her own sledge, and wrapped the fur round him, he felt as if he sank into a snowdrift.

"Are you still cold?" asked she, and then she kissed him on the forehead. Oh, that was colder than ice; it went quite through to his heart, half of which was already a lump of ice; he felt as if he were going to die; but only for a moment; for then he seemed quite well, and he did not notice the cold all about him.

"My sledge! Don't forget my sledge." That was the first thing he thought of; and it was bound fast to one of the white chickens, and this chicken flew behind him with the sledge upon its back. The Snow Queen kissed Kay again, and then he had forgotten little Gerda, his grandmother and all at home.

"Now you shall have no more kisses," said she, "for if you did I should kiss you to death."

Kay looked at her. She was so beautiful, he could not imagine a more sensible or lovely face; now she did not appear to him to be made of ice as before, when she sat at the window and beckoned to him. In his eyes she was perfect; he did not feel at all afraid. He told her that he could do mental arithmetic, as far as fractions; that he knew the number of square miles and the number of inhabitants in the country. And she always smiled, and then it seemed to him that what he knew was not enough, and he looked up into the wide sky, and she flew with him high up upon the black cloud, and the storm blew and whistled; it seemed as though the wind sang old songs. They flew over woods and lakes, over sea and land; below them roared the cold wind, the wolves howled, the snow crackled; over him flew the black scream-ing crows; but above all the moon shone bright and clear, and Kay looked at the long, long winter night; by day he slept at the feet of the Queen.

THIRD STORY
The flower garden of the woman who could conjure

But how did it fare with little Gerda, when Kay did not return? What could have become of him? No one knew, no one could give informa-tion. The boys only told that they had seen him bind his sledge to another very large one, which had driven along the street, and out at the town-gate. Nobody knew what had become of him; many tears were shed, and little Gerda especially wept long and bitterly—then she said he was dead; he had been drowned in the river which flowed close by their school; oh, those were very dark long winter days! But now spring came, with warmer sunshine.

"Kay is dead and gone!" said little Gerda.

"I don't believe it!"—said the sunshine.

"He is dead and gone!" she said to the sparrows.

"We don't believe it!" they replied; and at last little Gerda did not believe it herself.

"I will put on my new red shoes,"—she said, one morning,—"those that Kay has never seen; and then I will go down to the river, and ask for him!"

It was still very early; she kissed the old grandmother, who was still asleep, put on her red shoes, and went quite alone out of the town-gate towards the river.

"Is it true, that you have taken away my little playmate from me? I will give you my red shoes, if you will give him back to me!"

And it seemed to her as if the waves nodded quite strangely; and then she took her red shoes, that she liked best of anything she possessed, and threw them both into the river; but they fell close to the shore, and the little wavelets carried them back to her, to the land; it seemed as if the river would not take from her the dearest things she possessed because he had not her little Kay; but she thought she had not thrown the shoes far enough out; so she crept into a boat that lay among the reeds; she went to the other end of the boat, and threw the shoes from thence into the water; but the boat was not bound fast, and at the movement she made, it glided away from the shore. She noticed it, and hurried to get back, but before she reached the other end the boat was a yard from the bank, and it drifted away faster than before.

Then little Gerda was very much frightened, and began to cry: but no one heard her except the sparrows, and they could not carry her to land; but they flew along by the shore, and sang, as if to console her, "Here we are, here we are!" The boat drove on with the stream; little Gerda sat quite still, with only her stockings on her feet; her little red shoes floated along behind her, but they could not come up to the boat for that made more way.

Gerda and the strange woman

It was very pretty on both shores; there were beautiful flowers, old trees and slopes, with sheep and cows; but not one person was to be seen.

"Perhaps the river will carry me to little Kay," thought Gerda; and then she became more cheerful, and rose up, and for many hours she watched the charming green banks; then she came to a great cherry orchard, in which stood a little house with remarkable blue and red windows; it had a thatched roof, and without stood two wooden soldiers, who presented arms to those who sailed past.

Gerda called to them, for she thought they were alive; but of course they did not answer: she came quite close to them; the river carried the boat, towards the shore.

Gerda called still louder, and then there came out of the house an old woman leaning on a crutch; she had on a great velvet hat painted over with the finest flowers.

"You poor little child!" said the old woman; "how did you manage to come on the great rolling river, and to have floated thus far out into the world?" And then the old woman went quite into the water, seized the boat with her crutch-stick, drew it to land, and lifted little Gerda out. And Gerda was glad to be on dry land again, though she felt a little afraid of the strange old woman.

"Come and tell me who you are, and how you came here," said the old lady. And Gerda told her everything; and the old woman shook her head, and said "Hem, hem!" and when Gerda had told everything, and asked if she had not seen little Kay, the woman said that he had not yet come by, but that he probably would still come. Gerda was not to be sorrowful, but to look at the flowers, and taste the cherries, for they were better than any picture-book, for each one of them could tell a story. Then she took Gerda by the hand and led her into the little house, and the old woman locked the door.

The windows were very high, and the panes were red, blue, and yellow; the daylight shone in a remarkable way, with different colours. On the table stood the finest cherries, and Gerda ate as many of them as she liked, for she had leave to do so. While she was eating them, the old lady combed her hair with a golden comb, and the hair hung in ringlets of pretty yellow, round the friendly little face which looked as blooming as a rose.

"I have long wished for such a dear little girl as you," said the old lady. "Now you shall see how well we shall live with one another;" and as the ancient dame combed her hair, Gerda forgot her adopted brother Kay more and more; for this old woman could conjure, but she was not a wicked witch. She only practised a little magic for her own amusement, and wanted to keep little Gerda. Therefore she went into the garden, stretched out her crutch towards all the rose-bushes, and, beautiful as they were, they all sank into the earth, and one could not tell where they had stood. The old woman was afraid that if the little girl saw roses, she would think of her own, and remember little Kay, and run away.

Now she led Gerda out into the flower-garden. What fragrance was there, and what loveliness! Every conceivable flower was here in full bloom; there were some for every season; no picture-book could be gayer and prettier. Gerda jumped high for joy, and played till the sun went down behind the high cherry-trees; then she was put into a lovely bed with red silk pillows stuffed with blue violets; and she slept there, and dreamed as gloriously as a Queen on her wedding day.

One day she played again with the flowers in the warm sunshine;

and thus many days went by. Gerda knew every flower; but as many as there were of them, it still seemed to her as if one were wanting; but which one she did not know. One day she sat looking at the old lady's hat with the painted flowers; and the prettiest of them all was a rose. The old lady had forgotten to efface it from her hat when she caused the others to disappear. But so it is, when one does not keep one's wits about one. "What! are there no roses here?" cried Gerda; and she went among the beds, and searched and searched, but there was not one to be found. Then she sat down and wept; her tears fell just upon a spot where a rose-bud lay buried, and when the warm tears moistened the earth, the tree at once sprouted up as blooming as when it had sunk; and Gerda embraced it and kissed the roses, and thought of the beautiful roses at home, and also of little Kay.

"Oh, how I have been detained!" said the little girl. "I wanted to seek for little Kay! Do you not know where he is?" she asked the roses. "Do you think he is dead?"

"He is not dead," the roses answered. "We have been in the ground. All the dead people are there. But Kay is not there." "Thank you," said little Gerda; and she went to the other flowers, looked into their cups, and asked: "Do you not know where little Kay is?" But every flower stood in the sun thinking of her own story or fancy tale: Gerda heard many, many of them; but not one knew anything of Kay.

And what did the tiger-lily say?

"Do you hear the drum 'Rub-dub!' There are only two notes, always rub-dub! Hear the morning song of the women, hear the call of the priests. The Hindoo widow stands in her long red mantle on the funeral pile; the flames rise up around her and her dead husband; but the Hindoo woman is thinking of the living one here in the circle, of him whose eyes burn hotter than flames, whose fiery glances have burned in her soul more ardently than the flames themselves, which are soon to burn her body to ashes. Can the flame of the heart die in the flame of the funeral pile?"

"I don't understand that at all!" said little Gerda. "That's my story," said the lily.

What says the convolvulus?

"Over the narrow road looms an old knightly castle, thickly the ivy grows over the crumbling red walls, leaf by leaf up to the balcony, and there stands a beautiful girl; she bends over the balustrade and glances up the road. No rose on its branch is fresher than she; no apple blossom wafted onward by the wind floats more lightly along. How her costly silks rustle. Comes he not yet?"

"Is it Kay, whom you mean?" asked little Gerda. "I'm only speaking of a story, my dream," replied the convolvulus.

What said the little snowdrop?

"Between the trees a long board hangs by ropes, that is a swing; two pretty little girls, with clothes white as snow, and long green silk ribands on their hats, are sitting upon it swinging; their brother, who is greater than they, stands in the swing, he has slung his arm round the rope to hold himself, for in one hand he has a little saucer, and in the other a clay pipe; he's blowing bubbles, the swing flies, and the bubbles rise with beautiful changing colours, the last still hangs from the pipe-bowl, swaying in the wind. The swing flies on, the little black dog light as the bubbles, stands up on his hind legs and wants to be taken into the swing; it flies on, the dog falls, barks, and grows angry, he is teased, and the bubble bursts. A swinging board, a bursting bubble, that is my song."

"It may be very pretty what you're telling, but you speak it so mournfully, and you don't mention little Kay at all."

What do the hyacinths say?

"There were three beautiful sisters, transparent and delicate, the dress of one was red, that of the second blue, and that of the third quite white; hand in hand they danced by the calm lake in the bright moonlight. They were not elves, they were human beings. It was so sweet and fragrant there; and the girls disappeared in the forest, the sweet fragrance became stronger; three coffins, with the three beautiful maidens lying in them, glided from the wood-thicket across the lake; the glow-worms, flew gleaming about them like little hovering lights. Are the dancing girls sleeping, or, are they dead? The flower-scent says they are dead, the evening-bell tolls their knell."

"You make me quite sorrowful," said little Gerda. "You scent so strongly, I cannot help thinking of the dead maidens! Ah! Is little Kay really dead? The roses have been down in the earth, and they say no."

"Kling, klang!" tolled the hyacinth bells; "we are not tolling for little Kay, we don't know him, we only sing our song, the only one we know."

And Gerda went to the buttercup, gleaming forth from the green leaves. "You are a little bright sun," said Gerda. "Tell me if you know where I may find my companion?"

And the buttercup shone so gaily, and looked back at Gerda. What song might the buttercup sing? It was not about Kay.

"In a little courtyard the clear sun shone so warm on the first day of spring. The sunbeams glided down the white wall of the neighbouring house; close by grew the first yellow flower, glancing like gold in the bright sun's ray, the old grandmother sat out of doors in her chair; her granddaughter, a poor handsome maid servant, was coming home from a short visit, she kissed her grandmother; there was gold, heart's gold, in that blessed kiss, gold in the mouth, gold in the south, gold in the morning hour. See that's my little story," said the buttercup.

"My poor old grandmother!" sighed Gerda. "Yes she is surely longing for me, and grieving for me, just as she did for little Kay. But I shall soon go home and take Kay with me. There is no use of my asking the flowers, they only know their own song, and give me no information, and then she tied her little frock round her that she might run the faster; but the jonquil struck against her leg, as she sprang over it, and she stopped to look at the tall yellow flower, and asked, "Do you perhaps know anything?" And she bent quite down to the flower, and what did it say?

"I can see myself! I can see myself!" said the jonquil. "Oh, oh! how I smell! Up in the little room, in the gable, stands a little dancing girl, she stands sometimes on one foot, sometimes on both; she seems to tread on all the world, she's nothing but an ocular delusion, she pours water out of a teapot on a bit of stuff, it is her bodice. Cleanliness is a fine thing, she says; her white frock hangs on a hook, it has been washed in the teapot too, and dried on the roof, she puts it on and ties her saffron handkerchief round her neck, and the dress looks all the whiter. Point your toes, look how she seems to stand on a stalk. I can see myself! I can see myself!"

"I don't care at all about that," said Gerda. "You need not tell me that," and then she ran to the end of the garden.

The door was locked, but she pressed against the rusty lock and it broke off, the door sprang open, and little Gerda ran with naked feet out into the wide world. She looked back three times, but no one was there to pursue her, at last she could run no longer, and seated herself on a great stone, and when she looked round, the summer was over; it was late in autumn, one could not notice that in the beautiful garden, where there was always sunshine, and the flowers of every season.

"Alas! how I have loitered," said little Gerda. "Autumn has come. I may not rest again," and she rose up to go on.

Oh! How sore and tired her little feet were. All around it looked cold and bleak; the long willow leaves were quite yellow, and the dew fell down like water; one leaf after another dropped; only the sloe-thorn still bore fruit, but the sloes were sour, and set the teeth on edge. Oh! How grey and gloomy it looked, the wide world.

FOURTH STORY
Prince and Princess

Gerda was compelled to rest again; then there came hopping across the snow, just opposite the spot where she was sitting, a great crow. This crow stopped a long time to look at her, nodding its head—now it said, "Krah, krah! Good day! Good day!" It could not pronounce better, but it felt friendly towards the little girl, and asked where she was going all alone in the wide world. The word *alone* Gerda understood very well, and felt how much it expressed, and she told the crow the whole story of her life and fortunes, and asked if it had not seen Kay.

And the crow nodded very gravely, and said, "That may be, that may be!"

"What? Do you think so?" cried the little girl; and nearly pressed the crow to death, she kissed it so. "Gently, gently," said the crow; "I think I know; I believe it may be little Kay, but he has certainly forgotten you, with the Princess."

"Does he live with a princess?" asked Gerda. "Yes; listen," said the crow. "But it's so difficult for me to speak your language. If you know the crow's language I can tell it much better."

"No; I never learned it," said Gerda; "but my grandmother understood stood it, and could speak the language too. I only wish I had learned it."

"That doesn't matter," said the crow. "But it will go badly;" and then the crow told what it knew.

"In the country in which we now are lives a Princess who is quite wonderfully clever, but then she has read all the newspapers in the world and has forgotten them again, she's so clever. Lately she was sitting on the throne—and that's not so pleasant as is generally supposed—and she began to sing a song, and it was just this, 'Why should I not marry yet?' You see there was something in that," said the crow; "and so she wanted to marry, but she wished for a husband who could answer when he was spoken to, not one who only stood and looked handsome, for that was wearisome. Now she had all her maids of honour summoned, and when they heard her intention they were very glad. 'I like that,' said they. 'I thought the very thing the other day.' You may be sure that every word I'm telling you is true," added the crow. "I have a tame sweetheart who goes about freely in the castle, and she told me everything."

Of course the sweetheart was a crow, for one crow always finds out another, and birds of a feather flock together.

"Newspapers were published directly, with a border of hearts and the Princess's initials. One could read in them that every young man

Gerda and the crow

who was good-looking might come to the castle and speak with the princess, and him who spoke so that one could hear he was at home there, and who spoke best, the Princess would choose for her husband. Yes, yes," said the crow, "you may believe me. It's as true as I sit here. Young men came flocking in, there was a great crowding and much running to and fro, but no one succeeded the first or second day. They could all speak well when they were out in the streets, but when they entered at the palace gates, and saw the guards standing in their silver lace, and went up the staircase, and saw the lackeys in their golden liveries, and the great lighted halls, they became confused. And when they stood before the throne itself, on which the Princess sat, they could do nothing but repeat the last word she had spoken, and she did not care to hear her own words again. It was just as if the people in there had taken some narcotic and fallen asleep, till they got into the street again, for not till then were they able to speak. There stood a whole row of them, from the town-gate to the palace-gate. I went out myself to see it," said the crow. "They were hungry and thirsty, but in the palace they did not receive so much as a glass of lukewarm water. A few of the wisest had brought bread and butter with them, but they would not share with their neighbours, for they thought, 'Let him look hungry, and the Princess won't have him.'"

"But Kay, little Kay?" asked Gerda. "When did he come? Was he among the crowd?"

"Wait, wait! We're just coming to him. It was on the third day that there came a little personage, without horse or carriage, walking quite merrily up to the castle; his eyes sparkled like yours, he had fine long hair, but his clothes were shabby." "That was Kay!" cried Gerda, rejoicingly. "Oh, then I have found him!" and she clapped her hands.

"He had a little knapsack on his back," observed the crow. "No, that must certainly have been his sledge," said Gerda; "for he went away with a sledge."

"That may well be," said the crow. "I did not look to it very closely. But this much I know from my tame sweetheart, that when he passed under the palace gate and saw the Life Guards in silver, and mounted the staircase and saw the lackeys in gold, he was not in the least embarrassed. He nodded, and said to them, 'It must be tedious work standing on the stairs—I'd rather go in.' The halls shone full of lights; Privy

Councillors and Excellencies walked about with bare feet, and carried golden vessels; anyone might have become solemn; and his boots creaked most noisily, but he was not embarrassed."

"That is certainly Kay!" cried Gerda. "He had new boots on; I've heard them creak in grandmother's room."

"Yes, certainly they creaked!" resumed the crow. "And he went boldly into the Princess herself, who sat on a pearl that was as big as a spinning wheel; and all the maids of honour with their attendants, and the attendants' attendants, and all the cavaliers with their followers, and the followers of their followers, who themselves kept a page a piece were standing round; and the nearer they stood to the door, the prouder they looked. The followers' followers' pages, who always went in slippers, could hardly be looked at, so proudly they stood in the door-way!"

"That must be terrible!" faltered little Gerda. "And yet Kay won the Princess?"

"If I had not been a crow, I would have married her myself, notwithstanding that I am engaged. They say he spoke as well as I can when I speak the crow's language; I heard that from my tame sweetheart. He was merry and agreeable; he had not come to marry, but only to hear the wisdom of the Princess; and he approved of her, and she of him."

"Yes, certainly that was Kay!" said Gerda. "He was so clever, he could do mental arithmetic up to fractions. Oh! Won't you lead me to the castle too?"

"That's easily said," replied the crow. "But how are we to manage it? I'll talk it over with my tame sweetheart; she can probably advise us; for this I must tell you. A little girl, like yourself, will never get leave to go completely in!"

"Yes, I shall get leave," said Gerda. "When Kay hears that I'm there he'll come out directly, and bring me in."

"Wait for me yonder at the grating," said the crow; and it wagged its head and flew away.

It was already late in the evening, when the crow came back "Rax, Rax," it said. "I'm to greet you kindly from my sweetheart, and here's a little loaf for you. She took it from the kitchen. There's plenty of bread there, and you must be hungry. You can't possibly get into the palace, for you are barefoot, and the guards in silver and the lackeys in gold would not allow it. But don't cry; you shall go up. My sweetheart knows a little back staircase that leads up to the bed-room, and she knows where she can get the key."

And they went into the garden, into the great avenue, where one leaf was falling down after another; and when the lights were extinguished in the palace, one after the other, the crow led Gerda to a back-door, which stood ajar.

Oh, how Gerda's heart beat with fear and longing! It was just as if she had been going to do something wicked; and yet she only wanted to know if it was little Kay. Yes, it must be he; she thought so deeply of his clear eyes, and his long hair, she could fancy she saw how he smiled as he had smiled at home when they sat among the roses. He would certainly be glad to see her; to hear what a long distance they had come for his sake; to know how sorry they had all been at home when he did not come back. Oh, what a fear and what a joy that was!

Now they were on the staircase; a little lamp was burning upon a cupboard; in the middle of the floor stood the tame crow turning her head on every side and looking at Gerda, who curtsied as her grand-mother had taught her to do.

"My betrothed has spoken to me very favourably of you, my little lady," said the tame crow. "Your history, as it may be called, is very moving. Will you take the lamp, then I will precede you. We will go the straight way, and then we shall meet nobody."

"I feel as if some one were coming after us," said Gerda and something rushed by her; it seemed like a shadow on the wall; horses with flying manes and thin legs, hunters, ladies and gentlemen on horseback.

"These are only dreams," said the crow, "they are coming to carry the high masters' thoughts out hunting. That's all the better, for you may look at them the more closely, in bed. But I hope, when you are taken into favour and get promotion, you will show a grateful heart."
"Of that we may be sure!" observed the crow from the wood.

Now they came into the first hall; it was hung with rose-coloured satin, and artifical flowers were worked on the walls, and here the dreams came already flitting by them, but they moved so quickly that Gerda could not see the high-born lords and ladies. Each hall was more splendid than the last; yes, one could almost become bewildered! Now they were in the bed-chamber. Here the ceiling was like a great palm-tree with leaves of glass, of costly glass, and in the middle of the floor two beds hung on a thick stalk of gold, and each of them looked like a lily; one of them was white and in that lay the Princess; the other was red, and in that Gerda was to seek little Kay. She bent one of the red leaves aside, and then she saw a little brown neck. Oh, that was Kay! She called out his name quite loud, and held the lamp towards him—the dreams rushed into the room again on horseback—he awoke, turned his head, and—it was not little Kay.

The Prince was only like him in the neck; but he was young and good-looking, and the Princess looked up, blinking, from the white lily, and asked who was there. Then little Gerda wept, and told her whole history, and all that the crows had done for her.

"You poor child!" said the Prince and Princess; and they praised the crows and said that they were not angry with them at all, but the crows were not to do it again. However, they should be rewarded.

"Will you fly out free?" asked the Princess, "or will you have fixed positions as court crows, with the right to everything that is left in the kitchen?" and the two crows bowed, and begged for fixed positions, for they thought of their old age and said, "It was so good to have some provisions for one's old days," as they called them.

And the Prince got up out of his bed, and let Gerda sleep in it, and he could not do more than that. She folded her little hands and thought: "How good men and animals are!" and then she shut her eyes and went quietly to sleep. All the dreams came flying in again looking like angels; and they drew a little sledge, on which Kay sat nodding; but all this was only a dream, and therefore it was gone again so soon as she awoke.

The next day she was clothed from head to foot in velvet; and an offer was made to her that she should stay in the castle and enjoy pleasant times; but she only begged for a little carriage with a horse to draw it and a pair of little boots; then she would drive out into the world and seek for Kay.

And she received not only boots, but a muff likewise; she was neatly dressed; and when she was ready to depart a coach made of pure gold stopped before the door. Upon it shone like a star the coat-of-arms of the Prince and Princess; coachmen, footmen and outriders, for there were outriders too, sat on horseback with gold crowns on their heads. The Prince and Princess themselves helped her into the carriage, and wished her all good fortune. The forest crow who was now married, accompanied her the first three miles; he sat by Gerda's side, for he could not bear riding backwards: the other crow stood in the door-way flapping its wings, it did not go with them, for it suffered from headache, that had come on since it had obtained a fixed position and was allowed to eat too much. The coach was lined with sugar-biscuits, and in the seat there were gingerbread-nuts and fruit.

"Farewell, farewell!" cried the Prince and Princess; and little Gerda wept, and the crow wept. So they went on for the first three miles; and then the crow said good-bye, and that was the heaviest parting of all; the crow flew up on a tree, and beat its black wings as long as it could see the coach which glittered like the bright sunshine.

FIFTH STORY
The little robber-girl

They drove on through the thick forest, but the coach gleamed like a torch, that dazzled the robber's eyes, and they could not bear it.

"That is gold, that is gold!" cried they; and rushed forward, and seized the horses, killed the postillions, the coachman and the footman, and then pulled little Gerda out of the carriage.

"She is fat, she is pretty, she is fed with nut-kernels!" said the old robber-woman, who had a very long matted beard, and shaggy eyebrows that hung down over her eyes. "She's as good as a little pet lamb; how I shall relish her!" and she drew out her shining knife that gleamed in a horrible way.

"Oh!" screamed the old woman, at the same moment; for her own daughter who hung at her back bit her ear in a very naughty and spiteful manner. "You ugly brat!" screamed the old woman; and she had not time to kill Gerda.

"She shall play with me!" said the little robber-girl. "She shall give me her muff, and her pretty dress, and sleep with me in my bed!" and then the girl gave another bite, so that the woman jumped high up, and turned right round, and all the robbers laughed and said, "Look how she dances with her calf."

"I want to go into the carriage," said the little robber-girl. And she would have her own way, for she was spoiled, and very obstinate; and she and Gerda sat in the carriage, and drove over stock and stone deep into the forest. The little robber-girl was as big as Gerda, but stronger and more broad-shouldered, and she had a brown skin; her eyes were quite black, and they looked almost mournful. She clasped little Gerda round the waist, and said, "They shall not kill you as long as I am not angry with you. I suppose you are a Princess?"

"No," replied Gerda. And she told all that had happened to her, and how fond she was of little Kay.

The robber-girl looked at her quite seriously, nodded slightly and said, "They shall not kill you even if I do get angry with you; for then I will do it myself." And then she dried Gerda's eyes and put her two hands into the beautiful muff that was so soft and warm.

Now the coach stopped, and they were in the court-yard of a robber-castle, it had burst from the top to the ground; ravens and crows flew out of the great holes, big bulldogs—and each of which looked as if he could devour a man—jumped high up, but they did not bark, for that was forbidden.

In the old, great smoky hall, a bright fire burned upon the stone floor, the smoke passed along under the ceiling, and had to seek an exit for itself. A great cauldron of soup was boiling; and hares and rabbits were roasting on the spit.

"You shall sleep to-night with me and all my little animals;" said the robber-girl. They got something to eat and drink and then went to a corner, where straw and carpets were spread out. Above these sat on laths and perches more than a hundred pigeons, they all seemed asleep but they turned a little when the two little girls came.

"All these belong to me!" said the little robber-girl; and she quickly seized one of the nearest, held it by the feet and shook it so that it flapped its wings. "Kiss it!" she cried, and beat it in Gerda's face. "There sit the wood-rascals!" she continued, pointing to a number of laths that had been nailed in front of a hole in the wall. "Those are wood-rascals, those two; they fly away directly, if one does not keep them well locked up, and here's my old sweetheart, "Ba," and she pulled out by the horn a reindeer, that was tied up, and had a polished copper ring round its neck. "We're obliged to keep him tight too, or he'll run away from us. Every evening I tickle his neck with a sharp knife, and he's very frightened at that," and the little girl drew a long knife from a cleft in the wall, and let it glide over the reindeer's neck; the poor creature kicked out its legs, and the little robber-girl laughed and drew Gerda into bed with her.

"Do you keep the knife while you're asleep?" asked Gerda, and looked at it in rather a frightened way.

"I always sleep with my knife," replied the little robber-girl. "One does not know what may happen. But now tell me again what you told me just now about little Kay, and why you came out into the wide world." And Gerda told again from the beginning, and the wood-pigeons cooed above them in their cage, and the other pigeons slept. The little robber-girl put her arm round Gerda's neck, held her knife in the other hand, and slept so that one could hear her; but Gerda could not close her eyes at all; she did not know whether she was to live or to die. The robbers sat round the fire, sang and drank, and the old robber-woman tumbled about. It was quite terrible to behold for a little girl.

Then the wood-pigeons said, "Coo, coo, we have seen little Kay. A white owl was carrying his sledge; he sat in the Snow Queen's carriage, which drove close by the forest as we lay in our nests; she blew upon us young pigeons, and all died except us two. Coo, coo!"

"What are you saying there," asked Gerda. "Whither was the Snow Queen travelling? Do you know anything about it?"

"She was probably journeying to Lapland, for there they have always ice and snow. Ask the reindeer that is tied to the cord."

"There is ice and snow yonder, and it is glorious and fine," said the reindeer. "There one may run about free in great glittering plains. There the Snow Queen has her summer tent; but her strong castle is up towards the North Pole, on the island that's called Spitzbergen."

"Oh, Kay, little Kay!" cried Gerda. "You must lie still," exclaimed the robber-girl, "or I shall thrust my knife into your body."

In the morning Gerda told her all that the wood-pigeons had said, and the little robber-girl looked quite serious, and nodded her head and said, "That's all the same, that's all the same! Do you know where Lapland is?" she asked the reindeer.

"Who should know better than I?" the creature replied, and its eyes sparkled in its head. "I was born and bred there; I ran about there in the snow-fields."

"Listen!" said the robber-girl to Gerda. "You see all our men have gone away. Only mother is here still, and she'll stay; but towards noon she drinks out of the big bottle, and then she sleeps for a little while; then I'll do something for you." Then she sprang out of bed and clasped her mother round the neck, and pulled her beard crying, "Good morning, my own old nanny-goat." And her mother filliped her nose till it was red and blue, and it was all done for pure love.

When the mother had drunk out of her bottle and had gone to sleep upon it, the robber-girl went to the reindeer and said, "I should like very much to tickle you a few times more with the knife, for you are very funny there; but it's all the same. I'll loosen your cord and help you out, so that you may run to Lapland; but you must use your legs well, and carry this little girl to the palace of the Snow Queen, where her playfellow is. You've heard what she told me, for she spoke loud enough, and you were listening."

The reindeer sprang up high for joy. The robber-girl lifted little Gerda on its back and had the forethought to tie her fast, and even to give her own little cushion as a saddle. "There are your fur boots for you," she said, "for it's growing cold; but I shall keep the muff, for that's so very pretty. Still, you shall not be cold for all that; here's my mother's big muffles, they'll just reach up to your elbows, creep in; now you look in the hands just like my ugly mother," and Gerda wept for joy.

"I can't bear to see you whimper," said the little robber-girl, "Now you just ought to look very glad; and here are two loaves and a ham for you, now you won't be hungry." These were tied on the reindeer's back; the little robber-girl opened the door, coaxed in all the big dogs and then cut the rope with her sharp knife, and said to the reindeer, "Now run, but take good care of the little girl."

And Gerda stretched out her hands with the big muffles towards the little robber-girl, and said, "Farewell!" and the reindeer ran over stock and stone away through the great forest, over marshes and steppes, as quick as it could go. The wolves howled and the ravens croaked. "Hiss! hiss!" it went in the air. It seemed as if the sky were flashing fire.

"Those are my old Northern lights!" said the reindeer. "Look how they glow!" And then it ran on faster than ever, day and night. The loaves were eaten, and the ham too; and then they were in Lapland.

Gerda preparing to start

SIXTH STORY
The Lapland woman and the Finland woman

At a little hut they stopped. It was very humble; the roof sloped down
almost to the ground, and the door was so low that the family had to
creep on their stomachs when they wanted to go in or out. No one
was in the house but an old Lapland woman cooking fish by the light
of a train-oil lamp; and the reindeer told Gerda's whole history, but it
related its own first, for this seemed to the reindeer the more important of the two; and Gerda was so exhausted by the cold that she could
not speak.

"Oh, you poor things!" said the Lapland woman, "you've a long way to run yet! You must go more than a hundred miles into Finmark, for the Snow Queen is there, staying in the country, and burning Bengal lights every evening. I'll write a few words on a dried cod, for I have no paper; I'll give you that as a letter to the Finland woman; she can give you better information than I."

And when Gerda had been warmed and refreshed with food and drink, the Lapland woman wrote a few words on a dried codfish, and telling Gerda to take care of these, tied her again on the reindeer, and the reindeer sprang away. Flash, flash! it went, high in the air; the whole night long the most beautiful blue Northern lights were burning;—and then they got to Finmark and knocked at the chimney of the Finland woman, for she had not even a hut.

There was such a heat in the chimney, that the woman herself went about almost naked. She at once loosened little Gerda's dress and took off the child's mufflers and boots; otherwise it would have been too hot for her to bear. Then she laid a piece of ice on the reindeer's head, and read what was written on the codfish; she read it three times, and

Gerda travelling in Lapland

then she knew it by heart, and popped the fish into the soup-cauldron, for it was eatable; and she never wasted anything.

Now the reindeer first told his own history, and then little Gerda's; and the Finland woman blinked with her clever eyes, but said nothing. "You are very clever," said the reindeer, "I know you can tie all the winds of the world together with a bit of twine; if the seaman unties one knot, he has a good wind; if he loosens the second, it blows hard; but if he unties the third and the fourth, there comes such a tempest that the forests are thrown down. Won't you give the little girl a draught so that she may get twelve men's power, and overcome the Snow Queen?"

"Twelve men's power?" repeated the Finland woman. "Great use that would be!" And she went to a bed, and brought out a great rolled-up fur, and unrolled it; wonderful characters were written upon it, and the Finland woman read, until the water ran down over her forehead.

But the reindeer again begged so hard for little Gerda, and Gerda looked at the Finland woman with such beseeching eyes full of tears, that she began to blink again with her own, and drew the reindeer into a corner, and whispered to him, while she laid fresh ice on his head: "Little Kay is certainly at the Snow Queen's, and finds everything there to his taste and liking, and thinks it the best place in the world; but that is because he has a splinter of glass in his eye, and a little fragment in his heart; but these must be got out, or he will never be a human being again, and the Snow Queen will keep her power over him."

"But cannot you give something to little Gerda, so as to give her power over all this?"

"I can give her no greater power than she possesses already; don't you see how great that is? Don't you see, how men and animals are obliged to serve her, and how she got on so well in the world, with her naked feet? She cannot receive her power from us; it consists in this that she is a dear innocent child. If she herself cannot penetrate to the Snow Queen and get the glass out of little Kay, we can be of no use! Two miles from here the Snow Queen's garden begins; you can carry the little girl thither; set her down by the great bush that stands with its red berries in the snow; don't stand gossiping, but make haste, and get back here!" And then the Finland woman lifted little Gerda on the reindeer, which ran as fast as it could.

"Oh, I haven't my boots! I haven't my mufflers!" cried little Gerda. She soon noticed that in the cutting cold; but the reindeer dared not stop; it ran till it came to the bush with the red berries; there it set Gerda down, and kissed her on the mouth, and great bright tears ran over the creature's cheeks; and then it ran back, as fast as it could. There stood poor Gerda without shoes, without gloves, in the midst of the terrible cold Finmark.

She ran forward as fast as possible; then came a whole regiment of snow-flakes; but they did not fall down from the sky, for that was quite bright and shone with the Northern light: the snow-flakes ran along the ground, and the nearer they came the larger they grew. Gerda still remembered how large and beautiful the snow-flakes had appeared when she looked at them through the burning-glass. But here they were certainly far larger and much more terrible; they were alive; they were the advanced posts of the Snow Queen, and had the strangest shapes. A few looked like ugly great porcupines; others like knots formed of snakes which stretched forth their heads; and others like little fat bears, whose hair stood on end; all were brilliantly white, all were living snow-flakes.

Then little Gerda said her prayer; and the cold was so great, that she could see her own breath, which went forth out of her mouth like smoke. The breath became thicker and thicker and formed itself into little angels, who grew and grew whenever they touched the earth; and all had helmets on their heads, and shields and spears in their hands; their number increased more and more, and when Gerda had finished her prayer, a whole legion stood round about her; they struck with their spears at the terrible snow-flakes, so that these sprang into a thousand pieces; and little Gerda could go forward afresh, with good courage. The angels stroked her hands and feet, and then she felt less how cold it was, and hastened on to the Snow Queen's palace.

But now we must see what Kay is doing. He certainly was not thinking of little Gerda, and least of all that she was standing in front of the palace.

SEVENTH STORY
Of the Snow Queen's castle, and what happened there at last

The walls of the palace were formed of the drifting snow, and windows and doors of the cutting winds; there were more than a hundred halls, all blown together by the snow: the greatest of these extended for several miles; the strong Northern light illumined them all, and how great and empty, how icily cold and shining they all were! Never was merriment here, not even a little bear's ball, at which the storm could have played the music, while the bears walked about on their hind-legs and showed off their pretty manners: never any little sport of mouth-slapping or bars-touch; never a little coffee gossip among the young lady white foxes. Empty, vast, and cold were the halls of the Snow Queen. The Northern lights flamed so brightly that one could count them when they stood highest and lowest. In the midst of this immense empty snow hall was a frozen lake, which had burst into a thousand pieces; but each piece was like the rest, so that it was a perfect work of art: and in the middle of the lake sat the Snow Queen when she was at home; and then she said that she sat in the mirror of reason, and that this was the only one, and the best in the world.

Little Kay was quite blue with cold,—indeed, almost black; but he did not notice it, for she had kissed the cold shudderings away from him, and his heart was like a lump of ice. He dragged a few sharp flat pieces of ice to and fro, joining them together in all kinds of ways, for he wanted to achieve something with them. It was just like when we have little tablets of wood, and lay them together to form figures,— what we call the Chinese game. Kay also went and laid figures, and, indeed, very artistic ones. That was the icy game of reason. In his eyes these figures were very remarkable; and of the highest importance; that was because of the fragment of glass sticking in his eye. He laid out the figures so that they formed a word, but he could never manage to lay down the word as he wished to have it,—the word "Eternity." And the Snow Queen had said, "If you can find out this figure, you shall be your own master, and I will give you the whole world, and a new pair of skates." But he could not.

"Now I'll hasten away to the warm lands," said the Snow Queen. "I will go and look into the black pots:" these were the volcanoes, Etna and Vesuvius as they are called. "I shall make them a little white! that's necessary; that will do the grapes and lemons good!" And the Snow Queen flew away, and Kay sat quite alone in the great icy hall that was miles in extent, and looked at his pieces of ice, and thought so deeply that it cracked inside him; one would have thought that he was frozen.

Then it happened that little Gerda stepped through the great gate into the wide hall. Here reigned cutting winds, but she prayed a prayer, and the winds lay down as if they would have gone to sleep; and she stepped into the great empty cold halls, and beheld Kay; she knew him, and flew to him and embraced him, and held him fast, and called out, "Kay, dear little Kay, at last I have found you!"

But he sat quite still, stiff and cold. Then little Gerda wept hot tears, that fell upon his breast; they penetrated into his heart, they thawed the lump of ice, and consumed the little piece of glass in it. He looked at her, and she sang:

> Roses bloom, and roses decay,
> But we the Christ-child shall see one day!

Then Kay burst into tears; he wept so that the splinter of glass came out of his eye. Now he recognized her, and cried rejoicingly, "Gerda, dear Gerda! Where have you been all this time? And where have I been?" And he looked all around him. "How cold it is here! How large and void!" and he clung to Gerda, and she laughed and wept for joy. It was so glorious that even the pieces of ice round about danced for joy; and when they were tired and lay down, they formed themselves just into the letters of which the Snow Queen had said that if he found them out he should be his own master, and she would give him the whole world, and a pair of new skates.

And Gerda kissed his cheeks, and they became blooming; she kissed his eyes, and they shone like her own; she kissed his hands and feet, and he became well and merry. The Snow Queen might now come home; his letter of release stood written in shining characters of ice.

And they took one another by the hand, and wandered forth from the great palace of ice. They spoke of the grandmother, and of the roses on the roof; and where they went the winds rested, and the sun burst

Gerda and Kay returning home

forth; and when they came to the bush with the red berries, the reindeer was standing there waiting; it had brought another young reindeer, which gave the children warm milk, and kissed them on the mouth.

Then they carried Kay and Gerda, first to the Finnish woman where they warmed themselves thoroughly in the hot room, and received instructions for their journey home; and then to the Lapland woman, who had made their new clothes and put their sledge in order.

The reindeer and the young one sprang at their side, and followed them as far as the boundary of the country. There the first green sprouted forth, there they took leave of the two reindeers and the Lapland woman. "Farewell!" said all. And the first little birds began to twitter, the forest was decked with green buds, and out of it, on a beautiful horse (which Gerda knew, for it was the same that had drawn her golden coach), a young girl came riding, with a shining red cap on her head, and a pair of pistols in the holsters. This was the little robber-girl, who had grown tired of staying at home, and wished to go first to the north, and if that did not suit her, to some other region. She knew Gerda at once, and Gerda knew her too; and it was a right merry meeting.

"You are a fine fellow to gad about!" she said to little Kay. "I should like to know if you deserve that one should run to the end of the world after you?"

But Gerda patted her cheeks, and asked after the Prince and Princess.

"They've gone to foreign countries," said the robber-girl. "But the crow!" said Gerda. "Why the crow is dead," answered the other. "The tame betrothed one has become a widow, and goes about with an end of black worsted thread round her leg. She complains most lamentably, and it's all talk. But now tell me how you have fared, and how you caught him." And Gerda and Kay told their story.

"Snipp-snapp-snurre-purre-baselurre!" said the robber-girl; and she took them both by the hand, and promised that if she ever came through their town, she would come up and pay them a visit. And then she rode away into the wide world. But Gerda and Kay went hand in hand, and as they went it became beautiful spring, with green and with flowers. The church bells sounded, and they recognized the high steeples, and the great town: it was the one in which they lived; and they went to the grandmother's door, and up the stairs, and into the room, where everything remained in its usual place. The big clock was going "Tick, tack!" and the hands were turning; but as they went through the rooms they noticed that they had become grown-up people. The roses out of the roof gutter were blooming in at the open window, and there stood the little children's chairs, and Kay and Gerda sat each upon their own, and held each other by the hand. They had forgotten the cold empty splendour at the Snow Queen's like a heavy dream. The grandmother was sitting in God's bright sunshine, and read aloud out of the Bible, "Except ye become as little children ye shall in no wise enter into the kingdom of God."

And Kay and Gerda looked into each other's eyes, and all at once they understood the old song,—

Roses bloom and roses decay,
But we the Christ-child shall see one day.

There they both sat, grown up, and yet children—children in heart—and it was summer, warm delightful summer.

The mother spinning the flax

THE FLAX

The flax stood in blossom; it had pretty little blue flowers, delicate as a moth's wings, and even more delicate. The sun shone on the flax, and the rain clouds moistened it, and this was just as good for it as it is for little children when they are washed, and afterwards get a kiss from their mother; they become much prettier, and so did the flax.

"The people say that I stand uncommonly well," said the flax, "and that I'm fine and long, and will make a capital piece of linen. How happy I am! I'm certainly the happiest of beings. How well I am off!

And I may come to something! How the sunshine gladdens, and the rain tastes good and refreshes me! I'm wonderfully happy; I'm the happiest of beings."

"Yes, yes, yes!" said the hedgestake. "You don't know the world, but we do, for we have knots in us;" and then it creaked out mournfully,

Snip-snap-snurre,
Bassellurre!
The song is done.

"No, it is not done," said the flax. "To-morrow the sun will shine, or the rain will refresh us. I feel that I'm growing, I feel that I'm in blossom! I'm the happiest of beings!"

But one day the people came and took the flax by the head and pulled it up by the root. That hurt; and it was laid in water as if they were going to drown it, and then put on the fire as if it was going to be roasted. It was quite fearful!

"One can't always have good times!" said the flax. "One must make one's experiences, and so one gets to know something!"

But bad times certainly came. The flax was moistened and roasted, and broken and hackled. Yes, it did not even know what the operations were called that they did with it. It was put on the spinning-wheel—whirr, whirr—it was not possible to collect one's thoughts.

"I have been uncommonly happy!" it thought, in all its pain; "One must be content with the good one has enjoyed! Contented! Contented! Oh!" and it continued to say that, when it was put into the loom, and so it became a large beautiful piece of linen. All the flax, to the last stalk, was used in making one piece.

"But this is quite remarkable! I should never have believed it! How favourable fortune is to me! The hedgestake was well informed, truly with its

Snip-snap-snurre,
Bassellurre!

The song is not done by any means. Now it's beginning in earnest. That's quite remarkable! If I've suffered something, I've been made into something! I'm the happiest of all! How strong and fine I am, how white and long! That's something different from being a mere plant; even if one bears flowers, one is not attended to, and only gets watered when it rains. Now I'm attended to and cherished, the maid turns me over every morning, and I get a shower bath from the watering pot every evening. Yes, the clergyman's wife has even made a speech about me, and says I'm the best piece in the whole parish. I cannot be happier!"

Now the linen was taken into the house, and put under the scissors; how they cut and tore it, and then pricked it with needles! That was not pleasant; but twelve pieces of body linen, of a kind not often mentioned by name, but indispensable to all people, were made of it—a whole dozen!

"Just look! Now something has really been made of me! So that was my destiny. That's a real blessing. Now I shall be of some use in the world, and that's right, that's a true pleasure! We've been made into twelve things, but yet we're all one and the same; we're just a dozen; how remarkably charming that is!"

Years rolled on, and now they would hold together no longer. "It must be over one day!" said each piece. "I would gladly have held together a little longer, but one must not expect impossibilities!"

They were now torn into pieces and fragments. They thought it was all over now, for they were hacked to shreds, and softened and boiled, yes, they themselves did not know all that was done to them, and then they became beautiful white paper.

"No, that is a surprise, and a glorious surprise," said the paper. "Now I'm finer than before, and I shall be written on, that is remarkable good fortune."

And really, the most beautiful verses and stories were written upon it, and only once there came a blot, that was certainly remarkable good fortune; and the people heard what was upon it, it was sensible and good, and made people much more sensible and better; there was a great blessing in the words that were on this paper.

"That is more than I ever imagined, when I was a little blue flower in the fields. How could I fancy that I should ever spread joy and knowledge among men. I can't yet understand it myself, but it is really so. I have done nothing myself but what I was obliged with my weak powers to do, for my own preservation, and yet I have been promoted from one joy and honour to another. Each time when I think 'the song is done' it begins again in a higher and better way. Now I shall certainly be sent about to journey through the world, so that all people may read me. That cannot be otherwise; it's the only probable thing. I've splendid thoughts, as many as I had pretty flowers in the old times; I'm the happiest of beings."

But the paper was not sent on its travels, it was sent to the printer, and everything that was written upon it was set up in type, for a book, or rather for many hundreds of books, for in this way a very far greater number could derive pleasure and profit from the book, than if the one paper on which it was written, had run about the world, to be worn out before it had got half way.

"Yes, that is certainly the wisest way," thought the written paper. "I really did not think of that, I shall stay at home, and be held in honour, just like an old grandfather, and I am really the grandfather of all these books. Now something can be effected; I could not have wandered about thus. He who wrote all this, looked at me, every word flowed from his pen right into me! I am the happiest of all!"

Then the paper was tied together in a bundle, and thrown into a tub that stood in the wash-house. "It's good resting after work," said the paper. "It is very right that one should collect one's thoughts. Now I'm able for the first time, to think of what is in me, and to know one's self is true progress. What will be done with me now? At any rate I shall go forward again; I'm always going forward, I've found that out."

Now one day all the paper was taken out and laid by on the hearth; it was to be burned, for it might not be sold to hucksters to be used for covering for butter and sugar, they said. And all the children in the house stood round about, for they wanted to see the paper burn, that flamed up so prettily, and afterwards one could see many red sparks among the ashes, careering here and there. One after another faded out quick as the wind, and that they called, "seeing the children come out of school," and the last spark was the schoolmaster, one of them thought he had already gone, but at the next moment there came another spark; "there goes the schoolmaster," they said. Yes, they all knew about it; they should have known who it was who went there; we shall get to know it, but they did not. All the old paper, the whole bundle was laid upon the fire, and it was soon alight. "Ugh!" it said, and burst out into bright flame. Ugh! that was not very agreeable, but when the whole was wrapped into bright flames, these mounted up higher than the flax had ever been able to lift its little blue flowers, and glittered as the white linen had never been able to glitter. All the written letters turned for one moment quite red, and all the words and thoughts turned to flame. "Now I'm mounting straight up to the sun," said a voice in the flame, and it was as if a thousand voices said this in unison, and the flames mounted up through the chimney and out at the top, and more delicate than the flames, invisible to human eyes, little tiny beings floated there, as many as there had been blossoms on the flax. They were lighter even than the flame, from which they were born, and when the flame was extinguished and nothing remained of the paper but black ashes, they danced over it once more, and where they touched the black mass, the little red sparks appeared. The children came out of school, and the schoolmaster was the last of all! That was fun, and the children sang over the dead ashes—

Snip-snap-snurre;
Bassellure;
The song is done.

But the little invisible beings all said, "The song is never done, that is the best of all, I know it, and therefore I'm the happiest of all!"

But the children could meither hear that nor understand it, nor ought they, for children must not know everything.

THE DROP OF WATER

Of course you know what is meant by a magnifying glass—one of those round spectacle glasses that make everything look a hundred times bigger than it is? When any one takes one of these and holds it to his eye, and looks at a drop of water from the pond yonder, he sees above a thousand wonderful creatures that are otherwise never discerned in the water. But they are there, and it is no delusion. It almost looks like a great plateful of spiders, jumping about in a crowd. And how fierce they are! They tear off each other's legs and arms, and bodies before and behind; and yet they are merry and joyful in their way.

Now there was once an old man whom all the people called Kribble-Krabble, for that was his name. He always wanted the best of everything, and when he could not manage it otherwise, he did it by magic.

There he sat one day, and held his magnifying glass to his eye, and looked at a drop of water that had been taken out of a puddle by the ditch. But what a kribbling and crabbling was there! All the thousand of little creatures hopped and sprung and tugged at one another, and ate each other up.

"That is horrible!" said old Kribble-Krabble. "Can one not persuade them to live in peace and quietness, so that each one may mind his own business!" And he thought it over and over, but it would not do, and so he had recourse to magic. "I must give them colour, that they may be seen more plainly!" said he; and he poured something like a little drop of red wine into the drop of water, but it was witches' blood from the lobes of the ear, the finest kind, at ninepence a drop. And now the wonderful little creatures were pink all over; it looked like a whole town of naked wild men.

"What have you there?" asked another old magician who had no name; and that was the best thing about him.

"Yes, if you can guess what it is," said Kribble-Krabble, "I'll make you a present of it." But it is not so easy to find out if one does not know.

And the magician who had no name looked through the magnifying glass. It looked really like a great town reflected there, in which all the people were running about without clothes! It was terrible! But it was still more terrible to see how one beat and pushed the other, and bit and hacked, and tugged and mauled him. Those who were at the top were being pulled down, and those at the bottom were struggling upwards. Look, look! His leg is longer than mine! Bah! Away with it! There is one who has a little bruise. It hurts him, but it shall hurt him still more. And they hacked away at him, and they pulled at him, and ate him up, because of the little bruise. And there was one sitting as still as any little maiden, and wishing only for peace and quietness. But now she had to come out, and they tugged at her, and pulled her about, and ate her up.

The two magicians

"That's funny!" said the magician.

"Yes; but what do you think it is?" said Kribble-Krabble. "Can you find that out?" "Why, one can see that easily enough," said the other. "That's Paris or some other great city, for they're all alike. It's a great city!"

"It's puddle water!" said Kribble-Krabble.

THE NIGHTINGALE

In China, you must know, the Emperor is a Chinaman, and all whom he has about him are Chinamen too. It happened a good many years ago, but that's just why it's worth while to hear the story, before it is forgotten! The Emperor's palace was the most splendid in the world; it was made entirely of porcelain, very costly, but so delicate and brittle that one had to take care how one touched it. In the garden were to be seen the most wonderful flowers, and to the costliest of them silver bells were tied, which sounded, so that nobody should pass by without noticing the flowers. Yes, everything in the Emperor's garden was admirably arranged. And it extended so far, that the gardener himself did not know where the end was. If a man went on and on, he came into a glorious forest with high trees and deep lakes. The wood extended straight down to the sea, which was blue and deep; great vessels could sail beneath the branches of the trees, and in the trees lived a nightingale, which sang so splendidly that even the poor fisherman, who had many other things to do, stopped still and listened, when he had gone out at night, to throw out his nets, and heard the nightingale. "How beautiful that is!" he said; but he was obliged to attend to his property, and thus forgot the bird. But when in the next night, the bird sang again and the fisherman heard it, he exclaimed again, "How beautiful that is!"

From all the countries of the world travellers came to the city of the Emperor and admired it, and the palace and the garden, but when they heard the nightingale, they said: "That is the best of all!"

And the travellers told of it when they came home; and the learned men wrote many books about the town, the palace, and the garden. But they did not forget the nightingale; that was placed highest of all; and those who were poets wrote most magnificent poems about the nightingale in the wood, by the deep lake.

The books went through all the world; and a few of them once came to the Emperor. He sat in his golden chair, and read, and read; every moment he nodded his head, for it pleased him to peruse the masterly descriptions of the city, the palace, and the garden. "But the nightingale is the best of all," it stood written there.

"What's that?" exclaimed the Emperor. "I don't know the nightingale at all! Is there such a bird in my empire, and even in my garden? I've never heard of that:—To learn such a thing for the first time from books!"

And hereupon he called his cavalier. This cavalier was so grand that if any one lower in rank than himself dared to speak to him, or to ask him any question, he answered nothing but P!—and that meant nothing.

"There is said to be a wonderful bird here called a nightingale!" said the Emperor. "They say, it is the best thing in all my great empire. Why have I never heard anything about it?"

"I have never heard him named," replied the cavalier. "He has never been introduced at court."

"I command that he shall appear this evening, and sing before me," said the Emperor. "All the world knows what I possess, and I do not know it myself!"

"I have never heard him mentioned," said the cavalier. "I will seek for him. I will find him."

But where was he to be found? The cavalier ran up and down all the staircases, through halls and passages, but no one among all those whom he met had heard talk of the nightingale. And the cavalier ran back to the Emperor, and said that it must be a fable invented by the writers of books. "Your Imperial Majesty cannot believe how much is written that is fiction, and something that they call the black art."

"But the book in which I read this," said the Emperor, "was sent to me by the high and mighty Emperor of Japan, and therefore it cannot be a falsehood. I will hear the nightingale! It must be here this evening! It has my imperial favour! And if it does not come, all the court shall be trampled upon after the court has supped!"

"Tsing-pe," said the cavalier; and again he ran up and down all the staircases, and through all the halls and corridors; and half the court ran with him, for the courtiers did not like being trampled upon.

Then there was a great inquiry after the wonderful nightingale, which all the world knew, excepting the people at court.

At last they met with a poor little girl in the kitchen, who said, "The nightingale? I know it well; yes, it can sing gloriously. Every evening I get leave to carry my poor sick mother the scraps from the table. She lives down by the strand, and when I get back and am tired, and rest in the wood, then I hear the nightingale sing! And then the water comes into my eyes, and it is just as if my mother kissed me!"

"Little kitchen-girl," said the cavalier, "I will get you a place in the kitchen, with permission to see the Emperor dine, if you will lead us to the nightingale, for it is announced for this evening."

So they all went out into the wood where the nightingale was accustomed to sing; half the court went forth. When they were in the midst of their journey a cow began to low.

"Oh!" cried the court pages, "now we have it! That shows a wonderful power in so small a creature! I have certainly heard it before."

"No; those are cows lowing!" said the little kitchen-girl. "We are a long way from the place yet!"

Now the frogs began to quack in the marsh. "Glorious!" said the Chinese court preacher. "Now I hear it—it sounds just like little church bells." "No; those are frogs!" said the little kitchen-maid. "But now I think we shall soon hear it." And then the nightingale began to sing.

"That is it!" exclaimed the little girl. "Listen, listen! and yonder it sits," and she pointed to a little grey bird up in the boughs.

"Is it possible?" cried the cavalier. "I should never have thought it looked like that! How simple it looks! It must certainly have lost its colour at seeing such grand people around."

"Little nightingale!" called the little kitchen-girl, quite loudly, "our gracious Emperor wishes you to sing before him!" "With the greatest pleasure!" replied the nightingale, and began to sing most delightfully.

"It sounds just like glass bells!" said the cavalier. "And look at the little throat, how it's working! It's wonderful that we should never have heard it before. That bird will be a great success at court."

"Shall I sing once more before the Emperor?" asked the nightingale, for it thought the Emperor was present.

"My excellent little nightingale!" said the cavalier, "I have great pleasure in inviting you to a court festival this evening, when you shall charm his Imperial Majesty with your beautiful singing."

"My song sounds best in the green wood!" replied the nightingale; still it came willingly when it heard what the Emperor wished.

The palace was festively adorned. The walls and the flooring, which were of porcelain, gleamed in the rays of thousands of golden lamps.

The most glorious flowers, which could ring clearly, had been placed in the passages. There was a running to and fro, and a thorough draught, and all the bells rang so loudly that one could not hear oneself speak.

In the midst of the great hall, where the Emperor sat, a golden perch had been placed, on which the nightingale was to sit. The whole court was there, and the little cook maid had got leave to stand behind the door, as she had now received the title of a real court cook. All were in full dress, and all looked at the little grey bird, to which the Emperor nodded.

And the nightingale sang so gloriously that the tears came into the Emperor's eyes. The tears ran down over his cheeks, and then the nightingale sang still more sweetly, that went straight to the heart. The Emperor was so much pleased that he said the nightingale should have his golden slipper to wear round its neck. But the nightingale declined this with thanks, saying it had already received a sufficient reward.

"I have seen tears in the Emperor's eyes, that is the real treasure to me! An Emperor's tears have a peculiar power. I am rewarded enough." And then it sang again with a sweet glorious voice.

"That's the most amiable coquetry I ever saw!" said the ladies who stood round about, and then they took water in their mouths to gurgle when any one spoke to them. They thought they should be nightingales too. And the lackeys and chambermaids reported that they were satisfied too; and that was saying a good deal, for they are the most difficult to please. In short, the nightingale achieved a real success.

It was now to remain at court, to have its own cage, with liberty to go out twice every day and once at night. Twelve servants were appointed when the nightingale went out, each of whom had a silken string fastened to the bird's leg, and which they held very tight. There was really no pleasure in an excursion of that kind.

The whole city spoke of the wonderful bird, and when two people met, one said nothing but "nightin," and the other said "gale;" and then they sighed, and understood one another. Eleven pedlars' children were named after the bird, but not one of them could sing a note.

One day the Emperor received a large parcel, on which was written "The Nightingale!"

"There we have a new book about this celebrated bird," said the

The courtiers find the nightingale

Emperor. But it was not a book, but a little work of art, contained in a box, an artificial nightingale, which was to be like a natural one, but was brilliantly ornamented with diamonds, rubies, and sapphires. So soon as the artificial bird was wound up, he could sing one of the pieces that he really sang, and then his tail moved up and down, and shone with silver and gold. Round his neck hung a little riband, and on that was written, "The Emperor of Japan's nightingale is poor, compared to that of the Emperor of China."

"That is capital!" said they all, and he who had brought the artificial bird, immediately received the title, Imperial Head-Nightingale-Bringer.

"Now they must sing together; what a duet that will be!" And so they had to sing together; but it did not go very well, for the real nightingale sang in its own way, and the artificial bird sang waltzes. "That's not his fault," said the playmaster, "he's quite perfect, and very much in my style." Now the artificial bird was to sing alone. He had just as much success as the real one, and then it was much handsomer to look at,—it shone like bracelets and breast-pins.

Three-and-thirty times over did it sing the same piece, and yet was not tired. The people would gladly have heard it again, but the Emperor said that the living nightingale ought to sing something now. But where was it? No one had noticed that it had flown away out of the open window, back to her green wood.

"But what is that?"—said the Emperor. And all the courtiers abused the nightingale, and declared that it was a very ungrateful creature. "We have the best bird after all," said they, and so the artificial bird had to sing again, and that was the thirty-fourth time that they listened to the same piece. For all that they did not know it quite by heart, for it was so very difficult, and the playmaster praised the bird particularly; yes, he declared that it was better than a nightingale, not only with regard to its plumage, and the many beautiful diamonds, but inside as well.

"For you see, ladies and gentlemen, and above all, your Imperial Majesty, with a real nightingale one can never calculate what is coming, but in this artificial bird everything is settled. One can explain it; one can open it and make people understand where the waltzes come from, how they go, and how one follows upon another."

"Those are quite our own ideas," they all said, and the speaker received permission to show the bird to the people on the next Sunday. The people were to hear it sing too, the Emperor commanded, and they did hear it, and were as much pleased as if they had all got tipsy upon tea, for that's quite the Chinese fashion; and they all said "Oh!" and held up their forefingers and nodded. But the poor fisherman, who had heard the real nightingale, said, "It sounds pretty enough, and the melodies resemble each other, but there's something wanting, I know not what!"

The real nightingale was banished from the country and empire. The artificial bird had its place on a silken cushion, close to the Emperor's bed; all the presents it had received, gold and precious stones, were ranged about it; in title it had advanced to be the High Imperial After-Dinner-Singer, and in rank to number one on the left hand; for the Emperor considered that side the most important on which the heart is placed, and even in an Emperor the heart is on the left side; and the playmaster wrote a work of five-and-twenty volumes about the artificial bird; it was very learned and very long, full of the most difficult Chinese words; but yet all the people declared that they had read it, and understood it, for fear of being considered stupid, and having their bodies trampled on.

So a whole year went by. The Emperor, the court, and all the other Chinese knew every little twitter in the artificial bird's song, by heart. But just for that reason it pleased them best; they could sing with it themselves, and they did so. The street boys sang "Tsi-tsi-tsi-glug-glug," and the Emperor himself sung it too. Yes! That was certainly famous.

But one evening, when the artificial bird was singing its best, and the Emperor lay in bed listening to it, something inside the bird said "Whizz!" Something cracked. "Whirr!" All the wheels ran around, and then the music stopped.

The Emperor immediately sprang out of bed, and caused his body physician to be called; but what could *he* do? Then they sent for a watchmaker, and after a good deal of talking and investigation, the bird was put into something like order; but the watchmaker said that the bird must be carefully treated, for the barrels were worn, and it would be impossible to put new ones in, in such a manner that the music would go. There was a great lamentation; only once in a year was it permitted to let the bird sing, and that was almost too much. But then the playmaster made a little speech, full of heavy words, and said this was just as good as before, and so of course it was as good as before.

Now five years had gone by, and a real grief came upon the whole nation. The Chinese really were fond of their Emperor, and now he was ill, and could not, it was said, live much longer. Already a new Emperor had been chosen, and the people stood out in the street and asked the cavalier how their old Emperor did.

"P!" said he, and shook his head.

Cold and pale lay the Emperor in his great gorgeous bed; the whole court thought him dead, and each one ran to pay homage to the new ruler. The chamberlains ran out to talk it over, and the ladies'-maids had a great coffee party. All about, in all the halls and passages, cloth had been laid down so that no footstep could be heard, and therefore it was quiet there, quite quiet. But the Emperor was not dead yet; stiff and pale he lay on the gorgeous bed with the long velvet curtains and the heavy gold tassels; high up, a window stood open, and the moon shone in upon the Emperor and the artificial bird.

The poor Emperor could scarcely breathe; it was just as if something lay upon his chest; he opened his eyes, and then he saw that it was Death who sat upon his chest, and had put on his golden crown and held in one hand the Emperor's sword and in the other his beautiful banner. And all around, from among the folds of the splendid velvet curtains, strange heads peered forth; a few very ugly, the rest quite lovely and mild. These were all the Emperor's bad and good deeds, that stood before him now that Death sat upon his heart.

"Do you remember this?" whispered one to the other. "Do you remember that?" and then they told him so much that the perspiration ran from his forehead.

"I did not know that!" said the Emperor. "Music! Music! The great Chinese drum!" he cried, "so that I need not hear all they say!" and they continued speaking, and Death nodded like a Chinaman to all they said.

"Music, music!" cried the Emperor. "You little precious golden bird, sing, sing! I have given you gold and costly presents; I have even hung my golden slipper around your neck—sing now, sing!" But the bird stood still; no one was there to wind him up, and he could not sing without that; but Death continued to stare at the Emperor with his great hollow eyes, and it was quiet, fearfully quiet!

Then there sounded from the window, suddenly, the most lovely song. It was the little live nightingale, that sat outside on a spray. It had heard of the Emperor's sad plight and had come to sing to him of comfort and hope. And as it sung the spectres grew paler and paler; the blood ran quicker and more quickly through the Emperor's weak limbs, and even Death listened, and said "Go on, little nightingale, go on!"

"But will you give me that splendid golden sword? Will you give me that rich banner? Will you give me the Emperor's crown?" And Death gave up each of these treasures for a song. And the nightingale sang on and on; and it sung of the quiet churchyard where the white roses grow, where the elder blossom smells sweet, and where the fresh grass is moistened by the tears of survivors. Then Death felt a longing to see his garden, and floated out at the window in the form of a cold white mist.

"Thanks, thanks!" said the Emperor. "You heavenly little bird! I know you well! I banished you from my country and empire, and yet you have charmed away the evil faces from my couch, and banished Death from my heart! How can I reward you?"

"You have rewarded me!" replied the nightingale. "I have drawn tears from your eyes, when I sang the first time, I shall never forget that. These are the jewels that rejoice a singer's heart; but now sleep and grow fresh and strong again; I will sing you something."

And it sang, and the Emperor fell into a sweet slumber. Ah! How mild and refreshing that sleep was. The sun shone upon him through the windows, when he awoke refreshed and restored; not one of his servants had yet returned, for they all thought he was dead; only the nightingale still sat beside him and sang.

"You must always stay with me!" said the Emperor. "You shall sing as you please; and I'll break the artificial bird into a thousand pieces."

"Not so," replied the nightingale. "It did well so long as it could! Keep it as you have done till now. I cannot build my nest in the palace to dwell in it, but let me come when I feel the wish; then I will sit in the evening on the spray yonder by the window, and sing you something so that you may be glad and thoughtful at once."

"I will sing of those who are happy, and of those who suffer. I will sing of good and of evil that remains hidden round about you. The little singing-bird flies far around, to the poor fisherman, to the peasant's roof, to everyone who dwells far away from you and from your court. I love your heart more than your crown, and yet the crown has an air of sanctity about it—I come, I shall sing to you—but one thing you must promise me."

"Everything!" said the Emperor; and he stood there in his imperial robes, which he had put on himself, and pressed the sword which was heavy with gold to his heart.

"One thing I beg of you; tell no one that you have a little bird who tells you everything. Then it will go all the better." And the nightingale flew away.

The servants came in, to look to their dead Emperor—and—yes, there they stood, and the Emperor said "Good-morning."

THE JUMPER

The flea, the grasshopper and the skipjack once wanted to see which of them could jump highest; and they invited the whole world, and who-ever else would come to see the grand sight. And there were three famous jumpers who met together in the room. "Yes, I'll give my daughter to him who jumps highest," said the King. For it would be mean to let these people jump for nothing."

The flea stepped out first; he had very pretty manners, and bowed in all directions: for he had young ladies' blood in his veins, and was accustomed to consort only with human beings; and that was of great consequence.

Then came the grasshopper; he was certainly much heavier, but he had a good figure, and wore the green uniform that was born with him. This person moreover maintained that he belonged to a very old family in the land of Egypt, and that he was highly esteemed there. He had just come from the field, he said, and had been put into a card-house three stories high, and all made of picture cards with the figures turned inwards. There were doors and windows in the house, cut in

The three candidates

the body of the queen of hearts. "I sing so," he said, "that sixteen native crickets, who have chirped from their youth up, and have never yet had a card-house of their own, would become thinner than they are with envy, if they were to hear me."

Both of them, the flea and the grasshopper, took care to announce who they were, and that they considered themselves entitled to marry a Princess.

The skipjack said nothing; but it was said of him that he thought all the more, and directly the yard dog had smelt at him, he was ready to assert that the skipjack was of good family, and formed from the breastbone of an undoubted goose. The old councillor who had received three medals for holding his tongue, declared that the skipjack possessed the gift of prophecy; one could tell by his bones whether there would be a severe winter or a mild one; and that's more than one can always tell from the breastbone of the man who writes the almanack.

"I shall not say anything more," said the old King. "I only go on quietly, and always think the best."

Now they were to take their jump. The flea sprang so high that no one could see him; and then they asserted that he had not jumped at all. That was very mean. The grasshopper only sprang half so high, but he sprang straight into the King's face, and the King declared that was horribly rude. The skipjack stood a long time considering; at last people thought that he could not jump at all.

"I only hope he's not become unwell!" said the yard dog, and then he smelt at him again. "Tap!" he sprang with a little crooked jump just into the lap of the Princess who sat on a low golden stool.

Then the King said, "The highest leap was taken by him who jumped up to my daughter; for therein lies the point, but it requires head to achieve that, and the skipjack has shown that he has a head." And so he had the princess.

"I jumped highest, after all," said the flea. "But it's all the same, let her have the goose bone with its lump of wax and bit of stick. I jumped at the highest; but in this world a body is required if one wishes to be seen."

And the flea went into foreign military service, where it is said he was killed.

The grasshopper seated himself out in the ditch, and thought and considered how things happened in the world. And he too said, "Body is required! Body is required!" and then he sang his own melancholy song, and from that we have gathered this story, which they say is not true, though it's in print.

THE ELF-HILL

A few great lizards race nimbly about in the clefts of an old tree; they could understand each other well, for they spoke the lizard's language.

"How it grumbles and growls in the old elf-hill," said one lizard. "I've not been able to close my eyes for two nights, because of the noise; I might just as well lie and have the tooth-ache, for then I can't sleep either."

"There's something wrong in there!" said the other lizard. "They let the hill stand on four red posts till the cock crows at morn. It is regularly aired, and the elf-girls have learned new dances. There's something going on!"

"Yes, I have spoken with an earthworm of my acquaintance," said the third lizard. "The earthworm came straight out of the hill, where he had been grubbing in the ground night and day; he had heard much; he can't see, the miserable creature, but he understands how to toss about and listen. They expect friends in the elf-hill—grand strangers; but who they are, the earthworm would not tell, and perhaps, indeed, he did not know. All the Will-o'-the-wisps are ordered to hold a torch-dance, as it is called; and silver and gold, of which there is enough in the elf-hill, is being polished and put out in the moonshine."

"Who may these strangers be?" asked all the lizards. "What can be going on there? Hark, how it hums! Hark, how it murmurs!"

At the same moment the elf-hill opened, and an old elf-maid,[1] hollow behind, came tripping out. She was the old Elf-King's house-keeper. She was a distant relative of the royal family, and wore an amber heart on her forehead. Her legs moved so rapidly—trip, trip! Patience! how she could trip; straight down to the sea, to the night-raven.

"You are invited to the elf-hill for this evening," said she; "but will you do me a great service, and undertake the invitations? You must do something as you don't keep any house yourself. We shall have some very distinguished friends, magicians, who have something to say; and so the old Elf-King wants to make a display."

---

[1] A prevailing superstition regarding the elf-maid, or elle-maid, is, that she is fair to look at in front, but behind she is hollow like a mask.

"Who's to be invited?" asked the night-raven.

"To the great ball the world may come, even men if they can talk in their sleep, or do something that falls in our line. But at the first feast there's to be a strict selection; we will have only the most distinguished. I have had a dispute with the Elf-King, for I declared that we could not even admit ghosts. The merman and his daughters must be invited first. They may not be very well pleased to come on the dry land, but they shall have a wet stone to sit upon, or something still better; and then I think they won't refuse for this time. All the old demons of the first class, with tails, and the wood-demon and his gnomes we must have, and then I think we may not have out the grave-pig, the death-horse,[2] and the church-twig: they certainly belong to the clergy, and are not reckoned among our people. But that's only their office; they are closely related to us, and visit us diligently. "Croak!" said the night-raven, and flew away to give the invitations.

The elf-girls were already dancing on the elf-hill, and they danced with shawls which were woven of mist and moonshine; and that looks very pretty for those who like that sort of thing. In the midst below the elf-hill the great hall was splendidly decorated; the floor had been washed with moonshine, and the walls rubbed with witches' salve, so that they glowed like tulips in the light. In the kitchen, plenty of frogs were turning on the spit, snail-skins with children's fingers in them, and salads of mushroom spawn, damp mouse muzzles, and hemlock; beer brewed by the marsh-witch, gleaming saltpetre wine from grave cellars: everything very grand; and rusty nails and church window glass among the sweets.

The old Elf-King had one of his crowns polished with powdered slate pencil; it was slate pencil from the first form, and it's very difficult for the Elf-King to get first-form slate pencil! In the bed-room curtains were hung up, and fastened with snail slime. Yes, there was a grumbling and murmuring there!

---

[2] It is a popular superstition in Denmark, that under every church that is built a living horse must be buried; the ghost of this horse is the death-horse, that limps every night on three legs to the house where some one is to die. Under a few churches a living pig was buried, and the ghost of this was called the grave-pig.

"Now we must burn horse-hair and pigs' bristles as incense here," said the elf-man; "and then I think I shall have done my part."

"Father dear!" said the youngest of the daughters, "shall I hear now who the distinguished strangers are?"

"Well," said he, "I suppose I must tell it now. Two of my daughters must hold themselves prepared to be married, two will certainly be married. The old gnome from Norway yonder, he who lives in the Dovre mountains, and possesses many rock castles of fieldstones, and a gold mine, which is better than one thinks, is coming with his two sons who want each to select a wife. The old gnome is a true old honest Norwegian veteran, merry and straightforward. I know him from old days, when we drank brotherhood with one another, he was down here to fetch his wife; now she is dead; she was a daughter of the King of the Chalk-rocks of Moen. He took his wife upon chalk, as the saying is. Oh! How I long to see the old Norwegian gnome. The lads they say are rather rude, forward lads; but perhaps they are belied, and they'll be right enough when they grow older. Let me see that you can teach them manners."

"And when will they come?" asked the daughters. "That depends, on wind and weather!" said the Elf-King. "They travel economically they come when there's a chance by a ship. I wanted them to go across Sweden, but the old one would not incline to that wish. He does not advance with the times, and I don't like that!"

Then two Will-o'-the-wisp's came hopping up, one quicker than the other, and so one of them arrived first. "They're coming! They're coming!" they cried. "Give me my crown, and let me stand in the moonshine," said the Elf-King; and the daughters lifted up their shawls and bowed down to the earth.

There stood the old gnome of Dovre, with the crown of hardened ice and polished fir cones; moreover, he wore a bearskin and great warm boots; his sons, on the contrary, went bare-necked and with trousers without braces, for they were strong men.

"Is that an acclivity?" asked the youngest of the lads; and he pointed to the elf-hill. In Norway yonder we should call it a hole."

"Boys!" said the old man, "hole goes down, mound goes up. Have you no eyes in your heads?"

The only thing they wondered at down here, they said, was that they could understand the language without difficulty. "Don't give your-selves airs!" said the old man, "One would think you were home nurtured."

And then they went into the elf-hill, where the really grand company were assembled, and that in such haste that one would really say they had been blown together. But for each it was nicely and prettily arranged. The sea folks sat at table in great washing tubs; they said it was just as if they were at home. All observed the ceremonies of the table, except the two young northern gnomes; they put their legs up on the table; but they thought all that suited them well.

"Your feet off the table cloth!" cried the old gnome; and they obeyed, but not immediately. Their ladies they tickled with pine cones that they had brought with them, and then took off their boots for their own convenience, and gave them to the ladies to hold. But the father, the old Dovre gnome, was quite different to them; he told such fine stories of the proud Norwegian rocks, and of the waterfalls which rushed down with white foam and with a noise like thunder and the sound of organs; he told of the salmon that leaps up against the falling waters when the Reck plays upon the golden harp; he told of the shining winter nights, when the sledge-bells sound, and the lads run with burning torches over the ice, which is so transparent that they see the fishes start beneath their feet. Yes! He could tell so finely, that one saw what he described; it was just as if the sawmills were going, as if the servants and maids were singing songs and dancing the kalling-dance; hurrah! All at once the old gnome gave the old elf-girl a kiss; that was a kiss, and yet they were nothing to each other.

Now the elf maidens had to dance, nimbly, and also with stamping steps, and that suited them well; then came the artistic and solo dance. Wonderful how they could use their legs; one hardly knew where they began and where they ended, which were their arms and which their legs; they were all mingled together like wood-shavings; and then they whirled round till the death-horse and the grave-pig turned giddy and were obliged to leave the table.

"Prur!" said the old gnome; "That's a strange fashion of using one's legs—but what can they do more than dance, stretch out their limbs, and make a whirlwind?" "You shall soon know!" said the Elf-King. And then he called forward the youngest of his daughters. She was as light

The Elf-King's feast

and graceful as moonshine; she was the most delicate of all the sisters. She took a white shaving in her mouth, and then she was quite gone; that was her art.

But the old gnome said he should not like his wife to possess this art, and he did not think that his boys cared for it.

The other could walk under herself, just as if she had a shadow, and the gnome people had none. The third daughter was of quite another kind; she had served in the brewhouse of the moor-witch, and knew how to stuff alder-tree knots with glow-worms.

"She will make a good housewife," said the old gnome; and then he winked a health with his eyes, for he did not want to drink too much.

Now came the fourth; she had a great harp to play upon, and when she struck the first chord all lifted up their left feet, for the gnomes are left-legged; and when she struck the second chord, all were compelled to do as she wished.

"That's a dangerous woman!" said the old gnome; but both the sons went out of the hill, for they had had enough of it.

"And what can the next daughter do?" asked the old gnome. "I have learned to love what is Norwegian!" said she; "and I will never marry unless I can go to Norway."

But the youngest sister whispered to the old King: "That's only because she has heard in a Norwegian song, that when the world sinks down the cliffs of Norway will remain standing like monuments, and so she wants to get up there, because she is afraid of sinking down."

"Ho, ho!" said the old gnome, "was it meant in that way? But what can the seventh and last do?" "The sixth comes before the seventh!" said the Elf-King; for he could count. But the sixth would not come out. "I can only tell people the truth!" said she. "Nobody cares for me, and I have enough to do to sew my shroud."

Now came the seventh and last, and what could she do? Why, she could tell stories, as many as she wished. "Here are all my five fingers," said the old gnome; "tell me one for each."

And she took him by the wrist, and he laughed, till it clucked within him; and when she came to the ring finger, which had a ring round its waist, just as if it knew that there was to be a wedding; the old gnome said, "Hold fast what you have, the hand is yours; I'll have you for my own wife."

And the elf-girl said that the story of the ring finger and of little Peter Playman the fifth, were still wanting.

"We'll hear those in winter," said the gnome, "and we'll hear about the pine tree, and about the birch, and about the spirits' gifts, and about the ringing frost. You shall tell your tales, for no one up there knows how to do that well; and then we'll sit in the stone chamber where the pine logs burn, and drink mead out of the horns of the old Norwegian Kings; Reck has given me a couple, and when we sit there, the nix comes on a visit, she'll sing you all the songs of the shepherds in the mountains. That will be merry. The salmon will spring in the waterfall, and beat against the stone walls, but he cannot come in."

"Yes, it's very good living in dear old Norway; but where are the lads?"

Yes, where were they? They were running about in the fields, and blowing out the Will-o'-the-wisps, which had come so goodnaturedly for the torch dance.

"What romping about is that?" said the old gnome. "I have taken a mother for you, and now you may take one of the aunts."

But the lads said that they would rather make a speech, and drink brotherhood, they did not care to marry; and they made speeches, and drank brotherhood, and tipped up their glasses on their nails, to show they had emptied them. Afterwards they took their coats off and lay down on the table to sleep, for they made no ceremony. But the old gnome danced about the room with his young bride, and he changed boots with her, for that's more fashionable than exchanging rings.

"Now the cock crows," said the old elf-girl, who attended to her housekeeping. "Now we must shut the shutters, so that the sun may not burn us;" and the hill shut itself up.

But outside the lizards ran up and down in the cleft tree, and one said to the other, "Oh! How I like that old Norwegian gnome."

"I like the lads better," said the earthworm. But he could not see, the miserable creature.

THE SHIRT-COLLAR

There was once a rich cavalier whose whole effects consisted of a boot-jack and a hair-brush, but he had the finest shirt-collar in the world, and about this shirt-collar we will hear a story. The collar was now old enough to think of marrying, and it happened that he was sent to the wash together with a garter.

"My word!" exclaimed the shirt-collar. "I have never seen anything so slender and delicate, so charming and genteel. May I ask your name?"

"I shall not tell you that!" said the garter.

"Where is your home?" asked the shirt-collar. But the garter was of rather a retiring nature, and it seemed a strange question to answer.

"I presume you are a girdle?" said the shirt-collar, "A sort of under-girdle. I see that you are useful as well as ornamental, my little lady."

"You are not to speak to me," said the garter. "I have not, I think given you any occasion to do so."

"Oh! When one is as beautiful as you are," cried the shirt-collar, "I fancy that is occasion enough." "Go!" said the garter, "don't come so near me; you look to me quite like a man."

"I'm a fine cavalier, too," said the shirt-collar. "I possess a boot-jack and a hair-brush." And that was not true at all, for it was his master who owned these things, but he was boasting.

"Don't come too near me," said the garter. "I'm not used to that." "Affectation!" cried the shirt-collar. And then they were taken out of the wash, and starched, and hung over a chair in the sunshine, and then laid on the ironing-board, and now came the hot iron.

"Mrs. Widow!" said the shirt-collar, "little Mrs. Widow, I'm getting quite warm. I'm being quite changed, I'm losing all my creases; you're burning a hole in me; ugh! I propose to you."

"You old rag!" said the iron, and rode proudly over the shirt-collar, for it imagined that it was a steam-boiler, and that it ought to be out on the railway, dragging carriages. "You old rag," said the iron.

The shirt-collar was a little frayed at the edges, therefore the paper scissors came to smooth away the frayed places. "O-ho!" said the shirt-collar, "I presume you're a first-rate dancer. How you can point your toes, no one in the world can do that like you." "I know that," said the scissors.

"You deserve to be a countess," said the shirt-collar. "All that I possess, consists of a genteel cavalier, a boot-jack and a comb. If I had only an estate!"

"What? Do you want to marry?"—cried the scissors, and they were angry, and gave such a deep cut that the collar had to be cashiered.

"I shall have to propose to the hair-brush," thought the shirt-collar.

The shirt-collar in its glory

"It is wonderful what beautiful hair you have, my little lady. Have you never thought of engaging yourself?" "Yes, you can easily imagine that," replied the hair-brush. "I am engaged to the boot-jack."

"Engaged!" cried the shirt-collar. Now there was no one left to whom he could offer himself, and so he despised love-making.

A long time passed, and the shirt-collar was put into the sack of a paper dealer. There was a terribly ragged company, and the fine ones kept to themselves, and the coarse ones to themselves, as is right. They had all much to tell, but the shirt-collar most of all, for he was a terrible Jack Brag.

"I have had a tremendous number of love affairs," said the shirt-collar. "They would not leave me alone; but I was a fine cavalier, a starched one; I had a boot-jack, and a hair-brush that I never used; you should only have seen me then, when I was turned down; I shall never forget my first love, it was a girdle, and how delicate, how charming, how genteel it was, and my first love threw herself into a washing-tub, and all for me! There was also a widow desperately fond of me, but I let her stand alone till she turned quite black. Then there was a dancer who gave me the wound from which I still suffer, she was very hot-tempered. My own hair-brush was in love with me, and lost all her hair from neglected love. Yes, I've had many experiences of this kind; but I am most sorry for the garter—I mean for the girdle, that jumped into the wash-tub for love of me. I've a great deal on my conscience. It's time I was turned into white paper."

And to that the shirt-collar came. All the rags were turned into white paper, but the shirt-collar became the very piece of paper we see here, and upon which this story has been printed, and that was done because he boasted so dreadfully about things that were not at all true, and this we must remember, so that we may on no account do the same, for we cannot know at all whether we shall not be put into the rag bag and returned to white paper, on which our whole history, even the most secret, shall be printed, so that we are obliged to run about and tell it, as the shirt-collar did.

THE NEIGHBOURING FAMILIES

One would really have thought that something important was going on by the duck pond; but nothing was going on. All the ducks lying quietly upon the water, or standing on their heads in it—for they could do that—swam suddenly to the shore. One could see the traces of their feet on the wet earth, and their quacking sounded far and wide. The water, lately clear and bright as a mirror, was quite in a commotion. Before every tree, every neighbouring bush, the old farmhouse with the holes in the roof and the swallow's nest, and especially the great rose-bush, covered with flowers, had been mirrored in it; this rose-bush covered the wall, and hung over the water, in which every-thing appeared as in a picture, only that everything stood on its head; but when the water was set in motion everything swam away and the picture was gone. Two feathers, which the fluttering ducks had lost, floated to and fro, and all at once they took a start, as if the wind were coming; but the wind did not come, so they had to be still, and the water became quiet and smooth again. The roses mirrored themselves in it again; they were beautiful, but they did not know it, for no one had told them. The sun shone among the delicate leaves; everything breathed in the sweet fragrance, and all felt as we feel when we are filled with the thought of our happiness.

"How beautiful is life!" said each rose. Only one thing I wish, that I were able to kiss the sun, because it is so bright and so warm. The roses, too, in the water yonder, our images, I should like to kiss, and the pretty birds in the nests. There are some up yonder too; they thrust out their heads and pipe quite feebly; they have not feathers like their father and mother. They are good neighbours, below and above. How beautiful is life!"

The young ones above and below; those below are certainly only shadows in the water—mere sparrows; their parents were sparrows too; they had taken possession of the empty swallow's nest of last year, and kept house in it as if it had been their own.

"Are those duck's children swimming yonder?" asked the young sparrows, when they noticed the duck's feathers upon the water.

"If you must ask questions, ask sensible ones," replied their mother. "Don't you see that they are feathers, living clothes stuff, like I wear, and like you will wear; but ours is finer. I wish, by the way, we had those up here in our own nest, for they keep one warm. I wonder what the ducks were so frightened at. Not at us certainly, though I said 'Piep' to you rather loudly. The thick-headed roses ought to know it; but they know nothing; they only look at one another and smell. I'm very tired of those neighbours."

"Just listen to those darling birds up there," said the roses. "They begin to want to sing, but are not able yet. But it will be managed in time; what a pleasure that must be; it's nice to have such merry neighbours."

Suddenly two horses came galloping up to water. A peasant-boy rode on one; he had taken off all his clothes, except his big broad straw hat. The boy whistled like a bird, and rode into the pond where it was deepest; and when he came past the rose-bush he plucked a rose, and put it upon his hat. And now he thought he looked very fine, and rode on. The other roses looked after their sister, and said to each other, "Whither may she be journeying?" but they did not know.

"I should like to go out into the world," said one; "but it's beautiful, too, here at home among the green leaves. All day the sun shines warm and bright, and in the night-time the sky is more beautiful still; we can see that, through all the little holes in it." They meant the stars; they knew no better.

"We make it lively about the house," said the mother sparrow; "and the swallow's nest brings luck," people say, "so they're glad to see us. But the neighbours! Such a rose-bush climbing up the wall causes damp. It will most likely be taken away; and then, at least, corn will perhaps grow here. The roses are fit for nothing but to be looked at, or at most one may be stuck on a hat."

"Every year, I know from my mother, they fall off. The farmer's wife preserves them, and puts salt among them; then they get a French name that I neither can nor will pronounce, and are put upon the fire to make a good smell. You see that's their life. They're only for the eye and the nose. Now you know it."

When the evening came, and the gnats played in the warm air and the red clouds, the nightingale came and sang to the roses, saying that the beautiful was like sunshine to the world, and that the beautiful lived for ever. But the roses thought the nightingale was singing of itself, and indeed, one might easily have thought so; they never imagined that the song was about them. But they rejoiced greatly in it, and considered whether all the little sparrows might become nightingales. "I understood the song of that bird very well," said the young sparrows; only one word was not clear. What is the *beautiful*?"

"That's nothing at all," replied the mother sparrow; "that's only an outside affair. Yonder, at the nobleman's seat, where the pigeons have their own house, and have corn and peas strewn before them every day—I've been there myself and dined with them; for tell me what company you keep, and I'll tell you who you are; yonder at the noble-man's seat, there are two birds with green necks and a crest upon their heads; they can spread out their tails like great shells, and then they play with various colours, so that the sight makes one's eyes ache. These birds are called peacocks, and that's the *beautiful*. They should only be plucked a little, then they would look no better than all the rest of us. I should have plucked them myself, if they had not been so large."

"I'll pluck them," piped the little sparrow, who had not any feathers yet.

In the farmhouse dwelt two young married people; they loved each other well, were industrious and active, and everything in their home looked very pretty. On Sunday morning the young wife came out, plucked a handful of the most beautiful roses, and put them into a glass of water, which she put upon the cupboard.

"Now I see that it is Sunday," said the husband, and he kissed his little wife. They sat down, read their hymn-book, and held each other by the hand; and the sun shone on the fresh roses and the young couple.

"This sight is really too wearisome," said the mother sparrow, who could look from the nest into the room; and she flew away.

The same thing happened the next Sunday, for every Sunday fresh roses were placed in the glass; but the rose-bush bloomed as beautiful as ever.

The young sparrows had feathers now, and wanted to fly out too, but the mother would not allow it, and they were obliged to stay at home. She flew alone; but, however it may have happened, before she was aware of it, she was entangled in a noose of horse-hair which some boys had fastened to the branches. The horse-hair wound itself fast round her legs, so fast as if it would cut the leg through. What pain, what a fright it was in! The boys came running up, and seized the bird; and indeed roughly enough.

"It's only a sparrow," said they; but they did not let her go, but took her home with them. And whenever she cried, they tapped her on the beak.

In the farm house stood an old man, who understood making soap for shaving and washing, in cakes as well as in balls. He was a merry, wandering old man. When he saw the sparrows, which the boys had brought, and for which they said they did not care, he said: "Shall we make it very beautiful?" The mother sparrow felt an icy shudder pass through her. Out of the box in which were the most brilliant colours, the old man took a quantity of shining gold leaf, and the boys were sent for some white of egg, with which the sparrow was completely smeared; the gold leaf was stuck upon that, and there was the mother sparrow gilded all over. She did not think of the adornment, but trembled all over. And the soap-man tore off a fragment from the red lining of his old jacket, cut notches in it, so that it looked like a cock's comb, and stuck it on the bird's head.

"Now you shall see the gold jacket fly," said the old man; and he released the sparrow, which flew away in deadly fear, with the sunlight shining upon it. How it glittered! All the sparrows, and even a crow, a knowing old boy, were startled at the sight; but still they flew after it to know what kind of strange bird this might be.

Driven by fear and horror, it flew homeward; it was nearly sinking powerless to the earth; the flock of pursuing birds increased, and some even tried to peck at it.

"Look at him! Look at him!" they all cried.

"Look at him! Look at him! cried the young ones, when the mother sparrow approached the nest. That must be a young peacock. He glitters with all colours. It quite hurts one's eyes, as mother told us. Piep! that's the beautiful!" And now they pecked at the bird with their little beaks, so that it could not possibly get into the nest; it was so much exhausted that it could not even say "Piep!" much less "I am your mother!" The other birds also fell upon the sparrow, and plucked off feather after feather till it fell bleeding into the rose-bush.

"You poor creature!" said all the roses; "be quiet, we will hide you! Lean your head against us!"

The sparrow spread out its wings once more, then it drew them tight to its body, and lay dead by the neighbour family, the beautiful fresh roses.

"Piep!" sounded from the nest. "Where can our mother be? It's quite inexplicable; it cannot be a trick of her's, and mean that we're to shift for ourselves; she has left us the house as an inheritance, but to which of us shall it belong, when we have families of our own?"

"Yes, it won't do for you to stay with me, when I enlarge my establishment with a wife and children," observed the smallest.

"I shall have more wives and children than you," cried the second.

The painter sketching the rose-bush

"But I am the eldest!" said the third. Now they all became excited. They struck out with their wings, hacked with their beaks, and flump! One after another was thrust out of the nest. There they lay with their anger; they held their heads on one side, and blinked with the eye that looked upwards. That was their way to look so stupid.

They could fly a little; by practice they improved, and at last they fixed upon a sign by which they should know each other when they met later in the world. This sign was to be the cry of "Piep," with a scratching of the left foot three times against the ground.

The young sparrow that had remained behind in the nest, made itself as broad as it possibly could, for it was the proprietor. But the proprietorship did not last long. In the night the red fire burst through the window, the flames seized upon the roof, the dry straw blazed brightly up, the whole house was burnt, and the young sparrow too; but the two others who wanted to marry, managed to escape with their lives.

When the sun rose again, and everything looked as much refreshed as if nature had had a quiet sleep, there remained of the farm-house nothing but a few charred beams, leaning against the chimney that was now its own master. Thick smoke still rose from among the fragments, but without stood the rose-bush quite unharmed, and every flower, every twig was immersed in the clear water.

"How beautifully those roses bloom before the ruined house," cried a passer-by. "I cannot imagine a more agreeable picture; I must have that." And the man took out of his portfolio a little book, with white leaves; he was a painter, and with his pencil he drew the smoking house, the charred beams, and the overhanging chimney, which bent more and more; quite in the foreground appeared the blooming rose-bush, which presented a charming sight, and indeed for its sake the whole picture had been made.

Later in the day, the two sparrows that had been born here, came by; "Where is the house?" asked they. "Where is the nest? Piep! All is burnt, and our strong brother is burnt too. That's what he has got by keeping the nest to himself. The roses has escaped well enough, there they stand yet, with their red cheeks. They certainly don't mourn at their neighbour's misfortune. I won't speak to them, it's so ugly here, that's my opinion," and they flew up and away.

On a beautiful sunny autumn day, when one could almost have believed it was the middle of summer, there hopped about in the clean dry court-yard of the nobleman's seat, in front of the great steps, a number of pigeons, black, and white, and variegated, all shining in the sunlight. The old mother pigeons said to their young ones, "Stand in groups, stand in groups, for that looks much better."

"What are those little grey creatures, that run about behind us?" asked an old pigeon, with red and green in her eyes. "Little grey ones, little grey ones," she cried.

"They are sparrows, good creatures. We have always had the reputation of being kind, so we will allow them to pick up the corn with us. They don't interrupt conversation, and they make such pretty curtseys."

Yes they curtsied three times each, with their left leg, and said "Piep." By that they recognized each other as the sparrows from the nest by the burnt house.

"Here's very good eating," said the sparrows. The pigeons strutted round one another, bulged out their chests mightily, and had their own secret views and opinions on things in general.

"Do you see that pouter pigeon?" said one, speaking of the others. "Do you see that one, swallowing the peas? She takes too many, and the best, moreover Curoo, Curoo! How she lifts up her crest, the ugly spiteful thing! Curoo, Curoo."

And all their eyes sparkled with spite. "Stand in groups, stand in groups! Little grey ones, little grey ones! Curoo, Curoo!" So their beaks went on and on, and so they will go on when a thousand years are gone.

The sparrows feasted bravely; they listened attentively, and even stood in the ranks of the pigeons, but it did not suit them well. They were satisfied, and so they quitted the pigeons, exchanged opinions concerning them, slipped under the garden railings, and when they found the door of the garden open, one of them, who was over-fed, and consequently valorous, hopped on the threshold. "Piep!" said he, "I may venture that."

"Piep!" said the other, "so can I, and something more too," and he hopped into the room. No one was present; the third sparrow saw that, and hopped still further into the room, and said, "Everything or nothing; by the way, this is a funny man's-nest, and what have they put up here? What's that?"

Just in front of the sparrows, the roses were blooming, they were mirrored in the water, and the charred beams leant against the toppling chimney. "Why, what is this? How came this in the room, in the nobleman's seat?"

And then these sparrows wanted to fly over the chimney and the roses, but flew against a flat wall. It was all a picture, a great beautiful picture, that the painter had completed from a sketch.

"Piep!" said the sparrows, "It's nothing, it only looks like something. Piep! That's the beautiful, can you understand it? I can't." And they flew away, for some people came into the room.

Days and years went by; the pigeons had often cooed, not to say growled, the spiteful things; the sparrows had suffered cold in winter and lived riotously in summer; they were all betrothed or married, or whatever you like to call it. They had little ones, and of course each thought his own the handsomest and the cleverest; one flew this way, another that, and when they met they knew each other by their "Piep," and the three curtseys with the left leg. The eldest had remained a maiden sparrow, with no nest and no young ones; her great idea was to see a town, therefore she flew to Copenhagen.

There was to be seen a great house painted with many colours, close by the castle and by the canal, in which latter swam many ships laden with apples and pottery. The windows were broader below than at the top, and when the sparrow looked through, every room appeared to her like a tulip with the most manifold colours and shades. But in the middle of the tulip were white people, made of marble; a few certainly were made of plaster, but, in the eyes of a sparrow, that's all the same. Upon the roof stood a metal carriage, with metal horses harnessed to it, and the Goddess of Victory, also of bronze, driving. It was THORWALDSEN'S MUSEUM.

"How it shines! How it shines!" said the little maiden sparrow. "I suppose that's what they call 'the beautiful' Piep! But this is greater than the peacock!" It still remembered what, in its days of childhood, the mother sparrow had declared to be the greatest among the beautiful. The sparrow flew down into the courtyard. There everything was very splendid; upon the walls palms and branches were painted; in the midst of the court stood a great blooming rose tree, spreading out its fresh branches, covered with many roses, over a grave. Thither the maiden sparrow flew, for there she saw many of her own kind. "Piep!" and three curtseys with the left leg—that salutation it had often made throughout the summer, and nobody had replied; for friends who are once parted don't meet every day, and now this form of greeting had become quite a habit with it. But to-day two old sparrows and a young one replied "Piep!" and curtsied three times, each with the left leg.

"Ah! Good day! Good day!" They were two old ones from the nest, and a little one belonging to the family. "Do we meet here again? It's a grand place, but there's not much to eat. This is the beautiful! Piep!"

And many people came out of the side chambers where the glorious marble statues stood, and approached the grave where slept the great master who had formed these marble images. All stood with radiant faces by Thorwaldsen's grave, and some gathered up the fallen rose leaves and kept them. They had come from afar: one from mighty England, others from Germany and France. The most beautiful among the ladies plucked one of the roses and hid it in her bosom. Then the sparrows thought that the roses ruled here, and that the whole house had been built for their sake; that appeared to them to be too much, but as all the people showed their love for the roses they would not be behindhand. "Piep!" they said, and swept the ground with their tails, and glanced with one eye at the roses; and they had not looked long at the flowers before they recognized them as old neighbours. And so the roses were really. The painter who had sketched the rose-bush by the ruined house had afterwards received permission to dig it up, and had given it to the architect, for nowhere could more beautiful roses be found. And the architect had planted it upon Thorwaldsen's grave, where it bloomed, an image of the beautiful, and gave its red fragrant leaves to be carried into distant lands as mementoes.

"Have you found a situation, here in the town?" asked the sparrows. And the roses nodded; they recognized their brown neighbours, and were glad to see them again. "How glorious it is to live and bloom, to see old faces again, and cheerful faces every day!" "Piep!" said the sparrows. "Yes, these are truly our old neighbours; we remember their origin by the pond. Piep! how they've got on. Yes, some people succeed while they're asleep! Why, yonder is a withered leaf—I see it quite plainly!" And they pecked at it till the leaf fell. But the tree stood there greener and fresher than ever; the roses bloomed in the sunshine by Thorwaldsen's grave, and were associated with his immortal name.

THE LITTLE MATCH-GIRL

It was terribly cold; it snowed and was already almost dark, and evening came on, the last evening of the year. In the cold and gloom a poor little girl, bareheaded and barefoot, was walking through the streets. When she had left the house she had certainly had slippers on; but of what use were they? They were very big slippers, and her mother had used them till then, so big were they. The little maid lost them as she slipped across the road where two carriages were rattling by, terribly fast. One slipper was not to be found again, and a boy had seized the other, and run away with it. He thought he could use it very well as a cradle, some day when he had children of his own. So now the little girl went with her little naked feet, which were quite red and blue with the cold. In an old apron she carried a number of matches, and a bundle of them in her hand. No one had bought anything of her all day, and no one had given her a farthing.

Shivering with cold and hunger she crept along, a picture of misery, poor little girl! The snow-flakes covered her long fair hair, which fell in pretty curls over her neck; but she did not think of that now. In all the windows lights were shining, and there was a glorious smell of roast goose, for it was New Year's Eve. Yes, she thought of that!

In a corner formed by two houses, one of which projected beyond the other, she sat down, cowering. She had drawn up her little feet, but she was still colder, and she did not dare to go home, for she had sold no matches, and did not bring a farthing of money. From her father she would certainly receive a beating, and besides, it was cold at home, for they had nothing over them but a roof through which the wind whistled, though the largest rents had been stopped with straw and rags.

Her little hands were almost benumbed with the cold. Ah! A match might do her good if she could only draw one from the bundle and rub it against the wall, and warm her hands at it. She drew one out. Ratch! How it sputtered and burned! It was a warm bright flame, like a little candle, when she held her hands over it; it was a wonderful little light! It really seemed to the little girl as if she sat before a great polished stove, with bright brass feet, and a brass cover. How the fire burned; how comfortable it was; but the little flame went out, the stove vanished, and she had only the little remains of the burnt match in her hand.

A second was rubbed against the wall. It burned up, and when the light fell upon the wall the wall became transparent like a veil, and she could see through it into the room. On the table a snow-white cloth was spread; upon it stood a shining dinner-service, the roast goose smoked gloriously, stuffed with apples and dried plums. And what was still more splendid to behold, the goose hopped down from the dish, and waddled along the floor, with a knife and fork in its breast, to the little girl. Then the match went out, and only the thick, damp, cold wall was before her. She lighted another match. Then she was sitting under a beautiful Christmas tree; it was greater and more ornamented than the one she had seen through the glass door at the rich merchant's. Thousands of candles burned upon the green branches, and coloured pictures like those in the print-shops looked down upon them. The little girl stretched forth her hand towards them; then the match went out. The Christmas lights mounted higher. She saw them now as stars in the sky; one of them fell down, forming a long line of fire.

"Now some one is dying," thought the little girl, for her old grandmother, the only person who had loved her, and who now was dead, had told her that when a star fell down a soul mounted up to God.

She rubbed another match against the wall; it became bright again, and in the brightness the old grandmother stood clear and shining, mild and lovely.

"Grandmother!" cried the child, "Oh! Take me with you! I know you will go when the match is burned out. You will vanish like the warm fire, the warm food, and the great glorious Christmas tree!" And she hastily rubbed the whole bundle of matches, for she wished to hold her grandmother fast. And the matches burned with such a glow that it became brighter than in the middle of the day; grandmother had never been so large or so beautiful. She took the little girl in her arms, and both flew in brightness and joy above the earth, very, very high, and up there was neither cold, nor hunger, nor care—they were with God!

But in the corner, leaning against the wall, sat the poor girl with red cheeks and smiling mouth, frozen to death on the last evening of the Old Year. The New Year's sun rose upon a little corpse! The child sat there, stiff and cold, with the matches of which one bundle was burnt.

The people find the little match-girl

"She wanted to warm herself," the people said. No one imagined what a beautiful thing she had seen, and in what glory she had gone in with her grandmother to the New Year's Day.

THE BUCK-WHEAT

Often when after a thunder-storm, one passes a field in which buck-wheat is growing, it appears quite blackened and singed. It is just as if a flame of fire had passed across it; and then the countryman says, it got that from the lightning. But whence has it received that? I will tell you what the sparrow told me about it, and the sparrow heard it from an old willow tree, which stood by a buck-wheat field, and still stands there. It is quite a great venerable willow tree, but crippled and old; it is burst in the middle, and grass and brambles grow out of the cleft; the tree bends forward, and the branches hang quite down to the ground, as if they were long green hair.

On all the fields round about, corn was growing, not only rye and barley, but also oats, yes, the most capital oats, that when it's ripe looks like a number of little yellow canary birds, sitting upon a spray. The corn stood smiling, and the richer an ear was, the deeper did it bend in pious humility.

But there was also a field with buck-wheat, and this field was exactly opposite to the old willow tree. The buck-wheat did not bend at all, like the rest of the grain, but stood up proudly and stiffly.

"I'm as rich as any corn-ear," said he. "Moreover, I'm very much handsomer; my flowers are beautiful as the blossoms of the apple-tree; it's quite a delight to look upon me and mine; do you know anything more splendid than we are, you old willow tree?"

And the willow tree nodded his head, just as if he would have said, "Yes, that's true enough!" But the buck-wheat spread itself out from mere vain glory, and said, "The stupid tree, he's so old that the grass grows in his body."

Now a terrible storm came on; all the field flowers folded their leaves together, or bowed their little heads, while the storm passed over them, but the buck-wheat stood erect in its pride.

"Bend your head, like us," said the flower. "I've not the slightest cause to do so," replied the buck-wheat.

"Bend your head, as we do," cried the various crops. "Now the storm comes flying on. He has wings that reach from the clouds just down to the earth, and he'll beat you in half before you can cry for mercy." "Yes; but I won't bend," quoth the buckwheat.

"Shut up your flowers, and bend your leaves," said the old willow tree. "Don't look up at the lightning, when the cloud bursts; even men may not do that, for in the lightning one may look into heaven, but the light dazzles even men; and what would happen to us, if we dared do so; we, the plants of the field, that are much less worthy than they."

The field of buck-wheat

"Much less worthy!"—cried the buckwheat. "Now I'll just look straight up into heaven," and it did so, in its pride and vain glory. It was as if the whole world were on fire, so vivid was the lightning.

When afterwards the bad weather had passed by, the flowers and the crops stood in the still, pure air, quite refreshed by the rain; but the buck-wheat was burnt coal-black by the lightning, and it was now like a dead weed upon the field.

And the old willow tree waved its branches in the wind, and great drops of water fell down out of the green leaves, just as if the tree wept; and the sparrows asked, "Why do you weep? Here everything is so cheerful; see how the sun shines, see how the clouds sail on; do you not breathe the scent of flowers and bushes? Why do you weep, willow tree?"

And the willow tree told them of the pride of the buck-wheat, of its vain glory, and of the punishment, which always follows such sin. I who tell you this tale, have heard it from the sparrows. They told it me one evening, when I begged them to give me a story.

THE OLD HOUSE

Down yonder, in the street, stood an old, old house. It was almost three hundred years old, for one could read as much on the beam, on which was carved the date of its erection, surrounded by tulips and trailing hops. There one could read entire verses in the characters of olden times, and over each window a face had been carved in the beam, and these faces made all kinds of grimaces. One story projected a long way above the other, and close under the roof, was a leaden gutter with a dragon's head. The rain water was to run out of the dragon's mouth, but it ran out of the creature's body instead, for there was a hole in the pipe.

All the other houses in the street were still new and neat, with large window-panes and smooth walls. One could easily see that they would have nothing to do with the old house. They thought perhaps: "How long is that old rubbish heap to stand here, a scandal to the whole street? The parapet stands so far forward that no one can see out of our windows what is going on in that direction. The staircase is as broad as a castle staircase, and as steep as if it led to a church tower. The iron railing looks like the gate of a family vault, and there are brass bosses upon it—it's too ridiculous!"

Just opposite stood some more new neat houses that thought exactly like the rest; but here sat at the window a little boy, with fresh red cheeks, with clear sparkling eyes, and he was particularly fond of the old house, in sunshine as well as by moonlight. And when he looked down at the wall where the plaster had fallen off, then he could sit and fancy all kinds of pictures; how the street must have appeared in old times, with parapets, open staircases, and pointed gables; he could see soldiers with halberts, and roof-gutters running about in the form of dragons and griffins. That was just a good house to look at; and in it lived an old man who went about in leather knee-smalls, and wore a coat with great brass buttons, and a wig which one could at once see was a real wig. Every morning an old man came to him, to clean his rooms and run his errands. With this exception the old man in the leather knee-smalls was all alone in the old house. Sometimes he came to one of the windows and looked out, and the little boy nodded to him, and the old man nodded back, and thus they became acquainted and became friends, though they had never spoken to one another; but indeed, that was not necessary.

The little boy heard his parents say, "The old man opposite is very well off, but he is terribly lonely."

Next Sunday the little boy wrapped something in a piece of paper, went with it to the house-door, and said to the man who ran errands for the old gentleman, "Harkye, will you take this to the old man opposite for me? I have two tin soldiers; this is one of them, and he shall have it because I know that he is terribly lonely."

And the old attendant looked quite pleased and nodded, and carried the tin soldier into the old house. Afterwards he was sent over, to ask if the little boy would not like to come himself and pay a visit? His parents gave him leave; and so it was that he came to the old house.

The brass bosses on the staircase shone much more brightly than usual; one would have thought they had been polished in honour of his visit. And it was just as if the carved trumpeters—for on the doors there were carved trumpeters, standing in tulips—were blowing with all their might; their cheeks looked much rounder than before. Yes, they blew "Tan-ta-ra-ra, the little boy's coming, tan-ta-ra-ra!" and then the door opened. The whole hall was hung with old portraits, with knights in armour and ladies in silk gowns; and the armour rattled, and the silk dresses rustled, and then came a staircase that went up a great way and down a little way, and then one came to a balcony which was certainly in a very rickety state, with long cracks and great holes; but out of all these grew grass and leaves for the whole balcony, the court-yard, and the wall, were overgrown with so much green that it looked like a garden, but it was only a balcony. Here stood old flower-pots that had faces with asses' ears; but the flowers grew just as they chose. In one pot pinks were growing over on all sides; that is to say, the green stalks, sprout upon sprout, and they said quite plainly, "The air has caressed me and the sun has kissed me, and promised me a little flower for next Sunday, a little flower next Sunday!"

And then they came to a room where the walls were covered with pigskin, and on the leather, golden flowers had been stamped:

Flowers fade fast,
But pigskin will last,

said the walls.

And there stood chairs with quite high backs, with carved work and elbows on each side. "Sit down!" said they. "Oh! how it cracks inside me. Now I shall be sure to have the gout, like the old cupboard! Gout in my back, ugh!"

And then the little boy came to the room where the old man sat.

"Thank you for the tin soldier, my little friend," said the old man. "And thank you for coming over to me." "Thanks, thanks!" or "Crick, crack!" said all the furniture; there were so many pieces that they almost stood in each other's way to see the little boy.

And in the middle, on the wall, hung a picture, a beautiful lady, young and cheerful in appearance, but dressed just like people of the old times, with powder in her hair, and skirts that stuck out stiffly. She said neither thanks, nor crack, but looked down upon the little boy with her mild eyes, and he at once asked the old man, "Where did you get her from?"

"From the dealer, opposite," replied the old man. "Many pictures are always hanging there. No one knew them or troubled himself about them, for they are all buried. But many years ago I knew this lady, and now she's been dead and gone for half a century."

And under the picture hung, behind glass, a nosegay of withered flowers; they were certainly also half a century old, at least they looked it; and the pendulum of the great clock went to and fro, and the hands turned round, and everything in the room grew older still, but no one noticed it.

"They say at home," said the little boy, "that you are always terribly solitary." "Oh," answered the old man, "old thoughts come with all that they bring, to visit me; and now you are coming too; I'm very well off."

And then he took from a shelf a book with pictures; they were long processions of wonderful coaches, such as one never sees at the present day; soldiers like the knave of clubs and citizens with waving flags. The tailors had a flag with shears on it, held by two lions, and the shoe-makers a flag without boots, but with an eagle that had two heads; for among the shoemakers everything must be so arranged that they can say, "There's a pair." Yes, that was a picture-book! And the old man went into the other room, to fetch preserves and apples and nuts. It was really glorious in that old house.

"I can't stand it," said the tin soldier who stood upon the shelf. "It is terribly lonely and dull here; when one has been accustomed to family life, one can't get accustomed to existence here. I cannot stand it! The day is long enough, but the evening is longer still! Here it is not at all like in your house opposite, where your father and mother were always conversing cheerfully together, and you and all the other dear children made a famous noise. How solitary it is here at the old man's! Do you think he gets any kisses? Do you think he gets friendly looks, or a Christmas tree? He'll get nothing but a grave! I cannot stand it!"

"You must not look at it from the sorrowful side," said the little boy. "To me all appears remarkably pretty, and all the old thoughts with all they bring with them, came to visit here."

"Yes, but I don't see them, and don't know them," objected the tin soldier. "I can't bear it." "You must bear it!" said the little boy.

And the old man came with the pleasantest face and with the best of preserved fruits and apples and nuts; and then the little boy thought no more of the tin soldier. Happy and delighted the youngster went home, and days went by, weeks went by; and there was much nodding from the boy's home, across to the old house and back, and then the little boy went over there again.

And the carved trumpeters blew: "Tanta-ra-ra, tanta-ra-ra, there's the little boy, tanta-ra-ra," and the swords and armour on the old pictures rattled, and the silken dresses rustled; and the leather told tales, and the old chairs had the gout in their backs. Ugh! it was just like the first time, for over there one day or one hour was just like another.

"I can't stand it!" said the tin soldier. "I've wept tears of tin! It's too dreamy here. I'd rather go to war and lose my arms and legs; at any rate, that's a change. I cannot stand it! Now I know what it means to have a visit from one's old thoughts and all they bring with them. I've had visits from my own, and you may believe me, that's no pleasure in the long run. I was very nearly jumping down from the shelf. I could see you all in the house opposite as plainly as if you had been here. It was Sunday morning, and you children were all standing round the table singing the psalm you sing every morning. You were standing reverently with folded hands, and your father and mother were just as piously disposed; then the door opened, and your little sister Maria, who is not two years old yet, and who always dances when she hears music or song, of whatever description they may be, was brought in. She was not to do it, but she immediately began to dance, though she could not get into right time, for the song was too slow, so she first stood on one leg and bent her head quite over in front, but it was not long enough. You all stood very quietly, though that was rather difficult, but I laughed inwardly, and so I fell down from the table and got a bruise which I have still; for it was not right of one to laugh. But all this, and all the rest that I have experienced, now passes by my inward vision, and those must be the old thoughts with everything they bring with them. Tell me, do you still sing on Sundays? Tell me something about little Maria. And how is my comrade and brother tin soldier? Yes, he must be very happy! I can't stand it!"

"You have been given away," said the little boy. "You must stay where you are. Don't you see that?"

And the old man came with a box in which many things were to be seen: little rouge-pots and scent-boxes; and old cards, so large and so richly gilt as one never sees them in these days; and many little boxes were opened, likewise the piano; and in this were painted landscapes, inside the lid. But the piano was quite hoarse when the old man played upon it; and then he nodded to the picture that he had bought at the dealer's, and the old man's eyes shone quite brightly.

"I'll go to the war! I'll go to the war!" cried the old soldier, as loud as he could; and he threw himself down on the floor.

Where had he gone? The old man searched, the little boy searched, but he was gone, and could not be found. "I shall find him," said the old man; but he never found him: the flooring was so open and full of holes. The tin soldier had fallen through a crack, and there he lay as in an open grave.

And the day passed away, and the little boy went home; and the week passed by, and many weeks passed by. The windows were quite frozen up, and the little boy had to sit and breathe upon the panes, to make a peep-hole to look at the old house; and snow had blown among all the carving and the inscriptions, and covered the whole staircase, as if no one were in the house at all. And, indeed, there was no one in the house, for the old man had died!

In the evening a carriage stopped at the door; and in that he was laid, in his coffin; he was to rest in a family vault in the country. So he was

The little boy visits the old man

carried away; but no one followed him on his last journey, for all his friends were dead. And the little boy kissed his hand after the coffin as it rolled away.

A few days later, and there was an auction in the old house; and the little boy saw from his window, how the old knights and ladies, the flower-pots with the long ears, the chairs and the cupboards were carried away. One was taken here, and then there; *her* portrait, that had been bought by the dealer, went back into his shop, and there it was hung; for no one cared for the old picture.

In the spring the house itself was pulled down, for the people said it was old rubbish. One could look from the street straight into the room with the leather wall covering, which was taken down, ragged and torn; and the green of the balcony hung straggling over the beams, that threatened to fall in altogether. And now a clearance was made.

"That did good!" said a neighbour. And a capital house was built with large windows and white smooth walls; but in front of the place where the old house had really stood, a little garden was planted, and by the neighbour's wall tall vine shoots clambered up. In the front of the garden was placed a great iron railing with an iron door; and it had a stately look. The people stopped in front, and looked through. And the sparrows sat down in dozens upon the vine branches, and chattered all at once as loud as they could; but not about the old house, for they could not remember that, for many years had gone by—so many, that the little boy had grown to be a man, a thorough man, whose parents rejoiced in him. And he had just married, and was come with his wife to live in the house, in front of which was the garden; and here he stood next to her while she planted a field-flower which she considered very pretty; she planted it with her little hand, pressing the earth close round it with her fingers. "Ah, what was that?" She pricked herself. Out of the soft earth something pointed was sticking up. Only think! That was the tin soldier, the same that had been lost up in the old man's room, and had been hidden among old wood and rubbish for a long time, and had lain in the ground many a year. And the young wife first dried the soldier in a green leaf, and then with her fine handkerchief, that smelt so deliciously. And the tin soldier felt just as if he were walking from a fainting fit.

"Let me see him!" said the young man. And then he smiled, and shook his head. "Yes, it can scarcely be the same; but it reminds me of an affair with a tin soldier, which I had when I was a little boy." And then he told his wife about the old house, and the old man, and of the tin soldier he had sent across to the old man whom he had thought so lonely: and the tears came into the young wife's eyes for the old house and the old man.

"It is possible, after all, that it may be the same tin soldier," said she. "I will take care of him, and remember what you have told me; but you must show me the old man's grave."

"I don't know where that is," replied he; "and no one knows it. All his friends were dead; none tended his grave, and I was but a little boy."

"Ah, how terribly lonely he must have been!" said she. "Yes, horribly lonely," said the tin soldier; "but it is glorious not to be forgotten."

"Glorious," repeated a voice close to them; but nobody except the tin soldier perceived that it came from a rag of the pig's leather hangings, which was now devoid of all gilding. It looked like wet earth, but yet it had an opinion, which it expressed thus:

Gilding fades fast,
Pigskin will last!

But the tin soldier did not believe that.

THE HAPPY FAMILY

The biggest leaf here in the country is certainly the burdock leaf. Put one in front of your waist and it's just like an apron, and if you lay it upon your head it is almost as good as an umbrella, for it is quite remarkably large. A burdock never grows alone; where there is one tree there are several more. It's splendid to behold! And all this splendour is snails' meat. The great white snails, which the grand people in old times used to have made into fricassees, and when they had eaten them they would say, "H'm, how good that is!" for they had the idea that it tasted delicious. These snails lived on burdock leaves, and that's why burdocks were sown.

Now there was an old estate, on which people ate snails no longer. The snails had died out, but the burdocks had not. These latter grew and grew in all the walks and on all the beds; there was no stopping them; the place became a complete forest of burdocks. Here and there stood an apple- or plum-tree, but for this nobody would have thought a garden had been there. Everything was burdock, and among the burdocks lived the two last ancient snails.

They did not know themselves how old they were, but they could very well remember that there had been a great many more of them, that they had descended from a foreign family, and that the whole forest had been planted for them and theirs. They had never been away from home, but it was known to them that something existed in the world called the *ducal palace*, and that yonder one was boiled, and one became black, and was laid upon a silver dish; but what was done afterwards they did not know. Moreover they could not imagine what that might be, being boiled and laid upon a silver dish; but it was stated to be fine, and particularly grand! Neither the cockchafer, nor the toad, nor the earthworm, whom they questioned about it, could give them any information, for none of their own kind had ever been boiled and laid on silver dishes.

The old white snails were the grandest in the world; they knew that! The forest was there for their sake, and the ducal palace too, so that they might be boiled and laid on silver dishes.

They led a very retired and happy life, and as they themselves were childless, they had adopted a little common snail, which they brought up as their own child. But the little thing would not grow, for it was only a common snail, though the old people, and particularly the mother, declared one could easily see how he grew. And when the father could not see it, she requested him to feel the little snail's shell, and he felt it, and acknowledged that she was right.

One day it rained very hard.

"Listen, how it's drumming on the burdock-leaves, rum-dum-dum, rum-dum-dum!" said the father snail. "That's what I call drops," said the mother. "It's coming straight down the stalks. You'll see it will be wet here directly. I'm only glad that we have our good houses, and that the little one has his own. There has really been more done for us than for any other creature; one can see very plainly that we are the grand folks of the world! We have houses from our birth, and the burdock forest has been planted on our account; I should like to know how far it extends, and what lies beyond it."

"There's nothing," said the father snail, "that can be better than here at home; I have nothing at all to wish for." "Yes," said the mother, "I should like to be taken to the ducal palace and boiled, and laid upon a silver dish; that has been done to all our ancestors, and you may be sure it's quite a distinguished honour."

"The ducal palace has perhaps fallen in," said the father snail, "or the forest of burdocks may have grown over it, so that the people can't get out at all. You need not be in a hurry. But you always hurry so, and the little one is beginning just the same way. Has he not been creeping up that stalk these three days! My head quite aches when I look up at him."

"You must not scold him!" said the mother snail. "He crawls very deliberately. We shall have much joy in him; and we old people have nothing else to live for. But have you ever thought where we shall get a wife for him? Don't you think that further in the wood there may be some more of our kind?"

The grand old snails

"There may be black snails there, I think," said the old man—"black snails without houses! But they're too vulgar; and they're conceited, for all that. But we can give the commission to the ants; they run to and fro, as if they had business; they're sure to know of a wife for our young gentleman."

"I certainly know the most beautiful of brides," said one of the ants; "but I fear it would not do, for she is the Queen!" "That does not matter!" said two old snails. "Has she a house?"

"She has a castle!" replied the ant. "The most beautiful ant's castle, with seven hundred passages." "Thank you!" said the snail-mother; "our boy shall go into an ant-hill. If you know of nothing better, we'll give the commission to the white gnats; they fly far about in rain and sunshine. They know the burdock wood, inside and outside!"

"We have a wife for him!" said the gnats. "A hundred man-steps from here a little snail with a house is sitting on a gooseberry bush; she is quite alone, and old enough to marry. It's only a hundred man-steps from here!"

"Yes, let her come to him!" said the old people. "He has a whole burdock forest, and she has only a bush." And so they brought the little maiden snail. Eight days passed before she arrived; but that was the rare circumstance about it, for by this one could see that she was of the right kind.

And then they had a wedding. Six glow-worms lighted as well as they could: with this exception it went very quietly, for the old snail people could not bear feasting and dissipation. But a capital speech was made by the mother-snail. The father could not speak, he was so much moved. Then they gave the young couple the whole burdock forest for an inheritance, and said, what they had always said, namely, that it was the best place in the world, and that the young people, if they lived honourably, and increased and multiplied, would some day be taken with their children to the ducal palace and boiled black, and laid upon a silver dish. And when the speech was finished, the old people crept into their houses, and never came out again, for they slept. The young snail pair now ruled in the forest, and had a numerous progeny. But as the young ones were never boiled and put into silver dishes, they concluded that the ducal palace had fallen in, and that all the people in the world had died out. And as nobody contradicted them, they must have been right. And the rain fell down upon the burdock leaves to play the drum for them; and the sun shone to colour the burdock forest for them; and they were happy, very happy,—the whole family was happy, uncommonly happy!

THE SHADOW

In the hot countries the sun burns very strongly; there the people become quite mahogany brown, and in the very hottest countries they are even burnt into negroes. But this time it was only to the hot countries that a learned man out of the cold regions had come. He thought he could roam about there just as he had been accustomed to do at home; but he soon altered his opinion. He and all sensible people had to remain at home; the window-shutters and doors were shut all day long; and it looked as if all the inmates were asleep or had gone out. The narrow street with the high houses in which he lived was, however, built in such a way that the sun shone upon it from morning till evening; it was really quite unbearable! The learned man from the cold regions was a young man and a clever man; it seemed to him as if he was sitting in a glowing oven; that exhausted him greatly, and he became quite thin; even his shadow shrivelled up and became much smaller than it had been at home; the sun even took the shadow away, and it did not return till the evening when the sun went down. It was really a pleasure to see this; so soon as a light was brought into the room the shadow stretched itself quite up the wall, farther even than

The visit of the shadow

the ceiling, so tall did it make itself; it was obliged to stretch to get strength again. The learned man went out into the balcony to stretch himself; and so soon as the stars came out in the beautiful clear sky, he felt himself reviving. On all the balconies in the streets—and in the hot countries there is a balcony to every window—young people now appeared, for one must breathe fresh air, even if one has got used to becoming mahogany brown; then it became lively above and below; the tinkers and tailors—by which we mean all kinds of people—sat below in the street; then tables and chairs were brought out, and candles burned, yes, more than a thousand candles; one talked and then

sang, and the people walked to and fro; carriages drove past, mules
trotted "Kling-ling-ling!" for they had bells on their harness. Dead
people were buried with solemn songs; the church bells rang, and it
was indeed very lively in the street. Only in one house, just opposite to
that in which the learned man dwelt, it was quite quiet, and yet somebody lived there for there were flowers upon the balcony, blooming
beautifully in the hot sun, and they could not have done this if they had
not been watered, so that some one must have watered them. Therefore, there must be people in that house. Towards evening the door was
half opened, but it was dark, at least in the front room; farther back, in
the interior, music was heard. The strange learned man thought this
music very lovely, but it was quite possible that he only imagined this,
for out there in the hot countries he found everything requisite, if only
there had been no sun. The stranger's landlord said that he did not
know who had taken the opposite house; one saw nobody there, and so
far as the music was concerned it seemed very monotonous to him. "It
was just," he said, "as if some one sat there, always practising a piece
that he could not manage—always the same piece. He seemed to say, 'I
shall manage it after all;' but he did not manage it, however long he
played."

Will the stranger awake at night? He slept with the balcony door
open; the wind lifted up the curtain before it, and he fancied that a
wonderful radiance came from the balcony of the house opposite; all
the flowers appeared like flames of the most gorgeous colours, and in
the midst, among the flowers, stood a beautiful slender maiden. It
seemed as if a radiance came from her also; his eyes were quite dazzled;
but he had only opened them too wide just when he awoke out of his
sleep. With one leap he was out of bed; quite quietly he crept behind
the curtain; but the maiden was gone, the splendour was gone; the
flowers gleamed no longer, but stood there as beautiful as ever. The
door was ajar, and from within sounded music, so lovely, so charming,
that one fell into sweet thought at the sound. It was just like magic
work. But who lived there? Where was the real entrance? For towards
the street and towards the lane at the side the whole ground-floor was
shop by shop, and the people could not always run through there.

One evening the stranger sat upon his balcony; in the room just
behind him a light was burning, and so it was quite natural that his

shadow fell upon the wall of the opposite house; yes, it sat just among the flowers on the balcony, and when the stranger moved, his shadow moved too.

"I think my shadow is the only living thing we see yonder," said the learned man. "Look, how gracefully it sits among the flowers. The door is only ajar, but the shadow ought to be sensible enough to walk in and look round, and then come back and tell me what it has seen."

"Yes, you would thus make yourself very useful!" said he, as if in sport. "Be so good as slip in. Now, will you go?" And then he nodded at the shadow, and the shadow nodded back at him. "Now go, but don't stay away altogether!" And the stranger stood up, and the shadow on the balcony opposite stood up too, and the stranger moved round, and if any one had noticed closely he would have remarked how the shadow went away in the same moment, straight through the half-opened door of the opposite house, as the stranger returned into his room, and let the curtain fall.

Next morning the learned man went out, to drink coffee and read the papers. "What is this?" said he, when he came out into the sunshine. "I have no shadow! So it really went away yesterday evening, and did not come back; that's very tiresome."

And that fretted him, but not so much because the shadow was gone as because he knew that there was a story of a man without a shadow. All the people in the house knew this story, and if the learned man came home and told his own history, they would say that it was only an imitation, and he did not choose them to say that of him. So he would not speak of it at all, and that was a very sensible idea of his.

In the evening he again went out on his balcony; he had placed the light behind him, for he knew that a shadow always wants its master for a screen, but he could not coax it forth. He made himself little, he made himself long, but there was no shadow, and no shadow came. He said, "Here, here!" but that did no good.

That was vexatious, but in the warm countries everything grows very quickly, and after the lapse of a week he remarked to his great joy that a new shadow was growing out of his legs, when he went into the sunshine, so that the root must have remained behind. After three weeks he had quite a respectable shadow, which, when he started on his return to the north, grew more and more, so that at last it was so long and great that he could very well have parted with half of it.

When the learned man got home he wrote books about what is true in the world, and what is good, and what is pretty; and days went by, and years went by, many years.

He was one evening sitting in his room when there came a little quiet knock at the door. "Come in!" said he; but nobody came. Then he opened the door, and there stood before him such a remarkably thin man that he felt quite uncomfortable. This man was, however, very respectably dressed; he looked like a man of standing.

"Whom have I the honour to address?" asked the professor.

"Ah!" replied the genteel man, "I thought you would not know me; I have become so much a body that I have got real flesh and clothes. You never thought to see me in such a condition. Don't you know your old shadow? You certainly never thought that I would come again. Things have gone remarkably well with me since I was with you last; I've become rich in every respect; if I want to buy myself free from servitude I can do it!" And he rattled a number of valuable charms, which hung by his watch, and put his hand upon the thick gold chain he wore round his neck; and how the diamond rings glittered on his fingers! and everything was real!

"No, I cannot regain my self-possession at all!" said the learned man. "What's the meaning of all this?"

"Nothing common," said the shadow. "But you yourself don't belong to common folks; and I have, as you very well know, trodden in your footsteps from my childhood upwards. So soon as you found that I was experienced enough to find my way through the world alone, I went away; I am in the most brilliant circumstances. But I was seized with a kind of longing to see you once more before you die; and I wanted to see these regions once more, for one always holds by one's fatherland. I know that you have got another shadow; have I anything to pay to it, or to you? You have only to tell me."

"Is it really you?" said the learned man. "Why, that is wonderful! I should never have thought that I should ever meet my old shadow as a man!"

"Only tell me what I have to pay," said the shadow; "for I don't like to be in any one's debt."

"How can you talk in that way?" said the learned man. "Of what debt can there be a question here? You are as free as any one! I am exceedingly pleased at your good fortune! Sit down, old friend, and tell me a little how it has happened, and what you saw in the warm countries, and in the house opposite ours!"

"Yes, that I will tell you," said the shadow; and it sat down. "But then you must promise me never to tell any one in this town, when you meet me, that I have been your shadow! I have the intention of engaging myself to be married; I can do more than support a family."

"Be quite easy," replied the learned man; "I will tell nobody who you really are. Here's my hand. I promise it; and my word's as good as my bond."

"A shadow's word in return!" said the shadow, for he was obliged to talk in that way. But, by the way, it was quite wonderful; how complete a man he had become. He was dressed all in black, and wore the very finest black cloth, polished boots, and a hat that could be crushed together till it was nothing but crown and rim, besides what we have already noticed of him, namely, the charms, the gold neckchain, and the diamond rings. The shadow was indeed wonderfully well clothed; and it was just this that made a complete man of him.

"Now I will tell you," said the shadow; and then he put down his polished boots as firmly as he could on the arm of the learned man's new shadow that lay like a poodle dog at his feet. This was done perhaps from pride, perhaps so that the new shadow might stick to his feet; but the prostrate shadow remained quite quiet, so that it might listen well, for it wanted to know how one could get free and work up to be one's own master.

"Do you know who lived in the house opposite to us?" asked the shadow. "That was the most glorious of all; it was Poetry! I was there for three weeks, and that was just as if one had lived there a thousand years, and could read all that has been written and composed. For this I say, and it is truth, I have seen everything, and I know everything!"

"Poetry!" cried the learned man. "Yes, she often lives as a hermit in great cities. Poetry! Yes; I myself saw her for one single brief moment, but sleep was heavy on my eyes; she stood on the balcony gleaming as the northern light gleams, flowers with living flames. Tell me, tell me! You were upon the balcony. You went through the door, and then—"

"Then I was in the ante-room," said the shadow. "You sat opposite, and were always looking across at the ante-room. There was no light; a kind of semi-obscurity reigned there; but one door after another in a whole row of halls and rooms stood open, and there it was light; and the mass of light would have killed me, if I had got as far as to where the maiden sat. But I was deliberate; I took my time; and that's what one must do."

"And what did thou see then?" asked the learned man. "I saw everything! And I will tell you that; but—it is really not pride on my part—as a free man, and with the acquirements I possess, besides my good position and my remarkable fortune, I wish you would say you to me."

"I beg your pardon," said the learned man. "This thou is an old habit, and old habits are difficult to alter. You are perfectly right, and I will remember it. But now tell me everything you saw." "Everything," said the shadow; "for I saw everything, and I know everything."

"How did things look in the inner room?" asked the learned man. Was it there as in a cool grave? Was it there like in a holy temple? Were the chambers like the starry sky, when one stands on the high mountains?"

"Everything was there," said the shadow. "I was certainly not quite inside; I remained in the front room, in the half darkness; but I stood there remarkably well. I saw everything, and know everything. I have been in the ante-room at the Court of Poetry."

"But what did you see? Did all the gods of antiquity march through the halls? Did the old heroes fight there? Did lovely children play there, and relate their dreams?"

"I tell you that I have been there, and so you will easily understand that I saw everything that was to be seen. If you had got there you would not have remained a man; but I became one: and at the same time I learned to understand my inner being, and the relation in which I stood to Poetry. Yes, when I was with you, I did not think of these things; but you know that whenever the sun rises or sets I am wonderfully great. In the moonshine I was almost more noticeable than you yourself. I did not then understand my inward being: in the ante-room it was revealed to me. I became a man! I came out ripe; but you were no longer in the warm countries. I was ashamed to go about as a man in the state I was then in: I required boots, clothes, and all this human varnish, by which a man is known. I hid myself: yes, I can confide the secret to you; you will not put it into a book. I hid myself under the cake-woman's gown; the woman had no idea how much she concealed! Only in the evening did I go out; I ran about the streets in the moonlight; I stretched myself quite long up the wall; that tickled my back quite agreeably. I ran up and down, looked through the highest windows into the halls and through the roof, where nobody could see, and I saw what nobody saw, and what nobody ought to see. On the whole it is a bad world; I should not like to be a man, if it were not allowed to be of some consequence. I saw the most incomprehensible things going on among men and women, and parents, and 'dear, incomparable children.' I saw what no one else knows, but what they all would be very glad to know, namely, bad goings on at their neighbours. If I had written a newspaper, how it would have been read! But I wrote directly to the persons interested, and there was terror in every town to which I came. They were so afraid of me, they were remarkably fond of me. The professor made me a professor; the tailor gave me new clothes (I am well provided); the coining-superintendent coined money for me; the women declared I was handsome: and thus I became the man I now am! And now, farewell! Here is my card; I live on the sunny side, and am always at home in rainy weather." And the shadow went away.

"That was very remarkable!" said the learned man.

Years and days passed by, and the shadow came again. "How goes it?" he asked.

"Ah!" said the learned man, "I'm writing about the true, the good, and the beautiful; but nobody cares to hear of anything of the kind: I am quite in despair, for I take that to heart."

"That I do not," said the shadow. "I'm becoming fat and stout, and that's what one must try to become. You don't understand the world, and you're getting ill; you must travel. I'll make a journey this summer; will you go too? I should like to have a travelling companion; will you go with me as my shadow? I shall be very happy to take you: I'll pay the expenses!"

"I suppose you travel very far," said the learned man. "As you take it," replied the shadow. "A journey will do you a great deal of good.

Will you be my shadow? Then you shall have everything on the journey for nothing."

"That's too strong!" said the learned man. "But it's the way of the world," said the shadow, and so it will remain!" And he went away.

The learned man was not at all fortunate. Sorrow and care pursued him, and what he said of the true and the good and the beautiful was as little valued by most people as a nutmeg would be by a cow. At last he became quite ill.

"You really look like a shadow!" said people to him; and a shudder run through him at these words, for he attached a peculiar meaning to them.

"You must go to a watering place!" said the shadow, who came to pay him a visit. "There's no other help for you. I'll take you with me, for the sake of old acquaintance. I'll pay the expenses of the journey, and you shall make a description of it, and shorten time for me on the way. I want to visit a watering place. My beard doesn't grow quite as it should, and that is a kind of illness; and a beard I must have. Now be reasonable, and accept my proposal; we shall travel like comrades."

And they travelled. The shadow was master now, and the master was shadow; they drove together, they rode together, and walked side by side, and before and behind each other, just as the sun happened to stand. The shadow always knew when to take the place of honour. The learned man did not particularly notice this, for he had a very good heart, and was moreover particularly mild and friendly. Then one day the master said to the shadow, "As we have in this way become travelling companions, and have also from childhood's days grown up with one another, shall we not drink brotherhood? That sounds more confidential."

"You're saying a thing there," said the shadow, who was now really the master. "That is said in a very kind and straightforward way; I will be just as kind and straightforward. You who are a learned gentleman, know very well how wonderful nature is. There are some men who cannot bear to smell brown paper, they become sick at it; others shudder to the marrow of their bones, if one scratches with a nail upon a pane of glass, and I for my part have a similar feeling when any one says "thou" to me; I feel myself, as I did in my first position with you, oppressed by it. You see that this is a feeling, not pride. I cannot let you say 'thou'[1] to me, but I will gladly say 'thou' to you; and thus your wish will be at any rate partly fulfilled."

And now the shadow addressed his former master as "thou." "That's rather strong," said the latter, "that I'm to say you, while he says 'thou,'" but he was obliged to submit to it.

They came to a bathing place, where many strangers were, and among them a beautiful Princess, who had this disease, that she saw too sharply, which was very disquieting. She at once saw that the new arrival was a very different personage to all the rest. "They say he is here to get his beard to grow, but I see the real reason, he can't throw a shadow."

She had now become inquisitive, and therefore she at once began a conversation with the strange gentleman on the promenade. As a Princess, she was not obliged to use much ceremony, therefore she said outright to him at once, "Your illness consists in this, that you can't throw a shadow."

"Your Royal Highness must be much better," replied the shadow. "I know your illness consists in this, that you see too sharply; but you have got the better of that. I have a very unusual shadow; don't you see the person who always accompanies me? Other people have a common shadow, but I don't love what is common. One often gives one's servants finer cloth for their liveries, than one wears oneself, and so I have let my shadow deck himself out like a separate person; yes, you see I have even given him a shadow of his own. That cost very much, but I like to have something peculiar."

"How?" said the Princess, "can I really have been cured? This bathing place is the best in existence; water has wonderful power now-a-days. But I'm not going away from here yet, for now it begins to be amusing; the foreign Prince—for he must be a Prince—pleases me remarkably well; I only hope his beard won't grow, for if it does he'll go away."

That evening the Princess and the shadow danced together, in the great ball-room. She was light, but he was still lighter; never had she seen such a dancer. She told him from what country she came, and he knew the country, he had been there, but just when she had been

---

[1] On the Continent, people who have "drank brotherhood," address each other as "thou," in preference to the more ceremonious "you."

absent. He had looked through the windows of her castle, from below as well as from above; he had learned many circumstances, and could therefore make allusions, and give replies to the Princess, at which she marvelled greatly. She thought he must be the cleverest man in all the world, and was inspired with great respect for all his knowledge. And when she danced with him again, she fell in love with him, and the shadow noticed that particularly, for she looked him almost through and through with her eyes. They danced together once more, and she was nearly telling him, but she was discreet; she thought of her country, and her kingdom, and of the many people over whom she was to rule. "He is a clever man," she said to herself, "and that is well, and he dances capitally, and that is well too; but has he well-grounded knowledge?—That is just as important, and he must be examined." And she immediately put such a difficult question to him, that she could not have answered it herself; and the shadow made a wry face.

"You cannot answer me that," said the Princess. "I learned that in my childhood," replied the shadow; and I believe my very shadow, standing yonder by the door, could answer it."

"Your shadow!" cried the Princess, "that would be very remarkable."

"I do not assert as quite certain that he can do so," said the shadow, "but I am almost inclined to believe it. But your Royal Highness will allow me to remind you, that he is so proud of passing for a man, that, if he is to be in good humour, and he should be so, to answer rightly, he must be treated just like a man." "I like that," said the Princess.

And now she went to the learned man at the door; and she spoke with him of sun and moon, of the green forests, and of people near and far; and the learned man answered very cleverly and very well.

"What a man that must be, who has such a clever shadow?" she thought. "It would be a real blessing for my country, and for my people, if I chose; and I'll do it!" And they soon struck a bargain—the Princess and the shadow; but no one was to know anything of it till she had returned to her kingdom.

"No one—not even my shadow!" said the shadow; and for this he had especial reasons. And they came to the country where the Princess ruled, and where was her home.

"Listen, my friend," said the shadow to the learned man. "Now I am as lucky and powerful as any one can become. I'll do something particular for you. You shall live with me in my palace, drive with me in the royal carriage, and have a hundred thousand dollars a year; but you must let yourself be called shadow by everyone, and may never say that you were once a man; and once a year, when I sit on the balcony and show myself, you must lie at my feet as it becomes my shadow to do. For I will tell you I'm going to marry the princess; and this evening the wedding will be held."

"Now, that's too strong," said the learned man. "I won't do it; I won't have it; that would be cheating the whole country and the Princess too. I'll tell everything; that I'm the man and you are the shadow, and that you only wear men's clothes!"

"No one would believe that," said the shadow; "be reasonable, or I'll call the watch."

"I'll go straight to the Princess," said the learned man.

"But I'll go first," said the shadow; "and you shall go to prison." And that was so; for the sentinels obeyed him, of whom they knew that he was to marry the Princess.

"You tremble," said the Princess, when the shadow came to her. "Has anything happened? You must not be ill to-day, when we are to have our wedding."

"I have experienced the most terrible thing that can happen," said the shadow. "Only think—such a poor shallow brain cannot bear much—only think, my shadow has gone mad; he fancies he has become a man; and, only think! That I am his shadow."

"That is terrible!" said the Princess. "He's locked up, I hope!"

"Certainly. I'm afraid he will never recover."

"Poor shadow," cried the Princess. "He's very unfortunate; it would be a really good action to deliver him from his little bit of life. And when I think how prone the people are, now-a-days, to take the part of the low against the high, it seems to me quite necessary to put him quietly out of the way."

"That's certainly hard, for he was a faithful servant," said the shadow; and he pretended to sigh.

"You've a noble character," said the Princess, and she bowed before him.

In the evening the whole town was illuminated, and cannon were fired—bang! And the soldiers presented arms. That was a wedding! The Princess and the shadow stepped out on the balcony to show themselves and receive another cheer.

The learned man heard nothing of all this festivity, for he had already been executed.

THE ROSE-ELF

In the midst of the garden grew a rose-bush, which was quite covered with roses; and in one of them, the most beautiful of all, there dwelt an elf. He was so tiny, that no human eye could see him. Behind every leaf in the rose he had a bedroom. He was as well formed and beautiful as any child could be; and had wings that reached from his shoulders to his feet. Oh, what a fragrance there was in his rooms, and how clear and bright were the walls! They were made of the pale-pink rose petals.

The whole day he rejoiced in the warm sunshine, flew from flower to flower, danced on the wings of the flying butterfly, and measured how many steps he would have to take to pass along all the roads and cross-roads that are marked out on a single hidden leaf. What we call veins on the leaf were to him high-roads and cross-roads. Yes, those were long roads for him! Before he had finished his journey, the sun went down; for he had begun his work too late!

It became very cold, the dew fell, and the wind blew; now the best thing to be done was to come home. He made what haste he could, but the rose had shut itself up, and he could not get in; not a single rose stood open. The poor little elf was very much frightened. He had never been out at night before; he had always slumbered sweetly and comfortably behind the warm rose petals. Oh, it certainly would be the death of him.

At the other end of the garden there was, he knew, an arbour of fine honey-suckle; the flowers looked like great painted horns; he wished to go down into one of them to sleep till the next day.

He flew thither. Silence! Two people were in there; a handsome young man and a young girl. They sat side by side, and wished that they need never part. They loved each other better than a good child loves its father and mother.

"Yet we must part!" said her young man. "Your brother does not like us, therefore he sends me away on an errand so far over mountains and seas. Farewell, my sweet pride, for that you shall be!"

And they kissed each other, and the young girl wept and gave him a rose. But before she gave it him, she impressed a kiss so firmly and closely upon it, that the flower opened. Then the little elf flew into it, and leaned his head against the delicate, fragrant walls. Here he could plainly hear them say "Farewell, farewell!" and he felt that the rose was placed on the young man's heart. Oh! How that heart beats; the little elf could not go to sleep, it thumped so.

But not long did the rose rest undisturbed on that breast. The man took it out, and as he went lonely through the wood, he kissed the flower so often and so fervently that the little elf was almost crushed. He could feel through the leaf how the man's lips burned, and the rose itself had opened, as if under the hottest noonday sun.

Then came another man, gloomy and wicked; he was the bad brother of the pretty maiden. He drew out a sharp knife, and while the other kissed the rose, the bad man stabbed him to death, and then, cutting off his head, buried both head and body in the soft earth under the linden tree.

"Now he's forgotten and gone!" thought the wicked brother; "he will never come back again. He was to take a long journey over mountains and seas; one can easily lose one's life, and he has lost his. He cannot come back again, and my sister dare not ask news of him from me."

Then with his feet he shuffled dry leaves over the loose earth, and went home in the dark night. But he did not go alone, as he thought; the little elf accompanied him. The elf sat in a dry, rolled-up linden leaf that had fallen on the wicked man's hair as he dug. The hat was now placed upon the leaf; it was very dark in the hat, and the elf trembled with fear and with anger at the evil deed.

In the morning hour the bad man got home; he took off his hat, and went into his sister's bedroom. There lay the beautiful blooming girl, dreaming of him whom she loved from her heart, and of whom she now believed that he was going across the mountains and through the

The girl and the flower-pot

forests. And the wicked brother bent over her, and laughed hideously, as only a fiend can laugh. Then the dry leaf fell out of his hair upon the coverlet; but he did not remark it, and he went out to sleep a little himself, in the morning hour. But the elf slipped forth from the withered leaf, placed himself in the ear of the sleeping girl, and told her, as in a dream, the dreadful history of the murder; described to her the place where her brother had slain her lover and buried his corpse; told her of the blooming linden tree close by it, and said; "That you may not think it is only a dream that I have told you, you will find on your bed a withered leaf!" And she found it when she awoke.

Oh, what bitter tears she wept! The window stood open the whole day: the little elf could easily get out to the roses and all the other flowers. But he could not find it in his heart to quit the afflicted maiden. In the window stood a plant, a monthly rose-bush: he seated himself in one of the flowers, and looked at the poor girl. Her brother often came into the room, and in spite of his wicked deed, he always seemed cheerful, but she dared not say a word of the grief that was in her heart.

So soon as the night came, she crept out of the house, went to the wood to the place where the linden tree stood, removed the leaves from the ground, turned up the earth, and immediately found him who had been slain. Oh, how she wept, and prayed that she might soon die also!

Gladly would she have taken the corpse home with her,—but that she could not do. Then she took the pale head with the closed eyes, kissed the cold mouth, and shook the earth out of the beautiful hair. "That I will keep!" she said. And when she had laid earth upon the dead body, she took the head, and a little sprig of the jasmine that bloomed in the wood where he was buried, home with her.

So soon as she came into her room, she brought the greatest flower-pot she could find; in this she laid the dead man's head, strewed earth upon it, and then planted the jasmine twig in the pot. "Farewell, farewell!" whispered the little elf: he could endure it no longer to see all this pain, and therefore flew out to his rose in the garden. But the rose was faded; only a few pale leaves clung to the wild bush.

"Alas! how soon everything good and beautiful passes away!" sighed the elf. At last he found another rose, and this became his house; behind its delicate fragrant leaves he could hide himself and dwell.

Every morning he flew to the window of the poor girl, and she was always standing by the flower-pot weeping. The bitter tears fell upon the jasmine spray, and every day, as the girl became paler and paler, the twig stood there fresher and greener, one shoot after another sprouted forth; little white buds burst out, and these she kissed. But the bad brother scolded his sister, and asked if she had gone mad? He could not bear it, and could not imagine why she was always weeping over the flower-pot. He did not know what closed eyes were there, what red lips had there faded into earth. And she bowed her head upon the flower-pot, and the little elf of the rose-bush found her slumbering there. Then he seated himself in her ear, told her of the evening in the arbour, of the fragrance of the rose, and the love of the elves. And she dreamed a marvellously sweet dream, and while she dreamed her life passed away. She had died a quiet death, and she was in heaven, with him whom she loved.

And the jasmine opened its great white bells. They smell quite peculiarly sweet; it could not weep in any other way over the dead one.

But the wicked brother looked at the beautiful blooming plant, and took it for himself as an inheritance, and put it in his sleeping room, close by his bed, for it was glorious to look upon, and its fragrance was sweet and lovely. The little Rose-elf followed, and goes from flower to flower—for in each dwelt a little soul—and told of the murdered young man, whose head was now earth beneath the earth, and told of the evil brother and of the poor sister.

"We know it!" said each soul in the flowers. "We know it; have we not sprung from the eyes and lips of the murdered man? We know it! we know it!" And then they nodded in a strange fashion with their heads.

The Rose-elf could not at all understand how they could be so quiet, and he flew out to the bees that were gathering honey, and told them the story of the wicked brother. And the bees told it to their Queen, and the Queen commanded that they should all kill the murderer next morning. But in the night—it was the first night that followed upon the sister's death—when the brother was sleeping in his bed, close to the fragrant jasmine, each flower opened, and invisible, but armed with poisonous spears, the flower-souls came out and seated themselves in his ear, and told him bad dreams, and then flew across his lips and pricked his tongue with the poisonous spears. "Now we have revenged the dead man!" they said, and flew back into the jasmine's white bells.

When morning came and the windows of the bed-chamber was opened, the Rose-elf and the Queen Bee and the whole swarm of bees rushed in to kill him.

But he was dead already. People stood around his bed and said, "The scent of the jasmine has killed him!" Then the Rose-elf understood the revenge of the flowers, and told it to the Queen and to the bees, and the Queen hummed with the whole swarm around the flower-pot. The bees were not to be driven away. Then a man carried away the flower-pot, and one of the bees stung him in the hand so that he let the pot fall, and it broke in pieces.

Then they beheld the whitened skull, and knew that the dead man on the bed was a murderer.

And the Queen Bee hummed in the air, and sang of the revenge of the bees, and of the Rose-elf, and said that behind the smallest leaf there dwells ONE, who can bring the evil to light, and repay it.

THE ANGEL

Whenever a good child dies an angel from heaven comes down to earth and takes the dead child in his arms, spreads out his great white wings, and flies away over all the places the child has loved, and picks quite a handful of flowers, which he carries up to the Almighty, that they may bloom in heaven more brightly than on earth. And the father presses all the flowers to his heart; but he kisses the flower that pleases him best, and the flower is then endowed with a voice, and can join in the great chorus of praise!

"See," this is what an angel said, as he carried a dead child up to heaven, and the child heard, as if in a dream, and they went on over the regions of home where the little child had played, and they came through gardens with beautiful flowers. "Which of these shall we take with us to plant in heaven?" asked the angel.

Now there stood near them a slender, beautiful rose-bush; but a wicked hand had broken the stem, so that all the branches, covered with half-opened buds, were hanging around, quite withered.

"The poor rose-bush!" said the child. "Take it, that it may bloom up yonder." And the angel took it, and kissed the child, and the little one half opened his eyes. They plucked some of the rich flowers; but also took with them the despised buttercup and the wild pansy.

"Now we have flowers," said the child, and the angel nodded; but he did not yet fly upward to heaven. It was night; it was quite silent, they remained in the great city; they floated about there in a small street, where lay whole heaps of straw, ashes, and sweepings, for it had been removal day. There lay fragments of plates, bits of plaster, rags and old hats, and all this did not look well. And the angel pointed amid all this confusion to a few fragments of a flower-pot, and to a lump of earth which had fallen out, and which was kept together by the roots of a great dried field-flower, which was of no use, and had therefore been thrown out into the street.

"We will take that with us," said the angel. "I will tell you why, as we fly onward."

"Down yonder in the narrow lane, in the low cellar, lived a poor sick boy; from his childhood he had been bedridden. When he was at his best he could go up and down the room a few times, leaning on crutches; that was the utmost he could do. For a few days in summer

The sick boy and the little flower

the sunbeams would penetrate for a few hours to the ground of the cellar, and when the poor boy sat there and the sun shone on him, and he looked at the red blood in his three fingers, as he held them up before his face he would say, "Yes, to-day he has been out!" He knew the forest with its beautiful vernal green only from the fact that the neighbour's son brought him the first green branch of a beech tree, and he held that up over his head, and dreamed he was in the beech wood when the sun shone and the birds sang. On a spring day the neighbour's boy also brought him field-flowers, and among these was, by chance, one to which the root was hanging; and so it was planted in a flower-pot, and placed by the bed close to the window. And the flowers had been planted by a fortunate hand; it grew, threw out new shoots, and bore flowers every year. It became as a splendid flower-garden to the sickly boy—his little treasure here on earth. He watered it, and tended it, and took care that it had the benefit of every ray of sunlight, down to the last that struggled in through the narrow window; and the flower itself was woven into his dreams, for it grew for him, and gladdened his eyes, and spread its fragrance about him; and towards it he turned in death, when the Father called him. He has now been with the Almighty for a year; for a year the flower has stood forgotten in the windows, and is withered; and thus, at the removal, it has been thrown out into the dust of the street. And this is the flower, the poor withered flower, which we have taken into our nosegay; for this flower has given more joy than the richest flower in a Queen's garden!"

"But how do you know all this?" asked the child which the angel was carrying to heaven. "I know it," said the angel; "for I myself was that little boy who walked on crutches! I know my flower well!"

And the child opened his eyes, and looked into the glorious happy face of the angel; and at the same moment they entered the regions where there is peace and joy. And the Father pressed the dead child to his bosom, and then it received wings like the angel, and flew hand-in-hand with him. And the Almighty pressed all the flowers to his heart; but he kissed the dry withered field-flower, and it received a voice and sang with all the angels hovering around; some near, and some in wider circles, and some in infinite distance, but all equally happy. And they all sang; little and great, the good happy child, and the poor field-flower that had lain there withered, thrown among the dust, in the rubbish of the removal-day, in the narrow dark lane.

TWELVE BY THE MAIL

It was bitterly cold; the sky gleamed with stars, and not a breeze was stirring.

"Bump!" An old pot was thrown at the neighbour's house doors. "Bang, bang," went the gun; for they were welcoming the New Year. It was New Year's Eve! The church clock was striking twelve!

"Tan-ta-ra-ra!" the mail came lumbering up. The great carriage stopped at the gate of the town. There were twelve persons in it; all the places were taken.

"Hurrah! hurrah!" sang the people in the houses of the town; for the New Year was being welcomed, and as the clock struck they stood up with the filled glass in their hand, to drink success to the new comer.

The arrival of the mail

"Happy New Year!" was the cry. "A pretty wife! Plenty of money! And no sorrow or care!"

This wish was passed round, and then glasses were clashed together till they rang again, and in front of the town-gate the post-carriage stopped with the strange guests, the twelve travellers.

And who were these strangers? Each of them had his passport and his luggage with him; they even brought presents for me and for you, and for all the people of the little town. Who were they? What did they want, and what did they bring with them?

"Good morning!" they cried to the sentry at the town gate. "Good morning!" replied the sentry, for the clock had struck twelve.

"Your name and profession!" the sentry inquired of the one who alighted first from the carriage.

"See yourself, in the passport," replied the man. "I am myself!" and a capital fellow he looked, arrayed in a bearskin and fur boots. "I am the man on whom many persons fix their hopes. Come to me to-morrow; I'll give you a New Year's present. I throw pence and dollars among the people, I even give balls, thirty-one balls; but I cannot devote more than thirty-one nights to this. My ships are frozen in, but in my office it is warm and comfortable. I'm a merchant. My name is JANUARY, and I only carry accounts with me."

Now the second alighted, he was a merry companion; he was a theatre director, manager of the masque balls, and all the amusements one can imagine. His luggage consisted of a great tub.

"We'll dance the cat out of the tub at carnival time," said he. "I'll prepare a merry tune for you and for myself too. I have not exactly long to live,—the shortest, in fact, of my whole family; for I only become twenty-eight days old. Sometimes they pop me in an extra day, but I trouble myself very little about that, hurrah!"

"You must not shout so!" said the sentry.

"Certainly, I may shout!" retorted the man. "I'm Prince Carnival, travelling under the name of FEBRUARY!"

The third now got out; he looked like Fasting itself, but carried his nose very high, for he was related to the "Forty Knights," and was a weather prophet. But that's not a profitable office, and that's why he praised fasting. In his button-hole he had a little bunch of violets, but they were very small.

"MARCH! MARCH!" the fourth called after him, and slapped him on the shoulder: "Do you smell nothing? Go quickly into the guardroom; there they're drinking punch, your favourite drink; I can smell it already out here. Forward, Master MARCH!" But it was not true; the speaker only wanted to let him feel the influence of his own name, and make an APRIL fool of him; for with that the fourth began his career in the town. He looked very jovial, did little work, but had the more holidays. "If it were only a little more steady in the world!" said he; "but sometimes one is in a good humour, sometimes in a bad one, according to circumstances; now rain, now sunshine. I am a kind of house and office letting agent; also a manager of funerals; I can laugh or cry, according to circumstances. Here in this box I have my summer wardrobe, but it would be very foolish to put it on. Here I am now! On Sundays I go out walking in shoes and white silk stockings, and with a muff!"

After him, a lady came out of the carriage. She called herself Miss MAY. She wore a summer costume and overshoes, a light-green dress, and anemones in her hair, and she was so scented with wild thyme that the sentry had to sneeze. "God bless you!" she said, and that was her salutation. How pretty she was! And she was a singer, not a theatre singer nor a ballad singer, no, a singer of the woods; for she roamed through the gay green forest and sang there for her own amusement.

"Now comes the young dame!" said those in the carriage, and the young dame stepped out, delicate, proud and pretty. It was easy to see that she was Mistress JUNE, accustomed to be served by drowsy marmots. She gave a great feast on the longest day of the year, that the guests, might have time to partake of the many dishes at her table. She, indeed, kept her own carriage; but still she travelled in the mail with the rest, because she wanted to show that she was not high-minded. But she was not without protection; her younger brother JULY was with her.

He was a plump young fellow, clad in summer garments, and with a panama hat. He had but little baggage with him, because it was cumbersome in the great heat; therefore he had only provided himself with swimming trousers, and those are not much.

Then came the mother herself, Madam AUGUST, wholesale dealer in fruit, proprietress of a large number of fishponds, and land cultivator

The passengers dismounting

in a great crinoline; she was fat and hot, could use her hands well, and would herself carry out beer to the workmen in the fields. "In the sweat of thy face shalt thou eat bread," said she; that is written in the *Book*. Afterwards come the excursions, dance and playing in the greenwood, and the harvest-feasts! She was a thorough housewife.

After her, a man came out of the coach, a painter, Mr. Master-colourer SEPTEMBER; the forest had to receive him; the leaves were to change their colours, but how beautifully, when he wished it; soon the wood gleamed with red, yellow and brown. The master whistled like the black magpie, was a quick workman, and wound the brown-green hop plants round his beer-jug. That was an ornament for the jug, and he had a good idea for ornament. There he stood with his colour-pot, and that was his whole luggage!

A landed proprietor followed him, one who cared for the ploughing and preparing of the land, and also for field-sports. Squire OCTOBER brought his dog and his gun with him, and had nuts in his game bag; "Crack! Crack!" He had much baggage, even an English plough; he spoke of farming; but one could scarcely hear what he said, for the coughing and gasping of his neighbour.

It was NOVEMBER who coughed so violently, as he got out. He was very much plagued by a cold; he was continually having recourse to his pocket-handkerchief, and yet, he said, he was obliged to accompany the servant-girls, and initiate them into their new winter service. He said he should get rid of his cold when he went out wood-cutting, and had to saw and split wood, for he was sawyer-master to the firewood guild. He spent his evenings cutting the wooden soles, for skates, for he knew he said, that in a few weeks there would be occasion to use these amusing shoes.

At length appeared the last passenger, old Mother DECEMBER, with her fire-stool; the old lady was cold, but her eyes glistened like two bright stars. She carried on her arm a flower-pot, in which a little fir-tree was growing.

"This tree I will guard and cherish, that it may grow large by Christmas-Eve, and may reach from the ground to the ceiling, and may rear itself upward with flaming candles, golden apples, and little carved figures. The fire-stool warms like a stove. I bring the story-book out of my pocket, and read aloud, so that all the children in the room become quite quiet, but the little figures on the trees become lively, and the little waxen angel on the top spreads out his wings of gold-leaf, flies down from his green perch, and kisses great and small in the room, yes, even the poor children who stand out in the passage and in the street, singing the carol about the Star of Bethlehem.

"Well, now the coach may drive away!" said the sentry, "we have the whole twelve. Let the chaise drive up."

"First let all the twelve come in to me!" said the captain on duty. "One after the other! The passports I will keep here. Each of them is available for a month; when that has passed, I shall write the behaviour on each passport. Mr. January, have the goodness to come here," and Mr. January stepped forward.

"When a year is passed I think I shall be able to tell you what the twelve have brought me, and to you, and to all of us. Now I do not know it, and they don't probably know it themselves; for we live in strange times."

THE RACERS

A prize, or rather two prizes, had been appointed—a great one and a little one—for the greatest swiftness, not in a single race, but for swiftness throughout an entire year.

"I got the first prize!" said the hare; "there must be justice when relations and good friends are among the prize committee; but that the snail should have received the second prize, I consider almost an insult to myself."

"No!" declared the fence-rail, who had been witness at the distribution of prizes, "reference must also be had to industry and perseverance. Many respectable people said so, and I understood it well. The snail certainly took half a year to get across the threshold of the door; but he did himself an injury, and broke his collar-bone in the haste he was compelled to make. He devoted himself entirely to his work, and he ran with his house on his back! All that is very charming! And that's how he got the second prize!"

"I might certainly have been considered too!" said the swallow. "I should think that no one appeared swifter in flying and soaring than myself, and how far I have been around—far—far—far!"

"Yes, that's just your misfortune," said the fence-rail. "You're too fond of fluttering. You must always be journeying about, into far countries, when it begins to be cold here. You've no love of fatherland in you. You cannot be taken into account."

"But if I lay in the moor all through the winter?" said the swallow, "suppose I slept through the whole time; should I be taken into account then?"

"Bring a certificate from the old moor-hen that you have slept away half the time in your fatherland, and you shall be taken into account."

"I deserved the first prize, and not the second," said the snail. "I know so much, at least, that the hare only ran from cowardice, because he thought each time there was danger in delay. I, on the other hand, made my running the business of my life, and have become a cripple in the service! If any one was to have the first prize, I should have had it; but I don't understand chattering and boasting; on the contrary, I despise it!" And the snail looked quite haughty.

"I am able to depose with word and oath that each prize, at least my vote for each, was given after proper consideration," observed the old boundary post in the wood, who had been a member of the college of judges. "I always go on with due consideration, with order, and calculation. Seven times before I have had the honour to be present at the distribution of prizes, and to give my vote; but not till to-day have I carried out my will. I always went to the first prize from the beginning of the alphabet, and to the second from the end. Be kind enough to give me your attention, and I will explain to you how one begins at the beginning. The eighth letter from A is H, and there we have the hare, and so I awarded him the first prize; the eighth letter from the end of the alphabet is S, and therefore the snail received the second prize. Next time I will have its turn for the first prize, and R for the second; there must be due order and calculation in everything! One must have a certain starting point!"

"I should certainly have voted for myself, if I had not been among the judges," said the mule, who had been one of the committee. "One must not only consider the rapidity of advance, but every other quality also that is found,—as for example, how much a candidate is able to draw; but I would not have put that prominently forward this time, nor the sagacity of the hare in his flight, or the cunning with which he suddenly takes a leap to one side to bring people on a false track, so that they may not know where he has hidden himself. No! There is something else on which many lay great stress, and which one may not leave out of the calculation. I mean what is called the beautiful; on the beautiful I particularly fixed my eyes; I looked at the beautiful well-grown ears of the hare; it's quite a pleasure to see how long they are; it almost seemed to me as if I saw myself in the days of my childhood, and so I voted for the hare."

"But!"—said the fly,—"I'm not going to talk, I'm only going to say that I have overtaken more than one hare. Quite lately I crushed the hind-legs of one; I was sitting on the engine in front of a railway train— I often do that, for thus one can best notice one's own swiftness. A young hare ran for a long time in front of the engine; he had no idea that I was present—but at last he was obliged to give in and spring aside—but then the engine crushed his hind-legs, for I was upon it. The

The racers

hare lay there, but I rode on. That certainly was conquering him! But I don't count the prize!"

"It certainly appears to me,"—thought the wild rose—but she did not say it, for it is not her nature to give her opinion, though it would have been quite well if she had done so. "It certainly appears to me that the sunbeam ought to have had the first prize, and the second too. The sunbeam flies with intense rapidity along the enormous path from the sun to ourselves, and arrives in such strength that all nature awakes at it; such beauty does it possess that all we roses blush, and exhale fragrance in its presence! Our worshipful judges do not appear to have noticed this at all! If I were the sunbeam, I would give each of them a sunstroke—but that would only make them mad, and that they may become, as things stand. I say nothing!" thought the wild rose. "May peace reign in the forest! It is glorious to blossom, to scent, and to live,—to live in song and legend! The sunbeam will outlive us all!"

"What's the first prize?" asked the earthworm, who had overslept the time, and only came up now.

"It consists in a free admission to a cabbage garden!" replied the mule. "I proposed that as the prize. The hare was decidedly to have it, and therefore I as an active and reflective member took especial notice of the advantage of him who was to get it; now the hare is provided for. The snail may sit upon the fence and lick up moss and sunshine, and has further been appointed one of the first umpires in the racing. That's worth a great deal, to have some one of talent in the thing men call a committee. I must say I expect much from the future—we have made a very good beginning!"